Gender and Representation
in Latin America

Gender and Representation in Latin America

EDITED BY LESLIE A. SCHWINDT-BAYER

Oxford University Press is a department of the University of Oxford. It furthers
the University's objective of excellence in research, scholarship, and education
by publishing worldwide. Oxford is a registered trade mark of Oxford University
Press in the UK and certain other countries.

Published in the United States of America by Oxford University Press
198 Madison Avenue, New York, NY 10016, United States of America.

Library of Congress Cataloging-in-Publication Data
Names: Schwindt-Bayer, Leslie A., editor.
Title: Gender and representation in Latin America / edited by Leslie A. Schwindt-Bayer.
Description: New York, NY : Oxford University Press, [2018] |
Includes bibliographical references and index.
Identifiers: LCCN 2017028954 (print) | LCCN 2017041596 (ebook) |
ISBN 9780190851248 (Updf) | ISBN 9780190851255 (Epub) |
ISBN 9780190851231 (pbk. : alk. paper) | ISBN 9780190851224 (hardcover : alk. paper)
Subjects: LCSH: Women—Political activity—Latin America. |
Women public officers—Latin America. | Women legislators—Latin America.
Classification: LCC HQ1236.5.L37 (ebook) | LCC HQ1236.5.L37 G454 2018 (print) |
DDC 320.082/098—dc23
LC record available at https://lccn.loc.gov/2017028954

9 8 7 6 5 4 3 2 1

Paperback printed by WebCom, Inc., Canada
Hardback printed by Bridgeport National Bindery, Inc., United States of America

To all who work toward gender equality in politics

CONTENTS

ACKNOWLEDGMENTS

This book is truly a group effort. I've had the idea for this book for a very long time, but it was only after moving to Rice University in 2013 that the idea came to life. I secured funding from the Dean of Social Sciences to host a conference to evaluate the state of women's representation in Latin America and develop an edited volume on the topic. I began to ask some of the top scholars on women, gender, and political representation in Latin America to contribute to the conference and volume in various ways, and the enthusiastic response I got was more than I could have hoped for. In the Spring of 2015, we came together at Rice University for two days to present our initial analyses, critique each other's work, develop a compelling framework, evaluate the state of the field, and determine ways to push the field forward. The organic nature of our work together, the enthusiasm for the idea, and the constructive way in which everyone worked together was inspiring. My job was merely to channel the energy and organize our path forward. The outcome of the efforts of this amazing group of authors is this edited volume.

We have many people to thank for helping to make this volume possible. First and foremost, I thank the twenty authors who contributed to this volume. Each and every one of them was critical to making this volume what it is. I can't thank them enough for buying into this idea and working so hard to bring it to fruition. We would also like to thank the anonymous reviewers of our book prospectus and the full manuscript. Your critiques helped us develop our ideas and frame the volume, and your support for publication showed us that we were on the right track. I would like to thank the School of Social Sciences at Rice University and Dean Lyn Ragsdale for the funding that supported our book conference and the faculty in the Department of Political Science at Rice University who participated in our conference as discussants and informal commentators on the chapters. This conference was critical to shaping our ideas, and the book would not exist without it. Additionally, we thank the discussants and audience participants at our two panels at the 2016 Annual Meeting of the American Political Science Association who gave us excellent comments and suggestions as we finalized our manuscript. Specifically, we thank Caroline Beer, Miki Kittilson, Veronica Montecinos, and Diana O'Brien. I also greatly appreciate the insights of Melody Valdini who read not one but several drafts of my chapters. Thank you! Finally, I thank one of our new graduate students with a very bright future, Kaitlin Senk, for her help in the final stages of compiling and editing this book.

I especially want to thank Angela Chnapko, our acquisitions editor at Oxford University Press, for her support and guidance through this entire process. I approached her with the idea for this book before even mentioning it to the chapter authors and her encouragement for the idea and suggestions on how to best move forward were critical to our success. Because of the outstanding set of gender and politics books that Angela has helped put together over the past few years, I cannot imagine publishing this book anywhere else.

Finally, I thank my family, Jeff and Ethan, for their support through yet another book writing process. As always, I couldn't do this without them.

Santiago Alles is a postdoctoral researcher in the Department of Political Science at the Universidad del Rosario (Colombia). He specializes in comparative politics with an emphasis on Latin American politics and gender. His research has been published in *The Journal of Politics, Electoral Studies, América Latina Hoy*, and *Revista de Ciencia Política*. He received his PhD in Political Science at Rice University, his M.A. in Latin American Studies from the University of Salamanca (Spain), and his B.A. in Political Science from the Catholic University of Argentina.

Clara Araújo is a research professor in the postgraduate program in social sciences at the University of Rio de Janeiro State—UERJ/BRAZIL, and has a PhD in sociology from the Federal University of Rio de Janeiro in Brazil. She is a research fellow at the National Research Council/CNPq and is coordinator of the Research Group on Contemporary Inequalities and Gender Relations/NUDERG/UERJ. Her primary research areas and main interests are gender relations; citizenship and political participation; and gender, political representation, and power.

Tiffany D. Barnes is an associate professor at the University of Kentucky. Her research focuses on women's representation, Latin American politics, and comparative political institutions. She was previously a research fellow at the Kellogg Institute for International Studies at the University of Notre Dame. Her published work appears in *American Journal of Political Science, Journal of Politics, Comparative Political Studies, Politics & Gender, Governance*, and *Election Law Journal*. Her first book, *Gendering Legislative Behavior: Institutional Constraints and Collaboration*, was published in 2016 (Cambridge University Press).

Anna Calasanti is a doctoral candidate in the Department of Political Science at the University of New Mexico. Her research interests include political ethnography (with fieldwork experience in disadvantaged communities), the politics of abortion access, and comparative gender politics. She received a B.A. in political science from Guilford College in 2010, and an M.A. in public and international affairs from George Mason University in 2013. Her work has been published in the *Journal of Women, Politics, and Policy*.

Maria C. Escobar-Lemmon is a professor of political science at Texas A&M University. Her research focuses on political institutions, women's representation, local government, and public administration with a regional emphasis on Latin America. Her work has been published in the *American Journal of Political Science*,

Journal of Politics, Political Research Quarterly, Electoral Studies, Policy Studies Journal, and *Publius: The Journal of Federalism,* among others. With Michelle M. Taylor-Robinson she is the co-editor of *Representation: The Case of Women* (Oxford University Press, 2014) and co-author of *Women in Presidential Cabinets: Power Players Or Abundant Tokens?* (2016) also published by Oxford University Press.

Susan Franceschet is a professor of political science at the University of Calgary (Canada). Her research focuses on women's representation in legislatures and cabinets, gender quotas, and gender and the executive branch. She is the author of *Women and Politics in Chile* (Rienner, 2005) and co-editor of *The Impact of Gender Quotas* (Oxford University Press, 2012) and *Comparative Public Policy in Latin America* (University of Toronto Press, 2012). Her research has appeared in *Comparative Political Studies, Politics & Gender, Latin American Research Review,* and *Publius: The Journal of Federalism.*

Kendall D. Funk is a postdoctoral scholar at Arizona State University. She received her Ph.D. from Texas A&M University in 2017. Her research focuses on gender representation, political institutions, local governments, and public administration with a geographic concentration in Latin America. Her work has been published in *Political Research Quarterly, Politics & Gender, Administration & Society, Politics, Groups, and Identities, Revista Uruguaya de Ciencia Política,* and several edited volumes.

Meredith P. Gleitz is a recent graduate of Texas A&M University with a Bachelor of Arts in International Studies and Spanish. Her research interests include gender and politics, particularly in Latin America. While at Texas A&M, Meredith cofounded a committee dedicated to promoting gender equality on campus and was nominated for the Jameson Prize for most outstanding undergraduate research paper on women's issues. She hopes to pursue a career in academic research after serving in Peace Corps Ecuador from 2017–2019.

Magda Hinojosa is an associate professor of political science in the School of Politics and Global Studies at Arizona State University. Her research examines the political participation of women in Latin America, and in particular, institutional barriers to descriptive representation. She is the author of *Selecting Women, Electing Women: Political Representation and Candidate Selection in Latin America,* which was published by Temple University Press in 2012. Her work has also appeared in *Political Research Quarterly, Latin American Politics & Society,* and *Politics & Gender.*

Mala Htun is a professor of political science and deputy director of ADVANCE at the University of New Mexico. Her work focuses on the causes and effects of state efforts to overcome disadvantages of gender, race, and class. She is the author of three books: *Inclusion Without Representation: Gender Quotas and Ethnic Reservations in Latin America* (Cambridge University Press, 2016), *Sex and the State: Abortion, Divorce, and the Family under Latin American Dictatorships and Democracies* (Cambridge University Press, 2003), and *The Logics of Gender Justice: State Action on Women's Rights around the World* (forthcoming in 2018 from Cambridge University Press and co-authored with Laurel Weldon).

Niki Johnson is a lecturer and researcher in political science at the Universidad de la República, Uruguay. Her research centers on women's political representation, the feminist movement and the state in Uruguay and Latin America. She has had work published in *Government and Opposition, Parliamentary Affairs, América Latina Hoy,* the *Revista Uruguaya de Ciencia Política, Revista Política* of the University of Chile, and *Sociologia: Problemas e Práticas.* She has recently published a chapter on candidate selection and gender bias in Latin America in Nélida Archenti and María Inés Tula (eds), *La representación imperfecta. Logros y desafíos de las mujeres políticas* (Eudeba, 2014).

Mark P. Jones is the Joseph D. Jamail Chair in Latin American Studies, professor of political science, the James A. Baker III Institute for Public Policy's Fellow in Political Science, and the Faculty Director of the Master of Global Affairs Program at Rice University. He also is senior associate (Non-resident) in the Center for Strategic & International Studies (CSIS) Americas Program. His research focuses on the effect of electoral laws and other political institutions on governance, representation, and voting. His work has appeared in journals such as the *American Journal of Political Science, Comparative Political Studies,* and *The Journal of Politics* as well as in edited volumes published by Cambridge University Press, Oxford University Press, and Penn State University Press, among others. He also is a coauthor of *Texas Politics Today,* 2017–2018 Edition.

Santiago E. Lacouture is an economist and professional in government and public affairs from Universidad de los Andes. He currently works as a research assistant at the Center for Economic Development Studies (CEDE for its acronym in Spanish) of the Economics School at Universidad de los Andes. He is a graduate student of the Masters of Economics at Universidad de los Andes and has previously worked as a research assistant at the School of Government at Universidad de los Andes.

Jana Morgan is an associate professor of political science at the University of Tennessee and a visiting scholar at the Russell Sage Foundation. Her research considers issues of inequality, exclusion, and representation in the Americas. She is the recipient of the Van Cott Outstanding Book award given by the Latin American Studies Association for her book *Bankrupt Representation and Party System Collapse* (Penn State University Press, 2011). Her work has also been published in numerous journals including *American Political Science Review, Comparative Political Studies, Journal of Politics, Politics & Gender, Latin American Research Review,* and *Latin American Politics and Society.* Her work has been supported by grants from the Fulbright-Hays program and the Russell Sage Foundation, among others.

Mónica Pachón is Dean of the Faculty of Political Science, Government and International Relations at the Universidad del Rosario in Bogotá, Colombia. She was previously an associate professor at the School of Government Alberto Lleras Camargo at Universidad de los Andes, in Bogotá, Colombia. She received her PhD at University of California, San Diego, and her research and publications have focused on executive-legislative relations in Latin American presidential systems and legislative organization, with great emphasis on the Colombian case.

Jennifer M. Piscopo is an assistant professor of politics at Occidental College in Los Angeles, CA. Her research on representation, gender quotas, and legislative institutions in Latin America has appeared in numerous journals, including *Politics & Gender,*

Comparative Political Studies, The Latin American Research Review, Parliamentary Affairs, Publius: The Journal of Federalism, as well as several edited volumes. With Susan Franceschet and Mona Lena Krook, she is editor of *The Impact of Gender Quotas* (Oxford University Press, 2012). She received her PhD from the University of California in San Diego in 2011. A Gates Cambridge Scholar, she received her M.Phil. in Latin American studies from the University of Cambridge in 2003.

Catherine Reyes-Housholder is a postdoctoral fellow at the Centre for Social Conflict and Cohesion Studies (COES) in Santiago, Chile. She researches the presidency and gender with a regional focus on Latin America and received a Fulbright-Hays fellowship in 2015 to support dissertation research in Brazil and Chile. She is working on a book manuscript from her dissertation, which won the 2017 APSA Best Dissertation Award from the Women and Politics Research Section. She has published her work in *Latin American Politics & Society, Comparative Politics,* and *Politics, Groups, and Identities.* She also has published several book chapters.

Leslie A. Schwindt-Bayer is a professor of political science at Rice University. Her research focuses on women's representation, political institutions, and Latin America. She has published her work in the *American Journal of Political Science, The Journal of Politics, Politics & Gender, Electoral Studies, British Journal of Political Science, Comparative Political Studies,* and *Legislative Studies Quarterly,* among others. She also has published three books, two with Oxford University Press: *Political Power and Women's Representation in Latin America* (2010) and *The Gendered Effects of Electoral Institutions: Political Engagement and Participation* (2012, with Miki Caul Kittilson). The third book is *Clarity of Responsibility, Accountability, and Corruption* with Cambridge University Press (2016, with Margit Tavits).

Michelle M. Taylor-Robinson is a professor of political science at Texas A&M University. Her current research focuses on women's representation with a concentration on presidential cabinets in Latin America. She has published her work in the *American Journal of Political Science, The Journal of Politics, Electoral Studies,* and *Comparative Political Studies* among others. She also has published three books, *Do the Poor Count? Democratic Institutions and Accountability in a Context of Poverty* (Penn State University Press, 2010); *Negotiating Democracy: Transition from Authoritarian Rule* (University of Pittsburgh Press, 1996 with Gretchen Casper); and *Women in Presidential Cabinets: Power Players Or Abundant Tokens?* (Oxford University Press, 2016 with Maria Escobar-Lemmon). She also has an edited volume, *Representation: The Case of Women* (Oxford University Press, 2014 with Maria Escobar-Lemmon).

Gwynn Thomas is an associate professor of Global Gender Studies at the University at Buffalo, State University of New York. Her first book, *Contesting Legitimacy in Chile: Familial Ideals, Citizenship, and Political Struggle, 1970–1990* (Penn State University Press, 2011), examines the mobilization of familial beliefs in Chilean political conflicts. Her published work examining women's political activism, women's presidencies in Latin America, and institutional change supporting gender equality has appeared in *The Journal of Women, Politics and Policy; The International Feminist Journal of Politics;* the *ISA Compendium Project;* and the *Annals of the American Academy of Political and Social Science.* She received the Elsa Chaney Award in 2007 from the Gender and Feminist Studies section of the Latin American Studies Association.

Pär Zetterberg is an associate professor of political science and associate senior lecturer in the Department of Government at Uppsala University (Sweden). His research interests include candidate recruitment and political representation in a comparative perspective, with a particular focus on electoral gender quotas. He has published his research in journals such as *The Journal of Politics, Comparative Politics, Party Politics,* and *Political Research Quarterly.*

Gender and Representation
in Latin America

An Introduction to Gender and Representation in Latin America

LESLIE A. SCHWINDT-BAYER ∎

In the late 1970s and early 1980s, Latin American countries began the process of transitioning to democracy. Democracy took hold in nearly every country in the region by the end of the 1980s with high expectations for long-awaited political and economic modernization. Alongside the transitions to democracy were socioeconomic and cultural improvements in gender equality. The gap between women's and men's participation in the paid labor force decreased by almost half since 1990, and women's enrollment in higher education institutions started to outpace men's throughout the region.[1] The influence of the Catholic Church on politics and society declined after the transitions to democracy and the emergence of new evangelical movements helped loosen traditional gender role expectations and allowed for the development of more supportive attitudes toward gender equality in society and politics.[2]

According to modernization theories, these developments should be associated with increased representation of women in politics (Inglehart and Norris 2003). Focusing on regionwide averages and some exceptional countries, this appears to be the case. Since 1990, six women have been elected president of Latin American countries—Violeta Chamorro in Nicaragua (1990–1997), Mireya Moscoso in Panama (1999–2004), Michelle Bachelet in Chile (2006–2010; 2014–2018), Cristina Fernández de Kirchner in Argentina (2007–2011;

1. Based on data from the World Bank's World Development Indicators, women's labor force participation was 42% compared to 85% for men in 1990 and has increased to 57% compared to 84% for men in 2014. In 1970, women's tertiary enrollment in Latin America was half of men's, but today it is one-third larger: the Bank's Gender Parity Index averaged 0.59 in 1970 and averaged 1.30 in 2012 for the Latin American countries with data in those years.

2. As of 2008, only the Dominican Republic had less than half of its population disagree or strongly disagree that men make better political leaders than women (43%). All other countries ranged between 69% (Colombia) and 77% (Bolivia) in supporting women in politics (Morgan and Buice 2013).

2011–2015), Dilma Rousseff in Brazil (2011–2015; 2015–2016[3]), and Laura Chinchilla in Costa Rica (2010–2014). Presidents have increasingly appointed experienced women to cabinets, with a rare cabinet even achieving gender parity (e.g., Chile in 2006). The average percentage of Latin American legislatures that is female has more than doubled since 1995 to 25% (IPU 2016), and four Latin American countries are among the top 10 countries in the world in terms of women's representation in their national parliaments—Bolivia, Cuba, Nicaragua, and Mexico. All four have more than 40% of their congress being female (IPU 2017). Women's presence in subnational governments and in political parties averages about 25%, as well (Morgan and Hinojosa and Escobar-Lemmon and Funk, this volume).

Yet exploring variation across government arenas within individual countries reveals that culture and socioeconomics are not the full picture. Despite cultural and socioeconomic improvements in the region, twelve Latin American democracies have never elected a female president. Of the five countries that have had female presidents, three of them rank near the bottom in terms of women's representation in national legislatures—Panama, Chile, and Brazil. Chile has had a parity cabinet, but it is also one of the countries with the lowest representation of women in congress, its political parties, and its subnational offices. Similarly, whereas women's representation has nearly doubled in national legislatures, it has remained almost constant over time in subnational legislatures (see Escobar-Lemmon and Funk, this volume). Inside government arenas as well representation is highly gendered with rules and norms that advantage men and disadvantage women, limiting women's access to full political power. These inconsistencies in women's representation across different government arenas within countries and the unequal access to power for women working inside the political arena cannot be explained by country-level changes in socioeconomic and cultural gender inequality over the last thirty years.

This book argues instead that gender inequality in political representation in Latin America is rooted in institutions and the democratic challenges and political crises facing Latin American countries. Institutions and political context not only influence the number of women and men elected to office but also what they do once there, how much power they have, and how their presence and actions influence democracy and society more broadly. The book shows that formal and informal institutions and Latin America's recent crises of representation and democracy advantage men and disadvantage women in Latin American political representation, and it demonstrates how representation in Latin American democracies is gendered. We do this by drawing upon the expertise of top scholars of women, gender, and politics in Latin America to study the causes and consequences of women's representation in Latin America across five different "arenas of representation"—the presidency, cabinets, national legislatures, political parties, and subnational governments—and in seven countries—Argentina, Chile, Costa Rica, Mexico, Brazil, Colombia, and Uruguay.

3. Rousseff was impeached before her second term was completed.

STUDYING GENDER AND REPRESENTATION IN THE LATIN AMERICAN CONTEXT

Over the past three decades, scholars have analyzed representative democracy in Latin America by examining questions related to political institutions, parties and party systems, mass attitudes and behavior, and the functioning of democracy more generally. They have asked how executive and legislative institutions in Latin America's presidential systems influence the behavior of elected officials and the policymaking process (Carey 2009; Carey and Shugart 1998; Mainwaring and Shugart 1997; Morgenstern and Nacif 2002; Samuels 2003; Shugart and Carey 1992). They have explored parties and party systems to understand how they operate in Latin America and how they influence who gets elected and what they do once in office (Jones and Mainwaring 2003; Mainwaring and Scully 1995; Siavelis and Morgenstern 2008). More recently, scholars have examined how and why citizen support for democracy has declined, how and why party systems have fragmented, how and why new political actors—particularly leftist parties and politicians—have emerged on the political scene, what new political institutions have been created in response to the weakness of representative democracy, how these institutions operate, and how well (if at all) they have changed politics in the region (Alcántara Sáez 2008a; Brinks, Leiras, and Mainwaring 2014; Hagopian and Mainwaring 2005; Kitschelt et al. 2010; Lagos 2014; Levine and Molina 2011; Levitsky and Roberts 2011; Mainwaring, Bejarano, and Leongomez 2006; Mainwaring and Pérez-Liñán 2015).

Only rarely, however, have these studies considered gender. Rarely have they noted the fact that increases in women's representation occurred at the same time that the challenges to representative democracy were increasing. Rarely have they considered one of the most important institutional reforms of the past twenty-five years that has affected nearly all countries today—the adoption of gender quotas—and how this may have been shaped by the struggles with representation in the region. Rarely has this research evaluated the different consequences on male and female representatives of institutional rules and norms, such as decree or agenda-setting powers, rules about how powerful leadership posts are allocated, or norms about negotiating policy, and rarely has it considered how the region's democratic challenges may be intertwined with the increased presence of women and efforts to achieve greater gender equality in Latin American political offices.

This does not mean that a body of literature on women's representation in Latin America does not exist. Many scholars have studied women's movements and the roles they played in transitions to democracy and increasing women's access to new democratic governments (Baldez 2003; Bayard de Volo 2001; Jaquette 1994).[4] They have explored women's bureaucratic agencies and women's interactions with political parties (Franceschet 2005; Franceschet and Piscopo 2014; Macaulay 2006; Marx, Borner, and Caminotti 2007) as well as how the state attends to (or fails to attend to) policy outcomes for women (Htun 2003). Gender scholars became interested in

---

4. Women's movements continue to be an important piece of the puzzle of women's representation in Latin America, yet the interplay of women's movements and women's representation is complex and substantial enough to require attention beyond what this book can provide. We leave this for future research.

women's representation in legislatures as gender quotas emerged on the political scene and women began winning election in larger numbers in countries. Research, primarily on national legislatures, asked questions about what explains women's numbers in office (Araújo 2008; Archenti and Tula 2008a; Hinojosa 2012; Htun and Jones 2002; Jones 2009; Miguel 2008; Schmidt 2008a; Schwindt-Bayer 2010); how that influences elite behavior and policy outputs (Barnes 2016; Catalano 2009; Franceschet 2010a; Franceschet and Piscopo 2008; Heath, Schwindt-Bayer, and Taylor-Robinson 2005; Schwindt-Bayer 2006, 2010); and how women's presence improves citizens' attitudes toward politics and political participation (Barnes and Burchard 2013; Morgan and Buice 2013; Schwindt-Bayer 2010; Zetterberg 2009). As women's representation has spread into other Latin American political arenas, research has blossomed there too. Studies have emerged on the rising numbers of women in cabinets—their causes and consequences (Escobar-Lemmon and Taylor-Robinson 2005, 2009, 2016)—and the recent election of women to presidencies (Jalalzai 2015; Reyes-Housholder 2016b; Ríos Tobar 2008; Waylen 2016).

This book aims to build upon and contribute to both of these literatures. It brings the women's representation literature together with the literature on democracy, parties, and political institutions in Latin America to answer some important questions about women, gender, and representation while explicitly taking the context of the current political and institutional challenges that Latin American democracies face into account. It focuses on how representation in Latin America shapes and is shaped by formal and informal institutions; the latter having received much less attention (Helmke and Levitsky 2004; Krook and Mackay 2011). Additionally, it brings the perspective of "gender" to studying representation in Latin America to explore not just women's election to office and its consequences but the gendered nature of rules, norms, and political behavior. This helps to elucidate how representative democracy in Latin America came to advantage men and disadvantage women, how institutions perpetuate that, and how the influx of women into Latin American governments may help re-gender politics in a way that not only benefits women in politics but reshapes political representation as well. With this book, we hope to provide the most complete picture of gender and representation in Latin America to date and show that much new and important research remains to be done.

A CAUSES AND CONSEQUENCES FRAMEWORK
FOR WOMEN'S REPRESENTATION IN LATIN AMERICA

The central argument of this book is that political institutions and the political climate of democratic challenges and political crises are key for understanding the election and appointment of women to political arenas, the consequences their presence have inside the arenas, and the impacts women's inclusion has on democracy and society. We analyze this by disaggregating the study of gender and representation into three parts—the causes of women's representation, the consequences of women's representation inside arenas of representation, and the consequences of women's representation outside arenas of representation.[5]

5. Although research on women's representation has long-considered the causes and consequences of women's presence in political office, it does not usually use this terminology. Instead,

Causes of women's representation

Early thinking about women and political representation in Latin America suggested that changing cultural attitudes toward gender equality and increased integration of women into educational arenas and the labor force would increase gender equality in politics (Camp 1998; Craske 1999; Inglehart and Norris 2003; Staudt 1998). But, as noted at the beginning of this chapter, the cultural and socioeconomic changes that have occurred in Latin America have not correlated with comparable improvements in gender equality in all representational arenas in all Latin American countries. Qualified women are well-represented in the pool of potential officeholders, yet women have not achieved equal representation in Latin American political arenas. The chapters of this book explore the applicability of cultural and socioeconomic arguments in the five arenas of representation under study in this book and in specific Latin American countries.

Formal and informal political institutions should be much more important for explaining recent changes in women's representation in Latin America and for explaining continued variation across arenas of representation and across countries. We argue that formal and informal institutions are gendered and shape women's election and appointment to political office, even in the context of improved gender equality in cultural and socioeconomic environments. Specifically, the chapters explore the role of four main types of formal and informal institutions—candidate selection rules, election and appointment rules, gender quotas, and the rules and norms operating in the arenas themselves, such as the power and prestige of the arena and incumbency norms—for explaining variation in women's representation in Latin America. They also highlight additional formal and informal institutions that may matter for specific arenas or individual countries, such as cross-arena diffusion patterns and mechanisms.

The chapters further consider how the current political context in Latin America has both helped and hurt women's political opportunities and overall gender balance in representation. In the past twenty years, many Latin American countries have become mired in challenges to their democracies, such as lack of public support for and trust in governments (i.e., legitimacy), electoral volatility, party or party system fragmentation or collapse, the rise of the Left and the return of populists, decreased electoral participation by voters, and weak ideological attachments between voters and parties. These problems have been linked to "crises of representation" throughout the region (Carranza 2005; Domínguez 1997; Mainwaring, Bejarano, and Leongómez 2006; Miguel 2008; Morgan 2011). Argentina, for example, suffered a "crisis of representation" in the early 2000s, leading to the downfall of President De la Rúa and eventually the election of the leftist Peronist leaders, husband and wife team

---

the most popular approach has been to think about women's representation, particularly in legislatures and parliaments, in the language of Hanna Pitkin's (1967) "views" of representation—descriptive, substantive, and symbolic representation (see, e.g., Childs 2008; Schwindt-Bayer 2010; Schwindt-Bayer and Mishler 2005). We embrace Pitkin's language and views of representation, but we use a framework of causes and consequences because it encompasses more than just Pitkin's three views of representation, it is less specific to representation in legislatures and parliaments, and it provides a more holistic picture of gender and representation in Latin American politics.

Nestor Kirchner and Cristina Fernández de Kirchner (Carranza 2005). Their auto-cratic governing, economic mismanagement, and rampant corruption have contin-ued to challenge representative democracy in Argentina.

Although not all Latin American countries have reached "crisis" status, most have struggled with some degree of democratic and representative weakness over the past twenty years, even those where we might have least expected it, such as Costa Rica and Venezuela (Hagopian 2016; Luna 2016). Citizens have withdrawn support for representative democracy; long-standing two-party systems have eroded; political outsiders, particularly those from leftist parties, started winning elections through-out the region; and corruption scandals have broken out regionwide (Castañeda 2016). The book's chapters explore the linkages between these democratic challenges and gender and representation in Latin America.

Consequences of women's representation inside arenas of representation

For consequences inside the arena, we first argue that increased representation of women should increase policy attention to women's and gender equality issues and improve social policies in the region (Barnes 2016; Franceschet and Piscopo 2008; Htun and Weldon 2012; Kittilson 2008; Schwindt-Bayer 2010), but institutions and political context in specific arenas are likely to limit the extent to which women in different arenas can do this. For example, women in legislatures may be better able to carve out space in their agenda to promote issues of importance to women, as a constituency, whereas the constraints associated with a cabinet minister's portfolio (e.g., being in an economics or foreign affairs post) may make it much more difficult for female ministers to promote women's issues or social issues. The chapters evalu-ate the extent to which women are representing women's issues and social issues in different arenas of representation and in specific countries.

Second, formal and informal institutions within arenas are likely to limit wom-en's access to full political power once they are elected, restricting their impact on economic and traditionally "men's domain" policy areas and limiting their ability to address some of the larger political problems and crises that the countries are facing. Research has already shown that women elected to legislatures in Latin America, for example, do not gain access to men's domain committees to the same extent as do men and rarely have the opportunity to serve in chamber leadership posts (Heath, Schwindt-Bayer, and Taylor-Robinson 2005; Schwindt-Bayer 2010). Similarly, work on cabinets in Latin America suggests that cabinet appointment processes can be biased against women, limiting their access to some of the most powerful posts in a cabinet (Escobar-Lemmon and Taylor-Robinson 2005, 2016). Yet we have few stud-ies on how this plays out in other arenas of representation. The chapters in this vol-ume address the extent to which this dynamic occurs in those other arenas and how formal and informal institutions continue to facilitate women's unequal access to power in legislatures and cabinets.

Third, the inclusion of women in Latin American arenas of representation could have transformative effects on gender representation inside the arenas themselves but this too may be moderated by the institutional and political contexts of different arenas of representation. As gender equality increases in arenas of representation,

governments and governing should become more representative and more democratic because governments include greater diversity both descriptively and
substantively. This should facilitate changes to gendered institutions and the masculine norms that operate inside arenas (Kanter 1977). Yet the extent to which
that occurs may depend on the types of women and men elected or appointed
to office, the strength of the gendered arena norms, the presence or strength of
women's caucuses (*bancadas femininas*), the rules about how to change rules, and
the challenges governments face in the larger political environment. In legislatures
and parties, institutional change requires cooperation of large numbers of people,
which may limit the extent to which transformation of gendered arenas occurs.
In executives, institutional change is often in the hands of one or a small number
of people. Although this should make change easier, it requires a commitment
to gender equality from the leader and a leader who can navigate the larger constraints he or she may face in the form of a political party, coalition, opposition
legislature, constituents, and even the political, economic, and social climate. The
chapters evaluate the extent to which Latin American arenas of representation are
becoming less gendered as a result of women's election and appointment to office.

Consequences of women's representation outside arenas of representation

We also examine the consequences of women's representation outside government
arenas. The presence of women in political arenas may positively influence citizens'
views of gender equality in politics, political engagement, and political participation in Latin America, as a result of symbolic benefits of having women in politics (Desposato and Norrander 2009; Kerevel and Atkeson 2015; Morgan and Buice
2013; Schwindt-Bayer 2010; Zetterberg 2009). It also may improve citizens' attitudes
toward the state of Latin America's democracy and its political institutions, more
generally. Yet this too is likely to vary across arenas due to institutional and contextual differences among them. For example, the strength of these effects may vary
across arenas of representation because more powerful, prestigious, and visible arenas may yield bigger impacts than less powerful, prestigious, and visible arenas. The
election of a female president may have a stronger impact on citizen participation
in or evaluations of democracy than the election of a female mayor or city council
member. The chapters explore some of the societal and democratic effects of wom-
en's representation in different arenas of representation.

ORGANIZATION OF THE BOOK

The goal of this project is ambitious—to analyze the causes and consequences of
gender representation in five different representational arenas both regionwide and
within specific Latin American countries. It requires extensive expertise on Latin
American politics, women's representation in distinct political offices, and women's
representation in specific countries. The challenge of doing this well is more than
any one person could adequately handle. Thus this book draws upon a team of top

scholars with expertise in all of the different areas necessary to provide a holistic analysis of gender and representation in Latin America today.

The book is divided into two parts. The first part includes five chapters, each of which examines the causes and consequences of women's representation in a different arena of representation—the presidency, cabinets, the national legislature, political parties, and subnational governments. The second part of the book shifts the focus to country studies and presents seven chapters that analyze the causes and consequences of women's representation in all five arenas within individual countries—Argentina, Chile, Costa Rica, Uruguay, Mexico, Brazil, and Colombia.

To ensure consistency across the book, the arena and country chapters follow a similar organizational structure. Each chapter has an introduction that presents the main argument and a conclusion that summarizes the key points and articulates directions for future research on women's representation in the arena or country. The body of the chapter first describes either the arena of representation and women's representation in it (for the arena-specific chapters), or all five arenas and women's representation in them in the country under study (for the country-specific chapters). This provides a clear picture of these political offices in Latin America and the state of gender representation in each arena and country, drawing on extensive, and heretofore not always available, data. The chapters secondly focus on the causes of the levels of gender (in)equality in the arena or country and answers questions regarding the presence or absence of women in power, such as, what are the most relevant factors for increasing women's access to the government institution(s)? and how do these vary across countries or arenas of representation? The chapters thirdly explore what we know about the consequences of gender (in)equality in the arena or country both inside and outside the political arena. Many chapters also include a fourth part that highlights challenges that remain for gender and representation in the arena or country.

While ensuring consistency across chapters, we have tried not to induce repetition. Thus each chapter author(s) had their choice of how to evaluate the causes and consequences, what overarching arguments their chapters would make, and what methodology they would use. Some chapters provide a broad-brush analysis of causes and consequences, drawing on existing literature to make arguments about gender and representation in the arena or country. Others provide new original quantitative and/or qualitative analyses of specific causes and consequences that are particularly relevant to their arena or country. Some cover causes and consequences with relatively equal attention paid to each part, whereas others spend more time on one or the other and highlight specific research that remains to be done on the other part.

The specific arenas of representation and countries that this book studies were not selected at random. The goal of the book was to consider gender and representation broadly in all of the different political offices in which representation can take place in order to highlight the importance of institutions and politics in the Latin American context. Presidents and cabinets represent the nation, although the latter is an indirect form of representation because cabinet ministers are not directly held accountable via elections. National legislatures represent districts and regions as well as the country as a whole. Political parties represent the individuals who affiliate with them or vote for their candidates. And subnational executives and legislatures represent regional departments, provinces, or states, or the local city or county. By selecting these five arenas of representation, this book provides a much more comprehensive look at representation than most studies do. These five arenas also combine those that have received a lot of scholarly attention already (legislatures and cabinets) with those that have received much less attention (presidents, parties, and subnational governments).

The countries studied in this volume represent much of the diversity across Latin America.[6] They represent varying political contexts—some countries face significant challenges to democratic representation whereas others do not. They are countries with varying degrees of gender balance in representation reflecting one of its key causes—gender quotas. The selected countries also provide variation in the formal and informal institutions that organize the five arenas of representation, specifically electoral rules such as district and party magnitude and the use of intraparty or interparty voting; candidate selection rules about the centralization of selection and nomination processes; and systemic rules about political decentralization and the prestige of political offices. This diversity in countries allows us to draw some conclusions about gender and representation in Latin America more generally.

THE CHAPTERS AND THEIR MAIN FINDINGS

The chapters of this volume elucidate the varied patterns of gender representation in Latin American countries and their arenas of representation, the different explanations for these patterns, the many consequences they have had, and the challenges that emerge from them.

Catherine Reyes-Housholder and Gwynn Thomas start off Part I by exploring gender and the presidency. They highlight the unexpected emergence of female presidents and presidential candidates in Latin America over the past fifteen years. The gendered history of the presidency in Latin America has long obstructed women's access to that office. The authors point out that theories explaining the election of female executives globally fail to account for the rise of female presidents in Latin America and argue that the transition to democracy and subsequent efforts at democratic consolidation, women's increasing political experience, the rise of the left, and recent political party crises have provided new opportunities for women in the presidency.

Once in office, however, female presidents face gendered obstacles while governing. On one hand, they have been just as successful governing as male presidents, using reelection rates as a measure of "success." In certain circumstances, they have been more likely than men to appoint women to their cabinets, and their presence in office has had some positive impacts on women's participation and engagement in politics. On the other hand, male presidents have higher approval ratings, and only one female president (Michelle Bachelet) has made gender equality a central component of her governing agendas. Reyes-Housholder and Thomas's analysis of the Latin American presidency reveals that numerous challenges and opportunities remain for women and gender equality in the presidency.

6. We define "Latin America" to be the nineteen Spanish- and Portuguese-speaking countries of the Western Hemisphere.

Michelle Taylor-Robinson and Meredith Gleitz analyze cabinets in Latin America from a gendered perspective. They show that the overall representation of women in cabinets has increased significantly since the transitions to democracy, but women and men tend to be represented in stereotypically gendered cabinet portfolios (women in "soft" portfolios, such as social affairs, and men in "hard" portfolios, such as economics) and the gendered nature of the cabinet appointment process has not changed (i.e., the women who get appointed look like men in experience, backgrounds, and other qualifications). Some of the causes of the increase in women's presence in cabinets include the recent political crises that have led to outsider, leftist, and female (to only a very small degree) presidents who select more women, as well as the increase in women's representation in national legislatures and subnational governments.

The consequences of greater gender balance in cabinets for women's issues and gender equality programs have been minimal. Female cabinet ministers find it difficult to promote women's issues because of the restrictions of their portfolios—they are often in posts with little access to resources or need to implement the president's priorities, which are only rarely about gender equality. At the same time, however, greater equality in the credentials and skills that male and female ministers bring to the table suggests improvements in gender integration into cabinets. The authors argue that more research needs to be conducted to explore these consequences and more work needs to be done on how women and men do their jobs differently as cabinet ministers, particularly in terms of balancing autonomy; how female cabinet ministers are treated in office; and what differential impacts male and female cabinet ministers may have on other elites, other government arenas, and citizens.

Santiago Alles and I explore gender and the much-researched arena of Latin American legislatures. We argue that the influx of women into Latin American legislatures has been substantial in many countries, but once in office, women have struggled to attain full access to political power. After describing the widely varying representation of women in Latin American legislatures, we present a statistical analysis that shows that the main explanations for this variation lie with formal institutions, specifically gender quotas, and, to a lesser extent, party system fragmentation. We then present evidence from existing literature that shows that women in legislatures have brought women's issues to the legislative arena through their sponsorship of bills, their committee participation, and their verbal support for these issues, and we provide a new analysis using the Parliamentary Elites of Latin America (PELA) survey to show that female legislators in Latin America are more supportive of gender equality, liberalizing abortion, and less restrictive divorce laws. However, we argue that women have not gained access to committee leadership posts on a diverse array of committees or served in top chamber leadership posts to the same extent as men. We use the PELA dataset again to show that women perceive greater threats to democracy, but we argue that it is not clear that they have acted on those any differently than have men. Finally, we use the Americas Barometer survey to show that the presence of women in legislatures has had important effects on citizen support for female political leaders, political engagement and participation, and supportiveness of representative democracy.

Jana Morgan and Magda Hinojosa analyze gender representation in Latin American political parties. They present data from a unique dataset that shows wide variation across countries in party representation of women as members, leaders, in women's wings, and as candidates and officeholders, and they argue that the primary explanation for gender inequality in party representation is party selection rules and norms. Gender quotas and party ideology matter less than we often expect. To improve gender equality in parties, they argue for better candidate selection and nomination processes, quotas for women in leadership, training programs for female candidates and aspirants, and increased state funding for female candidates. Moving to some of the consequences of having more gender balance in parties, they conduct an original analysis with data from the Americas Barometer to show that women are less likely to identify with parties than men, and parties frequently fail to offer substantive linkages for women beyond their recent advances in descriptive representation. Poor party representation of women has strong negative substantive consequences. Research on gender and representation inside of political parties is sparse thus far, but Morgan and Hinojosa move the literature in the right direction, make clear that more research is much needed, and offer important suggestions for future research in this area.

In the final chapter of Part I, Maria Escobar-Lemmon and Kendall Funk explore gender representation at the subnational level in both state ("intermediate") and local governments. They present an impressive amount of original data on subnational legislatures and executives in Latin America, revealing that women's representation at this level has not changed much over time even though it registers about 25% on average. The causes of different degrees of representation of women and men vary across level and type of office—legislative and executive—but they make clear with a novel statistical analysis that institutions and cross-arena diffusion are key explanations.

Escobar-Lemmon and Funk are positive about the consequences of having more women in subnational legislatures, showing evidence from numerous studies of the ways in which women in local executive and legislative offices have worked to promote gender equality and women's issues and worked to transform political arenas in ways that make them less biased toward women. They do, however, point out some significant challenges for gender equality in subnational politics—women are not getting into local executive offices to the same extent as they are legislative offices, subnational party politics has not been friendly to women (reinforcing Morgan and Hinojosa's arguments), and gender balance is far from assured in local judiciaries and bureaucracies. Much more research needs to be done on both the causes and consequences of increasing gender equality at the subnational level, but Escobar-Lemmon and Funk set the stage for future research.

Moving to Part II and the country chapters, Tiffany Barnes and Mark Jones provide an analysis of women's representation in the first country in the world to adopt a gender quota for legislative elections—Argentina. Although Argentina initiated the wave of quota adoptions that has overtaken Latin America (and the world) in the past twenty-five years, it no longer retains the title of the most successful case of women's representation in the region. Women's legislative representation today sits just over the quota threshold of 33%. Barnes and Jones point out that the country has had more female presidents than any other Latin American country[7] but lags

7. Cristina Fernández de Kirchner served two terms and Isabel Perón was president from 1974 to 1976.

behind in women's representation among subnational executives, in national and subnational cabinets, and in party leadership. Explanations for this vary across the arenas of representation—whereas gender quotas and electoral rules matter most for legislatures, political factors and informal institutions related to party selection processes for candidates and elected leadership positions are key for executives and parties.

According to Barnes and Jones, women's representation in Argentina has had important consequences. Women have helped get women's issues represented and have helped create policies that benefit poor women, and women's representation, particularly at the subnational level, has increased men's and women's trust in government and political engagement of women. Although Argentina is an oft-studied case in literature on gender and representation in Latin America because of its gender quotas, this chapter highlights that quotas have had pros and cons for women in the country and that many challenges for women and scholarship on gender and representation remain.

In the next chapter, Susan Franceschet explores the case of Chile and points out an interesting paradox—the very institutional and political factors that have made Chile one of the region's success stories have limited progress for women. Chile is one of the few countries in Latin America that has not seen large numbers of women enter the political system. Despite electing a female president, Michelle Bachelet, in 2006 (and reelecting her in 2014) and at one point achieving gender parity in cabinet appointments, women's presence in the national congress remains small (less than 20%), is only slightly higher at local levels, and is extremely limited among party and coalition leaders. A primary reason for women's poor legislative representation, Fraceschet argues, is the strong formal and informal institutions that limit the size of electoral districts, require large thresholds to win seats, and require coalition negotiation over candidates for elected office. These are the very institutions that helped Chile become the stable two-party (two-coalition) democracy it is today.

At the same time, according to Franceschet, increased public frustration with democracy and recognition of the problems those rules create for politics has helped women's representation in the executive branch. Even though women have a mixed record of getting into Chile's five arenas of representation, their presence has had important policy consequences. A gender-focused president has been critical for passage of gender-attentive policies. Women in Chile's legislative arenas have been more likely to bring gender issues to the agenda, even if they have not always had success getting them passed or implemented. Franceschet points out that Sernam, the women's ministry, has played a critically important role in this. Although challenges for gender equality in Chile remain, much progress has occurred and the 2015 institutional reforms create expectations of continued improvements to come.

Jennifer Piscopo highlights Costa Rica as a country that has done exceptionally well in terms of women's presence in various arenas of representation and in terms of women acting for women in office and the passage of female-friendly policies. A well-implemented gender quota and subsequent parity law had much to do with this. Yet Piscopo also points out that recent political crises in the country over the past decade have put a ceiling on gender equality in representation. Declining citizen confidence in government, decreased trust in parties, economic stagnation, and corruption scandals have led to a restructuring of the Costa Rican party system with the decline of the two traditional parties and rise of new and small parties. This increased party fragmentation makes it more difficult to elect multiple candidates from any one ballot, making top spots more prestigious and more likely to be protected by men (the majority of party leaders who select candidates are men) for men. This has made the election of women more difficult at the national and subnational level, in executive posts and legislative ones, and explains why gender parity has not been achieved, despite a parity gender quota law.

Piscopo also points out that, although the election of Costa Rica's first female president, Laura Chinchilla, in 2010 broke the highest glass ceiling, her term in office was much less heralded. Corruption scandals, party breakdown, citizen frustration, and economic problems tainted her presidency, and unlike female legislators, who have often worked to promote women's issues and feminist policies in Costa Rica, Chinchilla did not (although she did not obstruct them either). Her negative legacy may make it more difficult for other women to get into top political offices and could have negative consequences for views of women in politics and Costa Rican representation more generally. Piscopo notes the need for much more research on this.

Niki Johnson offers an impressively thorough analysis of women's representation in Uruguay and its causes. Building on her extensive knowledge of the case and incredibly detailed original data, she points out that despite Uruguay being a strong, stable, and institutionalized democracy with laws on equality and significant cultural and socioeconomic gender equality, women have struggled to make numerical progress in politics. Her chapter explores how and why this is the case. After a description of the Uruguayan system and women's representation in all five arenas of representation, she argues that the system is significantly gendered. Formal and informal institutions that are inherently intertwined with political biases limit women's representation. Small district and party magnitudes along with male-biased candidate selection rules hindered women's entry into office until women's groups finally pushed through a gender quota in 2009. Although successful, the main parties applied the quota minimally for national and departmental elections in 2014 and sought out loopholes, particularly through the election of substitutes (*suplentes*), where they could. Even with a quota, they still do not prioritize gender as a criterion, either formally or informally, for elected or appointed political offices.

Highlighting the consequences of women's limited numerical representation, Johnson points out that substantive representation of women has been historically strong. Uruguay has had a longstanding cross-party women's caucus in the national parliament that has helped pass significant policies to help women. This contrasts with other countries where small numbers of women has meant more limited policy progress for women. Yet women still face numerous challenges both in terms of numbers and operating as women in politics in Uruguay. Parties are perhaps the biggest obstacle, and as Johnson points out, the least studied. Future research on the gendered nature of parties in Uruguay is much needed.

Pär Zetterberg explores the gendered nature of political representation in Mexico. He points out that whereas women's legislative representation at the national and subnational level has increased dramatically (placing Mexico in the top twenty nations worldwide) and they have gained nearly 1/3 of seats on party executive bodies, women have done poorly in executive offices. Like many of the authors in this volume, he argues that formal and informal institutions are key to explaining this disparity. Gender quotas have increased women's legislative and party leadership presence, but at the same time, the quota adoption process has brought to light just how reticent male elites are to incorporate women into the political system. Much of this results from unique Mexican rules (term limits) and norms (centralized selection and decision making in parties) that prioritize long-standing male party backbenchers' political careers. These challenges persist when examining the institutional consequences of women's presence in office. Women have to walk a fine line between representing women and responding to formal and informal institutional incentives to protect their own political careers. This has resulted, Zetterberg argues, in a clear gendered division of labor in Mexican politics. Women represent women through policymaking, but they have not gained access to powerful political positions, such as "hard" cabinet portfolios or prestigious committees. Zetterberg also points out that the societal consequences of women's presence in office are understudied.

What Zetterberg makes very clear is that greater democratization and more inclusive formal and informal rules are necessary to change the gendered nature of Mexico's political system and further incorporate women. Recent institutional reforms may be one step in this direction but only time will tell whether Mexican women's exceptional progress in getting elected to legislative bodies will translate into greater representation in other arenas, greater access to political power, and more impact on democracy and society.

Clara Araújo, Anna Calasanti, and Mala Htun explore women's representation in the Brazilian democracy. Despite its democratic transition in 1985 and increased economic power as one of the BRIC's, Brazil has struggled more than any other country in this volume with bringing women into politics. Araujo, Calasanti, and Htun use the juxtaposition of the election of a female president in 2010 and the long-standing small number of women elected to the national congress and subnational legislatures and executives to motivate their chapter and explore the causes and consequences of women in Brazilian arenas of representation. They document women's small numbers in elected and appointed office over time and the increased number of female candidates after the revised 2009 quota reform. They argue that the primary explanations for women's limited representation is fourfold—the candidate-centered electoral system, party system fragmentation and weak institutionalization alongside decentralized selection processes, lack of access to financial resources to mount successful campaigns, and the interaction of incumbency and television in campaigns.

Despite the challenges that women have had getting into office in Brazil (and into positions of power in office), they have worked together through a women's caucus in the congress to put some women's issues on the political agenda. Social gender inequality and conservatism in the country, however, make promoting clearly feminist issues a challenge. Thus Brazil represents a country where arenas of representation, institutions, campaigns, and policy is still highly gendered and significantly disadvantages women. Sadly, recent economic troubles, corruption scandals, and political crises look set to create an even more pessimistic environment for women's representation in the future.

Finally, Pachón and Lacouture echo these conclusions in Colombia. Women's representation has been low and remains low in most arenas of representation and across national and subnational levels of government, and they identify institutions and the highly personalized Colombian political context as the primary reasons for this. No woman has been president and only a few have been credible candidates. This pattern is repeated with governors and mayors. Women's representation in cabinets has increased in recent years, largely as a result of the adoption of a cabinet-level administrative quota law, but the types of posts to which they get appointed remain gendered.

In legislatures, Pachón and Lacouture show that slow increases have occurred over time in women's representation in local councils and the national congress, but the pattern has been flat in department-level assemblies. They find that electoral reforms are mostly responsible for this, but institutional change (such as the adoption of a legislative quota in 2011) has had larger effects on women's representation on party ballots than on the actual proportion of women elected to office. Here, they suggest that Colombia's highly personalistic politics are partly to blame. Despite women's small numbers, they do bring women's issues to the political arena. Pachón and Lacouture show that women are more likely to sponsor bills on women-focused topics, which may lead to greater substantive representation of women in Colombia.

CONCLUSIONS ABOUT GENDER AND REPRESENTATION IN LATIN AMERICA

Overall, this book generates important conclusions about gender and representation in Latin America. We show that even though more women are entering political office than ever before, they are still far from parity in nearly all arenas of representation and countries. We show that the broader Latin American political context and its formal and informal rules about election and appointment to representative offices have had significant positive and negative effects on numerical representation of women and men. Gender quotas have been key to the increased representation of women in some arenas. Yet gender representation in all arenas continues to be hindered by gender-biased candidate selection and electoral, appointment, and arena-specific rules and norms that have long benefited male candidates over female ones. Political crises and scandals have helped bring women into Latin American presidencies but the party system fragmentation of recent years has hurt women's entry into national and subnational legislatures.

In office, increased representation of women has contributed to more policy attention to women's and gender equality issues and women have helped to bring about "some" improved social policies in the region. However, this is not true in all arenas of representation. The formal and informal constraints of some arenas make it much more difficult to address gender equality issues. Greater gender equality in political offices also has not translated into economic or political policies aimed at improving democracy or fighting back against the democratic struggles countries in the region face. Women often fail to gain access to leadership positions where they might have influence over those issues, and even where they do (e.g., the presidency, cabinets), countries have continued to struggle with economic recessions, corruption scandals, party system breakdown, and weak public support.

More generally, greater gender balance in arenas of representation has not had some of the transformational gender effects that could begin to fundamentally restructure Latin American politics in a way that makes the informal and formal institutions that comprise the various arenas of representation more gender equal. The presence of women has had some positive effects on the improvement of societal attitudes toward gender equality, particularly gender equality in politics, and increasing engagement and participation, but the more superficial treatment of this "consequence" in the chapters suggests that much more research needs to be done in this area. Thus increased gender representation has had some positive consequences, but those consequences are not always strong nor have they been consistent across countries and arenas of representation. The inclusion of women has not yet re-gendered representative democracy.

Myriad challenges remain for representative democracy in Latin America, and many of them are intertwined with gender representation. On the positive side, questions about the representativeness of government are now on the political agenda in many countries, and concern over women's underrepresentation in politics has spurred the adoption of gender quota policies in nearly every Latin American country. Political crises have increased representation of women as a result of women's political outsider status becoming more attractive to political elites and citizens. On the negative side, however, party system fragmentation has hindered greater gender balance in legislatures and limited women's rise in party leadership. Additionally, the inclusion of women in political arenas has not been associated with fewer crises or scandals or improved macroeconomic conditions in the region. Increased representativeness, particularly in the form of greater gender representation, is not a sufficient condition for diffusing Latin America's political problems.

Latin American representative democracies remain highly gendered: existing rules and norms advantage men and disadvantage women hampering women's ability to gain numerical parity in nearly all arenas and countries and hindering women's ability to fully exercise political power. Although women have a greater presence today than ever before, they do not necessarily gain access to leadership posts or highly prestigious offices. Institutions and the Latin American political context are a critical piece of the puzzle for understanding why this is the case. This book shows exactly how and why.

PART I

Arenas of Representation

2

Latin America's *Presidentas*

Overcoming Challenges, Forging New Pathways

CATHERINE REYES-HOUSHOLDER AND GWYNN THOMAS ∎

Women's rise to the presidency over the last twenty-five years in Latin America has been dramatic. Before 1990, no woman had ever democratically won the presidency, but between 1990 and 2000, two women did so.[1] From 2001 to 2010, four more women won the presidency, and three successfully competed for a second term. Women have made competitive runs for the presidency in fourteen out of eighteen Latin American countries and have been elected nine times in countries as diverse as Chile, Argentina, Brazil, Costa Rica, Panama, and Nicaragua. Table 2.1 lists in chronological order all female winners, runners-up, and viable candidates since 1990 and shows these candidates' wide range of ideologies and political backgrounds.[2]

Latin America stands out among world regions in terms of electing women to the highest political office. The growing number of women presidents and viable contenders highlights the need for a research agenda on the dynamic intersection of gender and presidential power in Latin America. This chapter outlines and advances such an agenda by analyzing three interrelated questions, each addressed in a separate section. First, what gendered challenges do women face in running for and winning the presidency? Second, what explains the recent rise of women presidents (*presidentas*)? Third, what are the consequences of *presidentas'* rise in terms of governing success, gender equality, and women's representation?

The authors would like to thank the anonymous reviewers, Leslie Schwindt-Bayer, and the other contributors to the volume for their insightful suggestions on this chapter. The chapter was equally co-authored.

1. Janet Jagan served as the first woman prime minister in Guyana in 1997, and then was elected president by the legislature, and served as president from 1997–1999. Guyana is not a presidential regime, but instead a mixed parliamentary-presidential regime, and belongs more to the political traditions of the Anglophone Caribbean than Spanish or Portuguese Latin America.

2. Most electoral systems in Latin America have a two-round voting system. We define "viable" candidates as those who received at least 15% of the first-round vote because candidates who reach this threshold often advance to a second round.

Table 2.1 FEMALE WINNERS AND VIABLE CANDIDATES 1990–2017

Year	Country	Candidate	First-Round Vote %	Ideology	Political Experience
1990	Nicaragua	Violeta Chamorro*	55	Center-right	Opposition leader
1997	Honduras	Nora de Melgar**	43	Right	Mayor, First lady
1997	Bolivia	Remedios Loza	17	Center-left	Congress
1998	Colombia	Noemi Sanin	27	Right	Minister
1999	Panama	Mireya Moscoso*	30	Right	Party leader
2001 / 2006	Peru	Lourdes Flores	24 / 24	Center-right	Congress
2005 / 2013	Chile	Michelle Bachelet*	46 / 47	Center-left	Minister
2007 / 2011	Argentina	Cristina Fernández de Kirchner*	45 / 54	Center-left	Congress, First lady
2007	Argentina	Elisa Carrió**	23	Center-left	Congress
2008	Paraguay	Blanca Ovelar**	32	Center-right	Minister
2009	Panama	Balbina Herrera	38	Center	Mayor, Congress, Minister
2010	Costa Rica	Laura Chinchilla*	47	Center-right	Minister
2010 / 2014	Brazil	Marina da Silva	19 / 21	Center-left	Congress
2011 / 2016	Peru	Keiko Fujimori**	21 / 39.8	Center-right	Congress, First lady[a]
2010 / 2014	Brazil	Dilma Rousseff*	41.6 / 41.1	Center-left	Minister
2012	Mexico	Josefina Vázquez	26	Right	Minister
2013	Honduras	Xiamara Castro de Zelaya	29	Center-left	First lady
2013	Chile	Evelyn Matthei**	25	Right	Congress, Minister
2014	Colombia	Marta Lucia Ramirez	16	Left	Congress, Minister
2014	Colombia	Clara López	17	Right	Mayor, Minister
2015	Guatemala	Sandra Torres**	19.8	Center-left	First lady
2016	Peru	Verónika Mendoza	18.8	Center-left	Congress
2017	Ecuador	Cynthia Viteri	16	Center-right	Congress

[a] The daughter of Alberto Fujimori, Keiko, served as Peru's first lady from 1994–2000.

* Elected

** Second-place finisher

SOURCE: Reyes-Housholder (2017).

We begin by arguing that the Latin American presidency developed as a gendered institution that poses formidable challenges for women's representation. Men's historical dominance of presidential power shaped societal expectations surrounding presidential leadership as well as the institution of the presidency itself. Even after women legally could participate at all levels of electoral politics, the presidency remained for decades a political office exclusively held by men. The current political opportunity structures that advantage men over women as presidential candidates cannot be separated from this history.

In section two, we ask: what political factors have helped women overcome these steep gendered barriers to democratically win the presidency? Recent changes in Latin America's political context, including processes of civil society mobilization, democratization, and democratic strengthening have fundamentally altered Latin American politics, providing new opportunities for women to gain the necessary experience and networks needed to run for president, and changing political meanings around women's representation and leadership. These factors have facilitated increases in the number of viable women candidates, posing serious challenges to men's previously uncontested control of the presidency. We argue that the combination of Latin America's "left turn" and challenges faced by institutionalized parties in maintaining political power produced an opportunity structure particularly propitious for talented women candidates. These dual factors helped certain women overcome gendered barriers to not only capture the presidency, but also clinch reelection. Although preliminary, this explanation of *presidentas'* rise challenges dominant theories on how women access chief executive office worldwide.

The third section addresses the consequences of women's presidencies. We look at *presidentas'* performance relative to their male counterparts, their efforts to enhance gender equality, and their impact on women's political participation. We argue that even though women presidents have been successful in terms of reelection, women presidents' slightly lower approval ratings compared to their male counterparts may be due to intense scrutiny of their role as the "first *woman* president." As a result, women presidents must continually manage gendered cultural expectations to maintain their popularity. We finally show that initial research into *presidentas'* impact on women's descriptive, substantive, and symbolic representation is mixed, and no clear trend emerges.

In our conclusion, we call for greater theoretical development and empirical investigation into the intersection of gender and the Latin American presidency. We argue for a reconceptualization of the presidency in this region as a gendered institution. This chapter's findings, while still preliminary given the small number of cases, delineate the contours of a rich research agenda on the challenges, causes, and consequences of Latin America's *presidentas*.

LATIN AMERICA'S GENDERED PRESIDENCIES: A UNIQUE CHALLENGE TO WOMEN'S REPRESENTATION

The presidency is by far the most influential and visible elected office in Latin America. All former colonies of Spain and Portugal eventually developed presidential constitutions during the 1800s, making presidentialism[3] the most dominant form of government in Latin America (Cheibub, Elkins, and Ginsburg 2011; Foweraker 1998; Mainwaring 1990; Shugart and Carey 1992). During the past two hundred years, Latin American countries created a form of presidentialism distinguished by the concentration of lawmaking powers in the executive (Payne 2007). As Cheibub, Elkins and Ginsburg (2011, 1079) argue, "Latin American constitutions are uniquely inclined to empower presidents," who in their "executive lawmaking authority," more closely resemble the executive in parliamentary systems.

While the centrality of the presidency in Latin American politics is widely acknowledged, how the presidency both shaped and was shaped by gender, race, class, and sexuality has not received the attention it deserves.[4] Specifically, the recent elections of women presidents expose the theoretical lacunae on the effects of men's dominance in the presidency. As we argue below, the long history of men's access to and women's exclusion from presidential power has fundamentally shaped the presidency as a political institution. Most scholarship in Latin America assumes, as Duerst-Lahti (2008) argued in reference to the case of the United States, that (1) a president's gender is not important to understanding presidential governance, and that (2) gender is not important in understanding the institutional functioning of the presidency. Scholarship on the Latin American presidency continues to develop absent any attention to gender, a glaring problem given the growing attention to how political institutions are gendered (see for example Dore and Molyneux 2000; Htun 2003; Waylen 2016).

Even a cursory look at the history of Latin America reveals foundational connections between elite men and presidential power. The creation of independent states is traditionally depicted through the lives of men such as Simón de Bolívar, Bernardo O'Higgins, José de San Martín, Miguel Hidalgo y Costilla, and José Gervasio Artigas, who are lauded as military heroes and fathers of new nations. More broadly, it was the male members of the newly dominant Creole elite (native born of European descent) who first crafted the presidential systems that fused liberalism with patriarchalism, the ideology of colonial rule (Dore 2000; Lynch 1986; Stern 1997). Latin America's emerging political order was often conceptualized as an extended family naturally ruled by a fraternity of elite, male leaders, rather than by a distant king (Collier 1967; Dore 2000; Felstiner 1983; Mallon 1995; Thomas 2011b). Thus, on the one hand, the new states' founding constitutions embraced liberal principles of equality, liberty, and consent among political equals. On the other,

---

3. Presidentialism is a system of government where the executive (the president) is elected directly by popular vote, in contrast to parliamentary systems, where the majority of the members of parliament elect the prime minister.

4. Lack of theoretical attention to the impact of these social categories marks not only the literature developed on the presidency in the 1990s and 2000s, such as the classic institutionalist debates around the "perils of presidentialism" (Linz 1994; Linz and Valenzuela 1994; Mainwaring 1993; Mainwaring, Shugart, and Linz 1997; and Stepan and Skach 1994), but also the recent scholarship on the rise of multiparty presidential regimes, the comparative differences between Latin American presidential systems, and the greater attention to presidential strategies in promoting their political agenda (Ames 2001; Amorim Neto 2006; Foweraker 1998; Pereira and Melo 2012; Raile, Pereira, and Power 2011).

elite male leaders were quick to restrict the meaning of "political equals" by limiting the participation and power of people they considered their natural inferiors (all women, indigenous peoples, and racial/ethnic minorities, as well as poor and working-class men). They justified the new structure of political power by invoking existing discourses around the naturalized raced and gendered superiority of elite men (Dore and Molyneux 2000).

Throughout the 19th century, ongoing civil unrest over the distribution of political power plagued fragile Latin American states. However, no serious alternative to the presidential system of government emerged. Historians instead argue that the weakness of state institutions during this period promoted the political dominance of networks of elite families and caudillos—charismatic leaders who gained power through armed force (Lynch 1986). Elite men's power and authority as patriarchs continued to shape presidential power, as invocations of the connections between the family and the state continued to legitimate political power and authority (Dore 2000; Dore and Molyneux 2000; Mallon 1995; Thomas 2011b).

A new form of organizing and exercising presidential power arose in the first half of the 20th century. Populist presidents sought to funnel the increasing political participation of non-elite men into their own power base (Kampwirth 2010). These presidents, like their predecessors, drew from, rather than challenged, pre-established connections between gender and political power (Kampwirth 2010). Populists such as Lázaro Cárdenas, Juan Perón, and Getúlio Vargas, reworked the links between paternalism and presidential power to emotionally appeal to citizens and justify their political agendas. Conniff argues that "virtually all populists assumed roles as paternal figures to their followers" (1999, 19). The enduring power of paternalist claims can be seen in the ideologically diverse presidential campaigns of Chilean socialist Salvador Allende in 1970, conservative candidates Joaquín Lavín and Sebastián Piñera in 2005–2006, and Brazil's left-leaning President Luiz Inácio "Lula" da Silva in 2002 and 2006 (Reyes-Housholder 2017; Thomas 2011a).

The gendered history of presidential power has severely limited women's abilities to compete for the presidency. While women started winning legislative political offices at the sub-national and national levels shortly after achieving full suffrage rights in the 1940s and 1950s (Chaney 1979; Lavrín 1995; Schwindt-Bayer and Alles in chapter 4, this volume, and Escobar-Lemmon and Funk in chapter 6, this volume), it was not until 1990 that the first woman democratically won a presidential election.[5] Women's representation at all levels of government currently outpaces women's access to the presidency (see chapters 4, 5, and 6, this volume). Female presidential candidates confront well-established ideological connections between men, masculinity, and presidential power, as well as negative gender stereotypes about women's political abilities and leadership. These stereotypes, in turn, shape both the media coverage of women candidates

---

5. Before 1990, two women had served as president without being popularly elected: Isabel Peron (Argentina, 1974–1976) and Lidia Gueiler Tejada (Bolivia, 1979–1980). We discuss these cases below.

and voters' perceptions (Franceschet and Thomas 2010; Hinojosa 2010; Murray 2010; Piscopo 2010; Thomas 2011a). For example, in her first campaign in 2005, Bachelet was routinely criticized for her more consensual approach to leadership that differed from an authoritative, directive style strongly associated with presidential power. Her opponents claimed she simply was not "presidential" or lacked competence (Thomas 2011a). In an example of the double-bind often faced by women candidates, the Argentine press criticized Fernández de Kirchner for acting "authoritarian, aloof, vain and self-centered," criticisms that show the difficulties she faced in appearing both properly "presidential" and properly "feminine" (Piscopo 2010, 201). The gendered media coverage of Fernández de Kirchner ultimately meant that she was not treated as a competent professional, but rather as either the "wife of" the current president or as a "spotlight-hungry starlet" (Piscopo 2010, 201, 205). In her unsuccessful bid for the presidency in Venezuela, Irene Sáez also received a barrage of sexist coverage that emphasized her femininity and past Miss Universe title, rather than her campaign platform and success as mayor (Hinojosa 2010).

In negotiating the pro-masculine bias around presidential power, women have sometimes invoked historical connections between women's political participation and maternal ideology. Maternalism is one of the few ideological "tools" women have historically used to justify their interest and participation in politics (see Franceschet, Piscopo, and Thomas 2016 for an overview). Maternalism might also present gendered advantages for women competing for the presidency in specific contests. For example, Violeta Chamorro, in her 1990 presidential campaign in Nicaragua, highlighted her skills as a mother in crafting peace among her ideologically diverse family to persuade voters of her capacity to end the armed conflict between the Sandinistas and Contras. She also portrayed herself as the "Mother of the Nicaraguans" and strategically used religious imagery associated with the Virgin Mary (Kampwirth 1996). Chamorro rhetorically leveraged characteristics associated with women (peacemakers, consensus builders, honest leaders) with issues that most mattered to Nicaraguans in 1990—the end of civil conflict and the military draft (Franceschet, Piscopo, and Thomas 2016).

Chamorro's case underscores the power of maternalism as a presidential campaign strategy for women, particularly given the existing masculine bias in definitions around presidential leadership and power. Twenty years later, Rousseff similarly leveraged a maternalist discourse in her first campaign, but she did so to soften her image as a "hard" leader and to establish a shared identity with women voters. As the figurative *mãe do Pac*, Rousseff and her team emphasized her technocratic capacities to continue the legacy of Lula, who had portrayed himself as a *pai do Brasil* (Reyes-Housholder 2017). However, the strategic use of maternalism should not be overstated. Franceschet, Piscopo, and Thomas (2016) argue that very few women recently elected at the national level position themselves as a "traditional *supermadre*," as Chamorro did, by justifying their entry into politics mostly through appeals to maternal identities. Instead, like Rousseff, most successful female candidates craft more complex gendered personas, highlighting their competence and experience, while also promoting their general interest in public welfare and care for society.

Nevertheless, women presidential candidates' nuanced approach to managing gendered political expectations is often distorted in media coverage that explains women's political power via familial frames. Often, these frames are used to question women's competency and legitimacy as leaders. For example, political pundits in Chile attributed Bachelet's record-breaking public support at the end of her first presidency (over 80%) not to the success or popularity of her policy accomplishments, or to her skill as a political leader, but to the *cariñocracia* (caring-ocracy) founded in her charisma and likability (Franceschet and Thomas 2010; Thomas 2011a). Thus long-standing connections between women's political participation and maternalism are renegotiated as women increasingly and more successfully contest their exclusion from presidential power.

THE RISE OF *LAS PRESIDENTAS*: CHALLENGING BARRIERS AND CREATING OPPORTUNITIES FOR WOMEN

Above, we explored the connections between presidential power, men's historical political dominance, and women's ongoing underrepresentation. However, from 2006–2014, Latin Americans elected and reelected women seven times to the presidency, a record unmatched in other world regions. This section will show that, beginning roughly in 1990, the gendered opportunities structure around democratic elections changed in ways that enhanced women's relative ability to win the presidency. First, region-wide conditions—namely, civil society mobilization, democratization, and democratic strengthening—helped create the necessary conditions for the rise of women presidents by creating more opportunities for women to develop the political experience and networks needed to position themselves as viable candidates. Second, Latin America's "left turn" and political opportunities granted by incumbent political parties were crucial factors in the rise of women presidents elected since 2006 in Latin America. Our analysis of Latin America's elected women presidents questions theories from existing studies on how women access executive power worldwide—namely the openings provided by regime crises and family ties. Yet, as with all studies of women executives, the small number of cases in any region, the wealth of idiosyncratic factors involved in elections, and the scarce existing scholarship limit our ability to exhaustively weigh the causes of *presidentas'* rise. This section nevertheless serves as a starting point for research on how and why women were elected president so many times in such a short period in Latin America.

Political context and political opportunity for women in the presidency

The spread of authoritarianism from 1950–1990 arrested both women's and men's possibilities to compete for the presidency. Only Costa Rica and Venezuela remained democracies during this period, while all other Latin American countries were at least partly governed by different forms of nondemocratic rule. During this time, women were the backbone of the social movements opposing military rule and demanding democracy (Jaquette 1994). Although social movements waned after the return of democratic elections, demands for the greater political inclusion of marginalized groups remained powerful.[6] A lasting legacy of the women's move-ments in Latin America has been the recognition of women's exclusion from the state and the need to increase women's representation in democratic governments (see for example, the country case studies for Chile [chapter 8], Argentina [chapter 7], Uruguay [chapter 10], and Brazil [chapter 12] in this volume).

While gender quotas for national legislatures have dramatically increased levels of women's national representation (see Schwindt-Bayer and Alles, chapter 4, this vol-ume), gains at the executive level have been slower. Male candidates continue to out-number female candidates, but women are making gains.[7] From 1990–2014, women made up 10% of presidential candidacies. In the 2010–2014 election cycle, women comprised about 17% of all candidacies.[8] Women have taken advantage of the oppor-tunities offered by the increasing stability of democratic rule in many countries to gain political experience and consolidate their networks—two assets that are often necessary for viable presidential runs. Case studies suggest that women's experiences and networks within institutionalized parties have helped position them as com-petitive contenders (see, again, Table 2.1). For example, many recent winners served as cabinet ministers in their respective countries; Bachelet as Minister of Health, then Defense under President Lagos; Chinchilla as Minister of Justice, and the First Vice President for President Arias; and Rousseff as Minister of Mines and Energy and later as President da Silva's chief of staff. As a powerful senator, Fernández de Kirchner led efforts in Congress and the Peronist party to advance the legislative agenda of then president (and her husband), Néstor Kirchner. In Panama, Moscoso led the Arnulfista Party both before and after her presidential term. Second-place presidential contenders, such as Nora de Melgar in Honduras, Keiko Fujimori in Peru (twice), Elisa Carrió in Argentina, Blanca Ovelar in Paraguay, Evelyn Matthei in Chile, and Sandra Torres in Guatemala, all possessed extensive experience within political parties.[9] Although women are often seen, or able to position themselves, as

6. Cuba remains the exception.

7. We built on Baker and Greene's (2011) presidential candidate dataset and coded the gender of over 750 candidates that competed in 101 elections from 1990–2014 in 18 Latin American countries. Unlike other databases used in literature on women executives around the world, this dataset examines actual as well as potential winners, female as well as male candidates. Our analysis of the first rounds of 101 presidential elections in 18 Latin American countries between 1990–2014 shows women's intensified presence in presidential contests over time.

8. While the overall trend is for greater participation, during the 2000–2004 election cycle, women ran less frequently than they had in previous or subsequent cycles, but the fewer women garnered more of the vote, perhaps reflecting the increasing viability of women as candidates.

9. Latin America has had three non-elected women presidents, two of whom also had extensive experience in national politics. Lidia Gueiler Tejada (Bolivia, 1979–1980) was a long-time politi-cal leader on the left. While serving as the elected president of Bolivia's Chamber of Deputies, she was appointed president in order to oversee new elections in the face of the contested results of the 1979 presidential election. Previously Minister of Education, Culture and Sports, Rosalía Arteaga Serrano (Ecuador 1997) was vice-president of Ecuador when Congress voted President Abdalá Bucaram Ortiz out of office in 1997. She served as president for just six days, after which Congress nominated Fabián Alarcón to replace her. Only Isabel Perón, who as vice-president, took over the presidency after the death of the elected president and her husband, Juan Perón, lacked extensive political experience in her own right.

political outsiders because of historical patterns of gender exclusion, the biographies of women presidential candidates suggest they were not political newcomers and had built extensive political careers through their own efforts, rather than relying on family connections or dramatic political events.

Women's increasing experience in political parties might also help explain a finding that emerges from our analysis of viable female candidates—women's growing success in garnering votes. Figure 2.1 shows a notable jump in women's average vote shares in terms of mean vote percentage by presidential candidates in the past five election cycles. Women's average vote share rose from 6.6% during the 1990–1994 election cycle to 8.4% in 1995–1999. From there, this average dipped during the third election cycle to 6.9%, only to jump again to 14.4% and then reached 20.3% during the most recent round of presidential competitions. While women increased their vote share, Figure 2.1 also shows that men outperformed women during the first three election cycles. Male candidates on average earned about 12.9% of the total vote while female candidates captured 7.0% from 1990–1994. Women's relative performance improved slightly during the next election cycle (12.0% for men and 8.4% for women from 1995–1999). During the third election cycle (2000–2004), women's average vote shares again dropped relative to men's (13.5% for men compared to women's 6.9%).

These statistics are not terribly surprising, given that the gendered opportunity structure historically has favored male presidential candidates. What is less expected, however, is that women presidential candidates outperformed men during the two most recent election cycles. From 2005–2009, women earned, on average, 1.4% more of the vote share than their male competitors, and during the most recent round

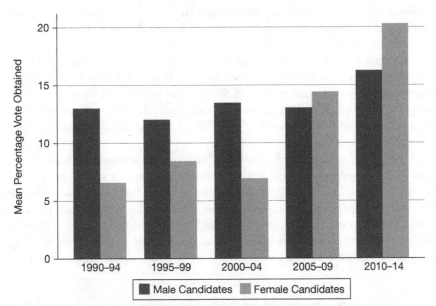

Figure 2.1 Mean Percentage of Vote Won by Candidate Gender and Election Years
NOTE: The mean percentage vote is the average of all presidential candidate vote shares across 18 Latin American countries for all elections that occurred during the specified time period.

of competitions (2010–2014), women captured 4.0% more of the vote share than men.[10] This analysis reveals that the growth in popular support for female candidates reflects the post-2005 surge in women's victories. Women triumphed in one presidential election in each of the first two cycles (1990–1994; 1995–1999); none in the third cycle (2000–2004); two in the fourth cycle (2005–2009) and then five in the last cycle (2010–2014). Yet the number of female candidates from 1990–2004 (38) is the same number of female candidates during the 2005–2014 period. The uptick in women's election success, therefore, has far outpaced the influx of female presidential contenders.

What accounts for the success of women winning the presidency starting in 2006? Women's growing political experience and political contexts more propitious for women's political representation seem to function as necessary rather than sufficient conditions for women's recent string of victories. As Table 2.1 shows, both winners and runners-up have boasted substantial political experience. Here, we argue that two recent changes—Latin America's left turn and challenges and opportunities related to incumbent parties—created the conditions that opened a path to victory for women presidents.

To begin, women presidential candidates may have been able to capitalize on what Baker and Greene (2011) argue was a regional shift in preferences for state intervention. Most scholars believe the string of presidential victories for the left (the so-called "pink tide") began in the late 1990s with Hugo Chávez in Venezuela (Levitsky and Roberts 2011). While the causes of the left turn are still debated, one prevailing theory is that popular support for free market reforms dwindled during this period as voters gave their presidential candidates a leftist mandate (Baker and Greene 2011).

A leftward shift in public preferences and potentially an increased salience of state provision for social welfare may have tipped the balance in favor of some female presidential candidates. We found that the ideological difference between all male and female contenders from 1990–2014 in Latin America is statistically significant, meaning that women have tended to run as slightly more progressive candidates than men.[11] While the difference is small in terms of magnitude (one point on a 20-point scale), it is important in light of the fact that presidential elections are often won by narrow margins. This means that female presidential candidates may have been seen as more in line with public demands around social welfare than their male counterparts.

Ideological orientation helps draw a line between female winners and almost winners. Since the beginning of the "left turn," three out of the four women presidents—Bachelet, Fernández de Kirchner, and Rousseff—have been standard bearers for the center-left. Looking back at Table 2.1, we see that, with the exception of Sandra Torres in Guatemala in 2016, every woman who has finished in second place has professed a more conservative ideology than the eventual winner: Nora de Melgar in Honduras in 1997, Blanca Ovelar in 2008 in Paraguay, Keiko Fujimori in Peru in

10. Nevertheless, none of the candidate sex differences in percent vote share are statistically significant for any of the election cycles. This is likely due to the small number of observations.

11. A score of 1 indicates extreme left and 20 indicates extreme right (Baker and Greene 2011). Female presidential candidates' scores average to 10.3, while males' are 11.3.

2011 and 2016, and Evelyn Matthei in Chile in 2013. These comparisons bolster our argument on the relationship between a leftward shift in preferences and women's recent successes. Ideology seems to have benefited left-leaning women and potentially hurt some conservative women.

Another consequence of the left turn—growing salience of social issues—could also have benefited some female presidential candidates relative to their male counterparts. Gender stereotypes that portray women as more concerned with and capable of handling issues of social protection could provide electoral advantages to women presidential candidates, even on the right. In Costa Rica, the center-right Chinchilla was able to distance herself from the deeply unpopular positions taken by her political predecessor and party leader (Óscar Arias) in supporting the Central American Free Trade Agreement by touting her concern for social provisions for children and the elderly. Chinchilla shored up her centrist claims by signaling her support of Costa Rica's welfare state (Thomas 2014). Women candidates from center or center-right parties might also have particular advantages when competing against similarly ideologically situated men within a political context marked by a desire for greater attention to social issues.

Josefina Vázquez in Mexico provides a "negative" case that supports the importance of the "left turn" as a factor. Mexico is one of the few Latin American countries that has not participated in the region-wide left turn. The increasingly center-right Institutional Revolutionary Party (PRI) governed Mexico for about seventy years until the center-right National Action Party (PAN) won two consecutive presidential elections (Vicente Fox in 2000 and Felipe Calderón in 2006). In 2012, Vázquez became the only Mexican woman to make a viable presidential run, emerging as the candidate for the PAN. She finished third, behind Andrés López Obredor of the left and Enrique Peña Nieto of the right, who went on to win in the second round.

In addition to the left turn, political challenges faced by incumbent parties also help explain the post-2005 emergence of *las presidentas*. Women might have gendered advantages as presidential nominees of incumbent parties in a context shaped by corruption scandals, voter fatigue with political elites, and the desire for change. As the introduction of this volume describes, growing popular discontent over democratic representation and accountability has spread across the region. At the same time, demands for the political inclusion of previously marginalized groups and their concerns continued. By 2005, it was often left-leaning presidents in office and who faced growing citizen dissatisfaction. Left political elites—even those who emerged from democratization movements—were seen as disinterested in and removed from the everyday concerns of citizens. The advantages offered by women candidates might be particularly attractive when the challenge for a party or coalition was not to gain but to *maintain* presidential power.

Women candidates, particularly as possible "first woman" presidents, seem to provide the desired—but often elusive—qualities of "continuity and change," as Bachelet's 2005 campaign slogan proclaimed (Adams and Thomas 2010; see Thomas 2014 for a discussion of this argument for Chinchilla's case). Corruption scandals recurring in many of Latin America's parties appear to structure opportunities in ways that may benefit female presidential candidates. Female candidates are stereotypically viewed as more honest and less corrupt than male politicians (Murray 2010). Elites from a sitting president's party or coalition may perceive nominating experienced women candidates as a strategy to maintain control of the presidency where a woman candidate is seen as responding to a desire for change in light of corruption accusations and when the sitting male president is prohibited from running for (consecutive) reelection.

Bachelet, Fernández de Kirchner, Chinchilla, and Rousseff all fit this pattern. Presidents from their own parties preceded them, and all received the backing of their male predecessors. In Chile, Bachelet's popularity during her first campaign was partly based on voters' perception of her emergence from "the people" rather than via elite party networks. She capitalized on growing dissatisfaction over political scandals and with the traditional political elites from the center-left coalition, the *Concertación*, which had governed for sixteen years (Franceschet and Thomas 2010; Thomas 2011a). Fernández de Kirchner in Argentina was clearly seen as the candidate that would continue her husband's *Kirchnerismo* policies that she had helped formulate and advance within the Senate while also offering political change (Piscopo 2010). In Costa Rica, Arias' reasons for supporting Chinchilla's nomination to succeed him as the *Partido Liberación Nacional*'s candidate were also gendered. In light of ongoing corruption scandals related to other members of Arias's government, Chinchilla's identity as a woman coupled with her lack of involvement in previous scandals boosted her presidential prospects (Thomas 2014).

Finally, Rousseff was one of the few high-level members of the Partido dos Trabalhadores (Worker's Party or PT), who was not implicated in the *mensalão* corruption scandal that rocked Brazil during Lula's second term, and this undoubtedly contributed to Lula's support for her nomination as the PT's presidential candidate. For a brief period, many perceived Rousseff as the *faxineira* or "cleaning lady" for Brazilian corruption. This politically advantageous, gendered image faded as the *lava jato* corruption scandal erupted during the beginning of her second term and helped pull her approval ratings down to 8%, opening the door for her eventual impeachment in 2016.

Furthermore, all *presidentas* in Latin America, with the exception of Chamorro, benefitted from the support of political parties already holding presidential power. If we look at all the presidential candidates from 1990–2014 who obtained at least 25% of the vote, we find initial statistical support for the importance of incumbent party support. Of the 176 candidates, (17 were women, 159 were men), women were candidates of incumbent political parties 65% of the time, whereas men were candidates of incumbent parties 39% of the time. These sex differences are statistically significant ($p=0.04$). Comparing female winners and runners-up in Table 2.1, we observe that five women finished as runners-up in presidential contests. Three of the five of the second-place female finishers were challengers: Alba Gúnera de Melgar (Honduras 1997), Carrió (Argentina 2007), and Fujimori (Peru 2011, 2016). In Chile, Evelyn Matthei (2013) emerged as a candidate for the right political coalition of the sitting president, Sebastián Piñera, after a number of political scandals led to the resignation of more well-known male candidates. However, in Matthei's case, she ran against former president Bachelet, who had returned to presidential politics with high levels of popular support after sitting out one constitutionally mandated term. Blanca Ovelar (Paraguay 2008) was the only other female candidate sponsored by the incumbent party who lost, and as noted above, she maintained a more conservative ideology than the female presidential candidates who won.

In short, we have argued that Latin America's broader social changes, including women's participation in social movements and political parties, and the sustained focus on increasing women's political representation created the conditions for more viable women candidates for the presidency. We also argued that the region-wide ideological shift toward the left and the opportunities found within the context of incumbent parties facing scandal were crucial factors that increased the likelihood of women candidates being able to overcome gendered barriers and win the presidency.

Latin America's challenge to existing research on women executives

Our argument for how women have accessed presidential power in Latin America, however, differs from existing explanations for female chief executives worldwide. That research points to the importance of facilitating factors such as weak or divided executive power, extreme political instability or democratic transition, and close familial ties, particularly as wives or daughters to past executive leaders, in overcoming gendered barriers (Jalalzai 2008; Jalalzai 2013; Jalalzai and Krook 2010). Yet, the recent success of women presidents in Latin America provides little support for these factors. To begin, presidents in this region possess some of the strongest formal powers of any chief executives in the world. Yet it is in this region that women have been democratically elected and reelected to the presidency the most often. Thus the barrier to women's election posed by the concentration of executive power and advantages offered by weak or divided executives seems a less relevant explanation than previously believed.

Our analysis also casts doubt on the global applicability of arguments that women access executive power during moments of extreme political instability where the rules—or tradition—of democratic succession are unclear, such as immediate post-conflict situations or during transitions from military rule. Of the elected women presidents, only Chamorro's election in 1990 was set in a context of ongoing conflict. Her candidacy was explicitly seen as a way to end ongoing armed conflict between the Contra rebels and the Sandinista government. Instead, since 1998, women presidential candidates and women presidents have emerged in the context of long-standing connections to institutional political parties. Women candidates in Latin America have benefitted from the electoral advantages offered within the context of institutional political parties seeking to hold onto political power.

Lastly, our analysis leads us to question the argument often made in reference to Latin America that leveraging family ties is a primary way that women overcome gendered barriers to presidential power. We would argue that of all women presidents in Latin America only in the case of the nonelected Isabel Perón were ties to her husband clearly explanatory in her gaining the presidency—he had appointed her as vice president. Other women may have had some family ties, but those ties were less important for explaining their elections than other factors, such as the left turn, ties to incumbent parties, and these women's own political prowess. While two out of six of the region's elected *presidentas*—Fernández de Kirchner and Moscoso— were married to former presidents (with Fernández de Kirchner serving as first lady before becoming president), both were accomplished politicians in their own right. Fernández de Kirchner and her husband Néstor Kirchner jointly accrued power, beginning in the 1970s until Kirchner's sudden death in 2010. While many have pointed to the ways in which her first lady status helped launch her presidential campaign, few have recognized how Fernández de Kirchner, a powerful Peronist legislator, helped her husband clinch victory by 2003. In other words, the family ties argument should work both ways in the case of Argentina—helping Kirchner and helping Fernández de Kirchner. Although it is true that Kirchner won the presidency before Fernández de Kirchner, existing family ties theories applied to Fernández de Kirchner tend to undermine the relevance of her own mastery of Argentine politics. Although she and her husband built their political careers together, Fernández de Kirchner's presidential victories are better explained by her political skill, by the electoral advantages offered by Latin America's left turn, and the advantages offered by the incumbent Peronist party.

Scholars have also used the cases of Moscoso and Chamorro to illustrate the family ties argument but neither case provides clear support for the theory. Moscoso ascended to the presidency eleven years after the death of her husband whom she had married after his short-lived third (and final) presidency of only eleven days. Her election was built on her work as a long-time party leader and power-broker in Panamanian politics. Chamorro was a well-known widow of a prominent newspaper editor who had been killed by the Somoza dictatorship, but she rose to political prominence because of her opposition to the Sandinista revolutionary government that had overthrown this dictatorship. In neither of these cases, does the existence of family ties provide a persuasive explanation for how they achieved the presidency. In addition, half of the *presidentas*—Bachelet,[12] Chinchilla, and Rousseff—had no marital or close family connections to powerful male political leaders. Like Fernández de Kirchner, their elections and re-elections are better explained by the factors explored above.

Family ties nevertheless do often affect the campaigns of female presidential candidates in both positive and negative ways, but this scholarship often focuses on how family ties always *help* female candidates. There is evidence that family ties to powerful male figures can be hurtful. Female candidates have faced media framing of family ties that distort their own self-branding as efficient, independent executives (Murray 2010). Family ties may act as a double-edged sword for some viable candidates, such as Keiko Fujimori who lost extremely close elections in Peru in 2011 and in 2016. The antidemocratic legacy of her father and past president, Alberto Fujimori, may ultimately have tipped the balance against her.

Finally, much of the family ties research fails to verify the extent to which men have used similar family connections to capture the presidency. This means that women are singled out in the scholarship for their family ties in contexts where presidential power itself could be embedded within political families, making

---

12. In some quantitative studies (Jalalzai 2008; Jalalzai 2013), Bachelet is wrongly coded as having family ties to a powerful male political figure. This error occurs because of the lack of country specific knowledge of Chile. While her father, Airforce Brigadier General Bachelet, had served in a minor appointed post at the end of President Allende's presidency, he was not considered a member of the Chilean political elite, and he had no political career. He was targeted for detention as a member of the "constitutionalist" officers who supported the principal of civilian rule during Pinochet's consolidation of military power shortly after the 1973 coup d'état. Before Bachelet served as Chile's first woman defense minister, when her personal biography—including her family connections to the military—became well-known, many Chileans had probably never heard of her father.

familial relationships important advantages for both men and women. For example, President Eduardo Frei in Chile (1994–1999) is the son of a former president; President Enrique Bolaños of Nicaragua (2002–2007) was married to a relative of three former presidents; President Martín Torrijos of Panama (2004–2009) is the son of a former dictator; and President Felipe Calderón of Mexico (2006–2012) is the son of a cofounder of the PAN. In short, our analysis advances the scholarship developing around women and executive leadership worldwide by providing greater insights into the specific factors that have helped women overcome gendered barriers in their election to the presidencies in Latin America.

WHEN A WOMAN LEADS: CONSEQUENCES OF *PRESIDENTAS*

Research around the consequences of women's presidencies, and specifically around issues of gender equality and women's political representation, is sparse given their relatively small numbers and recent presidencies. In addition, the media, voters, and political actors intensely scrutinize, and often judge, women presidents' governing abilities in relationship to their gender, an issue faced less by men whose gender is seen as an unremarkable factor. This poses difficulties in conducting more objective scholarly analysis into the successes and failures of women's presidencies. Given these limitations, we assess women's presidential performance relative to their male counterparts in three areas: (1) reelection rates and approval ratings; (2) the degree to which they promote gender equality in their government through appointments, policies, and legal changes; and (3) their symbolic impact, particularly on female citizens' political participation.

To begin, *presidentas'* reelection rates are generally on par with those of their male counterparts. Fernández de Kirchner and Rousseff successfully ran for immediate reelection and Bachelet sat out the constitutionally mandated one term before successfully winning a second term in a landslide. This means that every *presidenta* constitutionally enabled to run for reelection has done so and won. From 2005–2012, all male presidents who ran for immediate reelection were also successful (Zovatto 2014).

A second indicator of performance in office is popular support measured by opinion polling. Presidential approval can help capture public satisfaction between elections. We looked at LAPOP's biennial surveys in 18 Latin American countries that asked a presidential approval question from 2004–2014. These surveys thus capture snapshots of public opinion during the Moscoso government in Panama 2004; Bachelet in Chile 2006, 2008, and 2014; Fernández de Kirchner in Argentina 2008, 2010, 2012, and 2014; Rousseff in Brazil 2012 and 2014; and Chinchilla in Costa Rica 2010 and 2012. Male presidents governed the rest of the countries and years.

Overall, women presidents have sometimes struggled to maintain high approval ratings in public opinion polls. About 8% of citizens governed by male presidents rate their performance as "very good," whereas this number is about 5% for citizens living under female presidents (see Table 2.2). The difference between male and female presidents' average approval ratings is statistically significant, although fairly small: average approval for female presidents was 0.07 and 0.23 for male presidents, a difference of just 0.16 points on a 5-point ordinal scale from -2 ("very bad")

Table 2.2 PRESIDENTIAL APPROVAL RATES BY PRESIDENTIAL SEX,
2004–2014 IN 18 LATIN AMERICAN COUNTRIES

	Female Presidents	Male Presidents
Very Good	5.0%	7.9%
Good	28.5%	31.7%
Neither Good nor Bad	43.3%	42.6%
Bad	15.2%	11.8%
Very Bad	8.2%	6.1%
N	17,688	144,834

to 2 ("very good"). Interestingly, interaction models reveal that female respondents attribute *less lower*—that is, relatively higher—ratings than male respondents to female presidents, showing a possible interaction effect between the sex of the president and the sex of the respondent (models not shown). The slightly lower approval ratings for women presidents could be due to many factors, one of which may relate to gendered bias against women presidents, possibly because of media attention to the "first woman" frame, where male voters hold "first" women presidents to higher standards then men presidents.

Case studies provide some insights into the intersection between gender expectations, media framing, and public opinion of women presidents. In terms of public opinion, Bachelet during her first term would qualify as the most successful *presidenta*. She handed over power in 2010 as the most popular president since the advent of polling in Chile, with approval ratings over 80%, and won reelection in 2013 in one of the country's most lopsided elections. On the other hand, one of the least popular *presidentas* in recent history was Chinchilla, whose approval rating dipped almost to single digits. Criticisms of Chinchilla were disproportional to her actual presidential record and general social indicators (such as rate of economic growth and crime), and seemed at least partly rooted in sexism as she faced harsh criticisms from even elites in her own party (Thomas 2014; see also Piscopo in chapter 9, this volume).

The recent experiences of Bachelet and Rousseff also highlight how women presidents might face harsher public reactions to corruption accusations because of gendered expectations about women's honesty. During Bachelet's second term, Chile was rocked by a successive stream of political corruption scandals around the financing of political parties and election campaigns that implicated politicians from across the ideological spectrum. Within this context, she faced a political crisis due to accusations that her son and daughter-in-law used political connections to arrange a sweetheart loan and real estate deal that netted them millions. While there was no evidence of Bachelet's involvement in or knowledge of the deal, her poll numbers never recovered to previous levels and the scandal damaged Bachelet's political standing and her ambitious reform agenda.

In Brazil, from 2011–2016, Rousseff experienced extreme variations in her approval ratings—from as high as mid-60% approval to as low as single digits. In her second term, Rousseff was caught up in the *lava jato* scandal over the connections between Brazil's state-owned oil company Petrobras and her PT party. Although not personally implicated, Rousseff was impeached in August 2016 on technical charges of fiscal mismanagement. However, many political analysts interpreted this as the opposition taking advantage of public discontent over Brazil's growing economic crisis and widespread corruption to grab political power. Numerous commentators noted the irony of removing the president on corruption allegations given the corruption charges against many sitting congressmen, as well as the President of the Chamber of Deputies,[13] the President of the Senate, and the Vice President (and Rousseff's successor). Many Brazilian feminists took to the streets after the impeachment to protest sexism leveled against Rousseff by her opponents. Rousseff herself suggested that she might have finished her second term had she been a man rather than a woman (Lissardy 2016). Sexism thus complicates researchers' efforts in assessing public perceptions of women presidents.

In sum, much evidence suggests that women presidents face unique challenges in managing the public's gendered perceptions of their presidencies. But do women presidents make a difference in terms of appointing more women to ministries, promoting gender equality policies, and inspiring women to become politically active? One area of fruitful research examines whether women presidents have used one of the most important presidential powers—the ability to nominate ministers—to augment women's descriptive representation in executive cabinets. Here, the impact of *presidentas* appears mixed. In a study of all ministerial appointments in 18 Latin American countries between 1999 and 2015, Reyes-Housholder (2016b) found that *presidentas* are making a small, but statistically significant, difference in women's representation in cabinets (see also Taylor-Robinson and Gleitz in chapter 3, this volume). However, *presidentas* are also more likely than male presidents to name women to ministries with stereotypically feminine portfolios, such as social welfare, health, and culture. Thus, while appointing more women, *presidentas* might also be reinforcing gender stereotypes within the executive branch.[14]

More research has examined the extent to which *presidentas* have used their legislative prerogatives to promote women's equality. Scholars have focused on Bachelet's presidencies because of her explicit agenda to improve gender equality. During her first term, Bachelet increased the attention to legislation that promoted women's equality (Reyes-Housholder 2016a; Thomas 2016; Valdés 2012; Waylen 2016). She also pursued gender-mainstreaming goals during both terms by asking all ministers to develop specific gender equality goals and providing mechanisms to assess progress. These policies have helped, more broadly, to legitimize issues of gender equality within the Chilean state (Thomas 2016). Many of the signature achievements of Bachelet's first presidency (namely the massive expansion of state-supported childcare and pension reforms) targeted women given the unequal distribution of carework and access to formal employment (see Franceschet, chapter 8, this volume).

Other scholars are more critical about the extent to which Bachelet actually *achieved* her ambitious gender equality agenda, pointing to her failure to address more controversial areas of women's inequality, such as reproductive rights and

---

13. This former President of the Chamber of Deputies, now in jail, has received a fifteen-year sentence.

14. Bachelet named a gender parity cabinet at the beginning of her first term but not when she was reelected (Franceschet and Thomas 2015).

political representation (Borzutzky and Weeks 2010). Bachelet, in her second term, passed electoral reforms that include Chile's first quota legislation and legislation to liberalize Chile's complete ban on abortion. No other president (woman or man) has yet to match Bachelet's legislative successes in promoting gender equality nor has made gender equality central to their presidential agenda. Explanations for Bachelet's use of presidential power to advance gender equality point both to her feminist consciousness (Staab and Waylen 2014) and her constituencies. Bachelet seems unique among female presidents in that she successfully mobilized a core constituency of women behind a pro-women platform and networked heavily with elite feminists, meaning she possessed both the incentives and capacity to use her power to promote significant change favoring women (Reyes-Housholder 2017).

In addition to Bachelet, Rousseff's impact on women's status in society has also generated considerable debate. Jalalzai and dos Santos (2015) use evidence from personal interviews with elite officials to argue that Rousseff had a greater impact on women's status in society than her male predecessor Lula. Reyes-Housholder (2017) employs interviews with leaders of Brazilian women's movements and an original dataset of hundreds of legislative bills to find results that challenge Jalalzai and dos Santos' conclusions. While Rousseff did name more women to her inaugural cabinet than Lula, pro-women change policies were not a higher priority for Rousseff than for Lula in terms of legislation. This could be related to the fact that Lula and Rousseff maintained the same core constituencies and many of the same political advisers (Reyes-Housholder 2017). In short, more research is needed to explore the consequences of women's administrations in terms of legislative and policy gains for gender equality and women's status in society.

Finally, preliminary research suggests that women presidents might exert a symbolic impact by subtly shifting gender-related attitudes and behaviors at the mass level. Historically, women in Latin America have participated in politics less than men, but Reyes-Housholder and Schwindt-Bayer (2016) reveal that the presence of a woman president is correlated with higher campaign participation, intention to vote, and local meeting attendance among women. The exact causal mechanisms linking *presidentas* to enhanced participation among women are still unknown, but some evidence suggests that *presidentas* are associated with increases in men's and women's support for female political leadership, which in turn, could lead to greater female political participation.

For example, another experimental study conducted in Brazil examined whether a positive impact of female executives on citizen's symbolic representation could be due to their *presence* in office or their *novelty* as "first females" (Schwindt-Bayer and Reyes-Housholder 2017). The results showed different effects for presence and novelty, with presence emerging as the more important factor increasing women's symbolic representation. Thus just the presence of a woman president seems to represent a symbolic opening of presidential power to women. Electing a woman as president breaks the previous hold by men on the most powerful elected office in a country. Given persistent gender inequalities and barriers to women's political entry, a woman president can play a uniquely powerful symbolic role in advancing gender equality, an idea repeatedly mentioned to the authors during fieldwork in Chile, Brazil, and Costa Rica.

In sum, this analysis of the consequences of women's presidencies provides further evidence for this chapter's main arguments on the gendered nature of the presidency. Men and women presidents may enjoy similar "success" rates in terms of reelection. Yet female presidents must continually confront sexist expectations that may hurt their approval ratings and media evaluations of their political successes and failures vis-à-vis their male counterparts. Women and men presidents also often employ their appointment and legislative powers in different ways. Finally, *presidentas* appear to exert a symbolic impact on women's political participation as well as on citizens' support for female leadership.

CONCLUSIONS

We conclude by outlining future directions for the emerging scholarship on how gender shapes the causes and consequences of women's presidential representation. First, researchers could examine the gendered strategies presidents use to maintain public approval, pursue their legislative agenda, and seek possible reelection. For example, we have suggested ways and reasons why both men and women presidents strategically deploy gender ideology and symbols—including those related to paternalism and maternalism. This research would help trace the current gendered expectations around presidential office and how the experience of having a woman president might challenge the historical connections between masculinity, paternalism, and presidential power discussed above. This scholarship could enrich existing work on the functioning of Latin America's diverse presidential systems (Foweraker 1998; Raile, Pereira, and Power 2011). In focusing overwhelmingly on formal institutional mechanisms, the current literature has also positioned the president as a strategic actor unmarked by gender, race, class, or sexuality (e.g., Ames 2001; Amorim Neto 2006; Pereira and Melo 2012; Raile, Pereira, and Power 2011). Placing gender at the center of the analysis could direct more attention to both the role of informal institutional practices in promoting presidential agendas as well as how powerful social hierarchies shape the strategies of individual presidents.

Concomitantly, scholars should further analyze how gender ideologies have shaped political expectations about what qualities and characteristics presidents need to successfully govern. The existing work on the gendered media treatment of presidential candidates in Latin America could provide a basis for expanding research into the media's treatment of female and male presidents throughout their presidency. The fact that many recent *presidentas* have served two terms might help illuminate how traditional gender stereotypes around presidential leadership might be changing. More attention to the media's gendered treatment might also provide new insights into how gender, as well as race and class, helps shape public expectations around a presidency, as well as how different presidents manage these expectations. Finally, so little research has explored the effects of women's presidencies, including their successes and failures, that almost any kind of systematic study is welcome.

A more robust development of the comparative scholarship on the gendered presidency in Latin America could help correct explanations from global studies on women national executives. Scholars need to examine both men and women from

different regions of the world. Finally, a focus on the presidency as a gendered institution demands more attention to how male presidents also must negotiate gendered
proscriptions around presidential power, even though the historical development of
the presidency provides much greater opportunities and fewer challenges for men
vis-à-vis women. Our analysis has paved the way for several promising avenues for
future research. The study of women's representation and the Latin American presidency is wide open.

Women in Presidential Cabinets

Getting into the Elite Club?

MICHELLE M. TAYLOR-ROBINSON AND MEREDITH P. GLEITZ ∎

High-level executive branch posts have been described as "the most gendered of all political offices"—where "maleness" is an expected part of what it takes to do the job (Watson, Jencik, and Selzer, 2005, 55–56). Since women have been legally able to participate in politics, assessments of women's representation in government have concluded that "where power is, women aren't" (Vallance 1979, cited in Davis 1997, 28; also Putnam 1976, 33 and 36). In part, that evaluation reflects the traditional lack of women in cabinet posts, which is changing in many Latin American countries.

Cabinet posts are some of the most important posts for making and implementing policy. Women's presence in the cabinet is particularly important in Latin American countries because the executive typically sets the policy agenda and leads policy formulation, with the legislature playing a more reactive, yet still important policymaking role (Cox and Morgenstern 2002; Mainwaring and Shugart 1997). Representation of women in cabinets is also important so government can take advantage of the knowledge and perspective of the female half of the population.

This chapter outlines women's integration into Latin American cabinets, the ways in which integration is still limited, and the results of women's incorporation. We first introduce how cabinet appointments are made. We then evaluate the causes of women's representation in presidential cabinets and analyze the types of posts women hold within those cabinets, drawing on existing literature and new empirical data. We provide more recent data and an updated test of factors associated with increased representation of women, finding that factors that explained appointment of women in the past no longer appear to be significant. This indicates that it has become too costly for Latin American presidents to ignore women in their appointment calculus. Next, we examine the consequences of women gaining seats in the cabinet, how they are treated, and their effectiveness compared to men. We conclude with challenges for women in appointed posts and suggestions for a future research agenda as women break the highest glass ceilings in government.

GENDERED CABINETS AND WOMEN'S APPOINTMENT

Cabinets are elite clubs because cabinet posts are highly prestigious and thus valuable for ambitious politicians, the number of positions is limited, and appointments receive much media attention. Cabinets are also a gendered club where men, male values, and masculine behaviors have long been dominant. Change is difficult because the men who have traditionally held power in politics do not want to give up cabinet posts precisely because they are a scarce resource with the power to impact elite interests. Yet savvy politicians and parties that recognize when women's demands for representation have become too costly to ignore can respond by including women in the cabinet (Carroll 1984; Duke 1976; Gamson 1968, 117–120; Lukes 1974; Mills 1957; Zimmer 1988). A president can take this prudent response because all Latin American presidents have the discretion to make cabinet appointments without ratification by the congress (Alcántara Sáez 2008b, 2013). The main constraints on a president's appointments are the needs to build a governing coalition, within the president's party or with other parties, and to forge alliances with key sectors of society.

Presidential systems have no legal requirement that ministers come from the congress, and ministers often enter government directly from the private sector (Escobar-Lemmon and Taylor-Robinson 2016, chapter 5). Some ministers have well-established linkages to a political party, but others are *not* connected to a party and are appointed because of their technical credentials (Camerlo and Pérez-Liñán 2015). Ministers are often close confidants of the president—family members, friends, and campaign managers. An important topic for study about women in presidential cabinets is whether women are more or less likely than men to need to be "connected" to the president to be considered for cabinet appointments. Because presidents have discretion in who they appoint, when pressures mount to appoint women, presidents can appoint women who will not deviate greatly from the policy that would have been made by men. Such a strategy of appointing women who, other than their sex, are very much like the men who have long held cabinet posts, minimizes the likelihood of dramatic policy change that would threaten the interests of the dominant male groups typically in power. Yet it would also mean that the women are qualified for their post and not tokens who are marginalized in the cabinet (Borrelli 2002; Escobar-Lemmon and Taylor-Robinson 2016, chapter 1). Although women's numbers are increasing in cabinets, it is unclear if the gendered process of cabinet appointments has changed.

Latin American presidents are also not limited in the configuration of cabinet portfolios. Presidents can separate or combine ministries to draw attention to a policy area or limit the power of a post. They can add posts to the cabinet to give themselves more bargaining chips in coalition formation. These decisions can be used to incorporate more women into the government—possibly via new, small, less important portfolios— which is another way the appointment process can be gendered.

Many Latin American countries have been world leaders in representation of women in the legislature through successful implementation of gender quotas, but some countries and presidents are setting examples for inclusion of women in the cabinet. When democratic regimes spread across the region in the 1980s, Latin American presidents appeared to have a choice of whether to include any women in their cabinet. Over time, however, it became expected that there would be at least one woman, then more than one, and more recently it has become common for women to hold one, and sometimes more than one, of the most prestigious posts. The percentage of women in cabinets in the region expanded from 5% in 1980 to 7% in 1990 (Escobar-Lemmon and Taylor-Robinson 2005, 829).[1] Table 3.1 shows appointment patterns for initial cabinets of presidents elected from 1999 to 2003,[2] with 15% women on average, and from the initial cabinets of the presidents in office as of December 2014, averaging 25%. This expansion in representation of women has occurred regardless of cabinet size, which ranges from 12 to 31 members. But while the regional average for women ministers has risen, there is wide variance, from a low of 8.3% women in Uruguay in President Mújica's initial 2010 cabinet, to a high of 46.2% in Nicaragua for President Ortega's 2012 cabinet. Table 3.2 provides information about how many women hold nontraditional posts (outside of social welfare policy) and posts in stereotypically masculine policy domains. These data show that it has become more common for women to hold masculine policy domain posts, but women are still predominantly appointed to stereotypically feminine policy domain posts.

Cabinets are one of the bastions of male power that have taken the longest for women to enter, both in Latin America and around the world. Cabinets have also been gendered in terms of which posts have typically been held by women: posts that fit into stereotypically feminine policy domains, such as policymaking on topics related to care of children and family (e.g., education, health, social welfare, women's and family issues). Even today, while appointing women is becoming more common in stereotypically masculine policy areas and masculine gendered posts (Escobar-Lemmon and Taylor-Robinson 2009), the most prestigious posts in charge of the economy still appear to be a glass ceiling for women (see Table 3.2).

CAUSES OF INCREASED REPRESENTATION OF WOMEN IN PRESIDENTIAL CABINETS

As explained in chapter 1, causes of increased representation of women in government can be grouped into several categories, of which the literature about cabinets has focused on socioeconomic, political, and institutional explanations. However, repeated tests find that socioeconomic factors have weak explanatory power for women's representation in cabinet, as argued in chapter 1 of this volume.

Reyes-Housholder (2013) found that increasing GDP/capita and the percentage of women in the workforce are not correlated with more women in the cabinet. Escobar-Lemmon and Taylor-Robinson (2005) found that increased education of women (secondary school enrollment) was associated with fewer women in the cabinet. Whether this is due to measurement problems (e.g., tertiary education vs. secondary, women working in professional jobs vs. simply joining the workforce) or cultural attitudes about the proper role of women (at least in the early administrations

1. Most women ministers have been white, and few indigenous or Afro-descendant women have been appointed to the cabinet (Luna, Roza, and Vega 2008).

2. Initial cabinets are particularly interesting because they are typically photographed for the press and nowadays are subject to criticism if the picture lacks descriptive diversity.

Table 3.1 WOMEN IN THE INITIAL CABINETS OF LATIN AMERICAN PRESIDENTS INAUGURATED 1999–2003 AND 2010–2014

Country	Inaugurated 1999–2003					Inaugurated 2010–2014				
	President	Start of term: month/year	# of ministers Total	Women	% Women	President	Start of term: month/year	# of ministers Total	Women	% Women
Argentina	de la Rua	Dec/1999	12	1	8.3	Fernandez	Dec/2011	16	3	18.7
Bolivia	Quiroga	Aug/2001	16	1	6.3	Morales	Jan/2010	20	5	25.0
Brazil	da Silva	Jan/2003	25	3	12.0	Rousseff	Jan/2011	31	8	25.8
Chile	Lagos	Mar/2000	16	5	31.3	Bachelet	Mar/2014	23	9	39.1
Colombia	Uribe	Aug/2002	14	6	42.9	Santos	Aug/2010	13	4	30.8
Costa Rica	Pacheco	May/2002	20	6	30.0	Solis	May/2014	21	8	38.1
Dominican Rep.	Mejia	Aug/2000	18	2	11.1	Medina	Aug/2012	24	4	16.7
Ecuador	Noboa	Jan/2000	14	1	7.1	Correa	May/2013	29	13	44.8
El Salvador	Flores	June/1999	13	3	23.1	Sanchez	June/2014	14	3	21.4
Guatemala	Portillo	Jan/2000	12	1	8.3	Perez	Jan/2012	14	3	21.4
Honduras	Maduro	Jan/2002	21	3	14.3	Hernandez	Jan/2014	21	4	19.0
Mexico	Fox	Dec/2000	19	3	15.8	Peña	Dec/2012	17	3	17.6
Nicaragua	Bolaños	Jan/2002	14	2	14.3	Ortega	Jan/2012	13	6	46.2
Panama	Moscoso	Sept/1999	14	3	21.4	Varela	July/2014	15	3	20.0
Paraguay	Gonzalez	Mar/1999	11	0	0	Cartes	Aug/2013	14	3	21.4
Peru	Toledo	July/2001	16	1	6.3	Humala	July/2011	18	3	16.7
Uruguay	Batlle	Mar/2000	14	0	0	Mujica	Mar/2010	12	1	8.3
Venezuela	Chavez	July/2000	13	3	23.1	Maduro	Apr/2013	30	8	26.7
Regional average:			15.7		15.3			19.2		25.4

[Handwritten annotations in top margin: "some shitty low", "even", "Argentina which has v high", "women rep"]

NOTES: Data are from CIA *Chiefs of State and Cabinet Members of Foreign Governments* (https://www.cia.gov/library/publications/resources/world-leaders-1/index.html accessed August 15, 2017). Data for the Dominican Republic, Ecuador, El Salvador, Guatemala, Panama, and Paraguay are from the 2001 CIA publication *Countries of the World and Their Leaders: Yearbook 2001*. Both sources also report Vice President(s), President of the Central Bank, Ambassador to the United States and the country's United Nations Representative, but those posts are not included in the counts. For some countries the Prosecutor General is reported, as are some agency heads, and those posts are also not included.

Table 3.2 Types of Posts Held by Women in the Initial Cabinets of Latin American Presidents Inaugurated 1999–2003 and 2010–2014

| Country | Initial cabinet of presidents inaugurated 1999–2003 # of women by type of portfolio | | | | | Initial cabinet of presidents inaugurated 2010–2014 # of women by type of portfolio | | | | |
| | Broad Substantive Categories* | | | Stereotype of Policy Domain | | Broad Substantive Categories* | | | Stereotype of Policy Domain | |
	Economics	Social Welfare	Central	Masculine	Feminine	Economics	Social Welfare	Central	Masculine	Feminine
Argentina	0 of 1	1 of 5	0 of 6	0 of 8	1 of 4	1 of 5	1 of 5	1 of 6	2 of 12	1 of 4
Bolivia	0 of 5	1 of 5	0 of 6	0 of 12	1 of 4	2 of 8	0 of 3	3 of 8	4 of 16	1 of 4
Brazil	2 of 10	1 of 9	0 of 5	2 of 17	1 of 8	3 of 11	3 of 10	1 of 9	4 of 21	3 of 9
Chile	1 of 5	3 of 5	1 of 6	2 of 12	3 of 4	1 of 9	6 of 7	1 of 6	3 of 16	6 of 7
Colombia	2 of 8	1 of 2	2 of 3	4 of 11	2 of 3	1 of 7	1 of 2	1 of 3	2 of 10	2 of 3
Costa Rica	1 of 8	4 of 7	1 of 4	2 of 13	4 of 7	1 of 8	5 of 8	1 of 4	2 of 13	6 of 8
Dominican Rep.	0 of 6	2 of 6	0 of 5	0 of 12	2 of 6	0 of 9	4 of 7	0 of 7	1 of 17	3 of 7
Ecuador	1 of 6	0 of 5	0 of 3	1 of 10	0 of 4	5 of 13	3 of 6	3 of 9	8 of 22	5 of 7
El Salvador	1 of 4	1 of 3	1 of 6	2 of 11	1 of 2	1 of 6	2 of 3	0 of 5	2 of 12	1 of 2
Guatemala	0 of 5	0 of 3	0 of 3	0 of 9	1 of 3	1 of 6	1 of 3	1 of 4	2 of 11	1 of 3
Honduras	2 of 8	0 of 6	0 of 6	2 of 16	1 of 5	1 of 7	1 of 4	2 of 9	3 of 17	1 of 4
Mexico	2 of 8	1 of 4	0 of 7	2 of 16	1 of 3	1 of 8	2 of 4	0 of 5	1 of 14	2 of 3
Nicaragua	0 of 6	2 of 4	0 of 4	0 of 11	2 of 3	1 of 6	4 of 4	1 of 3	3 of 10	3 of 3
Panama	0 of 5	2 of 5	1 of 4	1 of 10	2 of 4	0 of 5	1 of 5	2 of 5	2 of 11	1 of 4
Paraguay	0 of 4	0 of 2	0 of 5	0 of 9	0 of 2	0 of 5	2 of 3	1 of 6	1 of 11	2 of 3
Peru	0 of 6	1 of 4	0 of 6	0 of 13	1 of 3	0 of 7	2 of 5	0 of 5	0 of 13	3 of 5
Uruguay	0 of 5	0 of 6	0 of 3	0 of 9	0 of 5	0 of 5	1 of 4	0 of 3	0 of 9	1 of 3
Venezuela	2 of 6	1 of 4	0 of 3	3 of 10	0 of 3	0 of 12	6 of 11	2 of 6	3 of 20	5 of 10
Region	14 of 106 (13.2%)	21 of 85 (24.7%)	6 of 85 (7.1%)	21 of 209 (10%)	23 of 73 (31.5%)	19 of 137 (13.9%)	45 of 94 (47.9%)	20 of 103 (19.4%)	43 of 255 (16.9%)	47 of 89 (52.8%)

NOTES: Data are from *CIA Chiefs of State and Cabinet Members of Foreign Governments* (https://www.cia.gov/library/publications/resources/world-leaders-1/index.html accessed August 15, 2017). Portfolios held by women are coded into categories based on Escobar-Lemmon and Taylor-Robinson (2016, chapter 3). Totals may sum to fewer than the number of women holding posts because culture portfolios are not assigned to any of these three broad categories.
*Broad Substantive Categories do not sum to the Stereotype of Policy Domain categories.

of Third Wave democracies) has not been determined. However, more women in the legislature *is* associated with increased representation of women in cabinets, indicating cross-arena diffusion in women's representation in Latin America (Escobar-Lemmon and Taylor-Robinson 2005, 835).

Institutional factors are also expected to encourage a more diverse cabinet. Extreme multipartism makes it likely that a president will need a coalition to work with congress, and may make it more costly to appoint women because scarce cabinet slots are given to party leaders, who are typically men (see Morgan and Hinojosa, chapter 5, this volume). Alternatively, partisan competition can create an incentive to reach out to women voters by appointing women. Yet empirical studies have found that the need for a coalition or a highly competitive electoral situation does not predict appointment of women (Escobar-Lemmon and Taylor-Robinson 2005). What can be beneficial for appointment of women is a president from outside the party system. Jacob, Scherpereel, and Adams (2014, 2) found in a global study that "leaders who are party outsiders are more likely to appoint women to cabinet posts." Escobar-Lemmon and Taylor-Robinson (2008) found that in Latin America, presidents of what Siavelis and Morgenstern (2008) call the "free-wheeling independent" type appoint more women.

Political factors, such as presidents with a leftist ideology, more consolidated democracy, or a strong women's movement that can prevent backsliding, are expected to be associated with the appointment of more women to cabinets (see Escobar-Lemmon and Taylor-Robinson 2005; Jacob, Scherpereel, and Adams 2014; Krook and O'Brien 2012; Tremblay and Bauer 2011, 184). Empirical studies of Latin America have found some association between left presidents and appointment of more women (Escobar-Lemmon and Taylor-Robinson 2005, 835 and 839; Reyes-Housholder 2013, 24–25). However, evidence in Latin America does not indicate empirical support for the idea that presidents who receive more votes from women appoint more women (Reyes-Housholder 2013, 11). Women presidents are more likely to appoint women ministers than are men, though whether they do so depends on if their country has a high level of cabinet gender inequality and on the appointments made by their male predecessor (Reyes-Housholder 2013, 36).

Diffusion of pro-women norms can change cultural attitudes about the proper role of women and create international incentives for a president to appoint more women. Doing so gives the government international credibility for being progressive (Reyes-Housholder 2013; Towns 2010; True and Mintrom 2001). Diffusion of norms is often measured in empirical studies by the passage of time. Escobar-Lemmon and Taylor-Robinson (2005), using data from 1980–2003, offer statistical support for the diffusion hypothesis. Reyes-Housholder's (2013, 22–23) analysis, with data through 2013, also supports this expectation. Additionally, as norms develop to appoint at least one woman, and then more than one woman, it becomes costly for a president to not meet the norm (Barnes and Jones 2011, 108; Htun and Jones 2002; Jacob, Scherpereel, and Adams 2014; Krook and True 2012). A topic for future research is whether Michelle Bachelet's parity cabinet at the beginning of her first term as president of Chile raised the expectations bar in Chile and possibly throughout the region.[3] Media coverage of Bachelet's

---

3. Bachelet fulfilled her campaign promise to appoint a parity cabinet, even including women in three of the top six cabinet posts. She was unable to sustain that promise throughout her term, however, due to the need to balance the parties within her Concertación coalition (Staab and Waylen 2014, 4).

initial cabinet for her second term raised questions about whether she should have again appointed a parity cabinet. Another subject for inquiry is whether changes in expectations about the minimum acceptable number of women in the cabinet only apply to presidents' initial cabinets. The importance of this question is underscored by the finding by Jacob, Scherpereel, and Adams (2014) that individual country analysis (compared to analysis of global trends) shows that representation of women in cabinets often experiences a significant increase in the first year of an administration, followed by a dramatic decrease in the next year or two (see also Luna, Roza, and Vega 2008).

There has been less empirical testing of when and why women receive appointments outside of stereotypically feminine policy domains. As mentioned in the chapter's introduction, one way that cabinets have appeared to be gendered institutions is that, in most cases, women entered cabinets in Latin America in posts that fit feminine gender stereotypes. It was also common for women to be appointed to the Labor and Social Security post. The first woman appointed to a full cabinet rank post in Latin America was María Santodomingo de Miranda who became Minister of Labor, Social Provision and Health in Panama in 1950. After that, two women were appointed to a Chilean cabinet in 1952: Adriana Olguin de Baltra as Justice Minister and María Teresa del Canto as Minister of Education (Luna, Roza, and Vega 2008).

Another way that women have entered the cabinet is as Minister of Women's Affairs. In Chile, the Dominican Republic, and Peru, the Minister of Women's Affairs has had a full cabinet-rank position in all initial cabinets since 2000. Bolivia, Costa Rica, Panama, Paraguay, and Venezuela have had a Women's Ministry in some administrations. The remaining countries have not had a Women's Ministry in their cabinet. This post is clearly a "woman's seat" because in all instances in which a Minister of Women's Affairs was present, the minister has been a woman.

A relevant question is whether Minister of Women's Affairs is a powerful post from which the minister can address "women's interests." Though Women's Ministries and women's agencies are described as playing an important role in educating the public, designing policy often made in other ministries, and coordinating across portfolios, it appears that these ministers are limited in their capacity to get women's interests adopted into law (Luna, Roza, and Vega 2008, 13). Chile's SERNAM is the most extensively examined Women's Ministry in the region, and research on SERNAM argues that informal institutions have made its ministers weak unless the president puts their political weight behind the ministry, as President Bachelet has done (Franceschet 2005; Staab and Waylen 2014; Thomas 2016). Nonetheless, SERNAM has been a stronger player in promoting women's rights in Chile than Chile's Congress (Haas 2010, 172).

The incidence of women holding posts outside of stereotypically feminine policy domains has increased (see Table 3.2), but men still are appointed to most of the stereotypically masculine policy domain posts. We also see evidence of what Jacob, Scherpereel, and Adams (2014) called a "see-saw" effect, where numeric gains are often followed by drops in women's representation. Women are breaking glass ceilings in cabinets, yet some posts are still only rarely held by women. In 2002, Chilean Michelle Bachelet was the first woman in the region appointed as Minister of Defense, and since then, the defense post has been held by other women in Chile and a woman has held the defense post in Argentina, Colombia, Ecuador, and Nicaragua. A few women have held masculine-gendered posts such as Security (e.g., Argentina, Costa Rica, Venezuela); Public Works/Transport (e.g., Brazil, Chile, Colombia, Ecuador); and Foreign Relations (e.g., Argentina, Chile, Colombia, Ecuador, El Salvador, Honduras, Mexico, Panama). Finance appears to have the thickest glass ceiling for women, as a woman has only held the Finance post in Argentina, Costa Rica, Ecuador, Guatemala, Honduras, and Venezuela, and none were in the initial cabinet of presidents inaugurated between 2010 and 2014.

Escobar-Lemmon and Taylor-Robinson (2005, 839) analyzed whether a cabinet would have at least one woman in a high prestige post using annual data from all Latin American democracies from 1980 to 2003. They found that the passage of time was predictive, as were the percentage of women in the legislature and the presence of left presidents. These latter two factors support the political context argument discussed in chapter 1. In another study, Krook and O'Brien (2012) developed a Gender Power Score (GPS) to measure the diversity and prestige of women's appointments. The GPS combines the proportion of cabinet posts held by women and the prestige and gendered nature of the posts women receive. With data from 117 countries in 2009, they found that women's presence among political elites (in the legislature and executive) received the most support in explaining Gender Power Scores (60% of countries), followed by the structure of political institutions ("form of government, ideology of the ruling party degree of democracy, and intensity of party competition" [850]) (20%).

Research has also examined women's cabinet representation across types of portfolios, routinely finding that women are concentrated in some types of posts more than others. One way of categorizing portfolios is masculine/feminine/neutral categories (see Drew 2000; Escobar-Lemmon and Taylor Robinson 2009; Krook and O'Brien 2012). More recently, Escobar-Lemmon and Taylor-Robinson (2016, chapter 3) have limited the gender stereotypes of cabinet posts to two broad groups: stereotypically masculine/feminine policy domains. These gendered categorizations are built on literature about legislative work originating in studies of US state and national legislatures.[4] For example, policy areas related to family, home, and social welfare are typically viewed as fitting traditional feminine gender stereotypes (and often criticized as helping stereotypes persist). However, policy areas such as the environment, which is typically placed in the feminine policy domain, are often key areas of the economy in Latin American countries and thus fit in the stereotypically masculine economic policy domain.

A binomial test of proportions compares the actual number of cases (e.g., appointment of women to a type of post) to the number of appointments that would be expected if women received all types of posts in proportion to their representation in the cabinet. Using the data about initial cabinet appointment from Table 3.2, a binomial test of proportions shows that women continue to be overrepresented in the feminine policy domain (most recent cabinets: 23 expected, 47 observed, $p=0.000$;

4. For a more extensive review of this literature and a new categorization for how "visible" a post is according to whether it is charged with handling problems that citizens indicate in public opinion polls as "the most important problem facing the country," see Escobar-Lemmon and Taylor-Robinson (2016, chapter 3).

earlier cabinets: 11 expected, 23 observed, $p=0.001$) and under-represented in stereotypically masculine policy domain posts (most recent cabinets: 65 expected, 43 observed, $p=0.001$; earlier cabinets: 32 expected, 21 observed, $p=0.034$). Other studies have echoed this finding (e.g., Escobar-Lemmon and Taylor-Robinson 2009). This ongoing overrepresentation of women in stereotypically feminine policy domains indicates that cabinets are still gendered institutions with informal norms about gender stereotypes influencing where women are likely to be policy leaders.

Portfolios can also be grouped into broad categories based on policy purview. Building on Keman's (1991) typology of portfolios in Western Europe, Escobar-Lemmon and Taylor-Robinson (2016, chapter 3) developed three broad categories of posts: **Central** posts handle topics of national and international policy responsibility that are not related to the economy but that impact the entire country: Defense, Foreign Relations, Justice/Security, and Presidency. These ministers are players on the national and international stage, representing the country at international meetings and managing relations with the legislature and other levels of government. They also often produce future presidential candidates. **Economics** posts have the management of the national economy and industry sectors as their purview: Agriculture, Commerce/Industry, Energy/Mining/Environment, Finance, Planning, and Transportation/Public Works.[5] The **Social Welfare** category includes portfolios that oversee the welfare programs managed by the state: Education, Health, Housing/Urban Development, Labor/Social Security, and Women's Affairs.

Escobar-Lemmon and Taylor-Robinson (2016, chapter 7) analyzed Argentina, Chile, Colombia, Costa Rica, and the United States for several presidential administrations and found that, while women still had not obtained parity, they were not statistically significantly underrepresented in Economics posts (except in Costa Rica) or in Central posts (except in Argentina and Chile) relative to their share of cabinet seats. Table 3.2 in this chapter provides more data about posts held by women for all countries in the region. Analysis of these data using a binomial test of proportions indicates that women are in fact underrepresented in Economics posts in the initial cabinets of presidents in office in 2010–2014 (35 expected, 19 observed, $p=0.002$), but not in the initial cabinets of presidents in office in 1990–2003 (16 expected, 14 observed, $p=0.685$). Representation of women in Central posts has improved some with only borderline underrepresentation in 2010–2014 cabinets (26 expected, 20 observed, $p=0.098$ 1-tailed) but clear underrepresentation in 1990–2003 cabinets (13 expected, 6 observed, $p=0.034$). Regarding Social Welfare posts, women are overrepresented in recent administrations (24 expected, 45 observed, $p=0.000$) and the turn-of-the-century cabinets (13 women expected, 21 observed, $p=0.023$).

To explore how the political context in Latin America may be associated with more women serving in the cabinet or more women holding "masculine" policy domain posts, we use the data in Tables 3.1 and 3.2 as our dependent variables and test the effect of several of the institutional, political, and socioeconomic variables that had predictive power in earlier years. Escobar-Lemmon and Taylor-Robinson (2005) used annual data for all democratic countries in Latin America from 1980–2003 and

---

5. A challenge to this categorization is that the Finance portfolio can also be "Central" due to its impact on the entire nation's economy and involvement in spending decisions by all other cabinet posts.

found that a greater percentage of women in the legislature, presidents who were ideologically to the left of the runner-up candidate, stronger Human Development Index (HDI) scores, and passage of time were associated with a greater percentage of women in the cabinet.[6] We use these variables but also include a measure of whether a president had to form a coalition to govern or if a single-party government was possible and a measure of whether the president's parchment powers make the executive strong or weak (see Mainwaring and Shugart 1997).[7]

As shown in Table 3.3, fewer explanatory variables are significant for the post-2000 period than the pre-2000 period. Bivariate analysis shows a significant and positive relationship between the percentage of women in the cabinet and the percentage of women in the chamber, presidents from left parties, HDI, and time period. Only percentage of women in the chamber was significant in a bivariate analysis of factors affecting the percentage of women holding masculine policy domain posts. In multivariate analyses, the only variable that has a significant relationship with the percentage of cabinet seats held by women is the percentage of women in the legislative chamber, which showed a positive relationship. Whether this indicates the importance of a pipeline of women with strong links to parties or is indicative of society becoming accustomed to having women in national-level positions of power, increasing representation of women in the legislature is still associated with increased representation in the cabinet. However, the percentage of women in the legislature is not significantly related to the percentage of masculine policy domain posts held by women. In both models, the rest of the variables, including time period, are not significant, indicating that women are not likely to hold more seats or more masculine policy domain posts in more recent years than they were at the beginning of the century.[8]

Our interpretation of this analysis of the more recent time period is that women's representation in diverse posts in the cabinet has become expected, so it no longer matters if a president is from the left or right, must form a coalition to govern, if the level of economic development is high, etc. Latin American presidents, both male and female, know that they must include several women in their cabinet regardless of political context.[9] Cultural attitudes toward gender equality in Latin America are much more accepting of women in the public sphere, and we would even argue that some women are "expected" at the highest levels of government. However, even

6. They also found that the percentage of women enrolled in secondary education was significant, but negative. We do not include that variable here because most cabinet ministers have at least a university education.

7. In models not shown, we included the number of cabinet posts, ethnic fractionalization, change in a country's Corruption Perception Index score, and whether the country had a gender quota law, but none met traditional levels of significance.

8. To explore why time period was not a significant factor when it was significant in analysis of earlier years (see Escobar-Lemmon and Taylor-Robinson 2005), we ran models adding one variable at a time. Time period was significant except when the percentage of women in the chamber was included. Models do not cluster by country.

9. Despite what appears to be a new norm, it is noteworthy that the cabinet appointed by Michel Temer in 2016 when he became acting president of Brazil during Dilma Rousseff's impeachment proceedings included no women.

Table 3.3 TYPE OF POLITICAL SITUATION ASSOCIATED WITH APPOINTMENT OF WOMEN TO THE CABINET (EXAMINATION OF INITIAL CABINETS OF PRESIDENTS INAUGURATED 1999–2003 AND 2010–2014)

	% of all cabinet seats held by women	% of all cabinet seats held by women	% masculine posts held by women	% masculine posts held by women
% of chamber composed of women	0.369*	0.409†	0.208	0.283
	(0.217)	(0.244)	(0.212)	(0.235)
President from left party	5.767	6.372	3.522	2.451
	(4.301)	(4.833)	(4.198)	(4.668)
HDI	−6.086	−9.078	−8.857	−19.651
	(21.215)	(24.816)	(20.708)	(23.970)
Coalition needed to govern		2.978		0.880
		(4.465)		(4.313)
Executive powers		0.049		4.450
		(4.607)		(4.450)
Late time period	4.018	3.826	2.554	2.447
	(4.812)	(5.104)	(4.697)	(4.930)
Constant	13.075	12.128	12.112	15.939
	(14.364)	(15.828)	(14.021)	(15.289)
N	35	34	35	34
R-square	0.296	0.302	0.134	0.165
Prob > F	0.028	0.109	0.350	0.515

OLS regression, standard errors in parentheses

* $p<0.10$, † $p=0.10$

though some female faces are expected in the cabinet, their numbers are still almost always far below parity, and they are predominantly in stereotypically feminine policy domain posts.

We expect some other factors could explain the ongoing glass ceilings in the cabinet, despite expectations that more women should be in the cabinet. One such factor could be clientelism with the hypothesis that women will be less likely to be appointed to posts that offer strong opportunities to distribute pork and patronage (see Franceschet and Piscopo 2014 for evidence from Argentina). Another possibility is that women will hold more posts in cabinets where other actors outside the cabinet are known to play a greater role in policymaking, marginalizing the cabinet. We could not test these hypotheses due to a lack of systematic data for all countries and over time. In addition, presidents who enjoy a stronger institutional setting (i.e., their party has a majority in congress, the executive has strong "parchment" powers and can make policy without obtaining the support of congress) are more *able* to appoint women (in agreement with the theoretical argument in chapter 1 regarding the importance of formal and informal institutions).[10] However, *whether* they appoint more women appears to be conditional on their interest in doing so, as was seen with the dramatic increase in posts held by women in Chilean President Bachelet's first cabinet (see Franceschet 2016; Thomas 2016).

CONSEQUENCES—WHAT HAPPENS WHEN MORE WOMEN ARE APPOINTED TO THE CABINET?

Consequences in government. An assumption is that more women in cabinets will produce increased representation of women's interests, especially in Latin America, where the executive is central to policymaking. But is it the job of cabinet ministers to represent a particular part of the population when they are charged with designing, implementing, and enforcing policies for the entire nation? A major part of a cabinet minister's job is to help the president pass and implement policy in the policy area(s) of their ministry. Does that give women ministers the latitude to emphasize women's interests? Annesley et al. (2014, 9) write "it is useful to think about cabinets and individual ministers as more than simply carriers of policy ideas, but also as representing other politically relevant identities, such as region, generation, ethnicity, and gender." This topic requires future research, which we expect will find support for the argument made in chapter 1 that women in office will promote women's issues but that this may be less in executive offices.

Cabinet ministers who clash with the president are often forced to resign. Thus, unless the president endorses a women's interest policy as part of their policy agenda (or maybe as not inconsistent with their agenda), it may be difficult for a woman minister to pursue a "women's agenda" from her post. In addition, as explained in chapter 1, if men are still controlling the majority of the decision making related

---

10. A few presidents find their appointment decisions shaped by quotas that apply to the executive branch, such as the gender quota in Colombia adopted in 2000 for appointed posts and the 2009 constitution in Bolivia that requires the cabinet to be "plurinational" and have gender equality (Alcántara Sáez 2013, 319).

no women in finances
no funding for women's MOU

to economic policy and social spending, then women's presence in the cabinet will produce little change in economic and social policy outcomes. As shown above, women are still underrepresented in economics posts but overrepresented in social welfare posts. Thus country-level analysis of where and by whom social spending policy is made is needed to determine whether women who hold social welfare posts make different policies than men regarding social spending. Morgan and Hinojosa, chapter 5 (this volume), show that women's issues are rarely included in party platforms in Latin America, so another factor that could impede women ministers from representing women's interests is opposition from their party.

What resources does a minister need to be able to successfully pursue their policy interests—women's interests, feminist goals, or policy in general? Annesley and Gains (2010) studied the capacity of women in the British cabinet to pursue feminist policy goals and concluded that being a feminist is not sufficient. A feminist must head a department with a large budget and have links to vested interests and key actors in the bureaucracy and government. Building on the idea that ministers need various types of political capital to be successful in their post, Escobar-Lemmon and Taylor-Robinson (2016, chapter 6) examine whether women and men appointed to cabinets in Argentina, Chile, Colombia, Costa Rica, and the United States are equally likely to bring multiple political capital resources (PCRs) to the administration. They coded as PCRs the minister's policy expertise, political skills, and links to ministry clients. They find that most ministers do not have all three types of PCRs. Women are as likely as men to have all three PCRs or two PCRs, but a greater percentage of women than men have none of the three PCRs coded.

Escobar-Lemmon and Taylor-Robinson (2016, chapter 11) also explore whether women are equally likely to be successful in their post when equally endowed with PCRs. They predict that if women have the same number of PCRs as men, they will be equally successful in their posts, indicating gender integration. If women have different resources than men but are equally successful, that indicates that women are being incorporated and are no longer tokens. They assess treatment and effectiveness of ministers by aggregating three measures: how a minister exits their post, duration in post, and legislative activity.[11] They find women are equally as successful as men when they bring multiple PCRs to the administration. Women with zero PCRs appear to have other valuable resources because many of these women also receive high treatment/effectiveness scores, whereas men with zero PCRs do not.

Whether women ministers in Latin America legislate on women's issues has received little empirical investigation. Escobar-Lemmon, Schwindt-Bayer, and Taylor-Robinson (2014) studied bill initiation by ministers in Colombia and Costa Rica and found that women ministers are not pursuing a women's interest agenda.[12] In Colombia, neither women nor men ministers initiate women's equality bills. Furthermore, women ministers did not sponsor children and family bills and were less likely than men to initiate pro-poor bills. In Costa Rica, ministers initiate some bills that fit within all three definitions of "women's interests," but women were not

---

11. Legislative activity is not applied to cabinet secretaries from the United States.

12. This finding about ministers contrasts with the parallel study of legislatures in both countries, and with findings in other work about women in legislatures. Women legislators are more active than men at proposing bills on women's issues.

significantly more likely than men to initiate those bills. Studies in more countries are needed to determine if this is the norm in Latin American cabinets. Possibly ministers, both men and women, are responding to the president's agenda, and thus are equally constrained or incentivized to legislate on women's issues. Legislators, by comparison, may have more autonomy to propose bills about which they personally have an interest.

Research should also explore whether women ministers represent women in other aspects of their job, such as how they spend their ministry's budget or how aggressively they implement policies beneficial to women. For example, Chilean Minister of Health, feminist María Soledad Barría, "significantly raised the profile of gender issues in the Ministry's work. . ." (Staab and Waylen 2014, 8), though she was mainly able to act where "changes could take place at the ministerial level—via guidelines, decrees and health programming—and hence did not require legislative approval" (9).

More women in the cabinet may also impact the chances women have of becoming viable presidential candidates. For example, Ríos Tobar (2008, 517) argues that Chilean President Michelle Bachelet "would never have been able to garner that support had she not had a successful career as minister in the Lagos government."

Consequences for society. Increased appointment of women to cabinets could enhance symbolic representation of women. The literature predicts that women and girls will be more interested in politics and more likely to participate if they see female role models in government, particularly holding high-profile posts. Schwindt-Bayer (2010) explored whether the percentage of women in the cabinet impacts citizens' attitudes about their government. She found that descriptive representation of women in the cabinet does not have an influence on satisfaction with democracy (170) or attitudes about government corruption (176), and it lowers the likelihood that people will trust the legislature or the government more generally (180, 182). Morgan and Buice (2013) explored whether mass public attitudes about women in politics are affected by the presence of women in government. Indicating support for the argument made in chapter 1 of this volume, they found that "When elites signal support for gender equality by nominating women to influential political offices such as cabinet positions, men respond to these cues by increasing their acceptance of female leadership" (653–654). But they also explain that "men are more susceptible to the negative signals transmitted when elites exclude women. Thus elite cues transmitted via cabinet appointments have the capacity to promote or impede support for female political leadership among men" (656). More research is needed to explore whether inclusion of women *in* government produces ongoing support for women to serve in government.

CHALLENGES FOR WOMEN'S REPRESENTATION IN CABINETS

While it is an improvement over the earlier informal norm of a single "woman's seat," the current level of representation of women falls short of parity. The finance portfolio remains a glass ceiling for women, and women are still underrepresented in economics posts. If economics policy is still largely closed to women, that signals a lack of broad gender integration. Will this change as more women acquire the private sector credentials and business group linkages often associated with economics portfolios (Escobar-Lemmon and Taylor-Robinson 2016, chapters 4 and 6), or will good old boys networks and gender stereotypes continue to advantage men such that cabinets continue to be gendered institutions?

Another challenge is whether women in the cabinet can pursue a women's agenda. While extensive examination has only been done for Argentina, Chile, Colombia, and Costa Rica, findings indicate that women are as likely as men to bring impressive policy background, political experience, and group linkages to their jobs (Escobar-Lemmon and Taylor-Robinson 2016, chapters 4–6). Paraphrasing from Borrelli's (2002) work about the United States, women are not just being showcased for their sex, but also respected for their abilities, signaling gender integration. But we still do not know whether ministers can make a name for themselves advocating for or aggressively implementing policies to address women's issues. If a minister wishes to work on women's interest policy or respond positively to lobbying from women's groups, future research needs to explore whether she can do so, and how those actions impact her political future. The limited evidence available calls into question whether women with known links to women's groups are likely to be appointed to the cabinet. Escobar-Lemmon and Taylor-Robinson (2016, chapter 6) found that only 13 of the 96 women (13.5%) appointed to recent presidential cabinets in Argentina, Chile, Colombia, and Costa Rica had known links to women's groups. Analysis of Chilean politics explains that women are more likely to reach top levels of government if they are not known for activism in women's groups (Franceschet 2005, 104; Weeks and Borzutzky 2012). That several of Chile's SERNAM ministers lacked linkages to women's groups underscores that the common route for women to the executive branch is not through women's channels (Haas 2010, 61).

What does this say for the chances that women's interest groups will gain greater access in the executive branch as more women are appointed to the cabinet and in more diverse posts? Haas (2010, 62) found that even with a Socialist holding Chile's presidency, SERNAM ministers still were constrained in pursuing a feminist agenda because they had to navigate the more conservative parties in the Concertación coalition. Paralleling Annesley and Gains (2010), Haas (2010, 33) wrote that "the number of women elected or appointed to office, the strength of the Left within the Congress and the executive branch, and the institutional balance of power between branches of government are critical factors in creating opportunities for feminist policymaking."

CONCLUSION AND AREAS FOR FUTURE RESEARCH

Women's descriptive representation in cabinets has increased in Latin American countries, though parity is rare and short-lived. By 2016, it appears that presidents view appointment of several women to their cabinet as an expectation that they must meet.[13] Additionally, more presidents are appointing women to more diverse posts outside of stereotypically feminine policy domains.

13. Uruguay was the last hold-out for appointing multiple women to the cabinet. However, President Vazquez, who took office in March 2015, appointed women to 38.5% of his cabinet seats, including some in economics posts.

Moving forward, several types of research are needed. Once women are in the cabinet, do they do their job differently than the men? For example, we need to theorize about when cabinet ministers, men or women, have the autonomy from the president to pursue their own agenda, versus when is acting independently likely to get a minister shuffled out of their post?[14] Then we can explore empirically whether a woman minister is more likely than a man to be punished for acting autonomously. Women elected officials are often viewed as being mandated to represent women (Reyes-Housholder 2013, 6), but is this the case for women in cabinets? Annesley et al. (2014, 10) propose additional questions such as "whether the proportion of women affects decision-making, whether hierarchies are more common when women are present in particular proportions, and whether decision-making styles change when there are more women in cabinet."

Staab and Waylen (2014, 1) call for research that examines "the interaction between actors and structures/institutions and on the institutions themselves" to help us to better understand when women in the executive can achieve "positive gender change." Where legislatures are becoming more professional, or where presidents have to build coalitions to pass legislation, we need to know if legislators react the same way to women and men working to shepherd the president's policy initiatives through congress, and how parties react to women ministers. Party leaders are still typically men (see Morgan and Hinojosa, chapter 6, this volume). When presidents need to manage parties, are women cabinet ministers treated the same as men by party leaders and are they as likely to be able to manage relations with political parties?[15] Do presidents' strategies regarding the size of their cabinet impact representation of women?

Research also needs to explore how women are treated in the cabinet. There are concerns, some expressed by women in cabinets, that they "have been excluded from centers of decision-making power" (Krook and O'Brien 2012, 853). Of course in some countries, all ministers likely have that complaint when the president does not make use of the cabinet, as has been said of Kirchner and Fernández de Kirchner in Argentina (Catterberg and Palanza 2012). Presidents value loyalty and may remove ministers with whom they have policy clashes. Systematic research should explore if women are more likely than men to be removed when there is a policy clash, or if other resources a minister brings with them to the administration—rather than the minister's sex—explain who survives such conflicts (e.g., being what in British politics has been called a "big beast of the jungle" [King 1994]). When the cabinet meets as an advisory committee are women ministers equally likely as men to have their

14. Leaders are thought to prize loyalty over other traits when appointing ministers. They also want ministers who they believe share their policy interests because they want to avoid agency loss and policy slippage (Andeweg 2000; Annesley et al. 2014; Camerlo and Pérez-Liñán 2015; Edwards 2001; Huber and Martínez-Gallardo 2008; Indridason and Kam 2008; Lewis 2008).

15. Lack of women party leaders is noted as a barrier to women's advancement in Chile. Party elites in the Concertación coalition negotiate nominations for Congress and the cabinet, insuring that each party gets its "quota" of slots. When Bachelet was forming her cabinet "Party bosses would suggest names for 'their' cabinet posts and few women were likely to have the requisite elite party background to be in the frame (PNUD 2010)" (Franceschet 2016; Staab and Waylen 2014, 4–5).

point of view heard and valued in the discussion? Escobar-Lemmon and Taylor-Robinson (2016, chapters 8 and 9) show that women ministers in Argentina, Chile, Colombia, Costa Rica, and the United States are treated equally, but their treatment measure is based on time spent in office and how ministers exit, not treatment in cabinet discussions. The finding is encouraging, but more research is needed to determine how women are treated in policy negotiations or if a woman minister attempts to promote women's interests.

These are questions that we can now begin to answer as women become more numerous in cabinets and are more frequently appointed to more diverse posts. Greater descriptive representation of women in cabinets sets the scene for theorizing and testing how cabinets can still operate as gendered institutions, for which types of women, and under what types of circumstances.

Women in Legislatures

Gender, Institutions, and Democracy

LESLIE A. SCHWINDT-BAYER AND SANTIAGO ALLES ■

The influx of women into Latin American legislatures has been substantial in many countries since the transitions to democracy in the 1980s. In 1980, only 5% of Latin American legislatures were female, but today, the regional average is just over 25% (IPU 1995, 2016). Four Latin American countries are among the top ten worldwide—Bolivia, Cuba, Mexico and Nicaragua—and all four have more than 40% of their congresses being female (IPU 2017). The growth in women's legislative representation in Latin America has been a bright spot in a region struggling with a host of political, economic, social, and democratic problems, but the relationship between women's representation and this broader context in Latin American legislatures has not been fully explored. In this chapter, we examine the causes, consequences, and challenges of women's representation in national legislatures in Latin America taking gender, institutions (both formal and informal), and political context into account.

Using the vast literature on women's legislative representation in Latin America and new empirical analyses, we highlight the ways in which formal and informal institutions, gender, and democratic challenges interact in legislative politics in the region. First, we show the overwhelming importance of gender quotas for the election of women in Latin America and demonstrate that this institution has helped minimize negative consequences that some democratic challenges, such as corruption, party system fragmentation, and electoral disproportionality, can pose for women. Second, we describe the important legislative consequences that greater gender equality in the legislature has had for legislative work on women and women's rights, and we show that male and female legislators have distinct views of gendered policy issues and some of the democratic challenges the region faces. This could potentially help to improve the functioning of representative democracy in the region; however, whether women's presence in legislatures actually makes a difference in the form of new policy on these issues, less gendered institutional environments, and better democratic outcomes remains to be seen. Third, we show that greater gender equality in legislative representation has had important effects on society—specifically, how accepting citizens are of gender equality in politics, levels of citizen engagement and participation in politics, and citizen views of democracy.

LATIN AMERICAN LEGISLATURES AND WOMEN'S REPRESENTATION

Up until the 1980s, when the majority of Latin America's transitions to democracy occurred, Latin American legislatures were considered to be weak political institutions (Mainwaring and Shugart 1997; Mezey 1979). Yet, the transitions to democracy brought with them a new balance of executive and legislative power in many countries. The rise of powerful presidents—Hugo Chavez in Venezuela, Evo Morales in Bolivia, and the Kirchners in Argentina—have again raised the question of just how independently powerful some legislatures in the region are. For the most part, however, Latin American legislatures are independent governing and policymaking institutions that elect representatives in free and fair elections and act as important checks on presidential power.

Half of Latin America's national legislatures are bicameral with upper chambers that hold real political power. Elections are used for both chambers, although the type of electoral system varies significantly. All lower houses use either proportional representation (PR) electoral rules or a mixed system with some seats elected via PR and some via single-member district plurality. Bolivia, Mexico, and Venezuela have mixed systems. Ballots in most countries are closed and blocked, meaning that parties determine the order of candidates on the ballot and voters may not disturb the party's ranking of candidates. A few countries, however, use open-list or flexible-list PR (specifically, Brazil, Colombia,[1] Ecuador, Honduras, Panama, and Peru), which gives voters the opportunity to choose candidates rather than just parties. Nearly all of the upper chambers are elected under some type of majoritarian electoral rules with two to three seats allocated to each state or province. Colombia and Uruguay are exceptions—they use proportional representation in nationwide districts to elect senators.

Legislatures do substantial policymaking work in most countries (Mezey 1979; Morgenstern and Nacif 2002). Legislators (and the executive) submit bills for legislative consideration, sit on committees that debate and amend proposed legislation, participate in plenary debates discussing bills and procedural matters of the government, and pass legislation (Carey 2009; Morgenstern and Nacif 2002; Payne 2007). They work outside the legislature as well, representing their political party, campaigning, conducting constituency service and casework, and learning about constituent preferences. At the same time, Latin American legislatures have also developed reputations for some less professional and exemplary behaviors. Corruption concerns and accusations have long dominated politics in Latin America, with legislators often at the forefront of political scandals (Blake and Morris 2009; Gingerich 2013; Morris and Blake 2010; Power and Taylor 2011). Clientelism and patronage politics have characterized legislative politics in many Latin American countries (Kitschelt et al. 2010; Weyland, Madrid, and Hunter 2010). In a region long dominated by two-party systems, party system fragmentation in legislatures has increased dramatically (Mainwaring, Bejarano, and Leongómez 2006). Legislative professionalism has been low, comparatively, in Latin America, indicated by the high legislative turnover from election year to election year in many countries (Carey 1996; Samuels 2003). All of

1. In Colombia, parties choose closed or open list in each district.

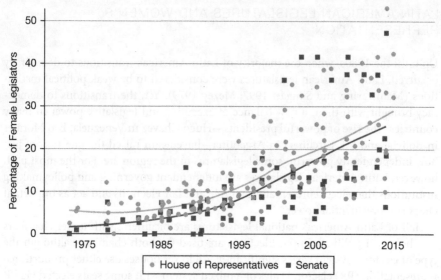

Figure 4.1 Evolution of the Percentage of the Legislature that is Female in Latin American Congresses, 1973–2015
NOTE: The figure plots the percentage of the legislature that is female at election years. The lines represent a LOESS prediction of trends based on these data.

these characteristics of Latin American legislatures have contributed, to some extent, to overall low levels of public trust in legislatures in Latin America (Lagos 2001). This creates significant obstacles to representative democracy in the region.

It is in this context that we consider gender as an important, but often overlooked lens through which to examine legislative representation in Latin America. Latin American legislatures have long been gendered political environments. Women have been significantly underrepresented, and the exclusion of women has perpetuated institutions that are dominated by masculine values and norms of behavior. Change has begun to occur, however. Figure 4.1 presents the percentage of Latin American legislatures that elected women from 1973–2015 and shows a clear increase over time.[2] The growth has been exponential rather than linear. In the fifteen years between 1980 and 1995, the figure's prediction line shows an increase of only 6 percentage points, but from 2000 to 2015, the increase more than doubled to 13 percentage points.

The increases over time have not been the same from country to country. Bolivia achieved parity with 52% of its congress being female and is one of only a few countries in the world that have ever been majority female. As of 2015, Ecuador, Nicaragua, Mexico, Argentina, and Costa Rica were also well above the regionwide average with women comprising more than 30% of the congress in each country. Other countries have faced more challenges, however. Brazil had less than 10% of its congress being female in 2015, and Uruguay and Guatemala were similarly weak, with 11.5% and 13.3%, respectively. Ten countries fell below the regionwide average of 25%. *Still countries below average*

2. The authors collected these data from election results and the Inter-Parliamentary Union (IPU).

CAUSES: THE CENTRAL ROLE OF GENDER QUOTAS

When attention to women's underrepresentation in Latin American legislatures first emerged, most research focused on cultural, socioeconomic, political, and formal electoral rule obstacles that women faced. As Saint-Germain (1993, 119) summarized from her research on women in the Costa Rican and Nicaraguan national assemblies, some of the most prominent obstacles for women emerged from the "political history of each country, including the development of women's legal rights, certain characteristics of the electoral system, the role of the state as an actor in gender politics, women's political activity, and important international bodies and events." Latin America's strong *machista* attitudes and traditional views of women's role in society (reinforced by the Catholic Church) created gender norms that promoted women's role as being in the private sphere and not in the formal political sphere of legislatures. This also excluded women from social institutions, such as higher education and the formal labor force, making it difficult for them to get the educational and occupational experience necessary to pursue political careers.[3]

This has changed significantly, however, over the past thirty years. By 2005, over half of the women in Latin American countries participated in the paid labor force, and women outnumbered men in higher education in many countries (World Bank 2007). The role of the Catholic Church has declined and the rise of evangelical movements has cut into Church participation. Political attitudes toward gender changed, such that by 2004, less than a third of Latin Americans thought men make better political leaders than women (Latinobarómetro 2004). These societal changes only led to incremental increases in women's numbers in some legislatures. However, they did contribute to the adoption of gender quotas, which in turn, has had a significant impact on women's legislative representation.

In 1991, Argentina became the first country in the world to pass a law requiring all political parties running candidates for the national legislature to ensure that at least 30% of the ballot in every district was female (Jones 1996).[4] The adoption of "gender quotas" spread throughout Latin America over the next twenty-five years. Table 4.1 shows the Latin American countries that have gender quota laws for their national legislatures and the year adopted. Every country, except Guatemala and Venezuela (as of 2015), had some kind of law mandating women's representation on party ballots for national legislative elections. In the first years after quotas were adopted, they had surprisingly little effect. As Htun and Jones (2002, 51) reported in one of the first comparative studies on the effectiveness of quotas, "With the exception of Argentina, quotas have been a relatively painless way to pay lip service to women's rights without suffering the consequences." Quota effectiveness has increased significantly in recent years, however.

3. As late as the 1970's, women's participation in the workforce was far below men's—only one-third of women participated in the paid labor force compared to nearly 85% of men (World Bank 2007).

4. Until 2001, the quota only applied to the House of Representatives because Senators were appointed from provincial legislatures. Beginning with the popular election of the Senate in 2001, the quota applied to the Senate too.

Table 4.1 GENDER QUOTAS IN LATIN AMERICA, AS OF MARCH 2015

Country	Year Adopted	Legislative Chamber to Which Quota Applies	Size	Placement Mandate	Enforcement Mechanism
Argentina	1991	Lower and Upper	30	Yes	Strong
Costa Rica[1]	1996	Unicameral	50	Yes	Strong
Paraguay	1996	Lower and Upper	20	Yes	Strong
Bolivia[2]	1997	Lower and Upper	50	Yes	Strong
Brazil	1997	Lower	30	No	Weak
Dominican Republic	1997	Lower	33	Yes	Strong
Panama[3]	1997	Unicameral	50	No	Weak
Peru	1997	Unicameral	30	No	Strong
Ecuador	1997	Unicameral	50	Yes	Strong
Honduras[4]	2000	Unicameral	40/50	No	Weak
Mexico[5]	2002	Lower and Upper	50	Yes	Strong
Uruguay	2008	Lower and Upper	33	Yes	Strong
Colombia	2011	Lower and Upper	30	No	Strong
Nicaragua	2012	Unicameral	50	Yes	None
El Salvador	2013	Unicameral	30	No	Weak
Chile	2015	Lower and Upper	40	No	Strong

NOTES: For more information, see Schwindt-Bayer (2009, 2010, 2015).

1. Increased to 50% and alternation in 2009 electoral reform.
2. Increased to 50% and alternation in 2010. The law applies to the list PR election and the single-member district constituencies (at least half of the constituencies have to have a female candidate representing the party).
3. Applies to party primaries only. Increased to 50% in 2012.
4. In 2012, Honduras increased the required quota size to 40% and added a fine (5% of their state funding) for parties that violate the quota. The law increases the quota to 50% for the 2016 elections.
5. Mexico passed a constitutional amendment in 2014 requiring parties to pass gender quotas. The 50% with alternation reflects this 2014 change.

Wide variation exists across quota laws in Latin America. A common way to compare quotas is by their size, placement mandates, and the types of enforcement mechanisms included in the law (see Table 4.1 for how Latin American quota laws vary on these dimensions). Argentina's quota law, for example, stipulates that women comprise 30% of candidate lists and that women must be in "electable" positions on the party ballot. Party lists that do not comply with the gender quota are not registered for the election. Honduras, however, passed a gender quota law in 2000 that required 30% of party list positions be allocated to women but did not mandate that women be placed in winnable ballot positions nor stipulate any enforcement mechanism by which the electoral commission could ensure that parties abide by the law.

The effectiveness of quota laws relates to their design. In Argentina, 33% of the Senate and 31% of the House of Deputies were female after the 2001 election, and the law was widely considered to be a success (Jones 1996, 2009). In the Honduran Congress, women won only 5.5% of legislative seats. It was largely unsuccessful at increasing the election of women in Honduras in 2001.[5] Scholarly research on quotas in Latin America also finds that quota design matters (Araújo and García 2006; Archenti and Tula 2008b; IDEA 2003; Jones 2009; Marx, Borner, and Caminotti 2007; Miguel 2008; Schmidt and Saunders 2004; Schwindt-Bayer 2010). For example, Jones (2009) assesses a quota's size, placement mechanism, and type of electoral system in which it operates in Latin America and finds that a well-designed quota with a size larger than 30% and having a placement mechanism outperforms quotas without those characteristics regardless of electoral system but that the effect of well-designed quotas is larger in closed-list PR systems than open-list PR systems.

need closed -list PR systems with enforcement rules

The importance of formal institutions

In this section, we demonstrate the overwhelming importance of quotas in Latin America with the largest dataset to date on women's representation in Latin American legislatures. The dataset includes election-year data for all 18 Latin American democracies with data for both legislative chambers in bicameral systems from 1974 or the first election after the country became democratic through 2015.[6] We analyzed many of the common explanations for women's election to Latin American legislatures, specifically socioeconomic development (measured as GDP per capita, logged); level of democracy; gender quotas; the type of electoral system (measured as the percentage of seats elected via proportional representation); logged district magnitude; and time (measured as four decade dummy variables from 1980 to 2015).[7] We found several important things. First, cultural and socioeconomic explanations have little relationship to women's election to Latin American legislatures. Using gross domestic product per capita as a rough proxy for socioeconomics,[8] we show that it and level of democracy (a culture change proxy) have no significant effect on the percentage of women elected to national legislative chambers in Latin America, all else held constant. Second, proportional representation electoral rules and district magnitude have no independent effect on women's representation, with gender quotas included in the statistical models. Third, gender quotas do matter. They are the most important explanation for women's representation in Latin America. Figure 4.2 presents the predicted percentage of female legislators in legislative bodies elected with and

level of dem + socoecon sore - little effect

5. The number of women in the Honduran Congress increased significantly after the 2005 election when open-list PR was used for the first time (Taylor-Robinson 2007).

6. The appendix includes tables of all statistical models discussed in this chapter. Table A4.1 of the appendix presents descriptive statistics for all variables discussed in this section.

7. Statistical models are pooled OLS with robust standard errors. See appendix Table A4.2 for analysis results. Percentage of the legislature that is female data are from IPU (various years); GDP per capita is from the World Development Indicators (various years); level of democracy is averaged Freedom House political rights and civil liberties scores; and the quota data, electoral system, and district magnitude data were collected by the authors from election archives and government documents.

8. Much research finds that GDP per capita is highly correlated with women's paid labor force participation and tertiary education enrollment.

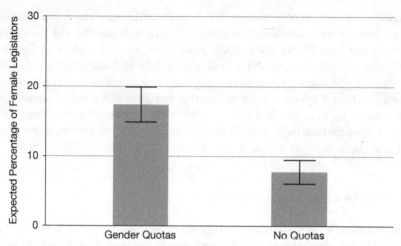

Figure 4.2 Expected Percentage of Legislators that are Women in Countries When Using and Not Using Gender Quotas
NOTE: Expected values predicted with all other variables in the model held at their means, modes, or referent category. Figure includes 95% confidence intervals.

without quotas that resulted from our analyses.[9] The presence of any type of national gender quota law yields an expected 17.4% of the legislature to be female, all else held at its means and modes, compared to 7.7% where quota laws are absent. This represents a difference of 10 percentage points in the two types of countries, on average.

We ran additional models to estimate the effects of differences in quota rules (see appendix Table A4.2, models 2–4). Countries using quotas with stronger rules elect more women than those with weaker rules. Our statistical models show that, in country elections with quotas, increasing the size of a gender quota by 1 percentage point corresponds with an increase in women's representation of 0.66% (model 3). Increasing from a 30% quota to a 50% quota, then, should lead to 13.2% more women in the legislature, on average. Quotas with a placement mandate produce 7% more women, on average, than quotas without placement requirements (model 3). Stronger enforcement mechanisms had no significant effect on women's representation. This may mean that it is not so much whether a quota has an enforcement mechanism that matters but whether enforcers and parties actually comply with that rule. Indeed, a multiplicative index of the three quota rules also significantly increases women's proportion of a legislative chamber in Latin America (model 4).[10]

Democratic context

Quotas and formal electoral rules are primary institutional explanations for the election of women in Latin America. Do the quality of democracy and the challenges

9. See model 1 in appendix Table A4.2.

10. Studies have also explored the role of preference voting on the effectiveness of quotas. Some studies find the preference voting reduces the effectiveness of quotas (Miguel 2008; Schwindt-Bayer 2010) whereas others find it has helped women get elected (Schmidt 2008b).

that it faces in Latin American countries provide unique obstacles or benefits to women? We conducted a statistical analysis of the role of five democratic challenges that could also help or hurt women's representation in the region—legislative professionalization; quality of government (i.e., corruption); clientelism; electoral disproportionality; and party system fragmentation. We found that the democratic context has little effect on the number of women represented in legislature above and beyond the effect of quotas, with the exception of party system fragmentation (see appendix Table A4.3).[11] Retention rates (as a measure of legislative professionalism), quality of government/corruption, electoral disproportionality, and programmatic structuration of parties (as a measure of clientelistic politics) had no significant relationship with women's numerical representation in Latin American legislatures. Also, in none of the analyses did the level of democracy relate to women's legislative presence either. The only factor that was statistically significant was the measure of party system fragmentation.

As highlighted in chapter 1, party system fragmentation has increased dramatically in Latin America and is one of the challenges that Latin American democracies face today. Highly fragmented party systems make governing and policymaking less efficient. For women's representation, it can be a challenge because the more parties that are winning seats, the smaller the number of representatives that get elected from each party. This can disadvantage women because parties have less incentive to balance the ticket with male and female candidates, and even where quotas are in place, women may miss out on being elected if they are not at the top of the ballot.

Indeed our analysis of the effect of party system fragmentation shows just that. We find that the effective number of parliamentary parties (ENPP) in a chamber is negatively associated with the percentage of the chamber that is female. More legislative fragmentation is related to reduced women's representation. This effect is exaggerated in quota elections compared to non-quota elections: in both cases the effect of ENPP is negative, but it is much larger when quotas are in use compared to when they are not (see appendix Table A4.3, models 6 and 7). Figure 4.3 shows the expected percentage of the chamber that would be female, on average, as party fragmentation increases, in an election using quotas and with all other variables held at their means (from appendix Table A4.3, model 5). Fragmentation clearly is detrimental to women's representation in Latin American legislatures with quotas: the predicted percentage falls from 19.1% in a system with two-party competition to 15.3% in a highly fragmented, five-party competition system. These are important findings for Latin America—increased party system fragmentation is associated

party system fragmentation

11. All models are OLS regression models with decade dummy variables included. Given widely varying data availability across the measures of democratic context, we estimate each factor separately. Some models include the full set of country elections (i.e., $n = 239$) whereas others are reduced to just the country years where data were available. Appendix Table A4.3 reports the results of all of the models. The data sources for these variables are as follows: retention as indicated in Schwindt-Bayer (2005); quality of government is an index that includes assessments of corruption, law and order, and democratic quality from the Quality of Government dataset (Dahlberg et al. 2015) that we converted from a 0–1 scale to a 0–10 scale; programmatic nature of parties is the inverse of clientelism and is a measure from the Democratic Accountability and Linkages Project (Kitschelt 2014) that we converted from a 0–1 scale to a 0–100 scale; electoral disproportionality and effective number of parliamentary parties is from Gandrud (2015), with missing observations filled in by the authors using country-specific resources.

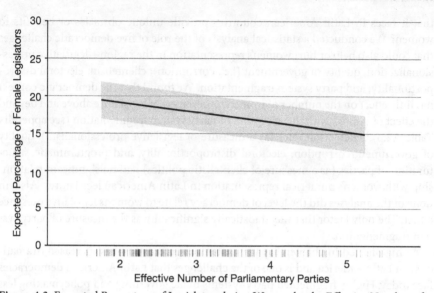

Figure 4.3 Expected Percentage of Legislators being Women by the Effective Number of Parliamentary Parties
NOTE: Full statistical model presented in model 5 of appendix Table A4.3. Expected outcomes predicted with all other variables in the model held at their means, modes, or referent category. Shaded area represents the 95% confidence intervals.

with less representation of women and the effectiveness of quotas is hindered by party fragmentation.

In sum, gender quotas are the primary explanation for women's increased representation in Latin American legislatures. They outperform cultural, socioeconomic, and other formal institutional factors in the Latin American context. Characteristics of the democratic context in Latin America are not highly correlated with women's representation in the region, with one exception: the increased party fragmentation in legislatures. More highly fragmented legislative party systems correspond to less representation of women, particularly in quota systems. Although quotas play a powerful role in women's descriptive representation in Latin America, their impact is somewhat weakened in countries facing challenges from increased party system fragmentation in politics.

CONSEQUENCES: GENDER INEQUALITY IN LEGISLATIVE POLITICS

The influx of women into Latin American legislatures has raised a host of questions about how gender shapes legislative politics. Research on these questions can be traced to Elsa Chaney's pioneering work on women in various political offices in Chile and Peru in the 1960's and 1970's (Chaney 1979). Even then, long before quotas were discussed or women had made significant inroads into elected office, the presence of just a few women prompted questions about what difference (if any) they would make in office. Chaney found that women in Latin American politics during that time did make a difference but did so by representing "feminine issues"

not many laws passed about women's lives (handwritten annotation)

and working to find solutions to the problems women faced daily in the private sphere. Women were maternalistic in their representative behavior and focused on more maternalistic issues (Jaquette 1976). Gender differences in legislative behavior appeared early, just after women's legislative entry.

More recent research on the consequences of women's election to legislatures shows change in the role of women in office and has largely overturned the idea of female legislators as *supermadres,* pursuing only issues that stereotypically were associated with their gender (Schwindt-Bayer 2006). Instead, research today shows that women in legislatures are, in general, more "feminist" and focused on representing women's rights and gender equality issues, and they do so in a variety of ways—sponsoring legislation on these issues (Barnes 2012a, 2016; Htun, Lacalle, and Micozzi 2013; Jones 1997; Schwindt-Bayer 2006, 2010; Taylor-Robinson and Heath 2003); promoting these issues on legislative committees (Barnes 2014; Granara 2014; Heath, Schwindt-Bayer, and Taylor-Robinson 2005; Marx, Borner and Caminotti 2007; Rivera-Cira 1993; Saint-Germain and Metoyer 2008; Schwindt-Bayer 2010; Zetterberg 2008); and defending these issues during legislative debates (Piscopo 2011a; Schwindt-Bayer 2010; Taylor-Robinson and Heath 2003).

Research also shows that women in legislatures influence legislative politics in other ways. Schwindt-Bayer (2010), examines how frequently representatives travel to their districts, how often they attend public events in their districts, the amount of time they spend on constituency service, and the kinds of casework they do on behalf of their constituents, finding that women do these things more than men when they are targeting female constituents and/or women's groups. Gender also influences networking and coalition building, which is critical for building women's political power and furthering a feminist policy agenda (Rodríguez 2003). Marx, Borner, and Caminotti (2007) highlight the role of Brazil's *bancada feminina* in helping female representatives overcome some of the challenges produced by their small numbers. Similarly, Archenti and Johnson (2006) and Johnson (2014) describe how the *bancada feminina* in the Uruguayan congress allowed the few women in the congress to produce substantial legislation on women's rights.

One area where women's presence makes a less clear contribution is policy outputs. Several studies find little evidence to directly connect increased presence of women in legislatures to passage of women's rights policies and instead argue that producing feminist policy outputs requires much more than just increasing women's representation (del Campo and Magdaleno 2008; Franceschet 2010a; Friedman 2009; Franceschet and Piscopo 2008; Haas 2010; Htun, Lacalle, and Micozzi 2013; Lopreite 2015; Rodríguez Gustá, Laura, and Caminotti 2010; Stevenson 1999). For example, Lopreite (2014) points out that the preferences of female legislators can help women's rights policies get on the agenda—specifically, abortion and reproductive rights policy—but that the federal nature of political systems and party ideological leanings interact to help or hinder passage of those laws. Htun and Power (2006) show that party ideology is much more important than gender in explaining legislator attitudes in Brazil, and as a result, influencing policy passage, and Htun and Ossa (2013) show that it took not just women in office but the unification of women across gender, indigenous, class, and urban lines to get a gender quota passed in Bolivia.

This literature has made substantial contributions to our understanding of the gendered nature of women's behavior in legislative politics. Yet, it has not told us much about what greater gender equality in Latin American legislatures might mean

coalition building between women (handwritten marginal annotation, right side)

need to cross gender (handwritten marginal annotation, left side)

for dealing with the challenges that democracy faces in the region. We explore the interaction between gender, representation, and the current political context in Latin America, using data from the University of Salamanca's Parliamentary Elites in Latin America (PELA) Survey.[12] We examine how a legislator's gender affects attitudes toward, first, three policy issues of particular importance to women that are currently being debated and discussed in several countries—gender inequality, divorce, and abortion—and second, democratic stability and current threats to democracy.

Gendered policy issues

We used three questions from the PELA survey to explore gender differences in legislator attitudes toward gender inequality, divorce, and abortion rights.[13] The question on gender inequality asked legislators how important a problem they think gender inequality is for their country, and respondents could respond on a 1 to 10 scale in order of increasing importance. Only three countries asked this question—Chile, Peru, and Uruguay—but the findings are consistent within each country as well as across them.[14] We find a significant difference in men's and women's responses (see appendix Table A4.5 for full statistical model results). Figure 4.4 presents expected responses for women and men, with all other variables from the statistical model held at their means, modes, and referent categories. For women, the model predicts an average response of 5.5 for men but an average response of 6.9 for women, representing a difference of 1.45 between the two sexes. Women perceive gender inequality to be a much larger problem for democracy in Chile, Peru, and Uruguay than men do.

Exploring attitudes toward divorce and abortion, we find similar, but substantively smaller, results. The divorce question was simply how in favor of divorce are you, and it was asked in all Latin American countries. It had a 10-point response scale in order of increasing support for divorce. Analysis of this question shows that women are more supportive of divorce in Latin America than are men (appendix

12. PELA has surveyed legislators in every Latin American country for up to five survey waves (as of now) since the mid-1990's (Alcántara Sáez 2017). The website of the project provides information about the composition of surveys' samples and copies of the survey questionnaires. PELA data have commonly been used to identify the ideological position of political parties and the organization of legislators' positions across policy issues in a common space across countries (Alcántara Sáez 2008a; Rosas 2005; Saiegh 2009). The dataset used in this chapter is an integrated country and survey dataset compiled by the authors (Alles and Schwindt-Bayer 2015). The appendix provides a table of survey questions and descriptive statistics as well as tables presenting the statistical model results. All modeling uses OLS or logit with country-fixed effects and estimates the effect of legislator gender on their perception of the issue, controlling for the legislator's age, legislative experience, political ideology, education level, marital status, and in some models, perceptions of democratic instability.

13. Table A4.4 in the appendix reports descriptive statistics of the three variables of interest.

14. In the single-country analyses, the level of significance is smaller in Chile and Uruguay but still at the $p=0.12$ level, which is notable for a small sample size of 75 with a much smaller number of that being women. The effect is still at the $p<0.01$ level in Peru.

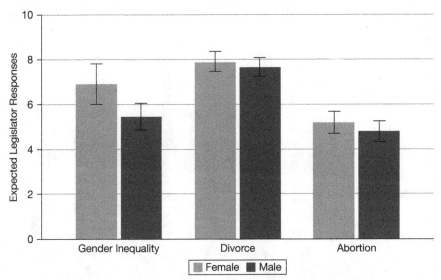

Figure 4.4 Expected Legislator Perceptions of Gendered Policy Issues by Respondent Sex (PELA Survey)

NOTE: The gender inequality question assesses the importance that legislators place on gender inequality in their country whereas the divorce and abortion questions are about support for more liberal divorce and abortion rights. Expected values estimated from OLS regression presented in appendix Table A4.5, models 1 to 3, with all other variables held at means, modes, or referent category. Figure includes 95% confidence intervals.

Table A4.5), although the effect is only borderline statistically significant (p=0.09). All else held at its mean, mode, or referent category, Figure 4.4 shows men's average response is 7.6 compared to women's average response being 7.9. Results are similar for views of abortion rights. Using a question asked in all Latin American countries on support for legislation that gives women the right to make their own reproductive choices (with a 10-point scale for responses), we see that women are more supportive of a woman's right to choose than are men. Referring again to Figure 4.4, women's average response is 5.2—all else held at means, modes, and the reference category—compared to 4.8 for men.

need more men involved
as not as much of an issue
for them

Challenges to democracy

Analyzing how gender affects legislator views of threats to democracy, we find some important differences between male and female legislators.[15] First, we examined a PELA question asking legislators for their views of how stable democracy is in their country, with four response options ranging from "not at all stable" to "very stable." We inverted the scale and dichotomized the response options to create a simple measure of perceptions of democratic *instability*. A statistical model estimating

15. Table A4.4 in the appendix reports descriptive statistics of these variables. The model results are reported in Table A4.6.

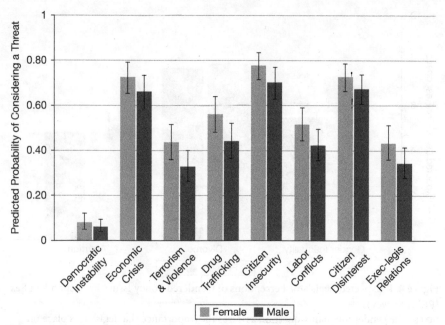

Figure 4.5 Predicted Probability of Democratic Threat Perceptions by Respondent Sex (PELA Survey)

NOTE: Predicted probabilities estimated from logit models presented in appendix Table A4.6, models 1 to 8, with all other variables held at their means, modes, or referent category. Figure includes 95% confidence intervals.

the relationship between legislator sex and democratic instability found that significantly more female legislators think that democracy is unstable compared to male legislators. The first two bars in Figure 4.5 show that the substantive size of this difference is rather small—the difference between the predicted percentage of male and female respondents who think democracy is unstable in their country is only about 0.02—but so too is the overall predicted percentage of women and men who think democracy is unstable. All else equal, democratic instability is not a huge concern to elected legislators in Latin America although slightly more women are concerned about this than men.

Second, we explored gender differences among legislators in their perceptions of the biggest threats to democratic consolidation in Latin America. Using a PELA question that asked about eleven different types of threats, we found no significant (or very small) gender differences on four of them—the relationship between the government and the armed forces, foreign debt, the poor functioning of the judiciary, and poverty and marginalization—whereas we found statistically significant and substantively larger differences on economic crises, terrorism and political violence, drug trafficking, citizen insecurity, labor conflicts, public disinterest in politics, and executive-legislative relations. Women rated all of these issues as bigger threats to democracy than men did, even after accounting for the fact that women think democracy is less stable overall. Figure 4.5 shows the predicted probability of men and women viewing each of these issues as threats to democracy. Gender differences are highly salient on all of the issues, with the predicted probability for women being about 0.07 higher than for men on most issues. The largest differences are for terrorism and drug trafficking, where the statistical model estimates a difference in predicted probabilities of 0.11 and 0.12, respectively. Why women perceive greater threats to democracy is unclear and needs future research attention. But one clue might come from the next chapter by Morgan and Hinojosa that finds women not feeling represented by parties or incorporated in them. That disconnectedness may transfer into the legislative arena leading women to perceive larger problems with democracy and representation than men do.

Third, we examined several PELA questions about corruption as a political problem (full models not reported here). These were only asked in a small subset of five countries—Argentina, Brazil, Chile, Peru, and Uruguay—but three of these countries have had large corruption scandals of late, making the question very relevant in Argentina, Brazil, and Chile. No significant gender differences existed in how legislators perceived corruption as a threat to democracy, what they thought characterized a corrupt politician, or how much corruption they perceived in different branches of government or societal entities. However, women legislators perceive more corruption in the legislature than do men: the predicted percentage of women reporting "a lot" of corruption is 11.1% (and 43.9% reporting either "a lot" or "some" corruption), whereas it is only 4.7% (and 35.1%) among men, all else held at means and modes. It is not clear why women would perceive more corruption in the very environment in which they work than men, but this certainly needs more analysis both to understand why it exists and what the consequences of it might be.

SOCIETAL CONSEQUENCES: WOMEN'S REPRESENTATION AND CITIZEN ATTITUDES AND BEHAVIOR

Of the issues about women's representation being evaluated in this chapter, the societal consequences of greater attention to gender and political representation are the most understudied. Although a variety of country-specific and cross-national studies have emerged in recent years, work that focuses on Latin America has been less common. Additionally, much of the research on gender and mass politics in Latin America has focused more on understanding the nuances of gender differences and societal attitudes and a myriad of factors relating to it than exploring the specific role of women's legislative representation. The key studies in this area have examined citizens' views of men and women as political leaders (Kerevel and Atkeson 2015; Morgan and Buice 2013), gender gaps in political engagement and participation (Desposato and Norrander 2009; Espinal and Zhao 2015; Zetterberg 2009), and citizen attitudes toward Latin American democracies (Schwindt-Bayer 2010; Walker and Kehoe 2013). In this section, we bring these three groups of research together to provide a comprehensive picture of whether and how women's legislative representation relates to support for female political leaders, engagement and participation, and democratic attitudes in Latin America, using the Latin American Public Opinion Project's (LAPOP) Americas Barometer biennial survey data from 2004–2012.

The adoption of gender quotas in Latin America and subsequent dramatic increase in women's legislative representation in some countries is argued to have a symbolic role model effect on citizens, making them feel more represented and included in the political process and, as a result, increasing their engagement and participation in politics and improving their attitudes toward representative democracy. Important research has found support for this theory. Desposato and Norrander (2009) find that higher representation of women in legislatures leads to smaller gender gaps in "conventional participation," specifically measures of following politics in the news, discussing politics with others, and persuading others of one's political opinion. Schwindt-Bayer (2010) finds a relationship between women in the legislature and citizens' democratic satisfaction and legislative trust. Yet research also makes clear that women's legislative representation is only one of many contextual factors that relates to mass attitudes, engagement, and participation (Morgan and Buice 2013), and it has not always had positive and significant effects on citizens (Zetterberg 2009).

We explore this relationship with pooled data from five waves of the Americas Barometer survey and reveal an important set of societal consequences for women's legislative representation.[16] First, we examined the relationship between women's legislative representation and support for women political leaders and five measures of political engagement.[17] Appendix Table A4.8 reports the results of the statistical models that we summarize here. We found that women's legislative representation has a positive effect on both men's and women's support for female leaders and engagement in politics, but on support for female leaders, political interest, and persuading others, the relationship is stronger for women than for men. Interestingly, for following politics in the news, the association is slightly weaker for women than for men.

Next, we examined how women's representation in Latin American legislatures relates to four measures of some of the challenges democracy faces in the region (see Schwindt-Bayer, chapter 1, this volume, for more details on these challenges)—low levels of support for democracy, reduced satisfaction with democracy, lack of confidence in the legislature, and pervasive corruption. LAPOP provides a seven-point scale for all but the democratic satisfaction question, which is a four-point scale. As Figure 4.6 shows, the expected mean response for all four democratic support and performance measures is higher when more women are in the national legislatures of Latin American countries than when fewer women are represented, all else held at means, modes, and referent categories. Citizens report more support for democracy, greater satisfaction with democracy, more trust in the legislature, and they perceive cleaner government (less corruption) when more women are in the national legislature. This relationship exists after accounting for the higher levels of economic development in some countries, the presence of gender quotas, and greater electoral disproportionality in legislative outcomes. Notably, there are no substantive differences between men and women on this relationship.[18]

16. Appendix Tables A4.8 and A4.9 present the full statistical models for the LAPOP analyses. Models were either logit or OLS regression, depending on whether the dependent variable in the model was dichotomous (support for female leaders, political interest, persuading others, government assistance, campaigning, and following politics in the news) or ordinal/continuous (democratic stability, democratic satisfaction, legislative trust, and corruption perceptions). All models included country- and time-fixed effects. Results were similar in models with random effects, those analyzed individually within country, and in year-specific models.

17. Table A4.7 of the Appendix provides descriptive statistics on the independent and dependent variables included in these models.

18. None of the statistical models had significant interaction terms between women's legislative representation and respondent sex.

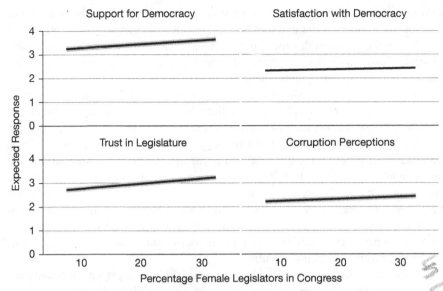

Figure 4.6 Expected Values of Survey Respondents' Views of Democracy (LAPOP Survey)
NOTE: Expected values estimated from models in appendix Table A4.9, with all other variables held at means, modes, or referent category. Shaded areas are 95% confidence intervals.

Although a much smaller body of research has examined the societal conse-quences of women's legislative representation in Latin America, research does sug-gest that the presence of women in national legislatures correlates with more support for political gender equality, greater political engagement and participation, and more positive feelings toward democracy in the region. Of course this does not nec-essarily mean that the presence of women in national legislative politics will change public attitudes or behavior enough to overcome the negative effects of the poor political and democratic performance that have plagued the region. Women's legisla-tive representation is no magic bullet for solving broader political problems in the region. That said, its positive effects, even if small, should not be ignored in either the gender and politics literature or the Latin American democracy, institutions, and behavior literature. In fact, it should be more explicitly considered and more atten-tion should given to exactly how and why the relationships reported here and in pre-vious literature exist. Much more work remains to be done in this area of the study on the consequences of women's legislative representation.

CHALLENGES FOR WOMEN IN LATIN AMERICAN LEGISLATURES

Women in Latin American legislatures still face myriad challenges. First, gender quotas have significantly improved women's opportunities to win election to national legislatures in Latin America. However, the election process is still gendered in a way that disadvantages women. Women struggle to obtain access to party ballots, for example. Despite quotas, gender bias persists among party leaders who may or may not support gender quotas and look for opportunities to bypass quota laws or find ways to implement them that minimize women's participation as much as reasonably possible. Research on party primaries, for example, suggests that parties have used them as a way to bypass quotas (Baldez 2004, 2007).[19]

Scholars have also suggested that parties use *suplente* positions to hinder women's representation (Costa Benavides 2003), although Hinojosa and Gurdián (2012) find no evidence that substitutes undermine women's access to legislatures in Nicaragua. Other indicators of the gendered nature of party selection processes are that male candidates are predominantly nominated to the first position on party ballots, and most ballots are still less than 50% female, even when gender quotas are in place. Women also face challenges getting into political networks that are male-dominated and filled with gendered rules and behaviors that disadvantage women. Thus to continue improving women's access to legislative office, Latin American countries need to focus on party-level politics and ways to make the candidate selection and nomination processes more gender-neutral.[20]

Second, as discussed previously, women in legislatures have played important roles bringing women's rights and gender equality issues to the legislative arena, and our analyses above show that they have distinct preferences on today's hotly debated gendered public policies and concerns about democratic stability and its threats. Yet once in office, research has shown that women have far less political power than men and this is likely to hinder significant policy changes that help women, gender equality, and democracy. Legislatures and the rules and norms that operate inside them are male-dominated institutions that were formed over years and years of women's exclusion. Reforming legislatures to be gender-inclusive institutions has proved challenging.

Third, the presence of women in legislatures has a positive association with how Latin American citizens view gender equality in politics, their engagement and participation in politics, and their views of democracy and its challenges. Yet if women's policy and legislative power is weaker than the symbolic power of their political presence, then the full extent of the societal benefits of greater gender equality in politics is not being realized. The societal effects of women's legislative incorporation has much more potential than just symbolism (Schwindt-Bayer 2010), but women's full access to legislative power is necessary for that to happen. The positive relationship between women in legislatures and citizen attitudes and political behaviors has significant room for growth but also regression.

CONCLUSION

This chapter has used the vast array of literature on gender and legislatures in Latin America and new empirics incorporating the Latin American political context to make three main points about the causes and consequences of women's legislative

19. Interestingly, one study found that women actually did better than men in primary elections in Mexico (Baldez 2004).

20. Hinojosa (2012) offers a seminal study of candidate selection rules and women's access to party ballots in Latin America.

representation. First, institutions, such as gender quotas, and fragmentation of party systems, are important determinants of the number of women elected to Latin American legislatures. Quotas facilitate women's election whereas increased party system fragmentation works against it. Women's legislative representation could, on average, be higher in Latin America if significant party system fragmentation had not occurred in the recent democratic past. Second, women in Latin America legislate differently than men, promoting women's rights and gender equality issues and bringing different views of democracy and its threats to the legislative agenda. Third, a positive correlation exists between women's presence in legislatures and democratic attitudes and behavior in society.

Much work on gender and legislative representation in Latin America remains to be done. First, research on women's substantive representation in Latin American legislatures needs to move beyond the handful of countries that have received the most attention thus far—Argentina, Brazil, and Costa Rica, for example. Data availability has often hampered efforts to study legislative politics in the region but new legislative websites and greater transparency in the archives of many Latin American legislatures have made this easier. Technological advances have greatly increased access to legislative information, such as bills, committees, legislative debates, and voting, even in some of the smaller and less developed Latin American countries.

Second, scholarship needs to consider some of the more subtle and nuanced ways in which gender affects legislative politics. We need detailed analysis of the pathways and mechanisms by which gender shapes and is shaped by legislative institutions, both formal ones and informal ones. This means moving beyond establishing mere correlations between phenomena and theorizing and testing how and why those correlations exist. One example of this is the recent study by Kerevel and Atkeson (2013) that aimed to parse out the different reasons for marginalization of women in legislatures and testing one of those in the context of the Mexican congress.

Third, scholarship that further incorporates the realities of representative democracy in Latin America is necessary to understand not just broad connections between gender and legislative representation but those connections in the context of weak democracy and serious threats to it from corruption, weak parties, cyclical economic crises, and populist presidents, which are characteristic of many Latin American democracies. This chapter has made an initial effort to do that but more research along these lines is necessary.

Women in Political Parties

Seen But Not Heard

JANA MORGAN AND MAGDA HINOJOSA ■

descriptive not led to substantive

Nadine Heredia. Susana Villarán. Keiko Fujimori. It is impossible to speak of Peruvian politics today without mentioning the names of these women, who currently lead or have recently led political parties.[1] Across the region, women occupy seats of power within parties: Cecilia Romero occupies the top seat in Mexico's *Partido Acción Nacional*, Isabel Allende leads Chile's *Partido Socialista*, and Mónica Xavier headed Uruguay's *Frente Amplio* from 2012–2016. Women are increasingly being *seen* as political actors within parties, but are they *heard*? To what extent does female presence in parties translate into making them effective agents for women's interests? This chapter presents data on women's representation within parties and discusses how this descriptive representation has generally not been associated with gains for the substantive representation of women's interests.

Latin American parties and party systems are an eclectic mix of types of organizations (e.g., mass parties, elite parties, personalist vehicles); linkage strategies (e.g., programmatic, clientelist, etc.); and patterns of interactions (e.g., conciliatory vs. conflictual, institutionalized vs. inchoate) (Kitschelt et al. 2010; Mainwaring and Scully 1995). Parties serve as the primary conduits for representation in democratic systems (Hagopian 1998). However for women, "parties constitute one of the most important barriers . . . to access formalized political power" (del Campo 2005, 1705). Despite the vital role of parties for representation, little work has examined how parties impose formal or informal obstacles to women's descriptive or substantive representation, and the literature has overwhelmingly overlooked how parties behave as gendered institutions. And while parties have the potential to play a pivotal part "in correcting the current gender imbalance" in representation (Hinojosa 2012, 12), the limited existing work in this area typically focuses on individual parties or countries

1. Heredia is president of *Partido Nacionalista Peruano*, Villarán is president of *Partido Descentralista Fuerza Social*, and Fujimori is president of *Fuerza Popular*.

without attention to the significant variation in women's representation across parties. We tackle these important issues head on.

This chapter first examines causes, by exploring women's representation within political parties as leaders, candidates, and officeholders. We find that Latin American parties are increasingly accessible to women. Women like Nadine Heredia and Isabel Allende now lead parties, and women are obtaining other powerful (and visible) positions within parties and as representatives of their parties in public office. But are these women heard? Here there is less reason for optimism. Few parties prioritize or even maintain organizational ties to women's groups, and women's concerns rarely figure prominently in party platforms. While a handful of party systems in the region feature parties that take progressive stances on social issues primarily affecting women, many countries have no party speaking out on such issues. Given these patterns, it is not surprising that women are much less likely to identify with parties than their male counterparts, and women's descriptive representation has done little to counteract this trend. The consequences, therefore, for women's substantive representation are dire. The full incorporation of women into political parties remains a challenge; the final section of this chapter provides suggestions for political parties to incorporate women into their organizations both descriptively and substantively.

CAUSES: WOMEN'S UNDERREPRESENTATION IN POLITICAL PARTIES

We begin by assessing the extent to which Latin American parties offer opportunities for women to participate within their organizations.[2] Academic work examining women's representation within parties has been limited (but see del Campo 2005; Franceschet 2005; Macaulay 2006). While data on candidates and officeholders are more accessible, the difficulty in collecting information on female party membership and leadership has limited our understanding of women within parties. Thus there is a considerable gap in our knowledge of both the causes of women's representation within parties and the consequences these patterns have for the ways that women relate to parties and policymaking.[3] Because parties often act as gatekeepers that control who gains access to positions of political influence, structure the kinds of issues that achieve salience in the political arena, and serve as the principle avenues through which citizens obtain voice and influence in the formal policy process, understanding women's ability to attain positions of influence within parties offers important insight into the dynamics of women's descriptive and substantive representation not only in political parties but across many domains of politics and policymaking.

2. There have been a few women-only parties in Latin America. Roza (2010) documents fourteen women's parties, which emerged between 1900 and 1970, often to promote female suffrage efforts.

3. We especially need more work examining "feminist groups who refuse all forms of interaction with parties" (Franceschet 2005, 12) and how this affects women's representation within parties.

Women in their parties: Leadership posts and women's sections

In order to examine women's representation within parties, we draw on original data from GEPPAL, the Gender and Political Parties in Latin America database, compiled by the Inter-American Development Bank and International IDEA, which is a uniquely comprehensive source of cross-national data on women in parties. The database provides information for all parties that obtained a minimum of 5% representation[4] in the lower (or only chamber) of congress in eighteen Latin American countries for 2009, which allows us to assess the variation that exists across countries and parties.

The degree of women's representation in these leadership positions offers an indication of parties' commitment to gender equality (Sacchet 2009a). But, as Table 5.1 demonstrates, women are less likely than men to be represented in the highest echelons of power, both as leaders within parties and as nominees for and representatives in national-level public office. Women's presence in parties' highest national-level executive committees (column 1), averages just 23% across the region despite the fact that a significant number of parties have instituted internal quotas to boost women's representation in these positions.[5] We observe tremendous variation here both across countries—with Panama averaging just 13% and Costa Rica at 41%—and within countries. For instance, in Costa Rica, the best overall performer, *Partido Unidad Social Cristiana* (PUSC), reports women in just 25% of its leadership posts while *Partido de Liberación Nacional* (PLN) boasts gender parity. On the opposite end of the spectrum, some parties in the region reported no women in their organization's top decision-making body. Of course, these data only tell us whether women occupy leadership positions; they do not offer insight into women's actual influence. And not all of these positions are equal, as Teresa Sacchet has indicated, "women tend to be selected for positions that are labour-intensive but not for those of real political clout." (Sacchet 2009a, 158).

Of course, presence in party leadership is not the only avenue for women's descriptive representation; some parties in the region maintain women's sections that might offer some opportunity for influence (as shown in the final column of Table 5.1). Moreover, there is considerable variation in the role these women's sections play, while some offer meaningful opportunities for representation, others merely serve as tokens or even as institutions meant to keep women in subservient roles "isolated from the main partisan structures" (Friedman 2000; Sacchet 2009a, 155; Saint-Germain and Metoyer 2008). In fact, the presence of women's sections does not enhance women's opportunities to fill influential party leadership positions, obtain candidacies, or get elected to office (Roza 2010). Regardless, Roza argues that these sections can have an impact and that "the profile of many women's units throughout the region is changing, from the traditional conception that assigned women's sections functions that mirrored their roles in the private sphere to sections charged with promoting gender equality and equal opportunities" (Roza 2010, 200). Women's sections may prove a double-edged sword, capable of advocating for women, yet also

---

4. For countries in which fewer than five parties surpassed this threshold, data for the five largest parties were collected.

5. The national executive committee represents each party's highest administrative authority; these go by a variety of names (e.g., *Comité Ejecutivo Nacional* or *Directorio Nacional*). Average is a simple cross-national average.

Table 5.1 WOMEN'S PARTICIPATION IN LATIN AMERICAN PARTIES

	% Leaders, Female (Total Leaders)	% Congressional Candidates, Female	% Legislators, Female (Total Elected)	Existence of Women's Section
ARGENTINA				
Afirmación para una República Igualitaria	44% (9)	39%	50% (14)	
Partido Justicialista	12% (75)	38%	36% (67)	✓
Partido Socialista	31% (13)	44%	36% (33)	✓
Propuesta Republicana/Compromiso Cambio	20% (5)	38%	50% (6)	✓
Unión Cívica Radical	12% (24)	40%	29% (17)	✓
WEIGHTED AVERAGE	17%	40%	37%	
BOLIVIA				
Movimiento al Socialismo	60% (10)	20%	14% (72)	✓
Poder Democrático y Social	—	17%	19% (43)	
WEIGHTED AVERAGE	40%	19%	17%	
BRAZIL				
Partido da Social Democracia Brasileira	14% (37)	15%	5% (66)	✓
Partido Democrático Trabalhista	14% (21)	11%	4% (24)	✓
Partido do Movimento Democrático Brasileiro	17% (12)	11%	10% (89)	✓
Partido dos Trabalhadores	33% (27)	12%	8% (83)	✓
Partido Progressista	8% (90)	8%	7% (41)	✓
Partido Socialista Brasileiro	23% (31)	13%	22% (27)	✓
WEIGHTED AVERAGE	16%	12%	8%	

← even with quotas still lacking leaders

(Continued)

Table 5.1 CONTINUED

	% Leaders, Female (Total Leaders)	% Congressional Candidates, Female	% Legislators, Female (Total Elected)	Existence of Women's Section
CHILE				
Partido Demócrata Cristiano	18% (11)	11%	10% (20)	✓
Partido por la Democracia	20% (10)	26%	24% (21)	✓
Partido Radical Social Demócrata	8% (12)	0	0% (7)	✓
Partido Renovación Nacional	0 (7)	16%	16% (19)	
Partido Socialista	10% (10)	29%	20% (15)	✓
Unión Demócrata Independiente	15% (13)	8%	12% (33)	
WEIGHTED AVERAGE	13%	14%	15%	
COLOMBIA				
Partido Cambio Radical	0 (6)	17%	10% (20)	
Partido Conservador Colombiano	18% (11)	11%	3% (29)	
Partido Liberal Colombiano	30% (10)	13%	11% (35)	✓
Partido Social de Unidad Nacional	— (11)	15%	14% (29)	
WEIGHTED AVERAGE	34%	13%	9%	
COSTA RICA				
Acción Ciudadana	33% (3)	49%	41% (17)	✓
Liberación Nacional	50% (6)	44%	40% (25)	✓
Movimiento Libertario	44% (9)	42%	17% (6)	✓
Unidad Social Cristiana	25% (4)	44%	40% (5)	✓
WEIGHTED AVERAGE	41%	45%	38%	
DOMINICAN REPUBLIC				
Partido de la Liberación Dominicana	12% (24)		24% (96)	✓
Partido Reformista Social Cristiano	16% (31)		14% (22)	✓
WEIGHTED AVERAGE	14%		19%	

ECUADOR				
Movimiento País o Acuerdo País	25% (12)	49%	41% (59)	
WEIGHTED AVERAGE	17%	48%	33%	
EL SALVADOR				
Alianza Republicana Nacionalista	23% (13)	15%	12% (32)	✓
Frente F. Martí para la Liberación Nacional	—	37%	31% (35)	✓
Partido de Conciliación Nacional	—	27%	0 (11)	✓
Partido Demócrata Cristiano	—	31%	20% (5)	✓
WEIGHTED AVERAGE	25%	26%	19%	
GUATEMALA				
Gran Alianza Nacional	9% (23)	18%	8% (37)	
Partido Patriota	15% (33)	13%	10% (29)	✓
Unidad Nacional de la Esperanza	25% (28)	16%	18% (51)	
WEIGHTED AVERAGE	16%	19%	12%	
HONDURAS				
Partido Liberal de Honduras	31% (13)		24% (62)	✓
Partido Nacional de Honduras	33% (12)		21% (56)	✓
WEIGHTED AVERAGE	38%		24%	
MEXICO				
Partido Acción Nacional	12% (17)	33%	23% (206)	✓
Partido de la Revolución Democrática	50% (18)	28%	21% (127)	✓
Partido Revolucionario Institucional	22% (36)	30%	16% (103)	✓
Partido Verde Ecologista de México	18% (11)	30%	53% (19)	✓
WEIGHTED AVERAGE	23%	31%	22%	

(Continued)

Table 5.1 CONTINUED

	% Leaders, Female (Total Leaders)	% Congressional Candidates, Female	% Legislators, Female (Total Elected)	Existence of Women's Section
NICARAGUA				
Frente Sandinista de Liberación Nacional	—	32%	32% (38)	✓
Movimiento Renovador Sandinista	22% (9)	21%	20% (5)	✓
Partido Liberal Constitucionalista	22% (9)	20%	8% (25)	✓
WEIGHTED AVERAGE	20%	28%	19%	
PANAMA				
Cambio Democrático	20% (10)	12%	17% (12)	✓
Partido Político Panameñista	7% (15)	3%	0 (21)	✓
Partido Revolucionario Democrático	11% (9)	14%	8% (26)	✓
Unión Patriótica	18% (17)	20%	25% (4)	✓
WEIGHTED AVERAGE	13%	12%	8%	
PARAGUAY				
Asociación Nacional Republicana	13% (90)	16%	7% (30)	✓
Partido Liberal Radical Auténtico	15% (55)	18%	10% (29)	✓
WEIGHTED AVERAGE	16%	26%	11%	
PERU				
Cambio 90	29% (7)	37%	38% (13)	✓
Partido Aprista Peruano	27% (15)	36%	22% (36)	
Partido Nacionalista del Perú	43% (7)	43%	33% (45)	
Partido Popular Cristiano	25% (16)	39%	29% (17)	✓
Unión por el Perú	35% (26)	43%	33% (45)	✓
WEIGHTED AVERAGE	31%	39%	30%	

URUGUAY			
Asamblea Uruguay-Frente Amplio	13% (15)	19%	12% (8)
Mov. de Participación Popular-Frente Amplio	13% (15)	16%	15% (27)
Partido Nacional-Alianza Nacional	0 (5)	13%	5% (21)
Partido Socialista-Frente Amplio	39% (23)	31%	18% (11)
WEIGHTED AVERAGE	19%	21%	10%
VENEZUELA			
Movimiento Primero Justicia	20% (41)	13%	0 (—)
Partido Socialista Unido	32% (31)	17%	18% (143)
WEIGHTED AVERAGE	21%	15%	18%

NOTE: The data contained here are for 2009. We present data *only* for those parties that obtained 5% of seats both in the elections immediately prior to 2009 (when GEPPAL collected their data) and in the most recent elections as of February 2015. When available for the most recent elections, data was obtained from Adam Carr's Election Archive: <http://psephos.adam-carr.net/>. For Bolivia, Brazil, Costa Rica, Honduras, Nicaragua, Panama, Paraguay, Peru, and Uruguay, legislative breakdown by political party was obtained from each country's legislative website. All websites were accessed in February 2015. "% Leaders, Female" refers to the percentage of female members of the party's national executive committee. The national averages are weighted based on the total seats on each party's national executive committee (not relative party size). "% Congressional Candidates, Female" refers to the percentage of female candidates that were nominated for lower houses/single house of the congress. "% Legislators, Female" refers to the percentage of female legislators in the lower house/single house of the congress. "Existence of Women's Section" refers to whether a women's section exists according to party statutes, as recorded in GEPPAL. The data was not available for the following parties: Chile's *Unión Demócrata Independiente*, Ecuador's *Movimiento País o Acuerdo País*, and Uruguay's *Partido Nacional-Alianza Nacional*.

SOURCE: Data compiled by authors from GEPPAL Database: http://www.iadb.org/research/geppal.

more women in leadership on the left but not more candidacies [handwritten]

keeping women away from true nuclei of power. Thus far, however, women's sections remain a largely untapped resource for identifying and recruiting female candidates and promoting women's interests within parties.

Parties and women's representation as candidates and officeholders

How frequently do parties nominate women for elected office? How often are female candidates successful? Data in Table 5.1 provide insight into the variation that exists across and within countries (even where national quota laws are in effect), presenting the percentage of each party's nominees and elected legislators who were women. The cross-national and within-country variation is significant and does not neatly follow patterns that might be predicted by the distribution of legislated gender quotas. In Chile, absent quotas,[6] female candidacies range from none to nearly 29%, and women's representation in the lower house ranges from zero to over 20%. In Brazil, which uses weak gender quotas, we still observe considerable variation with the *Partido Trabalhista Brasileiro* (PTB) having no female representation, while nearly a quarter of *Partido Socialista Brasileiro* (PSB) deputies were women. While gender quotas have had transformative effects on legislatures in the region (see Schwindt-Bayer and Alles, chapter 4, this volume) and to a lesser extent on women's representation in subnational government (see Escobar-Lemmon and Funk, chapter 6, this volume), women's incorporation into politics is often hampered, as the introductory chapter notes, by "other candidate selection, electoral, appointment, and arena-specific rules and norms."

Considering female candidacies together with women's abilities to gain seats illuminates conditions under which female candidacies are (un)successful. While women's representation as officeholders frequently mirrors their presence as candidates, the correlation is not perfect and deviating cases can be instructive. For example, in a closed-list system, if female candidacies outpace female officeholders this likely indicates that parties are placing women in unelectable spots. In open lists, a gap between female nominees and female officeholders could indicate voter bias against women. Additionally, if parties nominate women who are electorally unsuccessful, parties may be making rhetorical commitments to women's representation by selecting female nominees without making concomitant organizational changes designed to increase women's electability, such as providing women with the training or financing necessary to compete.

Somewhat surprisingly given that, as the introductory chapter explains, leftist parties have long been seen as promoting women into politics, women's representation as nominees and elected officials does not appear to be associated with the ideological positioning of their party. In a statistical analysis, Roza (2010) found that left parties were no more likely than those on the right to nominate or elect women, a conclusion also supported by Htun (2005). While left parties have more women in leadership than those on the right, this has not translated into more candidacies or elected positions for women. Like quotas, ideology offers an inadequate understanding of the variation we see.[7]

necessary financing? [handwritten]

6. Chile adopted a gender quota in 2015 that will first be applied in the 2017 elections.

7. This may be because parties of both left and right fail to represent women's issues and policy priorities, a point developed below.

We have sparse information on women's participation as candidates and officehold-ers by party at the subnational level in Latin America (see, however, Escobar-Lemmon and Funk, chapter 6, this volume). While recent work has examined women's represen-tation as candidates and officeholders in subnational legislatures by party (Barnes 2016) and in local elections (Hinojosa 2012; Hinojosa and Franceschet 2012; Shair-Rosenfield and Hinojosa 2014), this research has been largely constrained to single-country stud-ies. The unfortunate lack of data on women's electoral participation at the local level may mask some of women's political incorporation, since women may participate more locally where they see themselves as "tending the needs of [their] big family in the larger *casa* of the municipality" (Chaney 1979, 21) and where participation may be more com-patible with family responsibilities.[8]

What can parties do? Strategies to increase women's descriptive representation

While parties often lament the dearth of qualified or interested women to explain their failure to identify female nominees and their inability to meet external (or even internal) quotas, this supply side argument appears to have little merit. In Latin America, changes in women's domestic roles as well as increases in women's educational attainment and labor force participation are indicative of a large and growing pool of political talent, which parties could access (Hinojosa 2012). Additionally, parties frequently point to gender bias by voters as a rationalization for lack of female representation, but research on Latin American parties suggests voter bias is limited (Shair-Rosenfield and Hinojosa 2014). Despite parties' claims to the contrary, neither supply-side nor demand-side fac-tors explain women's underrepresentation. Instead, recent research has emphasized that candidate recruitment and selection processes are essential to explaining women's underrepresentation as both candidates and officeholders (e.g., Baldez 2004; Escobar-Lemmon and Taylor-Robinson 2008; Hinojosa 2009, 2012; Roza 2010). Indeed more academic attention needs to focus on the role parties have played in limiting women's political representation in Latin America.

These gendered patterns of candidate selection, which frequently snub capable women, are at odds with gender quota laws now common throughout the region. Since Argentina first adopted a gender quota in 1991, the use of quotas spread quickly through Latin America—today, only Guatemala lacks quotas for national elec-tions.[9] Quotas have had important implications for women's representation in Latin American legislatures (see chapter 4 in this volume), but they have also shaped parties' candidate selection procedures and internal recruitment practices across the region. Where parties are reticent to overhaul old recruitment and nomination strategies, meeting gender quotas has proven challenging (Hinojosa 2012). Parties have actively

8. The spread of subnational quotas has also led to increases in women's local level representation in recent years. Some work has indicated that parties are less likely to meet their internal quotas at the subnational level (see Sacchet 2009a).

9. Chile, Nicaragua, and Venezuela have not yet applied national level quotas, but will be doing so in upcoming elections. Venezuela previously used a gender quota, but it was ruled unconsti-tutional in 2000; in 2015, the National Electoral Council decreed that a gender quota would be applied in the December elections.

defied quota provisions, especially where effective enforcement mechanisms are lacking. Where parties fear sanctions for failing to comply, they "exploit loopholes in order to violate the spirit—if not the letter—of the laws" (Hinojosa and Piscopo 2013). For example, parties have tried to meet quota obligations by nominating women as alternates (*suplentes*) rather than titleholders (*titulares/principales*); in Mexico, where the law forbade this practice, parties imposed upon female titleholders to resign in favor of male alternates following the election (Hinojosa and Gurdián 2012).

On the other hand, some parties have instituted their own quotas to address women's underrepresentation in positions of power, and in many cases, party-level affirmative action measures pre-date national quotas. However, internal quotas have rarely yielded the expected results, as parties often fail to comply with their own rules. In Latin American parties that apply gender quotas to internal leadership posts, women on average occupy 19% of executive committee seats, while women fill 18% of leadership posts in parties without such measures (Roza 2010, 117).[10] Rather than strengthening women's representation, these measures frequently provide only lip service to gender equality.

Parties have taken other steps to address women's descriptive underrepresentation, such as providing women training to encourage their leadership potential and promote their effectiveness as candidates. By 2009, 65% of the parties included in the GEPPAL database were specifically training women, and some parties had rules in place to reserve a portion of their funding to promote female candidacies. While none of the largest parties in Argentina, Ecuador, or Guatemala have funds dedicated to training women, all four major parties examined in Costa Rica do, as do three of five Colombian parties and two of five Honduran parties. Some quota legislation has provided incentives for parties to engage in this type of training. For example, the Colombian quota rewards parties that nominate women by extending additional state funding (Hinojosa and Piscopo 2013), and the new Chilean quota will provide financial resources to parties based on the number of women they elect, incentivizing the nomination of women and the promotion of strong female candidacies.

While women comprise half the Latin American electorate, they remain minorities within parties. Women are inequitably represented in party leadership positions, and parties have underutilized or marginalized women's sections. The extreme variation in women's access to candidacies and elected positions is evidence that gendered candidate recruitment and selection procedures coexist with and contradict quota legislation aimed at leveling the playing field.

CONSEQUENCES FOR WOMEN'S SUBSTANTIVE REPRESENTATION IN PARTIES

Despite some uneven progress for women in terms of descriptive representation within their political parties, women often find little substantive voice in the region's parties. To flesh out this claim, this section takes on two primary questions. First, to what extent do parties in the region serve as meaningful arenas of representation by advocating for women's issues or employing strategies designed to incorporate women's concerns? Second, to what extent and through which mechanisms do women

10. The differences are not statistically significant.

in the region connect to parties? To address these motivating questions and thereby assess the extent to which Latin American parties offer substantive representation for women, we consider several kinds of evidence including expert surveys, the content of party programs, and public opinion data.

A considerable body of research has focused on exploring the ways in which subaltern groups in Latin America attain representation through parties. Analyses of party linkages with unions and the working class have long been a mainstay of this scholarship (Collier and Collier 1991; Levitsky 2003), and recently attention has turned to analyzing how the urban poor, the informal sector, and historically marginalized racial and ethnic groups (do not) find voice through parties (Anria 2016; Birnir 2007; Morgan 2011; Roberts 2003; Van Cott 2005). And while extensive work has analyzed how women attempt to achieve influence through social movements and women's organizations (Baldez 2002; Ewig 1999; Jaquette 1994), little research has focused on the extent to which parties link to these organizations or represent women's substantive concerns (despite parties' significance for promoting or inhibiting advancement of these interests [Osborn 2012]). The few studies that have analyzed Latin American *parties'* substantive ties with women focus on a few countries or issue domains, limiting our ability to assess regional patterns or draw broad conclusions (Haas 2001; Htun and Power 2006; Macaulay 2006).

This deficit in scholarly attention may be partially attributable to patterns discussed below, which indicate that most parties have made few overtures toward representing women's distinct concerns and that the region's party systems rarely manifest left-right polarization on feminist issues. Existing scholarship suggests that parties give little attention to women's issues when developing platforms or legislative agendas. When parties have reached out to women, they have primarily done so to advance party goals, not prioritize women's concerns (Haas 2001; Hipsher 2001, 140–146; Sacchet 2009a). Even in the rare system like Brazil where party elites hold (pro- and anti-) feminist attitudes that polarize along the left-right divide, tangible progress on feminist issues is limited (Htun and Power 2006). At the same time, women's organizations often favor autonomy over ties to parties, which they have perceived as gendered institutions that subordinate women's interests to other concerns (del Campo 2005; Franceschet 2005). In fact, Latin American parties are frequently depicted as barriers or gatekeepers as opposed to champions of women's concerns (Blofield 2006; Franceschet 2005, 85–90; Macaulay 2006). When women have advanced their substantive interests, they have done so most often through women's movements or through networks of individual female legislators collaborating across party lines, typically promoting descriptive representation or feminine concerns that affect all women (Haas 2010; Hipsher 2001, 150–156; Sacchet 2009a). Such cross-party or extra-party strategies have often proven more effective than working through parties, which are gendered institutions that tend to thwart rather than advance women's representation.

Here we flesh out the claim that Latin American parties have largely failed to develop substantive appeals designed with women in mind. The findings suggest that few parties maintain organizational ties to women's groups; women and their concerns rarely figure prominently in party platforms; and many countries feature no parties with feminist stances on issues like abortion and divorce. Supporting the argument made in the volume's introductory chapter, parties throughout Latin America remain gendered institutions in and through which women have made only limited gains. Perhaps not surprisingly then, women in the region are much less likely to identify with political parties than men.

Limited party efforts to connect with or advocate for women

To examine the extent to which parties strive to offer meaningful representation for women, we consider two potential linkage strategies (Kitschelt and Wilkinson 2007; Luna 2014). The first concerns party organizational ties to women's groups; the second emphasizes policy-based appeals. Organizational linkages through trade unions, business associations, or civil society groups have historically offered a major mechanism for interest representation in many Latin American party systems (Kitschelt et al. 2010; Morgan 2011). Parties often develop formal or informal organizational ties to groups that aggregate major interests, with the simultaneous goals of solidifying their electoral base, maintaining societal control, and offering representation or privileged access to certain sectors of society. Emblematic of this pattern are the close ties between organized labor and some parties of the left and between business or religious interests and some parties of the right (Collier and Collier 1991; Gibson 1996). As women's organizations have emerged and achieved (varying degrees of) influence across the region, parties may endeavor to form organization-based linkages with potential female supporters.

To explore parties' use of organizational ties as a mechanism for connecting to women, we use data from the Duke University Democratic Accountability and Linkages Project (DALP) expert survey. Two questions in the survey considered party organizational linkages. The first asked country experts which group each party connected to most strongly overall, and the second asked which type of group each party used to distribute benefits to supporters. Experts selected responses from a list of six groups: unions, business and professional associations, religious organizations, ethnolinguistic organizations, neighborhood organizations, and women's organizations. Table 5.2 lists all parties identified by at least one expert as having either type of organizational linkage to women's groups.[11] It is immediately apparent that few parties prioritize women as a target for this sort of linkage. Only seven parties in the region (from five countries) have strong ties to women's groups, and fifteen utilize women's organizations to distribute benefits. In more than a third of the countries, not a single expert identified even one party as prioritizing either sort of organizational linkage with women.[12] Of the nineteen parties with some ties to women's organizations, five supported a female presidential candidate in the election immediately preceding and/or immediately following the expert survey.[13] Numerous others that backed female candidates do not appear on the list, including those that supported Cristina Fernández de Kirchner (Argentina), Noemí Sanin

11. Chile's *Partido por la Democracia*, a party with a record of providing opportunities for women (Franceschet 2005, 77, 98–99), was the only party for which multiple experts specified women's organizations as the most important group.

12. By contrast, multiple experts identified many parties as having ties to unions and business associations.

13. These parties are Brazil's *Partido Progressista* and *Partido Socialista Brasileiro*, which supported Rousseff in 2010; Chile's *Partido por la Democracia*, which backed Bachelet in 2006; Panama's *Partido Revolucionario Demócratico*, which supported Herrera in 2009; and Peru's *Fujimoristas*, which backed Chávez in 2006 and Fujimori in 2011.

Table 5.2 LATIN AMERICAN PARTIES WITH LINKAGES TO WOMEN'S GROUPS

Country	(1) Parties with strong ties to women's groups[a]	(2) Parties that use women's groups to distribute benefits to supporters[b]
Argentina	—	—
Bolivia	—	—
Brazil	—	*P. Progressista (PP)*
	—	*P. Socialista Brasileiro (PSB)*
Chile	*Unión Demócrata Independiente (UDI)*	*Unión Demócrata Independiente (UDI)*
		Partido por la Democracia (PPD) (2)
Colombia	—	*Polo Democrático Alternativo*
Costa Rica	—	—
DR	—	—
Ecuador	—	—
El Salvador	—	*ARENA*
		FMLN
Guatemala	*P. Patriota (PP)*	*P. Solidaridad Nacional (PSN)*
	P. Solidaridad Nacional (PSN)	
Honduras	—	—
Mexico	—	*P. Verde Ecologista de Méx. (PVEM)*
Nicaragua	*Liberal*	—
Panamá	*P. Revolucionario Democrático (PRD)*	—
	P. Arnulfista (Panameñista)	
Paraguay	*P. País Solidario (PPS)*	*P. País Solidario (PPS)*
	—	*UNACE*
Peru	—	*Alianza por el Futuro (Fujimoristas)*
	—	*Frente del Centro (AP, Somos Perú)*
Uruguay	—	*P. Nacional*
	—	*P. Colorado*
Venezuela	—	—

NOTE: Only parties receiving at least 5% of the vote in the most recent legislative election are listed. Some parties with more than 5% of the vote may have not been included in the DALP data, which include only those parties with seats in the legislature at the time of the expert survey. Where parties or alliances have changed names since the time of the survey, the name at the date of the survey is listed here, with additional identifying information in parentheses. Numbers in parentheses after party name indicate number of experts that listed women's organizations, if more than one.

[a] Based on a question asking experts to identify the type of organization with which each party maintained the strongest ties: 1) unions, 2) business and professional associations, 3) religious organizations, 4) ethnic or linguistic organizations, 5) urban or rural neighborhood associations, and 6) women's organizations. Listed parties are those for which at least one expert specified women's organizations as their first mention.

[b] Based on a question asking experts to identify the type of organization each party trusted most as their agents to select recipients and deliver benefits to their electoral base, using the same set of response options as above. Parties listed are those for which at least one expert specified women's organizations as the most important channel for benefit distribution.

SOURCE: Author's calculations based on Duke Democratic Accountability and Linkages Project (DALP) expert survey data, collected May 2007 through February 2009.

(Colombia), Laura Chinchilla (Costa Rica), and Martha Roldós (Ecuador). Thus, experts were not especially likely to identify parties with female presidential candidates as having ties to women's groups.[14] Likewise, parties with more women in party leadership (see Table 5.1) were no more likely to be viewed as connecting to women's organizations—only three parties with ties to women's groups surpass the regional average female share of party leadership posts: *Partido Socialista Brasileiro* (Brazil), *Alianza Republicana Nacionalista* (El Salvador), and *Fujimoristas* (Peru). Thus, having women in positions of leadership within parties and as party nominees for president seems to do little to promote party organizational ties to women's organizations.[15]

A closer examination reveals that surprisingly few parties with ties to women's organizations are on the left; rather many maintain right-leaning tendencies, including Chile's *Unión Demócrata Independiente*, Peru's *Fujimoristas*, and Uruguay's *Colorados*. The only left-leaning parties identified as prioritizing ties with women's groups are Paraguay's *Partido País Solidario*, Brazil's *Partido Socialista Brasileiro*, Chile's *Partido por la Democracia*, Colombia's *Polo Democrático Alternativo*, and El Salvador's *Frente Farabundo Martí para la Liberación Nacional*. For most of these parties, linkages with women's groups are benefit driven, not substantive. Thus, in the few parties with ties to women's organizations, these linkages most likely occur either through conservative/religious groups or via material benefits rather than substantive feminist appeals.

Latin American parties also do not generally emphasize women's concerns during election campaigns. Although women constitute a large portion of the electorate (with female turnout matching male turnout throughout the region), issues such as domestic violence, female employment, and educational opportunities for women rarely figure prominently in campaign platforms. Analysis of recent platforms issued by major parties in four countries—Argentina, Brazil, Chile, and Uruguay—support this claim.[16] Using the campaign platforms for all the parties/candidates that contested the most recent presidential election in each country,[17] we conducted content analysis to identify how often each manifesto mentioned terms related to women and gender. We also assessed the number of times these terms were used specifically with reference to issue positions, as opposed to generic uses like "the men and women of Argentina." As a point of reference, we also counted terms related to employment, an economic issue typically emphasized by left-leaning parties.

Table 5.3 presents the percentage of words in each manifesto that falls into three categories—total gender mentions, relevant gender mentions, and total employment

14. Four women were elected president during the period under consideration (2005–2012); several others were major party nominees. But many parties that supported these candidates did not have ties to women's groups.

15. This pattern does not align with the argument made in the introduction to this volume, which anticipates that parties are an arena in which women's presence is expected to promote women's issues.

16. The Comparative Manifestos Project graciously provided the party manifestos.

17. In Brazil, Chile, and Uruguay, the most recent election was a runoff. In Argentina, Fernández de Kirchner won outright, so we present data for the top three competitors in the first round. For Brazil, the same two parties contested the 2010 and 2014 runoffs. Manifestos were only available for 2010, and we use those data here.

Table 5.3 Frequency of Attention to Women's Issues in Major Party Manifestos: Argentina, Brazil, Chile, and Uruguay

[handwritten note: not catering to women's issues]

Country	Year	Party (Candidate)	Gender mentions (Total)[a]	Gender mentions (Relevant)[b]	Employment mentions (Total)[c]
Argentina	2011	Frente Amplio Progresista (Binner)	0.14%	0.12%	0.30%
	2011	Frente para la Victoria (Fernández de Kirchner)	0	0	0.56%
	2011	Unión Cívica Radical (Alfonsín)	0.12%	0.07%	0.19%
Brazil	2010	Partido da Social Democracia Brasileira (Serra)	0.11%	0.08%	0.16%
	2010	Partido dos Trabalhadores (Rousseff)	0.13%	0.02%	0.44%
Chile	2013	Partido Socialista – Nueva Mayoría (Bachelet)	0.16%	0.13%	0.14%
	2013	Unión Demócrata Independiente—Alianza (Matthei)	0.08%	0.05%	0.21%
Uruguay	2014	Frente Amplio (Vázquez)	0.16%	0.13%	0.26%
	2014	Partido Nacional (Lacalle)	0.02%	0.01%	0.16%

NOTE: Parties included are those that contested the second round runoff, with the exception of Argentina where no second round was needed, and the top three vote-getters are included.

[a] Cells indicate the percent of total words in the manifesto that were from the following gender-related term list: *mujer, género, femenino, sexo*.

[b] Cells indicate the percent of total words in the manifesto that were from the gender-related term list and that were used in a context dealing with women's issues (as opposed to just mentioning women in a general way).

[c] Cells indicate the percent of total words in the manifesto that were from the following set of employment-related terms: *empleo, desempleo, trabajo*.

SOURCE: Author's calculations based upon original party programs provided by the Comparative Manifestos Project. Manifestos are from the most recent presidential election for which data are available.

mentions.[18] Chile's *Partido Socialista*, with Michelle Bachelet as its nominee, is the only party for which women's concerns were a major focus and mentions of gender slightly surpass employment references. Since taking office, this rhetorical emphasis has translated into policy, with Bachelet pushing feminist goals including gender quotas and abortion reform. Apart from this exception, the evidence emphasizes how women's issues receive considerably less rhetorical attention in party manifestos than employment concerns. In fact, the majority of parties in the table mentioned jobs and employment twice as often as they referenced women. One party, Argentina's *Frente para la Victoria*, made absolutely no mention of women or gender, despite having Cristina Fernández de Kirchner as its candidate. Thus having a female candidate at the helm does not consistently promote greater attention to women's concerns.

Among countries and parties in the region, this particular subset of party systems might be especially likely to include campaign platforms advocating on behalf of women's concerns. Three of the elections analyzed featured female candidates—Fernández de Kirchner (Argentina), Bachelet (Chile), and Rousseff (Brazil). Each of these party systems have serious competitors on the left, with left or center-left parties victorious in the analyzed elections (Wiesehomeier and Benoit 2009), and these countries are among the more developed, secular, and gender-egalitarian in the region.[19] If the platforms from this set of campaigns largely failed to prioritize women's concerns, it is unlikely that the more male-dominated candidacies and right-leaning party systems in the rest of the region would break from this pattern (Ewig 1999; Inglehart and Norris 2003; Moore and Vanneman 2003; Morgan and Buice 2013).

In examining the discussion of women's concerns more closely, several platforms, including those of Binner in Argentina, Bachelet in Chile, and Vázquez in Uruguay, maintained consistently feminist stances when discussing issues of particular relevance for women. In other cases, such as Uruguay's *Partido Nacionalista* and Argentina's *Unión Cívica Radical*, the discussion focused on feminine issues pertaining to women's traditional roles in the private sphere. This pattern offers some evidence of a left-right divide with more left-leaning parties favoring feminist articulations of women's concerns and right parties focusing on feminine issues. But across the board, women's issues of either type take a back seat to other concerns, and even having female presidential candidates at the helm has only rarely led to the transformation of party priorities toward feminist or even feminine concerns, a pattern that aligns with the expectations described in chapter 1 of this volume.

Expert surveys concerning party issue positions also support the view that many party systems fail to prioritize feminist concerns. The DALP survey asked experts to identify parties' positions on abortion rights, and Wiesehomeier and Benoit (2009) had experts evaluate parties' social policy stances pertaining to abortion and divorce as well as homosexuality and euthanasia. Table 5.4 displays all parties that experts identified as progressive on these issues. Less than half the countries have parties that favor

18. See notes in Table 5.3 for list of gender and employment-related search terms.

19. Based on data from the UNDP's Human Development Report and the AmericasBarometer survey.

Table 5.4 LATIN AMERICAN PARTIES WITH PROGRESSIVE POSITIONS ON WOMEN'S RIGHTS

Country	Parties with progressive stances on abortion[a]	Score, 10-pt scale	Parties with progressive stances on social issues[b]	Score, 20-pt scale
Argentina	Frente para la Victoria	3.7	Frente para la Victoria	6.5
			Unión Cívica Radical	7.4
Bolivia	—		—	
Brazil	Partido Socialista Brasileiro	3.4	Partido Socialista Brasileiro	5.7
	Partido dos Trabalhadores	3.8	Partido dos Trabalhadores	5.4
Chile	Partido por la Democracia	2.8	Partido por la Democracia	4.0
	Partido Socialista	3.2	Partido Socialista	3.5
Colombia	Polo Democrático Alternativo	2.1	Polo Democrático Alternativo	4.0
			Partido Liberal	7.6
Costa Rica	Movimiento Libertario	3.9	Movimiento Libertario	7.1
DR	—	—	—	
Ecuador	—		—	
El Salvador	—		FMLN	6.3
Guatemala	—		Encuentro por Guatemala	7.6
Honduras	—		—	
Mexico	PRD	1.8	PRD	4.5
Nicaragua	—		—	
Panamá	—		—	
Paraguay	—		Partido País Solidario	3.0
Peru	—		—	
Uruguay	Frente Amplio	3.4	Frente Amplio	5.7
Venezuela	—		MVR (PSUV)	7.2

NOTE: On both items, lower scores indicate more progressive stances. Only parties receiving at least 5% of votes in the most recent election are included.
[a] Question asked experts to place parties on a 10-point scale where 1 indicates strong agreement with the statement that "The woman has the right to decide whether or not to interrupt her pregnancy" and 10 indicates agreement with the statement that "Life is sacred, only God should decide." Parties are shown if expert scores averaged less than 4.
[b] Question asked experts to place parties on a 20-point scale where 1 indicates the party favors liberal policies on matters such as abortion, homosexuality, divorce, and euthanasia, and 20 indicates the party opposes liberal positions on these issues. Parties are included here if expert scores averaged less than 8. Exact score shown in parentheses.

SOURCE: Abortion data from DALP expert survey, collected May 2007 through February 2009. Social issue data from Wiesehomeier and Benoit Parties and Presidents in Latin America expert survey, collected 2006–2007.

abortion rights for women, and among those listed, only Colombia and Mexico feature parties with strong pro-choice stances. When considering a broader set of social policies (some of which are not women's issues), more parties appear progressive. However, even using this measure, seven systems lack even a single party taking permissive stands on issues like divorce, abortion, and homosexuality. On the abortion issue specifically, having women in positions of party leadership seems to make a difference. All the parties evaluated as taking feminist positions on abortion had either a female presidential candidate in the most recent election or women occupying at least one-third of party leadership posts, well above the regional average of 23% (GEPPAL 2014).[20] This pattern regarding abortion suggests that women's presence in parties has opened limited space for representing women through parties on this specific issue, providing some support for the argument made in the introductory chapter, which expects arenas like parties to provide more maneuvering room for advancing women's interests than other arenas of representation.[21] However, aside from the abortion dimension, we observe little correlation between female party leadership and pro-female advocacy by parties.

Overall, just a small set of Latin American parties connect with women through organizational linkages, prioritize women's concerns in their platforms, or take feminist policy positions. Thus, many women may view parties as failing to promote substantive representation on matters that specifically concern them.

Gender gaps in partisan ties

Given parties' relative inattention to women and their concerns, it is not surprising that women across the region are significantly less likely than men to identify with a party. Based on data from the AmericasBarometer survey in eighteen Latin American countries, 38% of men and 34% of women indicated that they sympathized with a party in 2014,[22] and this statistically significant gender gap dates to the mid-2000s.[23] We also calculated the gender gap in partisanship for each country, presented in Figure 5.1. Negative values indicate women sympathize with parties at lower rates than men. Only in Panama are women significantly more likely than men to affiliate with a party, while Brazil, Uruguay, Chile, Paraguay, Peru, Bolivia, Colombia, and Guatemala maintained negative gender gaps. In these systems, women were significantly less likely to identify with a party than were men, despite the fact that half these countries had women heading a major party's ticket in the most recent presidential election.

To explore whether these gaps in partisan identification might be explained by gender differences in socialization experiences, levels of economic and personal

20. This is similar to the finding in Schwindt-Bayer and Alles, chapter 4 (this volume), where female legislators are more likely to support abortion rights than are male legislators.

21. The only caveat is the case of Colombia's *Polo Democrático Alternativo*, for which we lack data concerning the gender composition of the party's executive committee.

22. This gap is statistically significant, $p<0.01$.

23. The question taps partisan identification: "At this time, do you sympathize with a political party?" Data from GEPPAL, which offer party membership rates by gender for eight countries in the region, do not point to a similar gender gap in membership. However, party membership

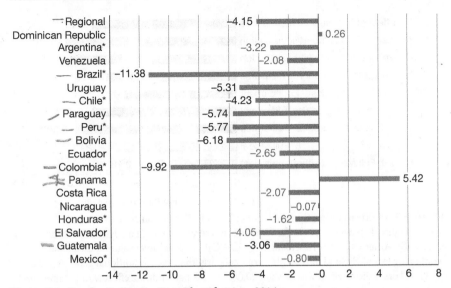

Figure 5.1 Gender Gap in Partisan Identification, 2014
NOTE: Negative values reect lower levels of partisan afliation among women than me.
Black numbers indicate a signicant gender gap; gray numbers indicate insignicant gap.
*Woman was a major presidential candidate in closest election preceding or during 2014.

autonomy, civic and political engagement, ideology, or gender attitudes, we use data from the 2012 AmericasBarometer[24] to conduct hierarchical logit analysis of partisan affiliation in eighteen Latin American countries. The intent is to assess how the gender gap varies after taking account of these potential explanations, drawn from previous research seeking to explain gender gaps in other attitudes and behaviors (e.g., Desposato and Norrander 2009; Klein 1984; Manza and Brooks 1998; Morgan 2015; Morgan and Buice 2013), as well as scholarship analyzing Latin American partisanship (e.g., Baker et al. 2016; Domínguez and McCann 1995; Lupu 2015; Medina Vidal et al. 2010; Morgan 2007; Pérez-Liñán 2002). In essence, we evaluate how the gender gap changes after controlling for each of these potential sources' difference between women and men. Figure 5.2 summarizes the results of this analysis, focusing on the effect of being female. The first row presents the coefficient for being female controlling for a basic set of individual demographics as well as some country-level features frequently thought to explain cross-national variations in partisanship.[25] The analysis reveals a significant negative effect for female estimated at –0.27.

rolls are frequently unreliable. This, together with the lack of region-wide data, limits our willingness to draw strong conclusions from GEPPAL membership data.

24. We use the 2012 survey because it included several questions about gender norms and attitudes not asked in 2014.

25. This model, as well as all subsequent models in the figure, includes a random coefficient for respondent sex as well as contextual-level controls for polarization of the party system, effective number of parties in the system, and whether the survey was conducted within 6 months of a national election. Including these variables allows for more accurate model specification but has no effect on the observed gender gap.

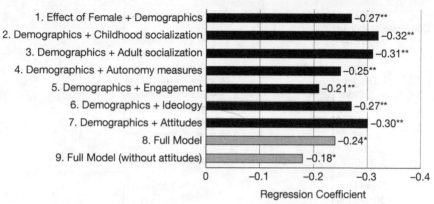

Figure 5.2 Multivariate Analysis of Gender Gaps in Partisanship
NOTES: Figure displays coeffcient for female from hierarchical logit analysis of party affliation in 18 Latin American countries, using 2012 LAPOP data. Negative values indicate that women are less likely to identify with a political party than men–traditional genders gaps.
 *Gray bars indicate effect with p-value<0.05. **Black bars indicate effect with p-value <0.01.
 All models include random coeffcients for respondent sex as well as contextual-level controls for polarization of the party system, effective number of parties in the system, and whether the survey way conducted within 6 months of a national election, the decision to include or exclude these contextual variables has no effect on the gender gap. Models 2–9 include demographic controls for respondent age, rural residence, chruch attendance, eduction, house hold wealth, and skin color.
 Model 1 includes sex plus contextual controls and individual demographics. Model 2 adds mother's education. Model 3 drops mother's education and includes parenthood. Model 4 drops parenthood and adds measure of autonomy–employment, marriage and gender equality in household incomes. Model 5 drops the autonomy measures and adds meausures of media attention, political knowledge and civic engagement. Model 6 drops the engagement items and measures of left-right ideology, ideological extremism, and ideological proximity to closest party in system. Model 7 drops ideology items and adds measures of attitudes about women's political leadership, abortion and views of female employment. Model 8 includes all variables in previous models except mother's education. Model 9 includes all items, except the attitude measures and mother's education.

Rows 2 through 7 present the logit coefficients for being female—that is, the effect being a woman has on partisan affiliation—after introducing six sets of individual-level independent variables. These variables assess how differences in demographic characteristics and childhood socialization (row 2), adult socialization (row 3), auton-omy (row 4), political and civic engagement (row 5), ideology (row 6), and gender attitudes (row 7) shape the size and significance of the partisan gender gap. Row 8 depicts the coefficient based on all of these categories, and row 9 shows all the catego-ries except gender attitudes. Examining the direction and significance of the coeffi-cient for respondent sex in models 2–9 reveals that the gap in partisan identification cannot be fully explained by gender differences in these factors. In every model, being a woman is associated with significantly lower odds of identifying with a party.[26]

26. Additional analysis, which we do not present here, also indicates that most of these factors do not have differential effects among women and men. The only significant interaction with respondent sex is for attentiveness to news, which reduces the gender gap.

Only in model 5, which controls for news attention, political knowledge, and civic engagement, do we observe a decline in the size (but not the significance) of the coefficient, suggesting a small amount of the gender gap is explained by differential levels of civic and political engagement between men and women. But much of the gap remains unexplained. Conversely, in model 6, which controls for left-right ideology, ideological extremism, and ideological proximity to a major party in the system, the magnitude of the sex coefficient goes back up. Even though women are *more* likely than men to be ideologically proximate to a major party and *less* likely to be ideologically extreme—two factors associated with higher rates of partisan identification—women remain significantly less likely to affiliate with a party. This pattern aligns with evidence presented above suggesting parties fail to advocate for policy concerns that are particularly relevant for women. Regardless of their different levels of education, employment, autonomy, or engagement, women are significantly less likely to affiliate with parties than men, even though women are generally ideologically closer to viable parties. Women seem to see parties as less concerned with the issues that interest them or as failing to deliver in ways that matter for their lives.

Moreover, evidence from the Americas Barometer regarding men and women's divergent preferences suggests that if parties pay attention to men on gender issues, they are likely to be ignoring women. Latin American women hold more feminist stances than men with regard to employment equality, gender quotas, and abortion rights.[27] The gap in attitudes toward women's employment is particularly wide and achieves significance in all but two countries in the region, Ecuador and Panama.[28] Yet among female respondents, support for employment equality has no significant relationship with partisan identification under any model specification. This issue, where women's interests diverge most from those of men and the majority of women hold feminist views, plays no role in motivating partisan attachments. This evidence lends further support to the claim that women's detachment from parties is at least somewhat rooted in their limited substantive representation through the region's party systems.

These conclusions align with previous research suggesting that many Latin American women do not find substantive representation within the existing set of political options and instead opt for descriptive representation, even when female candidates hail from ideologically distant parties (Morgan 2015). Additional analysis based on the 2014 AmericasBarometer survey, which included questions about party efforts to distribute clientelist benefits, reveals that women are also less likely to be targeted as the beneficiaries of clientelism. Parties are neglecting women in this simplest exchange.

We also considered how contextual factors pertaining to variations in women's economic opportunities and descriptive representation across the region might shape the observed gender gap in partisanship. However, we found no effects for the Gender Inequality Index, secularism, female labor force participation, presence of a female presidential candidate, percentage of female party leaders, and percentage of female legislative candidates (both based on GEPPAL data). Including these country-level indicators had no effect on the gender gap, and interacting them with the respondent's

27. While women in the region are on average more supportive of reproductive rights than men, there are several countries where the reverse is true.

28. The question asks whether men should be given priority for employment when jobs are scarce.

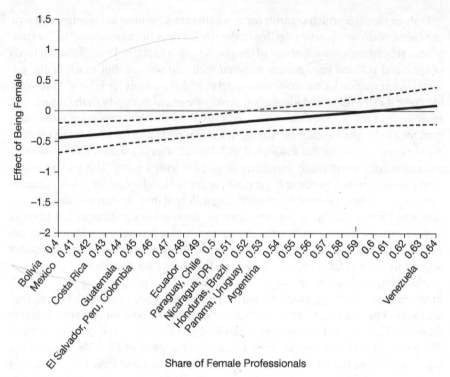

Figure 5.3 Effect of Being Female Conditioned on Share of Female Professionals
NOTE: Solid line indicates estimated effect; dotted lines indicate 90% confidence interval.

sex revealed that none influenced men and women's partisanship differentially.[29] The only contextual-level variable with a significant effect was the share of professionals who are women. Interacting the presence of female professionals with the respondent's sex reveals that having more women in higher status employment helps alleviate the gender gap in partisanship. As depicted in Figure 5.3, the gap in partisanship disappears in countries where women constitute at least 53% of professional workers. Four countries in the region surpass this threshold: Panama, Uruguay, Argentina, and Venezuela. Thus while the overall picture concerning women's substantive representation via parties is grim, this evidence suggests that having substantial female presence in higher-status jobs is associated with a slightly different dynamic, wherein women feel less disconnected from the political system. Society-wide female empowerment in the economic realm translates into greater political empowerment.

CHALLENGES TO WOMEN'S FULL INCORPORATION BY AND WITHIN PARTIES

Women today are visible actors within political parties. The data presented here on women's descriptive representation within and by parties points to an ever-increasing presence of women, but variation in women's access to candidacies and legislative

29. Full results available upon request.

positions suggests that parties have tremendous power to either incorporate or ignore women. Too many women are being left behind because parties are willing to disregard them. Women's gains are largely the result of gender quota laws that have *required* parties to seek out female candidates, but women continue to face parties that ignore their participation. Women within parties are suffering from neglect. Parties do not proactively adopt recruitment practices that would allow them to attract women. Likewise, parties fail to connect with women's groups and do not actively promote policies that appeal to women. This neglect appears to have substantive implications. The gender gap in party identification is evidence of the disconnect between women and parties in the region, and few factors, with the exception of women's economic empowerment (through professional employment) and informational empowerment (through media exposure), seem to bridge this gap.

What can be done to promote the full incorporation of women both descriptively and substantively? Candidate recruitment and selection procedures underlie efforts to increase descriptive representation. With regard to descriptive representation, parties must first create and maintain gender-disaggregated membership rolls, which will allow them to identify female talent. Second, parties can establish search committees charged with recruiting women for internal leadership positions or external candidacies. Parties with women's sections engaged in promoting equality can task these organizations with drawing up lists of potential candidates and forging relationships with organizations promoting women's interests, which may offer a broader recruitment pool. Third, quotas should also require parties to allocate funds for female candidate training and support. After all, quotas succeed not when they generate candidates, but when they beget legislators.

Women's substantive incorporation requires that parties address women's issues in their platforms and integrate women's concerns into their policymaking efforts. However, women's policy concerns appear largely absent when analyzing party platforms, and few parties take feminist stances in policy debates surrounding issues like abortion and divorce, which have profound implications for women's lives. Parties of the left, in particular, are well primed given their ideological affinities to construct promising relationships with organizations that advance women's policy concerns, but they are no more likely than parties of the right to nominate women, promote organizational ties with women's groups, or attract female partisans. In fact, women's ideological and policy interests seem largely disconnected from the contours of partisan contestation—although women are on average more ideologically proximate to parties than are men, women are less likely to affiliate with parties and less likely to vote. Moreover, female voters in Latin America frequently fail to see their concerns as integrated into existing axes of debates concerning ideology and policy (Morgan 2015). Thus women's concerns seem largely orthogonal to the established patterns of party competition, and as a result many women remain on the sidelines. This disconnect between women's concerns and the contours of policy debates suggest that parties must take intentional steps to craft policy and organizational linkages with women and to integrate women's priorities into their policy goals. Efforts in this vein could help move party systems toward aligning gender issues with existing partisan divides. Promoting this alignment would help assimilate women's issues into established patterns of competition and facilitate the pursuit of pro-female policies, rather than isolating gender issues from traditional debates that typically focus on economic, distributional, and security concerns.

Existing research on women's descriptive and substantive representation has largely overlooked political parties. Future work must identify the obstacles that exist within parties that prevent women's advancement in positions of power, assess the degree to which women are allowed to exercise power once they access leadership roles within party organizations, and explore whether women are able to wield positional power the way that their male counterparts do. Additionally, we should examine the extent to which accessing power via quotas marginalizes women within their parties, as Franceschet and Piscopo (2008) indicate. Moreover, the role that women's sections play within parties has been vastly understudied, and more work must be done to uncover the evolving role of these groups. We must also give attention to understanding why greater descriptive representation for women has, thus far, not translated into more meaningful substantive representation by parties. In other regions, women's issues map onto the left-right divide, which has the potential to facilitate articulation of women's concerns in policymaking, but most Latin American party systems fail to politicize women's issues, which often relegates them to the sidelines of political debate. In considering women's substantive representation, we should explore instances of success and failure to understand how women's concerns may become politicized and articulated through parties or whether extra-party mechanisms for representation (e.g., social mobilization) may be more effective.

Women's gains are clearly documented. Greater numbers of female candidates and legislators, however, should not obfuscate the fact that women remain underrepresented descriptively and that women's substantive concerns have been largely ignored by political parties. Women may be seen, but they are still not heard.

Women's Representation in Subnational Governments

Replicating National Institutions or Forging a Unique Path?

MARIA C. ESCOBAR-LEMMON AND KENDALL D. FUNK ■

In this chapter, we explore women's representation in subnational governments across Latin America. Exploring women's representation at the subnational level is important because responsibility for providing important social services, such as health and education, has been devolved to lower levels of government throughout much of Latin America. Subnational governments—especially in federal systems—can also create laws that affect the lives of women, such as laws regulating women's reproductive healthcare. Furthermore, if findings from studies of women in national-level governments hold in the case of subnational governments, this has important implications on a number of dimensions, including the expectation that women in subnational offices will produce different policies and outcomes than their male counterparts and better represent the interests of women.

We use the term "subnational governments" to refer to all levels below the national, including but not limited to, intermediate (e.g., state, provincial, departmental, regional) and local (e.g., municipal, cantonal, city) levels. Despite the importance of these governments, very little scholarly attention has focused on them. As a preliminary exploration, we examine women's representation in the executive and legislative branches of subnational governments. We focus on these institutions because they hold the primary locus of decision-making power. This is also where most scholarly attention has been devoted and these institutions are generally comparable across countries. However, other aspects of subnational government are equally important and future research should explore women's representation in other subnational venues (e.g., political parties, the judiciary, the bureaucracy).

The empowerment of local governments, through what Grindle (2000) calls a series of "audacious reforms," was one response to the crisis of representation. These reforms decentralized the state, creating opportunities for power to be exercised and representation to take place closer to the people.[1] This redistribution of power has taken place regionwide, not only in the four constitutionally federal states (Argentina, Brazil, Mexico, Venezuela). Many of the countries in the region adopted local elections either during the return to democracy in the 1980s or previously, although in some places intermediate-level executives remained appointed until later (see Willis, Garman, and Haggard 1999: Table 1). There were also significant efforts to reform the fiscal system to improve the financial position of subnational governments through the transfer of increased resources. Additionally, responsibility for providing public services (e.g., education, sanitation, and basic health) was transferred to subnational governments.[2] While there have been some moves toward the recentralization of services (and finances) across the region, intermediate and local governments remain important power centers and thus important venues for studying women's representation.

We begin by examining the causes of women's representation (or lack thereof) in the decentralized environment. Empowerment of subnational governments may have had gendered consequences. By creating direct opportunities for women to compete for policymaking authority—either by converting a previously appointed position into an elected one (e.g., Colombia) or by eliminating the fusion with legislative elections (e.g., Costa Rica)—mayors and governors had the chance to exercise real and independent political power. Ironically, this may have had the unintended, but nonetheless gendered, consequence of making it more difficult for women to actually win these offices. With real political power at stake, strong male candidates began to seek subnational offices and parties became more interested in controlling nominations for these positions, possibly producing lower levels of female representation, especially in executive offices. In considering the causes of women's representation (or underrepresentation) in subnational governments, we explore the implications of this as well as the extent to which factors found to be relevant in the election and selection of women to national office are applicable in subnational settings. We review the existing literature to identify how political, institutional, and socioeconomic factors shape representation. We then conduct—what is to our knowledge—the first cross-national and time-serial analysis of the determinants of women's representation in local legislatures and executive offices across Latin America to test how well the factors that have been identified in single-country

---

1. Decentralization is defined as "a process, as the set of policies, electoral reforms or constitutional reforms that transfer responsibilities, resources or authority from higher to lower levels of government" (Falleti 2010, 34). This includes both intermediate and local governments. Decentralization is multifaceted and may be relatively more advanced on one dimension than another. Political decentralization transfers political authority or creates subnational elections whereas administrative decentralization encompasses "policies that transfer the administration and delivery of social services such as education, health, social welfare, or housing to subnational governments." Fiscal decentralization increases financial resources flowing to subnational governments and encompasses legal changes designed to increase the revenues or fiscal autonomy of subnational governments. (Falleti 2005, 328–329).

2. There is an extensive literature on decentralization in Latin America. For a non-gender-focused summary, see Eaton (2012) and Montero and Samuels (2004). For more on the structure of local governments, see Nickson (1995).

studies and studies of women in national governments (see also Schwindt-Bayer, chapter 1, this volume) explain women's local representation across the entire region.

Next, we discuss the consequences of women's representation in subnational governments. Decentralization increased the salience of subnational governments in the lives of women, especially as education and healthcare were among the services most commonly devolved. Gendered consequences arose as decentralization interacted with existing state structures to create instances where intermediate-level authorities were able to block or expand women's reproductive rights (Franceschet and Piscopo 2013). Even when feminist policy was adopted, as Franceschet (2011, 274) notes, "federalism may create additional difficulties, particularly in the absence of oversight or coordinating mechanisms that ensure gender policies are implemented so that women can claim rights and benefits granted to them by law." While this literature is significantly less developed, it points to some important ways in which women in subnational offices might shape policy and also the way in which they might shape institutions to make them less gendered. Lastly, we consider how the inclusion of women might have consequences beyond the institution itself in terms of shaping society and perceptions of women.

In the third section, we look ahead to the challenges confronting women seeking access to subnational governments. As in many other settings, the challenges for women in subnational governments involve securing nomination from a viable political party, gaining enough votes to win political office, and obtaining the resources to govern effectively. While numbers are improving, women are still underrepresented as mayors, governors, council members, and state legislators. In the conclusion, we highlight some challenges for researchers and conclude with directions for future research in this important but understudied area.

HOW MUCH REPRESENTATION? SUBNATIONAL OFFICE HOLDING ACROSS THE REGION

One way that the "crisis of representation" (e.g., Mainwaring 2006) has manifested in Latin America is in the form of extremely low levels of women's representation at the subnational level. Though the previous literature has not considered whether the lack of gender parity in representation exacerbates the crisis of representation or is simply a symptom of it, examination of the percentage of women in subnational legislatures and executives shows that half of the population is not adequately represented. As of 2014, no country in the region had reached gender parity at the subnational level and only modest gains had been made over the course of nearly two decades. In addition, there is a significant gap between executive and legislative representation. In 2012, the regional average for women in the executive branch at the local level was about 12%, while the representation of women in the legislative branch was more than double this number at around 26%. At the intermediate level of government, usually only one or two governors are women, but having no women governors is not uncommon, and declines in women's executive representation are just as common as advances. Representation in state/provincial legislatures is much higher but still far below parity. The overall trend is thus consistent with single country studies indicating that measures to increase women's access to political office (e.g., quota laws, changes in electoral rules) have been more successful in the legislative than in the executive arena (Hinojosa and Franceschet 2012; Jiménez Polanco 2011).

Comparing women's local representation across countries and over time

Though the overall levels of women's representation in subnational arenas are low, there is significant variation both across institutions and across countries.[3] Figure 6.1 shows the percentage of women elected to local legislatures (i.e., city councils) for eighteen Latin American countries. Guatemala consistently has the lowest levels of representation (reaching just 8% in 2010), followed by Panama, Brazil, and Colombia. These counties' poor performance mirrors their legislative representation at the national level too (see Schwindt-Bayer and Alles, chapter 4, this volume). Furthermore, in most countries, legislative representation improved little, if any, between 1998 and 2014. Historically, Costa Rica has had the highest levels of women's representation in local legislatures; however, it was surpassed by Bolivia in 2010 due to the revision of Bolivia's gender quota law leading to near parity (44%) in 2014. Representation has also risen steadily in Mexico (to 38% in 2014). Overall, Figure 6.1 suggests that across this 16-year period women's representation has been largely static, with many countries still far from gender parity.

Figure 6.2 shows the percentage of elected local executives (i.e. mayors) who are women from 1998 to 2014. Generally, the representation of women in local executive offices has not exceeded 15%. In recent years, there have been substantial gains in Nicaragua, where women's representation increased from less than 10% to over 40% in a single election (2011). There were also significant increases in Uruguay (0% to 25% in 2010) and Venezuela (7% to 17% in 2009) and a more gradual increase over time in Cuba. Interestingly, of these countries, only Nicaragua has had a female president and that was only in 1990 (see Reyes-Housholder and Thomas, chapter 2, this volume). In Panama and Honduras, the percentage of female mayors has decreased slightly over time, suggesting that increases in women's representation are more difficult to achieve and sustain in the executive arena.

Comparing women's representation as legislators and executives

Comparing the general trends in Figures 6.1 and 6.2, it is clear that women's gains in the legislative branch have not translated into gains in the local executive arena. Women have been far more successful at gaining seats on city councils than they have been at winning the mayor's office. This trend persists in the intermediate (e.g., state, provincial) level of government as well. Women's representation in intermediate

3. Data on women's local representation are from the Economic Commission for Latin America and the Caribbean (ECLAC, or CEPAL with its Spanish acronym) (http://estadisticas.cepal.org/cepalstat/). Intermediate-level data were collected by the authors from government websites and various online sources. The authors thank Tiffany Barnes and Lilian Soto for providing additional provincial-level data on Argentina and Paraguay, respectively. Regional averages for all of Latin America were calculated by the authors.

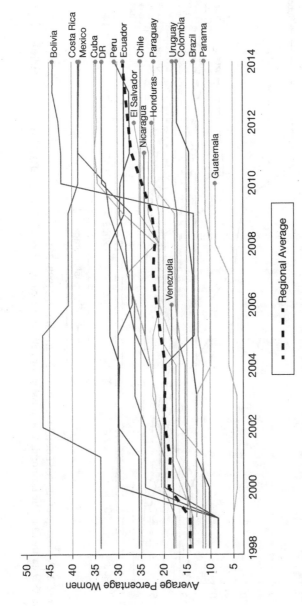

Figure 6.1 Percentage of Elected Local Legislators Who Are Women, 1998–2014

SOURCE: Data are from the Economic Commission for Latin America and the Caribbean (CEPALSTAT, http:// estadisticas.cepal.org/).

NOTE: Data for local level legislators in Argentina were not available.

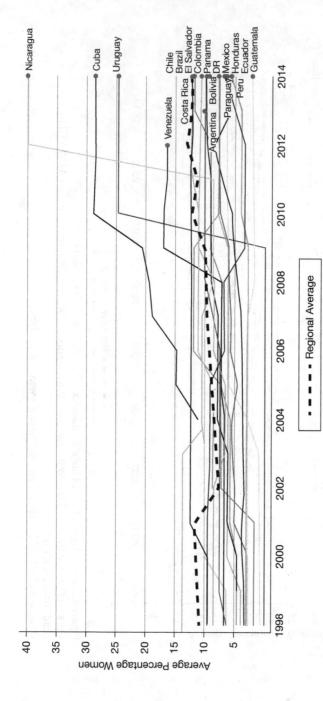

Figure 6.2 Percentage of Elected Local Executives who are Women, 1998–2014
SOURCE: Data are from the Economic Commission for Latin America and the Caribbean (CEPALSTAT, http://estadisticas.cepal.org/).

Table 6.1 WOMEN'S REPRESENTATION AT THE
INTERMEDIATE LEVEL IN 2012

Country	Percent Legislators	Percent Executives
Argentina	25.91*	8.70
Brazil	13.03	7.41
Colombia	17.94	9.38
Ecuador	—	3.45
Mexico	22.87	6.45
Paraguay	18.70	5.90
Peru	23.90	0.00
Venezuela	—	17.39
Regional Average	20.39	7.34

NOTE: Data collected by authors from various
sources. Countries lacking intermediate level
of government, data on women's intermediate
representation, or where executive is appointed
(as noted by Daughters and Harper 2007) are not
presented. *Data from 2010.

legislatures is much higher than in intermediate executive offices. Table 6.1 presents
a snapshot of women's average representation in intermediate legislative and executive offices in 2012. Women's average representation in intermediate legislatures is
around 20% (compare to 26% for local legislatures) and around 7% in intermediate
executive offices (compare to 12% for local executives).

Overall, the patterns we observe in Figures 6.1 and 6.2, as well as in Table 6.1,
are consistent with the literature, which has found that women are more likely to
obtain less powerful political offices. Since executive posts are often more powerful
and prestigious than legislative positions in Latin America, the finding that women
do better in legislative elections than in executive ones (Archenti and Albaine 2012;
Hinojosa and Franceschet 2012; Jiménez Polanco 2011) supports the notion that
women are more likely to be elected to less powerful offices than men.[4]

COMPARING WOMEN'S REPRESENTATION
ACROSS LEVELS OF GOVERNMENT

Vengroff, Nyiri and Fugiero (2003) find higher levels of women's representation in
intermediate than national legislatures, but they note this relationship is stronger
for older democracies than newer ones for whom the track record is more mixed.
Our data showing the percentage of women in the legislative branch at the national,

---

4. Jalalzai (2008) finds that women executives are likely to receive weaker political positions at
the national level of government as well.

intermediate, and local levels of government in 2010, presented in Figure 6.3, is also consistent with this trend. In the majority of countries we examine, women's representation is greater in local and/or intermediate legislatures than national ones. For instance, in Paraguay women comprise 21.9% of local legislatures, 18.7% of intermediate legislatures, and only 12.5% of the national legislature.

This pattern of decreasing representation moving from local to intermediate to national levels of government does not hold in all cases, however. In one set of cases, the pattern fails to hold because women obtain greater representation at the national level than at the local and/or intermediate level. In Argentina, for example, due to the adoption of an effective national-level gender quota law, women's representation in the national congress is relatively high (38.5% in 2010). However, since Argentine provinces adopted gender quota laws of various designs and at different times (Barnes 2014; Barnes and Jones, chapter 7, this volume), women's representation in provincial legislatures is much lower (averaging about 26% in 2010). The second break in the pattern is for countries such as Mexico, where women obtain the greatest representation in local legislatures (32.6%), but then win fewer seats in intermediate legislatures (21.7%) than in the national legislature (26.2%) (see also Zetterberg in chapter 11, this volume). Of course, in some cases electoral laws (in particular quotas) have been copied across levels of government minimizing differences between them, and leading to situations as in Costa Rica,

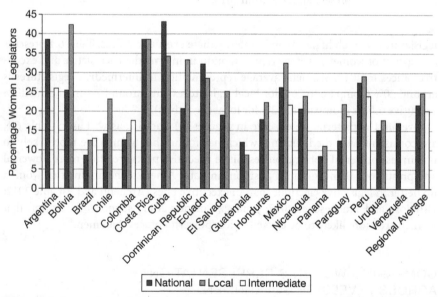

■ National ■ Local □ Intermediate

Figure 6.3 Comparison of the Percentage of Women in Legislatures at Different Levels of Government, 2010
NOTE: Intermediate-level data collected by the authors from government websites. Data for intermediate governments in Argentina were obtained from Barnes (2012b, 2014) and intermediate governments in Paraguay from Soto Badahui (2014). Data were not available for the local level of Argentina, intermediate levels of Bolivia and Ecuador, and all levels of Venezuela.
SOURCE: Data are from the Economic Commission for Latin America and the Caribbean (CEPALSTAT, http://estadisticas.cepal.org/).

where women win equally high percentages of seats in local and national legislatures (38.6%).

One possible explanation for why women obtain more seats in some national legislatures than in some intermediate ones is differences in levels of professionalization within a given country (see for instance, Schwindt-Bayer and Squire 2014). Alternatively, women may have greater ballot access at the local (or intermediate or national) level because of the political opportunity structure. That said, it is possible that women have greatest access to local and then to national governments, while generally lacking access to intermediate governments, because in some countries intermediate governments are more powerful than national-level institutions. Thus, state structure and the distribution of power among levels of government may partly explain the patterns observed in Figure 6.3 (see also Stockemer and Tremblay 2015; UNDP 2013). As we highlight below, however, this is an area where future research is needed.

Variation across different institutions at the same level of government (e.g., local legislators vs. local executives) and across the same institution at different levels of government (e.g., national legislature vs. local legislatures) leads us to question what explains the variation we observe.[5] Do the causes of women's representation that have been identified at the national level work in the same way for the subnational level, as most scholars who tested these in single cases found? In the next section, we survey the factors hypothesized to affect women's representation at the subnational level (i.e., the causes) and provide an empirical test focused on the local level.

FROM NATIONAL TO SUBNATIONAL: DETERMINING THE CAUSES OF WOMEN'S REPRESENTATION

Determinants of women's legislative representation have been explored extensively in the context of national-level institutions (see, for example, Schwindt-Bayer and Alles, chapter 4, this volume). Studies of women in subnational offices have also explored various causes including institutional, political, socioeconomic, and cultural explanations. Consistent with national-level studies, subnational studies have found the implementation of gender quotas is one of the main drivers of increases in women's representation—at least in the legislative branch. Table 6.2 shows the extent to which quota laws have been adopted at both national and subnational levels across the region (Hinojosa and Piscopo 2013). Studies in Argentina (Archenti and Tula 2007, 2011; Jones 1998), the Dominican Republic (Jiménez Polanco 2011), Costa Rica (Jones 2004), Peru (Schmidt 2003a, 2003b, 2011; Schmidt and Saunders 2004),

5. We remind the reader that there is important variation across municipalities within a country, which we do not examine here, and thus even if women seem to do well in winning local executive office overall, future research should ask *in which municipalities?* Research on Brazilian municipalities finds that women receive less powerful executive posts (Blay and Soeiro 1979), and women are more successful in municipal elections in the poorer, less developed regions of Brazil (Miguel and Monteiro de Queiroz 2006). However, Archenti and Albaine (2012) find the opposite is true in Argentina, where women seem to be more successful in executive elections in provincial capitals.

Table 6.2 FEDERALISM, DECENTRALIZATION, AND GENDER QUOTAS
IN LATIN AMERICA

Country	National Quota	Intermediate Quota	Local Quota	Federal Constitution	Level of Fiscal Decentralization
Argentina	Yes	Yes	No	Yes	Advanced
Bolivia	Yes	Yes	Yes	No	Moderate
Brazil	Yes	Yes	Yes	Yes	Advanced
Chile	Yes	N/A	No	No	Incipient
Colombia	Yes	Yes	Yes	No	Advanced
Costa Rica	Yes	N/A	Yes	No	Incipient
Cuba	No	N/A	No	No	None
Dominican Republic	Yes (Lower) No (Upper)	N/A	Yes	No	Incipient
Ecuador	Yes	Yes	Yes	No	Moderate
El Salvador	Yes	N/A	Yes	No	Incipient
Guatemala	No	N/A	No	No	Incipient
Honduras	Yes	N/A	Yes	No	None
Mexico	Yes	Mixed	Yes	Yes	Moderate
Nicaragua	Yes	N/A	Yes	No	None
Panama	Yes	N/A	No	No	None
Paraguay	Yes	Yes	Yes	No	None
Peru	Yes	Yes	Yes	No	Moderate
Uruguay	Yes	N/A	Yes	No	Incipient
Venezuela	No	No	No	Yes	Moderate

NOTE: Mixed = some intermediate governments have adopted quotas while others have not. N/A = not applicable because the intermediate level of government does not exist or exists but the executive is appointed and not elected (see Daughters and Harper 2007). Level of Fiscal Decentralization is coded by Daughters and Harper (2007). The authors coded Federal Constitution based on copies of constitutions obtained from the Political Database of the Americas. Data are accurate as of 2015.

SOURCE: Elaborated by authors from Quota Project Quota Database (http://www.quotaproject.org/searchDB.cfm), the Political Database of the Americas (http://pdba.georgetown.edu/Constitutions/constudies.html), and Daughters and Harper (2007).

Paraguay (Soto Badahui 2014), and Mexico (Correa 2014; Zetterberg 2011) find that the adoption of quotas increases the percentage of women in subnational offices (see also the country chapters in this volume).

However, as in studies of the national level, research on subnational offices finds that women must be placed in an electable position on the party list for quotas to be effective (Archenti and Tula 2011; Jones 1998; Jones 2004). Quotas are also found to be more effective in closed-list (vs. open-list) systems (Archenti and Tula 2007; Jones and Navia 1999)[6] and in the legislative branch (Jiménez Polanco 2011). Studies also suggest proportional representation systems produce greater representation than majoritarian or plurality systems (Hinojosa and Franceschet 2012). Higher district and party magnitudes also facilitate the election of more women at the subnational level (Schmidt and Saunders 2004; Schmidt 2003b). The findings from these studies are thus consistent with the findings from studies of women's representation in national legislatures (see Schwindt-Bayer and Alles, chapter 4, this volume).

Party control over candidate selection affects the election of women at the subnational level as well as the national (Archenti and Tula 2011). Particularly relevant to the subnational level is whether the candidate selection process is decentralized (i.e., local party members choose candidates for their district) or centralized (i.e., national party members choose candidates for all districts). Centralization of the candidate selection process has been argued to benefit women because it allows women to bypass local power enclaves (Hinojosa 2009, 2012). Parties that recruit candidates, versus those that require candidates to self-nominate, also improve the electoral chances of women since women are less likely than men to self-nominate (Hinojosa 2009). Furthermore, informal party rules and norms can shape women's representation as much as formal laws (Hinojosa and Franceschet 2012). For instance, the voluntary adoption of party quotas can increase women's access to political candidacy and the subsequent election of women (Jones 2004), as can the codification of rules, parties' ideology, and commitments to improving the representation of women (see also Morgan and Hinojosa, chapter 5, this volume).

Diffusion processes can also cause an increase in women's representation in subnational governments (see Gilardi 2015 on Switzerland). For example, the adoption of a quota law in one state might cause other states to initiate similar quota laws or even prompt the national government to adopt quota legislation, as occurred in Mexico (Correa 2014; Zetterberg 2011; Zetterberg, chapter 11, this volume). Once women are elected to public office, their presence might increase the probability that other women will be nominated and win election (Shair-Rosenfield and Hinojosa 2014).

Additional determinants of women's representation in subnational governments can be attributed to societal and cultural factors. The political mobilization of women and the organization of women's groups can play an important role in getting women elected to local offices (Barrera Bassols and Massolo 1998; Raczynski and Serrano 1992; Schmidt 2003a; Schmidt and Saunders 2004). However, cultural norms and traditional views about women's roles in society may decrease the chances that women will choose to run for office and successfully win election. In his research on Peruvian municipalities, Schmidt (2011) found that women in the rural and less developed parts of the country were reluctant to run for office because it was inconsistent with their traditional role in society, and they did not want to be viewed unfavorably. Other societal and cultural factors found to impact women's representation at the national level, such as women's caucuses (*bancadas femininas*), urbanization, women in the workforce, education levels, or ideology, have not been explored systematically at the subnational level in Latin America.

---

6. See Schmidt (2003a) for a challenge to this argument.

EXPLORING CAUSES OF WOMEN'S LOCAL REPRESENTATION WITH NEW DATA AND ORIGINAL ANALYSIS

We now turn to a test of whether the causes of women's representation in national-level institutions also explain women's representation at the local level by examining a dataset covering 18 Latin American countries from 1998 to 2013.[7] To our knowledge, this is the first time-serial, cross-national examination of women's representation at the local level of government.[8] We examine the three sets of factors that are hypothesized to affect women's descriptive representation (see Schwindt-Bayer, chapter 1, this volume): (1) cultural and socioeconomic (observed through female labor force participation, fertility rates, and urbanization), (2) political and institutional (including federalism, the presence of a local gender quota, fiscal decentralization, and number of years since the first local elections), and (3) diffusion effects (measured as percentage of women in the national legislature, woman president, and percentage of women in local institutions).[9] We estimate two hierarchical linear regressions (full results presented in appendix Table A6.1) to examine the determinants of women's representation in local legislatures (i.e., city councils) and local executive offices (i.e., mayors).

Many of these variables have been used in previous analyses of women's representation in national legislatures. However, we introduce three new variables that merit discussion: federalism, decentralization, and years since the first local elections. Federalism and decentralization are important because they determine the autonomy and importance of subnational governments. We have mixed expectations about the effect of federalism. Federalism might fragment women's movements and prevent the formation of national-level policies to promote women's representation. However, federal structures might allow innovative subnational governments to adopt their own policies that are beneficial to women's representation (like quotas). Alternatively, federalism may increase subnational variation in policy outcomes, leading to positive and negative effects that cancel out in the aggregate (see Franceschet [2011] and Franceschet and Piscopo [2013] for a longer discussion about the effects of federalism). We measure federalism using a dichotomous variable, where 1 indicates the country has a federal system (according to its constitution) and 0 indicates that the country is unitary.

Hypothesis 1a: Federalism increases women's local representation.
Hypothesis 1b: Federalism decreases women's local representation.

7. Argentina is not included in these analyses because data on the percent women in local legislatures is missing. Some years for some countries are not included due to missing data on one or more variables. The note on appendix Table A6.1 lists the countries and years that are included.

8. Vengroff, Nyiri, and Fugiero (2003) conduct a similar analysis; however, their research only considers meso (i.e., intermediate) and national-level legislatures and covers just one election period.

9. Data on female labor force participation, fertility rates, and urban population are from the World Bank's World Development Indicators. Local quota was coded (0 = no quota, 1 = quota) using information from the Quota Project (http://www.quotaproject.org). The percentage of women in the national legislature is from CEPAL STATS (http://estadisticas.cepal.org). Woman president was coded by the authors (0 = man, 1 = woman).

We expect decentralization to negatively impact women's representation since it increases the power, and thus the desirability, of subnational governments, which may subsequently increase the pool of interested male candidates and competition for subnational offices (Funk 2017; UNDP 2013). We measure decentralization using a categorical variable indicating whether the country has no (coded= 0), incipient (= 1), moderate (= 2), or advanced (= 3) fiscal decentralization based on Daughters and Harper (2007). We use fiscal decentralization (as opposed to political or administrative) because it better captures the extent to which decentralization increases the power of local offices. It is unclear whether increasing administrative or political decentralization in the absence of fiscal decentralization actually increases the power of local offices (Falleti 2005) and thus may not have the same hypothesized negative impact on women's local representation.

Hypothesis 2: Fiscal decentralization decreases women's local representation.

Finally, we expect that as a country's experience with local elections increases, the representation of women will increase as well. When elections first occur, existing (usually elite white male) power enclaves are likely to gain access to power before women, but over time it may become too costly or unnecessary to exclude women. We measure the number of years since the first local elections were held based on the dates of the first municipal elections provided by Daughters and Harper (2007, 218) relative to the years included in our dataset.

Hypothesis 3: Experience with local elections increases women's local representation.

Our results reveal that different factors predict when women gain access to legislative versus executive office at the local level. We find that higher labor force participation, lower fertility rates, more time since the first election, more women in the national legislature, and the presence of a quota all increase the percentage of women in local legislatures (see model 1, appendix Table A6.1). Other factors have no statistically significant effect. These results provide support for hypothesis 3 that experience with elections improves women's local representation, but not for hypotheses 1a or 1b, or hypothesis 2. To illustrate the substantive effect of these variables, we present predicted levels of representation for different values of statistically significant explanatory variables.

In Figure 6.4, we see that women's representation in local legislatures increases by 2.3 percentage points when there is a high versus low rate of female labor force participation, and decreases by 10.6 percentage points when there are high versus low fertility rates.[10] In addition, women's presence in local legislatures increases nearly 8 percentage points when there is a local gender quota in place. Finally, women's representation increases by 6.25 percentage points as a country moves from a few years of local elections to many. Even more impressive, going from few women in

---

10. High (low) values of continuous variables—female labor force participation, fertility rates, experience with local elections, percent women in national legislature—are defined as one standard deviation above (below) the mean.

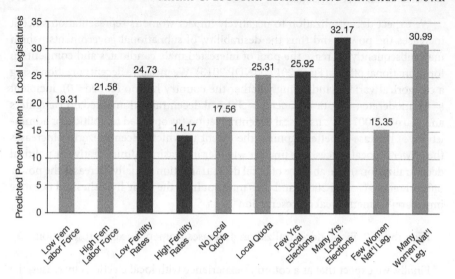

Figure 6.4 Average Predicted Percentage of Local Legislatures that is Women under Various Conditions
NOTE: Predicted values presented for statistically significant variables (at 90% confidence level). Predicted values were obtained using the "predict" post-estimation command in Stata 13 following the estimation of a multi-level model. The mean predicted value under each condition is presented. The hierarchical model also controlled for urban population, federalism, fiscal decentralization, woman president, and the percentage of mayors who were women. See appendix Table A6.1 for the full set of results. For continuous variables, low values indicate the average predicted value of Y for values of X lower than one standard deviation below the mean. High values indicate the average predicted value of Y for values of X greater than one standard deviation above the mean. For dichotomous variables, predicted values of Y are presented for each value of X.

the national legislature to many women nearly doubles women's representation in local legislatures (an increase of nearly 16 percentage points). These results echo the findings of national-level studies and suggest that there may be large diffusion effects across levels of government, although it is impossible to determine the direction of causality based on these results. Results also suggest, as hypothesized, that a longer history with local elections is beneficial for women's representation in local governments.

In terms of local female executives, local gender quotas and having a female president increase the percentage of female mayors, while more fiscal decentralization decreases it (see model 2, appendix Table A6.1). Figure 6.5 presents predicted levels of women's representation in local executive offices for these variables. The other variables did not have a statistically significant effect. In examining women's representation in local executive offices, we find support for hypothesis 2 that fiscal decentralization decreases women's local representation, but not for hypotheses 1a, 1b or 3. Women's representation in local executive (e.g., mayoral) offices increases by 1.6 percentage points when there is a quota, decreases by 4.6 percentage points when there is advanced fiscal decentralization, and increases by 3.9 percentage points when there is a woman president.

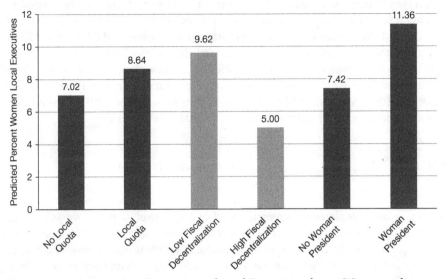

Figure 6.5 Average Predicted Percentage of Local Executives who are Women under Various Conditions

NOTE: Predicted values presented for statistically significant variables (at 90% confidence level). Predicted values obtained using the "predict" post-estimation command in Stata 13 following the estimation of a multi-level model. The mean predicted value under each condition is presented. The hierarchical model also controlled for female labor force participation, fertility rates, urban population, federalism, number of years since the first local elections, percentage of legislators who were women, and the percentage of city councilors who were women. See appendix Table A6.1 for the full set of results. For dichotomous variables (local quota, woman president), predicted values of Y are presented for each value of X. For fiscal decentralization, predicted values are presented for the lowest (0) and highest (3) levels of fiscal decentralization.

It is interesting that the presence of a local gender quota has a positive effect on women's representation in executive offices, given that quotas usually only apply to the legislature. However, some local governments have parliamentary-type election systems in which the executive is elected indirectly through legislative elections and that may account for some of this effect. Quotas may also produce spillover as more women gain experience qualifying them to run for mayor. As hypothesized, women's representation in the local executive office is higher in countries with very low levels of fiscal decentralization than in those with advanced fiscal decentralization.[11] Evidence of diffusion is also apparent through these results since the presence of a woman president increases the presence of women local executives.

In sum, the findings of these models suggest that some causes of women's representation at the national level are replicated at the local level. However, additional factors, such as federalism, decentralization, and experience with local elections may also impact the representation of women in subnational governments. Since

11. The predicted values are calculated for countries with no fiscal decentralization (0) and advanced fiscal decentralization (3).

local governments are nested within an existing polity and their power is capped by higher levels of government, future studies of women in local governments should account for the unique local context and attempt to measure variables that are likely to affect women's representation at this level. In addition, future studies should explore women's pathways to power in different countries (i.e., whether women have greater access to national institutions than intermediate ones, etc.) (see Beer and Camp 2016 on Mexico) and how and why diffusion or demonstration effects affect women's descriptive representation in subnational governments.

SHAPING SOCIETY AND INSTITUTIONS: WOMEN IN SUBNATIONAL POLITICAL OFFICE

When women are elected to subnational office, what effect do they have on political institutions and society at large? Relatively few studies have been conducted on the consequences of electing women to subnational political institutions. What work exists has focused on the legislative arena because women have been more success-ful in obtaining subnational legislative than executive positions (see for instance, Archenti and Albaine 2012). We begin by examining how women's representation shapes society in terms of policy and attitudes and then turn to how it affects the institutions themselves.

The inclusion of women is argued to be important because women politicians are expected to better represent women's interests than men politicians, and many studies have shown they behave differently. There are only a few studies that address this question at the subnational level in Latin America. Using data from Brazilian municipalities, Meier and Funk (2017) show that increasing the presence of women elected officials and public administrators increases the adoption of women-friendly policies in the municipality, such as services for victims of domestic abuse, daycare centers, and birthing centers. In a different study of Brazil, Funk, Silva, and Escobar-Lemmon (2017), find that women mayors are associated with smaller wage gaps between men and women in the municipal executive bureaucracy. Farah (2004, 2014) argues that in Brazil, gender issues have been better incorporated into local politics, citing recent local government initiatives in the areas of women's health, violence against women, generation of employment and sources of income for women, programs for at-risk girls, and education on reproduction and family planning.

Using data from Mexico, Kerevel and Atkeson (2015) find that women mayors change gender stereotypes in the short run, but more representation is needed to change long-term attitudes. Finally, Barnes (2016) finds that female provincial leg-islators in Argentina have closer ideal points to their female copartisans than their male copartisans. This proximity means women are more likely to work together to promote social issues and to jointly sponsor women, children, and family legislation. However, she also shows that parties can actually block collaboration by women by shifting incentives. Future research is needed to determine if these findings hold across countries, time, and institutions (e.g., bureaucracies, parties, and judiciaries), and if women use NGOs to affect local government policies as Barrera and Massolo (1998) find in Mexico.

Quotas may increase women's representation, but they may also constrain the ability of women to represent women's interests. In comparing Mexican state legislatures, Zetterberg (2008) finds no differences in the committee assignments or treatment of women elected in states with and without quotas. But, Barnes (2014) finds quota laws may (temporarily) limit the effectiveness of women in provincial legislatures in Argentina. She concludes that as women become more numerous in the chamber, they are less likely to be appointed to masculine committees like Economics and Trade and power committees. However, after quotas have been in place for an extended period, this effect diminishes, and women become more likely to receive appointments on masculine committees.

Women in office may also affect society by shaping evaluations of women. Shair-Rosenfield and Hinojosa (2014) provide evidence from Chile that women's electoral success changes how parties view women's candidacies. They find female incumbents are just as likely as males to be renominated and reelected. By proving women are electable, this paves the way for the party to nominate more women. Future research should identify if, as Jalalzai (2013) has argued at the national level, there is a snowball effect such that once a woman is elected, it is easier for other women to be elected, and if political parties who might not otherwise nominate women do so for all offices, especially in the absence of quotas.

There is some indication that the participation of women in subnational institutions is important because they can positively shape the institution. For instance, Castro (2014) finds that women's involvement in municipal councils in Salvador da Bahia, Brazil contributed to making the councils spaces for constructing citizenship and participatory democracy. However, in another study of over 5,000 Brazilian municipalities, Funk (2015) finds that women mayors' leadership styles are no more participatory than men mayors' styles as they are not more likely to adopt institutions that increase citizen's participation in municipal politics. Rather, Funk finds that both men and women mayors are strategic about when they increase opportunities for citizen participation, doing so in areas that make the mayor seem well rounded and appealing to constituents of the opposite sex.

There is some indication that electing women to local offices may lead to increases in women's representation in leadership posts in local bureaucracies as studies of Brazil find that women mayors have more women in bureaucratic leadership (Funk, Silva, and Escobar-Lemmon 2017; Meier and Funk 2017). Future work should confirm if this holds in other settings. Women may also change institutions beyond the one in which they participate. Zetterberg (2011) finds evidence that quotas may diffuse across subnational entities. The adoption of the first gender quota law in the Mexican state of Chihuahua in 1994 led almost all other Mexican states and the federal government to adopt quota laws. Subnational governments offer an ideal venue for testing diffusion effects because we expect states in a federation to be different and yet bounded by the same national institutions that shape how diffusion works.

Women's participation in subnational governments is critical not only because of the symbolic importance of parity, but because decentralization and reactivation of federal structures have made studying the consequences of women's representation at the subnational level important in their own right and not simply as a place to test theories developed at the national level. Firstly, decentralization of important social services such as healthcare and education means that control over subnational government has important consequences for women (and men). Franceschet and Piscopo (2013) urge caution in assuming that decentralization automatically increases the "women-friendliness" of policies, pointing to the increased variation in outcomes with regard to the availability of contraception in Argentina because of federalism and suggesting unitary states (like Chile) may produce more consistent outcomes.

Second, decentralization sought to bring government closer to the people and increase participation (Burki, Perry, and Dillinger 1999). This is especially important as increased participation represented a possible solution to the crisis of representation. Escobar-Lemmon and Ross (2014) show that decentralization led to greater perceptions of accountability for provincial government in Colombia, and Barnes and Beaulieu (2014) show women competing in elections reduce suspicions of fraud. Future research is needed to understand how women have been able to shape this venue, use it to serve their interests, and through their participation help address the crisis of representation.

CHALLENGES AT THE SUBNATIONAL LEVEL: GAINING ACCESS TO ALL VENUES

Women have made strides toward gaining representation in subnational government, especially in legislative branches; however, important challenges to equality remain. First, women's executive officeholding remains limited at the subnational level. Research consistently finds that women are more likely to be elected to legislative offices than executives ones (Archenti and Albaine 2012; Blay and Soeiro 1979; Hinojosa and Franceschet 2012; Jiménez Polanco 2011). This may reflect the unipersonal nature of the executive office and the difficulty of applying an effective quota in this setting. It may also result from horizontal centralization of power—the empowerment of the executive at the expense of the legislative and judicial branches—at the subnational level. While decentralization moved power downward from national to intermediate and local governments, it often left political power concentrated in the hands of the executive (mayor or governor). Thus decentralization made executive offices more attractive, but unintentionally may also have made it harder for women to gain access to these executive posts. Future research needs to examine the impact that women's lack of access to subnational executive offices has on their ability to compete for higher offices in the future.

Second, women have made important gains in subnational legislatures (e.g., municipal councils and provincial assemblies) especially where quotas are present, but challenges remain. Women's representation in these bodies often appears to be "capped" at a ceiling determined by the gender quota (see Archenti and Tula 2011 and Barnes and Jones, chapter 7, this volume). Additionally, subnational party politics are not always friendly to women. Morgan and Hinojosa (chapter 5, this volume) point out that political parties and party organizations do not attend to women's issues or women's organizations particularly well, and this could be problematic at the subnational level, as well. On municipal councils with a small number of seats, women's caucuses may be nonexistent. Moreover, parties may adopt unfavorable selection mechanisms, making it difficult for women to gain access to the ballot and have a chance of winning office.

Finally, Escobar-Lemmon and Taylor-Robinson (2014) challenge us to think about the way in which different political arenas may (or may not) be useful for the representation of women's interests in a particular country. This is especially true at the subnational level. The importance of subnational positions as a springboard to higher offices and the importance of subnational governments for policymaking means women must continue to push for equity in all subnational venues. Broad representation holds the best hope for long-term empowerment of women and protection of their interests.

MOVING FORWARD: CONCLUSIONS AND DIRECTIONS FOR FUTURE RESEARCH

There has been relatively limited scholarship on women's representation at the subnational level to date, making this a fruitful area for future study. Subnational research is challenging because of the difficulty of collecting reliable subnational data (especially for multiple countries) and making comparisons cross-nationally that account for the diversity of institutional structures across countries.[12]

Future research needs to take seriously the question of whether subnational institutions simply replicate national institutions and whether local and intermediate levels are fully comparable. On the one hand, women's representation at the subnational level does seems to be driven by many of the same factors that shape representation at the national level. In particular, the literature concurs on the robust and positive effect of gender quotas and certain socioeconomic factors. We confirm the importance of both in our analysis of women's representation in both legislative and executive arenas at the local level across Latin America. Our data also support the general conclusion of single-country studies—women gain executive offices at lower rates with potentially deleterious consequences for future advancement. There also seems to be powerful support for the diffusion of quotas across subnational units.

On the other hand, subnational politics may not mirror national politics. Federalism and decentralization, for instance, may shape women's representation in subnational governments in ways that do not apply to representation at the national level. Because federalism and decentralization shape the relative power of different levels of government and the policy areas that subnational governments control, they determine the salience of subnational governments for women's lives and also affect the political opportunity structure. Proximity to citizens, combined with the lack of sovereignty that a national government possesses, changes the game. Our analysis of women's representation in local governments across Latin America shows that fiscal decentralization has a negative effect on women's representation (at least in local executive offices) and that experience with local elections has a positive effect (at least in local legislative offices). Finally, our analyses suggest a demonstration effect may be present with more representation at the national level correlating with more representation at the local level for both executive and legislative branches, although

12. See Archenti and Tula (2007) for a detailed discussion of the challenges of subnational research.

we cannot determine whether more women in local office leads to more women in national office or vice versa.

There is some indication that women might represent women's interests in subnational governments and might change societal attitudes and institutional norms. However, very limited research exists, so we cannot decisively say whether this occurs across all subnational governments in Latin America. Women's representation in subnational governments (in executive offices, legislatures, and judicial branches, as well as bureaucracies) is important in guaranteeing a diverse and representative group governs at all levels and in all arenas of representation. As such, subnational governments offer one place where *if* women gain representation in all venues, they have a chance to make a real difference in the lives of their fellow citizens. Women's participation may help bolster not only descriptive representation, but also the substantive representativeness of local governments, perhaps helping to ameliorate the crisis of representation confronting the region.

Countries

Countries

Women's Representation in Argentine National and Subnational Governments

TIFFANY D. BARNES AND MARK P. JONES ■

Over twenty-five years has now passed since the birth of the world's first gender quota law in Argentina in 1991. Combining skillful mobilization and lobbying techniques with an appeal to the enduring legacy of the country's one-and-only Eva María Duarte de Perón, or Evita, Argentine women achieved the passage and subsequent implementation of what was at the time audacious and groundbreaking legislation. In doing so, they placed Argentina at the vanguard of the global quota movement and made it the country best suited for the present-day study of the medium- to long-term effects of quota legislation across a diverse set of experiences and settings.

The novel "Ley de Cupos" quota legislation signed into law by President Carlos Menem in 1991 dramatically increased the proportion of women legislators in the Argentine Chamber of Deputies and several Argentine provincial legislatures from the time of its very first use in the 1993 national and provincial midterm elections. This instant success converted Argentina into a shining example for Latin America and the world, and throughout the 1990s, Argentine women served as evangelists spreading the gospel of quotas at forums, conferences, and workshops in Latin America and the world. Trailblazers from across the political spectrum whose efforts were integral to the passage of the Ley de Cupos, such as Marcela Durrieu, Virginia Franganillo, María José Lubertino, and Zita Montes de Oca, found themselves traveling the hemisphere and globe to spread the word about Argentina's successful experience adopting and then implementing quotas. Simultaneously, Buenos Aires became a type of Mecca for activists from throughout the region who made a pilgrimage to

We thank Diana O'Brien, Michelle Taylor-Robinson, Leslie Schwindt-Bayer, and participants of the Women and Leadership in Latin America Conference at Rice University for very useful comments. We also thank Chloe Atwater for excellent research assistance.

learn about the new quota law and its passage, with the end goal of obtaining the adoption of similar legislation in their home countries.

The election of significantly more women legislators resulting from quota legislation in Argentina at the national, provincial, and municipal levels had three important effects. First, it enhanced the legitimacy of the country's democratic system, creating legislative bodies that more accurately mirrored the population they represent. Second, it improved the design, production, and implementation of public policies by better incorporating the views and contributions of women. Third, it helped to create a substantial cohort of female politicians with the power to influence political outcomes in both formal and informal settings.

Argentina's pathbreaking quota legislation without question had a profound impact on the nation's federal, provincial, and municipal legislatures, almost overnight transforming a majority of them from institutions with only a handful of female members to institutions where between one- and two-fifths of the members were women. At the same time however, women have continued to remain relatively absent from the influential subnational and municipal executive offices of governor and mayor. And, women lack access to some of the most powerful and prestigious political posts within legislative bodies. The 30% quota in some respects has become both a floor and a ceiling, with Argentina and all but a few of its provinces failing to keep up with global trends in gender quota legislation where parity is increasingly the norm. Although a 30% quota was earth-shattering in 1991, today it is rather dated and inadequate. Thus whereas Argentina was once a world leader in the promotion of gender equality, today it is decidedly in the middle of the pack, outshone in Latin America by countries such as Bolivia, Costa Rica, Ecuador, and Mexico (Piscopo 2015a). And finally, while without question the past twenty years have seen the passage of a wide variety of laws in Argentina that have positively addressed highly salient concerns in areas ranging from reproductive rights to sexual education to domestic violence to women's health, Argentina still suffers from serious problems of gender inequality, domestic violence, and sexual harassment, among others, underscoring the limits of gender quotas in addressing the myriad of gender-related societal ills in a polity.

Alone among the world's democracies, Argentina has more than two decades experience with well-designed and effective legislative gender quotas at the national, provincial, and municipal levels. For social scientists and other scholars concerned with the medium- and long-term impact of gender quotas, there is no better laboratory to understand the strengths and weaknesses of quotas than Argentina.

WOMEN IN GOVERNMENT IN ARGENTINA

Argentina is a presidential system in which the directly elected president is responsible for appointing the cabinet. Argentina is a federal republic composed of twenty-three provinces (states) and a federal district, each with its own constitution and electoral laws. The national government and all provinces are presidential systems with an elected executive (i.e., president or governor) and legislature. The head of the executive is responsible for appointing the cabinet. The national legislature is organized into a bicameral Congress; 72 senators and 257 deputies are directly elected

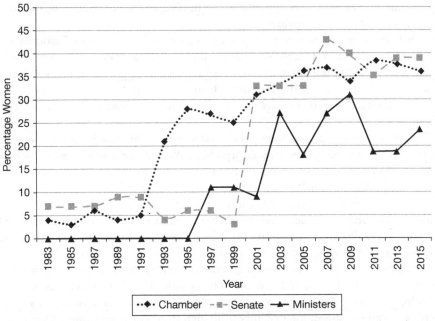

Figure 7.1 Women in the National Parliament and Executive Cabinet

Closed list

from closed-list proportional representation (PR) ballots to serve six- and four-year staggered terms respectively.

Historically, Argentina had a highly institutionalized two-party system (Mainwaring and Scully 1995), consisting of the Peronist Party (*Partido Justicialista*, PJ) and the *Unión Cívica Radcial* (UCR). Over the past two decades the party system has broken down and become increasingly fragmented (Jones and Micozzi 2013). Today, Argentine political parties are, with the partial exception of the UCR, mere shells and labels with party directorates that rarely, if ever, meet. Nonetheless, political parties—particularly provincial party leaders—remain key players in the candidate selection and recruitment process (De Luca 2008; Jones 2008).

Women's numeric representation in these five arenas of government has increased in Argentina over the past twenty years, but in varying degrees. Figure 7.1 graphs the evolution of women's numeric representation in the Argentine Chamber of Deputies and Senate (percentage elected in that year) as well as the presence of women in Argentine cabinet positions.[1] The values reflect the percentage of deputies elected that year who were women as well as the percentage of cabinet members who were women as of January of that year (see below for a discussion of cabinet posts). In 1991 at the national level, women held only 5% of seats in the Chamber of Deputies and 9% of seats in the Senate. Similarly, women had limited access to subnational

1. Legislative data was collected from the Inter-Parliamentary Union, data for cabinet posts come from the *Central Intelligence Agency's (CIA) online directory, Chiefs of State and Cabinet Members of Foreign Governments* (multiple years), and Escobar-Lemmon and Taylor Robinson (2005, 2009, 2016).

legislatures in the early 1990s (see Table 7.1). In 1990, women did not occupy a single legislative seat in some provinces.[2]

Over the course of the next twenty-five years, women's access to both national and subnational legislatures increased dramatically. As of 2015, women were remarkably well represented in the national and subnational legislatures in Argentina. Women held 37% of the seats in the National Chamber of Deputies, 40% of seats in the National Senate, and (on average) about 25% of the seats across all provincial level legislatures.

Women have also gained access to executive posts. Argentina is the only country in the region that has had two female presidents. And, this of course does not include the most powerful and influential woman in Argentine history, Evita. In 1973, Isabel Perón (Juan Perón's third spouse) was elected as Vice President on a ticket with her husband. Following Perón's death, she assumed office on July 1, 1974, becoming the world's first female president. She presided over an increasingly conflict-ridden and economically distressed Argentina, until being removed from office on March 24, 1976 by a military coup.

Despite Isabel Perón's rise to power, women's presence in the executive branch has lagged behind their gains in legislative politics. Indeed, with the exception of Isabel Perón, women did not serve in any executive posts (either as the president or as governors) until the twenty-first century. Although in recent years women have made gains in the executive branch, their overall representation here still lags behind the legislative branch. Following Isabel Perón, Argentina would not see another female president until Cristina Fernández de Kirchner was elected in 2007 for a four-year term, taking the reins from her spouse Néstor Kirchner who had served as president since 2003. She ran for reelection in 2011 where she won 54% of the vote, 37% ahead of her closest competitor. Constitutionally barred from seeking a third consecutive term, Fernández de Kirchner ended her eight-year tenure on December 10, 2015.

Women have made some electoral gains in executive positions in the provincial governments, but progress has been slow, and despite having broken the glass ceiling, women have rarely held the top executive posts in the Argentine provincial governments. To date, only four women have been elected to the office of governor in the Argentine provinces. Fabiana Ríos (of the minor center-left *Afirmación de una República Igualitaria*, ARI) in Tierra del Fuego (2007–2015) was the first woman to be elected to the governor's post in Argentina. She had previously served in the provincial and national legislatures. She was first elected in 2007, served a four-year term, and was reelected in 2011. Since that time, two other women have been elected to the post of governor: Lucia Corpacci (of the Peronist, *Frente para la Victoria*, FPV) in Catamarca in 2011, and then again in 2015, Claudia Ledesma Abdala de Zamora (or the provincial *Frente Cívico por Santiago*) in Santiago del Estero in 2013, and Rosana Bertone (of the PJ) in Tierra del Fuego in 2015. Corpacci was elected governor after serving in the national senate from 2009 to 2011. Like many powerful provincial leaders, she comes from a prominent political family. Her father served as the minister of government (the most powerful provincial cabinet appointment) under the Peronist Governors Vicente Saadi and Ramón Saadi. Ramón Saadi is her uncle. Ledesma Abdala also belongs to an influential political family. When elected

---

2. Data from Table 7.1 comes from Jones (1998) and Barnes (2016).

Table 7.1 WOMEN'S NUMERIC REPRESENTATION IN PROVINCIAL LEGISLATURES

Chamber	1990	1994	1998	2002	2006	2010	2014
Federal Capital	—	—	33.3	33.3	33.3	33.8	40.0
Buenos Aires House	6.5	6.5	21.7	26.1	21.7	26.0	31.0
Buenos Aires Senate	7.5	11.3	18.5	28.3	29.3	22.2	26.1
Catamarca Senate	0.0	12.5	6.3	6.3	12.5	12.5	12.5
Catamarca House	0.0	4.9	11.1	26.2	22.0	29.3	32.5
Chaco	12.5	18.2	28.0	28.1	25.0	34.4	40.6
Chubut	11.1	11.1	33.3	29.6	29.6	29.6	33.3
Cordoba Senate	1.7	0.0	10.0	30.8	—	—	—
Cordoba House	6.1	7.9	22.7	30.0	34.3	31.7	40.0
Corrientes Senate	7.7	7.7	7.6	30.7	30.7	38.5	46.7
Corrientes House	3.7	7.7	14.3	30.8	30.8	38.9	30.0
Entre Ríos Senate	0.0	0.0	0.0	0.0	11.8	0.0	11.8
Entre Ríos House	7.1	0.0	7.1	7.1	14.3	10.7	26.5
Formosa	17.9	13.3	20.0	33.3	33.3	30.0	30.0
Jujuy	12.5	20.8	25.0	25.0	27.1	31.3	33.3
La Pampa	8.7	9.5	26.9	30.8	34.6	30.8	30.0
La Rioja	13.3	3.6	10.0	2.3	30.4	22.2	50.0
Mendoza Senate	2.6	13.2	18.4	15.7	23.7	33.3	27.7
Mendoza House	6.3	14.6	18.8	22.5	22.5	29.2	24.4
Misiones	12.5	25.0	30.0	30.0	22.9	22.5	34.2
Neuquén	4.0	12.0	25.7	26.5	31.4	28.6	25.7
Río Negro	11.1	19.0	23.3	20.9	37.2	41.9	40.0
Salta Senate	4.3	9.1	8.7	13.0	13.0	13.0	12.0
Salta House	10.0	18.9	11.6	16.6	19.0	18.3	26.3
San Juan	0.0	14.6	13.3	11.1	14.7	14.7	23.5
San Luis Senate	0.0	22.2	22.2	11.1	22.2	22.2	33.3
San Luis House	2.4	9.3	18.6	31.0	32.6	23.0	27.9
Santa Cruz	13.6	20.8	16.7	4.6	12.5	20.8	16.7
Santa Fe Senate	5.3	0.0	0.0	0.0	10.5	7.1	5.3
Santa Fe House	0.0	4.0	28.0	26.0	26.0	32.0	32.0
Santiago del Estero	0.0	—	26.0	38.0	36.0	47.5	40.0
Tierra del Fuego	—	33.3	13.3	40.0	40.0	26.6	40.0
Tucumán Senate	0.0	—	—	—	—	—	—
Tucumán House	7.5	20.0	20.0	22.5	12.5	26.5	22.4
Average	**6.1**	**12.0**	**17.9**	**22.1**	**24.9**	**25.9**	**28.9**

NOTES: Tierra del Fuego became a province in 1992. The Federal Capital obtained a greater degree of autonomy, approaching that of a province, in 1996. Santiago del Estero had a federal government intervention in 1994. Córdoba and Tucumán possessed bicameral legislatures prior to 2001 and 1994 respectively.

to office, she replaced her husband (Gerardo Zamora) who held the gubernatorial post from 2005 to 2013 (and who could not seek a new term due to term limits) and who since 2005 has been the undisputed political boss of Santiago del Estero. Bertone had been a major political figure in Tierra del Fuego for more than a dozen years prior to being elected in 2015, with a political resume that included three four-year terms in the national chamber of deputies and subsequent election as a national senator in 2013. In 2011, she was narrowly defeated in a run-off election by Tierra del Fuego's first woman governor, Fabiana Ríos. Alicia Lemme of the PJ also served as governor in San Luis when Adolfo Rodríguez Saá, the elected governor, resigned in 2001. She held this post for two years and later served as a national deputy (2003–2007) and mayor of San Luis (2007–2011).[3]

With few exceptions women were virtually absent from national executive cabinet posts until the late 1990s. In May of 1989, Susana Ruiz Cerruti became the first female cabinet minister in Argentina. She was assigned the foreign relations portfolio. However, she was only appointed to occupy the post for the final six weeks of President Raúl Alfonsín's term in office after his longtime Minister of Foreign Relations, Dante Caputo (1983–1989), resigned (Barnes and Jones 2011).

It was not until the mid-1990s that Argentina had its next female cabinet appointment. In 1996, Susana Decibe was appointed Minister of Education and served for almost four years—until the end of President Carlos Menem's (1989–1995, 1995–1999) second term in 1999. Figure 7.1 charts increases in women's access to cabinet appointments over time. Although women were absent from the cabinet for the first half of the 1990s, the appointment of Susan Decibe marked the beginning of an upward trajectory. In the last fifteen years under presidents Eduardo Duhalde (2002–2003), Néstor Kirchner (2003–2007), and Cristina Fernández de Kirchner (2007–2015), women's numeric representation in cabinet posts has increased substantially, with women occupying 30% of all cabinet posts in 2009 (Barnes and Jones 2011). After this peak, women's presence in cabinet posts declined slightly and has hovered around 20% since. As of 2015, women held 23% of national cabinet posts.

Although women's initial appointments were to "feminine" or "low-prestige" posts such as education and social development, in the last decade women have been appointed to a few "masculine" and "high-prestige portfolios" (Escobar-Lemmon and Taylor-Robinson 2009, 2016). In November 2005, Nilda Garré was appointed Minister of Defense and, on the same day, Felisa Miceli was appointed Minister of Economy and Production under President Néstor Kirchner. Garré continued serving in the cabinet as Minister of Security under President Cristina Fernández de Kirchner. These appointments are consistent with broader trends in Latin America and across the globe (Barnes and O'Brien forthcoming; Barnes and Taylor-Robinson 2018; Escobar-Lemmon and Taylor-Robinson 2005, 2016; Krook and O'Brien 2012).

Similar to trends in the national government, women's representation has been slowly increasing in provincial ministerial posts. As Argentina is a federal system, and the policymaking process is decentralized to the provincial level, women's appointment to subnational cabinet ministries is important for understanding women's access to political power more generally and women's influence over policies that shape the quality of women's lives. In Argentina, subnational governments have jurisdiction over health, education, and social policies, giving them considerable influence over policies such as violence against women and reproductive

3. Two additional women were appointed to serve as provincial executive by President Carlos Menem. In 1991, prior to Tierra del Fuego achieving provincehood, Matilde Menéndez was appointed governor. In 1992 Claudia Bello was appointed to serve as the federal intervenor in the province of Corrientes after the federal government was forced to take over the provincial government as a result of a disputed gubernatorial election.

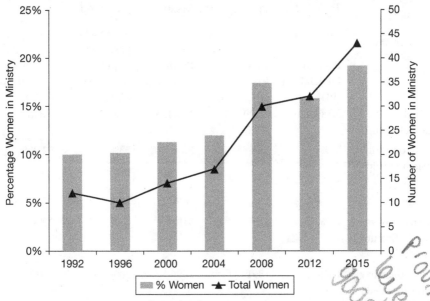

Figure 7.2 Women in Provincial-Level Cabinet Posts

rights (Barnes 2012b, 2016; Escobar-Lemmon and Funk, chapter 6, this volume; Franceschet 2011; Franceschet and Piscopo 2013; Lopreite 2014; Smulovitz 2015). Using original data from all twenty-four provinces, Figure 7.2 charts the number and percentage of women in provincial cabinet posts from 1992 to 2015. The percentage of women in each year is aggregated across provinces. In 1992, across all 24 provinces in Argentina, only 12 women held provincial-level cabinet portfolios. Women held about 10% of provincial-level ministerial posts throughout the majority of the 1990s and 2000s. Between 2005 and 2015, however, more women were included in the provincial-level executive branch, with women reaching a high of 19% in 2015. Consistent with the cross-national insights provided by Taylor-Robinson and Gleitz (chapter 3, this volume) women's access to cabinet posts—both at the national and subnational level in Argentina—indicate that it is becoming less acceptable to have male-only cabinets in Argentina.

Finally, women's participation in political parties is on par with men's. Still women lag behind in their access to leadership posts in the five largest political parties—particularly in the largest two parties. Table 7.2 shows the total party membership for the five largest parties in Argentina in 2009, and lists the percentage of members that are women by political party.[4] Women make up slightly more than half of the membership in all political parties. Yet, women hold only 12% and 13% of executive posts in the PJ and UCR, respectively. Women fare better in the smaller political parties, holding 31%, 44%, and 20% of positions in the executive body in the *Partido Socialista* (PS), ARI, and *Propuesta Federal* (PRO), respectively.

4. Data on party composition comes from the Género y Partidos Politicos en América Latina Database: http://www.iadb.org/research/geppal. See also Morgan and Hinojosa, chapter 5 in this volume.

Table 7.2 POLITICAL PARTY MEMBERSHIP IN 2009

not represented

	Partido Justicialista (PJ)	Unión Cívica Radical (UCR)	Partido Socialista (PS)	Afirmación para una República Igualitaria (ARI)	Propuesta Republicana (PRO)
Total Membership	3,586,326	2,500,237	115,423	48,063	1,848
% Women in Membership	51%	53%	52%	53%	52.90%
Total Executive Body	75	24	13	9	5
Percent Women in the Executive Body	12%	13%	31%	44%	20%
Year the Party was founded	1946	1891	1896	2004	2003

SOURCE: Género y Partidos Políticos en América Latina (GEPPAL).

CAUSES OF WOMEN'S NUMERIC REPRESENTATION

The causes of women's numeric representation in Argentina vary significantly across different political arenas. Whereas women's access to national and subnational legislatures is largely attributed to formal institutions, women's access to cabinet posts is better explained by cross-arena diffusion. In this section we examine the causes of women's representation in each of the five political arenas.

Causes of women's access to national and subnational legislatures

Formal institutions—namely the adoption and design of gender quotas as well as electoral systems—are critical for explaining increases in women's numeric representation in the legislative branch in Argentina. In 1991, Argentina became the first country in the world to adopt a legislative gender quota (Bonder and Nari 1995). Initially, the gender quota was implemented only in the National Chamber of Deputies (in 1993). It was not until 2001—when senators were directly elected for the first time—that a legislative gender quota was implemented in the national Senate. In 1992—the year after gender quotas were first adopted at the national level—many provinces began following suit and adopting provincial-level gender quotas of their own (Alles 2009; Archenti and Tula 2008b; Barnes 2012b; Caminotti 2009; Jones 1998). The adoption of quotas was staggered over the remainder of the 1990s, with the vast majority of provinces adopting a quota by 2000.[5] Quotas were however not adopted in the provinces of Jujuy and Entre Ríos until 2010 and 2011.

2001 Implemented in national senate

5. Moreover, gender quotas have enjoyed a high level of support among citizens. See Barnes and Córdova (2016) for a discussion of citizen support for quotas across Latin America.

With the adoption of legislative gender quotas, women's numeric representation grew dramatically in both national and subnational legislatures over the next ten years. Quota adoption, however, did not result in immediate or uniform increases in women's numeric representation in all legislatures due to significant variation in quota design and existing electoral rules. The three most important electoral rules influencing the success of gender quotas are variation in legislative election cycles, the use of placement mandates, and variation in district sizes (Jones 1998; see also Alles 2014; Jones 2009; Jones, Alles, and Tchintian 2012; Schwindt-Bayer 2009; and Schwindt-Bayer and Alles, chapter 4, this volume, for discussions of when gender quotas are most effective). Argentine chambers that renew every seat in the legislative chamber at once have tended to have large immediate gains upon implementing gender quotas, whereas chambers that renew only half of the legislative chamber in each election typically incurred only moderate increases in women's representation in the first election (Jones 1998). Quotas generally became fully effective in the second election in which the gender quota was employed. In both the immediate and long term, gender quotas were more effective when they were combined with districts that on average elected a medium to large number of legislators (Alles 2007, 2008; Htun and Jones 2002). Although almost all of the Argentine provinces use closed-list electoral systems to elect their legislators, the chambers vary significantly in district size (i.e., district magnitudes). This also accounted for a substantial portion of the variation observed in women's numeric representation across the Argentine chambers.

Variation in women's numeric representation in Argentina was also due to the design of the quota rules (Archenti and Tula 2008b; Barnes 2012b; Caminotti 2009; Granara 2014; Marx, Borner, and Caminotti 2007, 2009). Although the vast majority of legislative chambers in Argentina had adopted a legislative gender quota by 2000, not all quota designs were equally effective. Some quotas included a placement mandate—language stipulating that women must be included on the list of a political party's candidates and be placed in an electable position—whereas other quotas did not include this language. When quotas were adopted without a placement mandate, party leaders often placed women at the bottom of the list where they did not have a chance to be elected (Jones 2004). Over the course of the 1990s and early 2000s, quotas used in both national and provincial elections underwent a number of reforms aimed at improving their effectiveness (Barnes 2016). As a result, women occupied at least 20% of seats in the majority of provincial legislatures.

Despite the ubiquity of quotas across the lower houses in the Argentine provinces, multiple senates—including Catamarca, Entre Ríos, Salta, San Luis, or Santa Fe—are not elected using gender quotas. Each of these senates elects legislators using single member districts, which are by and large not compatible with legislative gender quotas.[6] As a result, whereas women's numeric representation has risen sharply in the Argentine provincial senates with quotas, women have not been well represented in senates without quotas. A direct comparison of women's numeric representation in the upper and lower chamber in the five provinces without quotas in the upper chamber provides further evidence that increases in women's access to legislatures

---

6. Other senates (i.e., Buenos Aries, Corrientes, and Mendoza) use multimember districts to elect legislators and do enforce the use of a gender quota.

in Argentina are due to formal institutions—namely gender quotas—and not cultural and socioeconomic or political factors. As cultural and socioeconomic factors, political factors, and women's representation in other political arenas are held constant within individual provinces, we would expect for women's numeric representation to attain similar levels in the upper and lower chamber within a single province if these factors were critical for explaining variation in women's representation in Argentina. Yet in four of the five provinces (with the San Luis senate, as a clear outlier) women's numeric representation in the Senate lags far behind the women's representation in the House. For example, in 2014 women only held 5% of seats in the Santa Fe Senate compared to 32% of seats in the Santa Fe House. Thus, similar to other parts of Latin America, and as argued in the introduction to this book, cultural and socioeconomic factors do not explain women's access or exclusion from legislative office. Instead, as Schwindt-Bayer and Alles (chapter 4, this volume) explain, gender quotas have "minimized the negative consequences" that other factors such as the conservative machismo culture can have for women. Instead, women's numeric representation is best explained by the adoption of well-designed quota legislation in combination with closed-list proportional representation electoral systems.

Causes of women's access to executive posts

Women have made fewer gains in national and subnational executive posts. In recent years, however, more women have risen to top executive posts. Gains in women's representation at the executive level are often associated with political factors. In particular, some scholars argue that women—typically political outsiders—are often elected to the presidency following political crises signaling change and renewal (Jalalzai 2004; Murray 2010). Yet the first woman elected to the presidency in Argentina was not a political outsider and did not ascend to power as a result of political crisis (Jalalzai 2015; Piscopo 2010). Prior to holding the presidential post, Fernández de Kirchner of the Peronist FPV had served in several prominent political positions. She was first elected as provincial deputy in 1989 and later elected to the national congress as both a national deputy and as a national senator (representing first the province of Santa Cruz and then later the province of Buenos Aires). Thus, rather than emerging as an outsider, Fernández de Kirchner's prior political experience in other political arenas and her insider status positioned her to be a credible candidate. Her election fits the broader Latin American pattern suggested by Reyes-Housholder and Thomas in chapter 2 of this volume.

Indeed, in many respects, Fernández de Kirchner's pathway to power is consistent with the premise that informal institutions—in this case a centralized selection procedure for the Front for Victory's 2007 presidential candidate—are key to explaining her election as president (Hinojosa 2012). In 2007 and again in 2011, it was a near certainty that the FPV's presidential nominee would win the general election. Thus when Fernández de Kirchner was selected as the FPV's presidential candidate by her predecessor and spouse, President Néstor Kirchner (2003–2007), her general election victory was almost a foregone conclusion (Barnes and Jones 2011).

Finally, although cultural factors were not important for explaining Fernández de Kirchner's election, public opinion toward women in office was at least conducive to the election of a female president in Argentina. Indeed, by the time the first female president was elected to office in Argentina, female politicians were seen as "commonplace" (Piscopo 2010, 199). Effective gender quotas had been in place for well over a decade and President Néstor Kirchner had recently appointed two women to the Supreme Court, a female minister of defense, and a female minister of economy. Public opinion was generally accepting of female political candidates.

Public opinion was good + she had pol exp.

Women's access to cabinet appointments

Women's representation in ministries has increased significantly over the past thirty years. Unlike women's access to the legislature, women's representation in the cabinet is not due to a change in formal rules. Although very few studies have centered specifically on women's appointments to cabinets in Argentina, time-series data analysis from the national Argentine cabinet shows that increases in women's cabinet appointments are associated with increases in the country's gender development index (Barnes and Jones 2011). Figure 7.1 also shows that increases in women's representation in cabinet posts have followed increases in women's numeric representation in the legislature. That said, earlier work by Barnes and Jones (2011) shows that increases in women's numeric representation in the national legislature are not a significant predictor of women's appointments to cabinet posts.

Similar to the national cabinet, at the subnational level, women's appointments to cabinet posts may be best explained by cross-arena diffusion. Specifically, the number of years that have passed since quota adoption in the legislature and the presence of a female governor are strongly correlated with the gender composition of provincial cabinets (Lopreite 2015). Despite the fact that few women have held the gubernatorial post in Argentina, when women govern the province, they are systematically more likely to appoint women to ministerial posts than are their male counterparts. Interestingly, Lopreite (2015) finds that the share of female legislators is negatively correlated with women's appointments to cabinet portfolios and that socioeconomic factors are not related to women's cabinet appointments in Argentina.

gov who are women more likely to appoint women

WOMEN'S ACCESS TO PARTY LEADERSHIP

What explains women's continued exclusion from party leadership in Argentina? Argentina is one of the most progressive countries in the region (Hinojosa 2012) and is generally accepting of female political leaders (Piscopo 2010). Feminist NGOs outside of government and female party activists organized to increase women's access to Congress (Waylen 2000). Moreover, Argentina has a wealth of qualified female candidates who have served in other branches of government (Franceschet and Piscopo 2014), and women make up the majority of political party members. Yet these factors have not translated to more women in party leadership positions. Women's marginalization from political party leadership is likely best explained by political factors and the informal and behind-the-scenes selection procedures that give rise to party leaders. Nonetheless, no systematic research has carefully considered the causes of women's exclusion from political party posts in Argentina.

CONSEQUENCES OF WOMEN'S REPRESENTATION

There are a number of consequences associated with women's numeric representation. Women bring new perspectives to bear on policies and introduce new issues to the legislative agenda. In conjunction with the rise of women in the national and provincial legislatures over the last two decades, Argentina has passed a number of landmark laws extending the scope of women's rights. In this section, we first review research on the substantive consequences of women's representation in Argentina. Then, using an original analysis of survey data, we examine the symbolic consequences of women's representation in subnational governments across Argentina. This is a novel contribution, as previous research has focused almost exclusively on the symbolic effects of women in national governments.

Substantive consequences of women's representation inside the political arena

One of the most important consequences of women's numeric representation in politics is that women bring to the table new ideas, perspectives, issues, and concerns. Indeed, female legislators in the Argentine Congress report that they have different priorities than their male colleagues (Schwindt-Bayer 2006, 2010), and evidence from cosponsorship patterns in the Argentine provincial legislatures shows that they exhibit a set of distinct policy preferences (Barnes 2012a). Women work diligently to advance their priorities and represent their constituents by authoring a large number of bills across the spectrum of issues. In fact, women tend to author more legislation than their male colleagues—women in the Chamber of Deputies, on average, sponsor seven more bills per session than their male colleagues (Schwindt-Bayer 2010). At the provincial level, women cosponsor almost 30% more bills than the average male legislator (Barnes 2016). Women's presence in decision-making bodies thus has important consequences for the representation of all constituents.

Women's numeric representation also has important consequences for the representation of women's interests. Women in the Argentine Congress report prioritizing women's rights more than do men (Schwindt-Bayer 2006, 2010) and many female legislators even feel obligated to act on behalf of women (Francheschet and Piscopo 2008). To accomplish these goals, female legislators use speeches and legislative debates to articulate women's interests (Piscopo 2011a), and they sponsor and cosponsor legislation intended to advance women's rights and advantage children and families more than do men (Barnes 2016; Jones 1997, Schwindt-Bayer 2006, 2010). Htun, Lacalle, and Micozzi (2013) shows that, in Argentina, many women desire to advocate women's rights through bill introduction, and their tendencies to do so increase as women's numeric representation increases (Htun 2016). Yet, only a minority of women in office are responsible for bills on women's rights—that is, not all women are equally active in introducing women's rights legislation (Htun 2016). Similarly, in the provincial legislatures, approximately a quarter of women refrain from coauthoring women's issues legislation (Barnes 2016). Whether or not female legislators choose to author and coauthor legislation on women's issues may vary depending on their personal ideas and religious beliefs, preferences over policy outcomes, policy priorities, and their party's current policy stance on issues (Barnes 2012a; Lopreite 2012, 2014; Piscopo 2011a). Finally, despite the large body of research on women's bill sponsorship in Argentina, scholars have not devoted sufficient attention to bill success. Future research should consider whether women's efforts to influence the policymaking process are successful beyond the agenda-setting phase (Htun, Lacalle, and Micozzi 2013).

Increases in women's legislative activity also motivate male legislators' interest in women's rights legislation (Htun 2016). Men were responsible for sponsoring and cosponsoring a few prominent women's issues bills in the national (Schwindt-Bayer 2010) and subnational (Barnes 2016) legislatures. For example, in the national congress, men sponsored bills to assist low-income pregnant mothers, provide monthly allowances to mothers with five or more children, and authored multiple bills focused on reproductive rights (Schwindt-Bayer 2010, 93). Further, women are strategic in seeking male allies to advance important legislation (Barnes 2016) and to oversee its implementation (Piscopo 2014a). Given women's ability to develop allies and work within the chamber to advance their interests, it is not surprising that the rise of women in parliament over the last two decades has been accompanied by the passage of a number of important laws extending the scope of women's rights in Argentina (Schwindt-Bayer 2010).

In Argentina, the executive branch—presidents and ministers—has been instrumental in defining women's rights (Lopreite 2015). Health Minister Ginés González García (appointed by President Eduardo Duhalde, 2002–2003) developed policies to reduce maternal and child mortality rates and to provide women access to contraceptive services. When President Néstor Kirchner was elected he continued the policies implemented under Duhalde to advance women's reproductive rights. In particular, he charged the Ministry of Justice with the task of designing legislation to decriminalize first trimester abortions. But, when President Cristina Fernández de Kirchner was elected as president, this progress halted—as she strongly opposed abortion (for details, see Lopreite 2015). Indeed, Fernández de Kirchner is typically seen as uncommitted to promoting progressive women's rights (Jalalzai 2015).

Fernández de Kirchner promoted women's issues that reinforced a "traditional conception of women as poor mothers rather than placing women on a more feminist path" (Jalalzai 2015, 117). She is credited with promoting the visibility of housewives, improving violence against women laws, introducing a childcare allowance, and extending the child allowance to pregnant women. Nonetheless, these policies are often criticized for reinforcing traditional gender roles and discouraging poor mothers from joining the work force (Lopreite 2015; Lopreite and Macdonald 2014). Despite her conservative stance on women's rights, President Fernández de Kirchner supported marriage equality and new progressive gender identity laws. Although she did not introduce the policies, the legislation would not have been passed into law without her explicit support (Jalalzai 2015). Overall, President Fernández de Kirchner is not seen as having spent her two terms in office championing women's rights, but she is recognized for working to improve the economic well-being of working class and poor women.

Consequences of women's representation outside the political arena

Women's presence in elite political positions may also have symbolic consequences. Although research on the symbolic effects of women's representation is mixed, numerous studies find that women's presence in politics improves citizen's perceptions of women's ability to govern (Alexander 2012; Morgan and Buice 2013; Reyes-Housholder and Schwindt-Bayer 2016; Schwindt-Bayer and Reyes-Housholder 2017), motivates more women to become politically engaged (Barnes and Burchard 2013; Reyes-Housholder and Schwindt-Bayer 2016; Schwindt-Bayer and Reyes-Housholder 2017; Wolbrecht and Campbell 2007), and engenders trust and satisfaction with democracy among citizens (Barnes and Beaulieu 2014; Schwindt-Bayer 2010; Schwindt-Bayer and Mishler 2005).

The majority of these studies, however, have focused on the symbolic effects of women's presence in national legislatures, and more recently, national executives (e.g., Barnes and Taylor-Robinson 2018; Reyes-Householder and Schwindt-Bayer 2016; Schwindt-Bayer and Reyes-Housholder 2017). Yet, in the opening chapter of this book, Schwindt-Bayer posits that this relationship may vary across arenas. On one hand, she suggests that the impact may be stronger when women are involved in the national political arena where they occupy more visible positions. On the other hand, in the same way that Escobar-Lemmon and Funk (chapter 6, this volume) argue that subnational governments may be more accessible to women's descriptive representation because they are closer to home, there is reason to believe that women's presence in subnational politics may also have powerful symbolic effects because individuals may be more likely to have personal contact with subnational government officials. Additionally, subnational governments have jurisdiction over policies that shape the quality of women's lives and other service provisions (e.g., healthcare and education) that profoundly affect ordinary citizens' daily lives (Barnes 2016; Franceschet 2011; Lopreite 2014). Thus we posit that the inclusion of women in subnational governments may also have positive effects on women's symbolic representation.

In this section, we provide the first systematic investigation of whether women's numeric representation in provincial level-legislatures and cabinets improves representation in Argentina by cultivating trust in the government and engendering political engagement. Using Latin American Public Opinion Project (LAPOP) data from twenty-three Argentine provinces across four waves of surveys from 2008 to 2014 for a total of seventy province-years (not every province is included in each survey wave), we examine two dependent variables to evaluate citizens' trust and engagement in subnational governments. First, to evaluate trust in the subnational government we use a survey question that asks citizens to respond to the following question by placing themselves on a scale of 1 (not at all) to 7 (a lot): "To what extent do you trust the local or municipal government?"[7] Second, to evaluate political engagement with subnational governments we use a survey question that asks: "In order to solve your problems have you ever requested help or cooperation from a local

---

7. The dependent variable for trust is ordinal (a 7-point scale), thus we estimate an ordered logistic regression.

public official or local government (for example, a mayor, municipal council, coun-
cilman, provincial official, civil governor, or governor)." Respondents could answer
yes or no.[8]

For both analyses we employ an interactive multilevel model (with random inter-
cepts for the province-year) that accounts for the sex of the respondent, percentage
of women in the provincial legislature, and the percentage of women in the provincial cabinet. Then to examine if these two provincial-level factors are associated with
both men's and women's political trust and engagement, we include an interaction
between each of these provincial level variables and the respondent sex (see appendix tables for description and measurement of variables [Table A7.1] and estimated
coefficients [Table A7.2]). Additionally, we control for important provincial-level
factors including development (HDI), gender equality (GDI), and income inequality (GINI), as well as individual-level demographics, socioeconomic characteristics,
and interests in politics.[9]

We find that increases in women's numeric representation in provincial-level legislatures are associated with increases in trust in local governments among both men
and women. Figure 7.3 shows that as women's numeric representation increases (x-
axis), the probability of citizens displaying the highest level of trust in local governments (a 7 on the 7-point scale; y-axis) increases significantly.[10] Among women, the
probability of having high levels of trust in the government is 5.2% for provinces with
the lowest level of women's numeric representation (10.7%), and rises to 16.8% (an
increase of 11.6 percentage points) in provinces with the highest level of women's
numeric representation (51.4%). A similar pattern holds for men. The probability of
displaying high trust in the government increases from 6.0% to 13.4% (an increase of
7.4 percentage points), as we move from provinces with the lowest to the highest level
of women's legislative numeric representation. Our analysis provides support for the
notion that increases in women's numeric representation improves trust in government among all citizens. We do not find, however, that increases in women's numeric
representation in cabinets is associated with higher levels of trust in government.

Next, turning to citizens' political engagement, whereas increases in women's
numeric representation in the legislature are not associated with the likelihood that
citizens contact their local government to solve a problem, increases in women's
numeric representation in the cabinet are associated with slightly higher levels of citizen engagement among women. Figure 7.4 graphs the predicted probability of contacting local government officials (y-axis) as women's representation in the cabinet
increases (x-axis). The left panel shows that at low levels of women's representation
(0%) the probability of the average female citizens contacting the local government
is 11.7%, whereas at high levels of women's numeric representation (50%) the probability increases to 18.7%, all else equal. This difference of 7 percentage points is

8. Given that this variable is binary, we use a logistic regression.

9. HDI refers to the Human Development Index, GDI refers to the Gender Development Index,
and GINI refers to the Gini coefficient.

10. Predicted probabilities were calculated using the Margins command in STATA 13. Following
Mitchell (2012) we calculate predicted probabilities across all of the cases in the sample and to
present the mean predicted probability. Thus, the predicted probabilities represent the average
value across individual predicted probabilities.

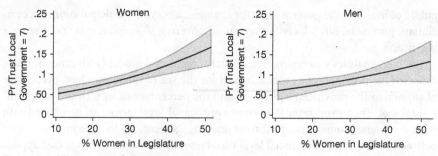

Figure 7.3 Trust in Local Governments
NOTE: This figure graphs the mean predicted probabilities of displaying high levels of trust
in the local government (trust=7) as women's numeric representation in the provincial
legislative chamber increases. Predicted probabilities are based on a multilevel mixed-
effects ordered logistic regression model with a random intercept for the province-year
(See Table A7.2, model 1 in the appendix). Shaded areas represent 95 percent confidence
intervals estimated using the Delta Method. Following Mitchell (2012) we calculate
predicted probabilities across all of the cases in the sample and present the mean predicted
probability. Thus, the predicted probabilities represent the average value across individual
predicted probabilities.

men less likely to contact local gov

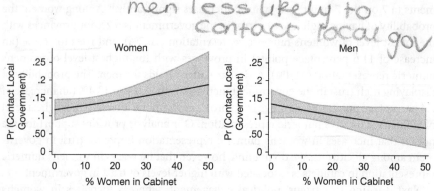

Figure 7.4 Contact Local Governments
This figure graphs the mean predicted probabilities of contacting local government
officials as women's numeric representation in subnational cabinets increases. Predicted
probabilities are based on multilevel mixed-effects logistic regression with a random
intercept for the province-year (See Table A7.2, model 2 in the appendix). Shaded areas
represent 95 percent confidence intervals estimated using the Delta Method. Following
Mitchell (2012) we calculate predicted probabilities across all of the cases in the sample
and present the mean predicted probability. Thus, the predicted probabilities represent the
average value across individual predicted probabilities.

statistically significant at the 0.10 confidence level. The relationship between wom-
en's numeric representation in the cabinet and men's political engagement is not statistically significant.

   In sum, this analysis makes several important contributions to the research on
women's representation. First, as very little research has examined how women's presence in government—and particularly subnational government—affects citizens'
attitudes and opinions, this analysis fills an important gap in the literature by systematically examining how increases in women's numeric representation in subnational

legislative and executive branches gives rise to trust in local governments and engenders citizens' political engagement. Second, this analysis provides evidence that increases in women's numeric representation in subnational governments works to improve trust in the government and engender political engagement. We find that women's representation in provincial legislatures is significantly correlated with trust in government (among both men and women), and women's representation in cabinets encourages political engagement specifically among female citizens. Thus our findings provide some evidence that women in the executive branch should have greater symbolic effects than women in the legislative branch. Furthermore, we find that in Argentina—where subnational governments have substantial policymaking power—women's presence in subnational governments has important consequences for symbolic representation. Finally, this analysis sets the agenda for future work on the symbolic effects of women's numeric representation—particularly at the subnational level where governments often have more influence over citizens' day-to-day lives.

CHALLENGES FACING WOMEN'S REPRESENTATION

Despite major gains in women's numeric representation at both the national and subnational levels of government and across the legislative and executive branches, challenges remain for women's representation in Argentina. As of yet, women entering historically male-dominated institutions are not being fully incorporated into the legislature, political party leadership, powerful ministerial posts, or informal political networks. Women are far less likely to hold legislative leadership posts such as the chamber president or vice president (Barnes 2016; Schwindt-Bayer 2010). Leadership posts in the National Chamber of Deputies have a disproportionate amount of power. The Chamber President (speaker), for example, determines which bills will come before the chamber for a vote. Yet, women have never held this powerful position in the Chamber and only one woman has ever assumed the office of Provisional President of the National Senate—the highest office in that body. Consistent with this trend, women have rarely held this position in the provincial-level legislatures (Barnes 2016). Female legislators are also proportionally underrepresented on powerful legislative committees such as the budget and economics committees and are virtually absent from the leadership on these powerful committees (Barnes 2014, 2016; Htun and Jones 2002); although, women's access to powerful committee posts varies dramatically by province (Granara 2014) and has improved over time (Barnes 2014).

Women are rarely appointed to powerful ministerial posts. We find that between 1992 and 2015, most women appointed to provincial-level cabinet posts held feminine, low-prestige appointments (similar to what Taylor-Robinson and Gleitz, chapter 3 of this volume, report for national cabinets regionwide). Specifically, women were frequently assigned the social development, health, education and culture, and tourism portfolios. Only a few women have been appointed to high-prestige portfolios that grant them substantial policy influence and access to resources. At the provincial level in Argentina, the two most powerful cabinet posts are Minister of Treasury and Finance and Ministry of Government. During this twenty-three-year period, women have only served in the former post in six of the twenty-three provinces, and only for short periods of time. Similarly, during this period, only six women have ever served as the Minister of Government, but none of them served for more than two years. All in all, women's access to prestigious and powerful cabinet posts at the provincial level has been minimal.

Furthermore, although gender quotas have been instrumental in affording women access to legislatures at both the national and provincial level, most political parties continue to comply with only the minimum requirements established by quota legislation. As such, women's numeric representation falls short of 30% in multiple provinces as well as in many municipalities. A case in point is found in the 135 municipal councils in the Province of Buenos Aires. Municipal councilors are elected from closed party lists in a single multi-member district (ranging in number of members from 3 to 12 with a median of 8) using the LR-Hare formula and a vote threshold equal to one Hare quota (parties that do not pass the threshold are ineligible to receive seats). The quota law requires that a minimum of 30% of the candidates be women and that, at a minimum, every third candidate be a woman. At present, 57 of the 135 municipal councils have a percentage of women below 30%.

To further investigate the challenge posed by political parties' minimal compliance with quota laws, we gathered original data on legislators' list positions. We find that of those legislators elected into the national Chamber of Deputies between 2003 and 2015, the *cabeza de lista* (i.e., the person at the top of the closed party list) was a woman on only 16% of party lists. By contrast 68% of legislators occupying the second place position on the ballot were women. Given that national level quota legislation requires political parties to place women in "electable positions" on the ballot, political parties/ alliances that do not have a realistic chance of winning more than two seats (demonstrated via their past electoral track record) are required to place women in second place on the ballot. Similar trends occur at the provincial level. Data from eight provinces indicate that the *cabeza de lista* was a woman in only 10% of cases, and the second position on the ballot was occupied by women in only 18% of cases. The exclusion of women from the *cabeza de lista* poses a major challenge for the election of women in districts with small district magnitudes. The vast majority of provinces elect no more than five representatives to the national congress in a given electoral cycle, with over half of the provinces electing three or fewer representatives. In such cases, even if women are placed second on the list, it is difficult for them to win a seat in congress.

Finally, women continue to be underrepresented in powerful party leadership positions. Viewing this alongside women's representation in other arenas, there appears to be a trend wherein women are gaining access to lower-level rank-and-file political posts, but they are rarely attaining political power.

CONCLUSION

Two decades ago, Argentina was the world leader in gender quota adoption and implementation. However, today, Argentina's national quota as well as that of two-thirds of its provinces no longer places it in the global vanguard (Piscopo 2015a).[11]

11. Eight provinces have adopted parity quota legislation (Buenos Aires, Chubut, Córdoba, Neuquén, Río Negro, Salta, Santiago del Estero, and Tierra del Fuego), although in Tierra del Fuego this legislation is combined with preference voting (open lists) which weakens its overall effectiveness in insuring parity in representation in the provincial legislature.

Efforts are presently being made to pass parity legislation for national legislative elections, although while parity enjoys substantial support, the parity legislation's passage has been delayed due to broader interparty disputes over other elements of the political reform package of which it forms a part (e.g., the adoption of electronic voting).

The natural experiment that has taken place in Argentina since the first use of gender quotas in 1993 underscores the tremendous potential of positive action to dramatically transform the composition of legislative bodies. The Argentine case makes clear that quotas represent a reliable and effective mechanism to significantly increase the proportion of women in national, provincial, and municipal legislatures. Evidence from Argentina also underscores that this improvement in descriptive representation has procedural and policy consequences, changing the way legislative politics is conducted as well as the impact of public policy on the lives of women.

Scholars have devoted significant attention to understanding the causes and consequences of women's representation in Argentina, yet a number of questions remain unexamined—particularly at the subnational level. As a result, Argentina provides promising avenues for future research. As subnational governments in Argentina are key actors in the political process, it is critical that scholars understand the causes and consequences of women's access to subnational political arenas. Beyond the analysis provided here, scholars have not considered the symbolic consequences of women's numeric representation in subnational Argentine governments. Future research should consider the extent to which women's representation in different political arenas in Argentina shapes attitudes toward gender equality.

8

Informal Institutions and Women's Political Representation in Chile (1990–2015)

SUSAN FRANCESCHET ■

Chile is clearly one of Latin America's success stories. Since the return of democracy in 1990, the country has achieved an enviable record of political stability and economic growth. Nonetheless, trends elsewhere in the region, such as declining party attachment, voter turnout, declining public trust in political institutions, and growing levels of social protest are evident in Chile too.[1] Exploring the gender dimensions of political representation in Chile can shed light on some of the broader political trends in the country since the transition to democracy. In this chapter, I argue that a gendered analysis of representation offers two key insights. First, the very same factors that have created political stability—namely, the emergence of informal institutions for candidate selection and political appointments—create obstacles to women's representation. Specifically, the chapter shows how institutional factors, and especially informal rules, rather than cultural or socioeconomic factors, are the key reasons for women's underrepresentation in electoral politics at both the national and subnational levels. A second insight is that growing public dissatisfaction with the status quo creates opportunities for women in politics. The historical election of Chile's first female president in 2006 demonstrates how gendered opportunities have emerged from citizen frustration with the political status quo.

Compared to the rest of the region, where electoral gender quotas have led to dramatic gains in the women's legislative presence, the number of women serving in Chile's congress remains woefully small. At 15.8% in the lower house, women's presence is well below the regional average of 26.1% (Piscopo 2016c;

---

1. In the 2013 presidential election, just 41.9% of the voting population participated, down from a high of 94.7% in 1989, the first democratic election after the dictatorship (Voter Turnout, Chile, http://www.idea.int/data-tools/question-countries-view/521/79/ctr, Accessed August 17, 2017). Notably, the 2013 election was the first under new rules in which voting was not compulsory.

see also, Schwindt-Bayer and Alles, chapter 4, this volume). Prior to passing a new electoral law in January 2015, Chile was one of just two countries in the region that had not legislated gender quotas. But despite women's underrepresentation in congress, significant progress on women's rights has been achieved. The first post-transition government created the Servicio Nacional de la Mujer (Sernam), and, unlike other women's policy agencies in the region, Sernam has seen steady increases in its budget, resources, and policy influence. In March 2015, Sernam was replaced with an even more powerful Ministry for Women. In contrast to their small numbers in elected office, women have fared relatively well in appointed positions in government, particularly since 2000, when the proportion of women in cabinet reached 30% (Franceschet and Thomas 2015). With the election of Chile's first female president in 2006, Michelle Bachelet, women achieved parity in cabinet representation, although that has not been sustained in subsequent governments.

The consequences of women's political presence are not determined solely by numbers, however. Instead, policy outcomes in gender equality are shaped by the institutional organization of the Chilean state, along with a well-established set of informal rules and practices within the coalition of parties that has governed for most of the post-transition period. Formal rules and informal but deeply entrenched norms and practices reduce the scope for action by legislators while increasing the policy capacity of the executive branch. Thus I argue that electing women to the presidency may be more consequential than electing women to congress.

Throughout this chapter, I make three arguments. First, I show that institutions, defined as formal rules and informal practices and norms, have shaped women's presence in all political arenas, including the legislature, the presidency, cabinet, and subnational governments. But formal rules and informal practices also shape the consequences of women's presence in politics. Second, I argue that presidents can have a far greater impact on public policy than can members of congress, given the constitutional division of powers between the presidency and the legislature. Finally, the broader political challenges facing Chile, such as declining party attachment and growing citizen dissatisfaction with the status quo, have ambiguous consequences for women. On the one hand, the ultimate source of citizens' frustration—namely, the elite and party-centric nature of Chilean politics—creates profound obstacles for women. Political stability in Chile has been achieved through the development of practices that reinforce the power of a small group of political elites in the main parties. Women are seldom present in these elite networks, thus reducing women's visibility and influence in politics. On the other hand, these very same dynamics created an opening for the country's first female president, who effectively positioned herself as outside of elite party networks.

A BRIEF OVERVIEW OF CHILEAN POLITICS

In March 1990, following seventeen years of highly repressive military rule by General Augusto Pinochet, a democratically elected government took office. President Patricio Aylwin, from the centrist Christian Democratic Party, led a coalition of center and left parties (the *Concertación*) that had come together during the dictatorship to demand the return of democracy and to organize the "No" vote in the 1988 plebiscite that ended Pinochet's rule. During the dictatorship, the country's Constitution was reformed and a new electoral law adopted. These reforms have shaped legislative politics in the post-dictatorship era. The new electoral system sought to transform Chile's traditional multiparty system into a two-party system, but its principal effect has been to compel the main parties to form two broad electoral coalitions. The *Concertación*, composed of four moderate left and center parties, won every set of congressional and presidential elections between 1990 and 2010. Their main competition is the coalition of rightist parties, formed by the National Renovation and the Independent Democratic Union. The coalition on the right is called the *Alianza* (Alliance). The *Alianza* won the presidency for the first time in 2010, governing for a single term before losing again to the center-left coalition. For the 2013 elections, the *Concertación* was replaced by an even larger group of parties, this time including those further to the left, like the Communists. The coalition changed its name to the *Nueva Mayoría*.

In terms of political structure, Chile is a centralized, unitary state with few offices open to electoral competition (Hinojosa and Franceschet 2012). At the national level, members of congress and the president are directly elected. Between 1990 and 2017, elections to both the chamber of deputies (120 seats) and the senate (38 seats) were based on open-list proportional representation with a small district magnitude (2 seats per district). A new electoral system, approved by the congress in January 2015, will take effect for the 2017 national elections. Both the number of seats and the district magnitude have increased. At the municipal level, councilors and mayors are directly elected. Councilors are elected through open-list proportional representation, and, since 2004, mayors have been directly elected. Even though there are other territorial administrations, such as regions and provinces, the top posts (*intendentes* and *gobernadores*) are appointed by the president, not elected by citizens. Although still a highly centralized country, elected offices at the local level are quite competitive, with many politicians beginning their careers at the local level. That said, local governments have little policymaking autonomy and few financial resources (Luna and Mardones 2010, 115).

Compared to other Latin American countries, political parties in Chile are strong and ideologically coherent. In fact, while party weakness, and in some cases, the collapse of traditional parties, has led to a crisis of representation in parts of the region, in Chile it is quite the opposite: it is the parties' dominance of politics (*partidocracia*) that produced growing levels of dissatisfaction with political institutions and record high incidences of social protest by 2011.[2] According to Siavelis, Chile's strong and institutionalized party system is a double-edged sword that has ensured a successful transition to democracy but also increased citizen discontent (2009, 20). Political parties remain the principle vehicles for organizing political life in Chile, despite declining

2. Jara (2014) reports survey data from the Centro de Estudios Públicos (CEP) finding that while 42% of Chileans trusted the government in 2010, the figure was down to 23% by 2012. Congress and political parties fared even worse: 28% of Chileans trusted congress in 2010, but only 10% did so in 2012, and a mere 6% of respondents trusted parties in 2012, compared to 15% in 2010.

levels of voter attachment to parties.[3] Each post-transition president has come from a well-established political party, the overwhelming majority of cabinet ministers are party representatives, and central party elites control access to nominations for elected posts at the national and even subnational levels. Yet while Chilean parties historically had among the strongest links to civil society, citizen attachment to parties has declined considerably in recent years (Luna and Mardones 2010). Relative to the rest of Latin America, however, citizen trust in political parties remains high (Carlin 2014, 66).

An important institutional feature of Chile's political system is the amount of legislative power concentrated in the executive branch. According to the Constitution, the executive enjoys exclusive rights to legislate in certain areas, as well as significant power to determine the legislative agenda (Siavelis 2006). The presidentialist nature of Chile's political system means that women in congress who wish to pursue gender equality legislation must get support from the president or a ministry (Haas 2010). Yet even supportive presidents like Michelle Bachelet and a well-resourced women's policy agency like Sernam have not always been able to improve women's rights, especially in controversial areas like reproductive rights. That is because Chile's institutional context also includes a set of informal norms and practices that constrain the executive branch and limit the use of the executive powers granted by the constitution. When it comes to policymaking, the most important informal rule is "democracy by agreement," the practice by which presidents seek consensus among the parties of the governing coalition before pursuing policy objectives (Siavelis 2006). Because the coalition that has most often formed government includes the Christian Democrats, a party that is more conservative on some gender issues, things like decriminalizing abortion were not pursued until Bachelet's second administration (2014–2018).

In sum, women's access to elected and appointed posts at all levels, as well as their impact in those posts, is shaped by the formal rules and organization of Chile's political system but, even more important, by well-established and deeply entrenched informal norms and practices.

CAUSES OF WOMEN'S DESCRIPTIVE REPRESENTATION

A striking pattern emerges when we examine women's presence in Chile's political institutions: at the national level, the proportion of women has been lower in elected posts than in appointed posts. Although the initial post-transition government had very few women in either elected or appointed posts, pressure for women's inclusion grew over the years, and was more easily addressed when offices were appointed. In those cases, a single selector could respond to calls for gender balance by appointing more women. On the other hand, the electoral system in place between 1990 and 2017 gave rise to a complex process of bargaining over candidacies among political parties who were compelled to compete in electoral coalitions, thereby increasing the number of selectors. As I argue below, the causes of women's presence in elected office are found in institutional factors rather than societal or cultural factors.

---

3. In 2008, 21% of Chilean identified with a political party (Luna and Maldones 2010, 112). By 2010, that figure was down to just 11% (Luna and Altman 2011, 10).

Women and elected office

The small number of female candidates for all post-transition national elections indicates that Chile's political parties are reluctant to select women. In 1989, the first post-dictatorship election, women were nominated to just 7.9% of candidacies for the Chamber of Deputies and 6.3%,for the Senate. These figures have grown, but not by much. Even in 2013, women represented less than 20% of candidates for both houses of congress (see Tables 8.1 and 8.2). The small number of female candidates translates into few women elected to congress. In 1989, women won 5.8% of seats in the Chamber of Deputies and 6.3% in the Senate. Those numbers have increased

Table 8.1 PATTERNS OF WOMEN'S CANDIDACIES AND ELECTION TO THE CHAMBER OF DEPUTIES, 1989–2013

	Year of Election						
	1989	1993	1997	2001	2005	2009	2013
Total Candidates	419	384	442	381	386	429	470
Number of Men (%)	386 (92.1)	334 (87)	358 (81)	326 (85.5)	323 (83.6)	356 (82.9)	379 (80.6)
Number of Women (%)	33 (7.9)	50 (13)	84 (19)	55 (14.4)	63 (16.3)	73 (17)	91 (19.4)
Total Deputies Elected	120	120	120	120	120	120	120
Number of Men (%)	113 (94.2)	111 (92.5)	107 (89.2)	105 (87.5)	102 (85)	103 (85.8)	101 (84.2)
Number of Women (%)	7 (5.8)	9 (7.5)	13 (10.8)	15 (12.5)	18 (15)	17 (14.2)	19 (15.8)

SOURCE: http://www.servel.cl/ss/site/elecciones_de_diputados_1989_al_2013.html

Table 8.2 WOMEN'S CANDIDACIES AND ELECTION TO SENATE, 1989–2013

	Year of Election						
	1989	1993	1997	2001	2005	2009	2013
Total Candidates	110	55	66	46	66	58	67
Number of Men (%)	103 (93.6)	52 (94.5)	56 (84.8)	44 (95.6)	57 (86.3)	50 (86.2)	55 (82.1)
Number of Women (%)	7 (6.3)	3 (5.5)	10 (15.2)	2 (4.3)	9 (13.6)	8 (13.7)	12 (17.9)
Total Senators Elected	38	18	20	18	20	18	20
Number of Men (%)	36 (94.7)	18 (100)	18 (90)	18 (100)	18 (90)	15 (83.3)	16 (80)
Number of Women (%)	2 (5.3)	0	2 (10)	0	2 (10)	3 (16.7)	4 (20)

SOURCE: http://www.servel.cl/ss/site/elecciones_de_diputados_1989_al_2013.html

to 19.4% and 15.8% respectively after the 2013 elections. As other chapters in this volume show, these figures are considerably lower than other countries in the region, particularly those with effectively designed quota laws.

Women have fared somewhat better at the municipal level: women's presence is greater among municipal councilors than deputies or senators. Women won 12% of seats in municipal councils in 1992, but by 2012, they held 25.2% of seats. There are still very few female mayors, however (only 12.4% by 2012). The difference between women's presence in municipal and national office shows the importance of institutions, namely electoral design, in shaping patterns of descriptive representation. Elections to subnational and national offices operate according to different rules. Prior to its reform in 2015, Chile used an electoral system for national elections known as binominal majoritarianism. This system was created during the Pinochet dictatorship with the twin goals of decreasing the number of political parties and overrepresenting the political right. The country was divided into sixty districts for the Chamber of Deputies and nineteen for the Senate, and each district elected two members using open lists. But in order for a party list to win both seats, it had to double the amount of votes received by the second-largest vote getter. Where it did not, the second seat went to the list receiving the second highest number of votes.

Chile's electoral rules for the national congress disadvantaged women in three ways (Franceschet 2005; Hinojosa and Franceschet 2012). First, the small number of seats and the likelihood that each coalition would win only one seat created fierce competition for nominations. Women, with the exception of those coming from well-known political families, rarely had the political resources or networks of supporters to prevail in such contests. Second, the need for coalitions to double the amount of votes of the competing coalition in order to gain both seats privileged high-profile candidates who were well known to voters. Again, with few exceptions, women were rarely perceived as safe bets. But incumbents were advantaged. As such, turnover in Chile's congress was remarkably low: From 1993 to 2001, more than 70% of legislators sought reelection and 82.2% of them won their seats (Navia 2008, 97).

A third disadvantage of Chile's electoral rules was that the most important negotiation over candidacies took place at the level of the coalition, not within the parties (Siavelis 2014). What is more, this bargaining was governed by informal but well-established practices among a group of party elites (*partido transversal*) who did not occupy formal offices. As such, it was difficult for gender equality advocates to intervene in the process of candidate nomination to promote formal institutional changes, like gender quotas, to increase the number of women selected. All of the *Concertación* parties have internal party quotas, yet they are relatively meaningless. Even if the parties applied quotas internally and chose more female candidates, these candidacies could be bargained away at the coalition negotiation stage.

Fortunately, women's representation should improve when the new electoral law takes effect. Over the years, the binominal rules grew increasingly unpopular and were blamed for all manner of weaknesses in Chile's democracy. Most of all, they were blamed for growing voter apathy. Citizens became increasingly uninterested in elections because the outcome was predetermined: in most districts, a member of each of the two coalitions was elected. The lack of meaningful competition and growing frustration that small parties who were not part of the two main coalitions were completely shut out of congress led to numerous efforts to reform the electoral system. After many failed attempts, a new electoral law introduced by President Bachelet in July 2014 was approved by congress in January 2015.

The new law replaces entirely the binominal system with a more proportional one, although still with open lists. The new law increases the size of both chambers of congress—from 120 to 155 seats in the lower house and from 38 to 50 seats in the upper house. In the Chamber of Deputies, members will be elected in 28 districts with a magnitude ranging from 3 to 8 seats. Most important, the new law includes a gender quota: parties cannot have lists where more than 60% of candidates are from a single sex. Effectively, that translates into a 40% quota for women. The first elections to which the new law will apply take place in 2017. It is difficult to predict with any certainty how effective the quota will be. Some studies find that open lists are disadvantageous for women, while other studies find no incompatibility between quotas and the use of open lists (Jones and Navia 1999; Schmidt 2003b). Chile's law permits parties to exempt themselves from the quota provision when selecting candidates through primaries, although the possibility of using this provision as a loophole is limited, since the law caps the number of candidates selected through primaries (precisely to prevent parties from using primaries to escape the quota requirement; see Zetterberg, chapter 11 in this volume for more on how parties did this in Mexico).[4]

At the municipal level, electoral rules are based on open-list proportional representation. Until 2004, mayoral and council elections were fused, and between 1992 (when municipal elections were democratized) and 2004, various mechanisms for electing mayors were implemented. Initially, the mayor would be the candidate with the greatest share of the vote (from the winning list) as long as that candidate had won at least 35% of the vote. If no candidate met the criteria, then councilors would select the mayor. The large number of parties competing made it unlikely that any candidate would pass the 35% threshold, with the effect that mayors were usually chosen by the municipal council. The rules were reformed a number of times (for example, lowering the threshold), but it was not until 2002 that a reform separated mayoral and council elections such that mayors would be directly elected on a separate ballot. The fact that women are far more likely to win election to a council seat rather than a mayoral post indicates the greater barriers women face in accessing elected office at the executive level (Hinojosa and Franceschet 2012).

In 2006, however, Michelle Bachelet overcame the gender barrier to win executive office at the national level (Ríos Tobar 2008; Thomas 2011a). And in 2013, the second round of presidential election was fought between two women, Bachelet (for the *Nueva Mayoría*) and Evelyn Matthei (for the *Alianza*).[5] According to

4. "Fin al binominal: el ardua y extensa session despachan nueva composición del Congreso y sistema electoral proporcional," *Senado, República de Chile*. http://www.senado.cl/fin-al-binominal-en-ardua-y-extensa-sesion-despachan-nueva-composicion-del-congreso-y-sistema-electoral-proporcional/prontus_senado/2015-01-13/101536.html, Accessed March 3, 2015.

5. For presidential elections, winners must receive more than 50% of the vote. If that does not occur, the two candidates with the greatest share of votes proceed to a second round of voting. Since the transition to democracy, all presidential elections have required two rounds of voting.

Reyes-Housholder and Thomas (chapter 2, this volume), Latin American executives are the most masculinized of political offices, posing significant hurdles to female candidates. How and why did Bachelet succeed? For election to national executive office, institutional factors are far less important than political factors. Indeed, Bachelet's historic election in 2006 suggests that political crises can create opportunities for female presidential candidates. Bachelet's success is clearly linked to Chile's unique "crisis" of representation, understood as growing public dissatisfaction with the status quo and with political parties. Bachelet was selected as the *Concertación's* candidate in 2005 even though she was not the favored candidate of the coalition leaders. Although she had served in former President Ricardo Lagos's cabinet, first as health minister and later as defense minister, she was perceived as outside of the parties' core elite whose members had rotated through various elected and appointed offices since the return of democracy. And that was precisely why she was so popular with ordinary Chileans.

After fifteen years in power, the *Concertación* was increasingly perceived as elitist, in large part because the norms and practices established within the coalition to maintain unity and avoid instability fed beliefs that important decisions were taken behind the scenes, and that the same group of individuals circulated through arenas of power (Siavelis 2014). In the lead up to the 2005 elections, public opinion polls consistently ranked Michelle Bachelet and Soledad Alvear (also a cabinet minister) as the most popular members of President Lagos' government. Sensing the need for political renovation, Lagos himself endorsed the idea that the coalition ought to select a female presidential candidate. According to Lagos, "the greatest indication of change would be to have the first female president in the country" (quoted in Franceschet 2005, 2).

In the end, a primary to select the candidate was not even needed, because the only other candidate (Soledad Alvear) withdrew from the competition, leaving Bachelet as the sole candidate. Her consistently high rankings in public opinion polls led coalition elites to support her, leading to comments that Bachelet was the "citizens' candidate" (Franceschet and Thomas 2010). But there were other factors that contributed to her popularity, too. The political and social context for the 2005 elections was one in which Bachelet's gender was actually an advantage. The main issues that concerned voters were precisely those on which women were perceived to be more competent: social welfare, education, and inequality. Issues that would give male candidates an edge, like crime or insecurity, were not ranked as primary concerns among voters. Chile's economy had performed relatively well since the return of democracy, but there were growing concerns that the fruits of economic growth were disproportionately distributed, leading to a growing gap between the wealthy and the poor. Bachelet's campaign perfectly captured these sentiments. She spoke about political renovation, social justice, and more citizen input into decision making (Franceschet and Thomas 2010; Thomas 2011a). Her campaign promises clearly resonated with women: for the first time in Chilean history, the gender gap disappeared. In all previous elections, more women than men favored candidates from the right. In 2005 (and in the 2006 run off) Bachelet polled equally well among women, and in fact, more women supported Bachelet than the conservative candidate, Joaquín Lavín, from the Independent Democratic Union (Morales 2008).

Women in appointed office

President Bachelet's electoral success notwithstanding, women have actually fared better in accessing appointed posts in the executive branch than elected posts. The first post-transition cabinet of Patricio Aylwin contained just one woman, Soledad Alvear, as the director of the National Women's Service. But the percentage of women in cabinets has steadily grown since then, reaching 50% after Bachelet's first election in 2006, but dropping below 40% in the subsequent governments (see Table 8.3). Women's presence in cabinets has grown for a few reasons. First, women in the parties of the *Concertación* were frustrated by men's dominance in politics, and in 2000, after the election of Ricardo Lagos, they lobbied him to appoint more women. He responded to their efforts, naming a record number of women to his initial cabinet (five women in a sixteen-member cabinet).

Second, unlike candidacies for elected office, which are decided through a process of complex coalition bargaining, cabinet appointments are decided by a single selector: the president. Although presidents are constrained by a host of informal rules, namely the practice of distributing cabinet posts proportionally across the coalition parties, presidents do not actually negotiate ministerial selection. Instead, party leaders submit lists of recommendations to the president, often in person. But the president does not always follow the parties' recommendations. President Bachelet is reported to have followed the informal rule of proportional distribution while not necessarily appointing people recommended by the parties (Franceschet and Thomas 2015). Most important, when soliciting recommendations from the parties, Bachelet made it clear that she wanted the parties to include women's names.

Third, inclusionary norms have gained popularity, particularly as concerns grew about voter apathy and citizen disengagement. Once again, this shows how perceptions of a crisis of representation create opportunities for women to enter politics. Political pundits and scholars were linking public disaffection to the elitist nature of Chilean politics, particularly electoral rules and executive appointment practices that undermined turnover and political renovation. There was growing frustration that the same circle of individuals in the *Concertación* was moving from congress to cabinet (and vice-versa) and these individuals were remarkably homogenous. For example, they all came from a small handful of private elite schools. Bachelet's

Table 8.3 WOMEN'S CABINET REPRESENTATION* (1990–2014)

President	Aylwin (1990)	Frei (1994)	Lagos (2000)	Bachelet (2006)	Piñera (2010)	Bachelet (2014)
Total Ministers	18	19	16	20	22	23
Men	17	16	11	10	15	14
Women	1	3	5	10	7	9
% Male	94.4	84.2	68.7	50	68.2	60.9
% Female	5.5	15.8	31.3	50	31.8	39.1

*These figures reflect women's inclusion in *initial* cabinets. The only exception is President Aylwin's cabinet, where the initial cabinet had no women at all, but when Sernam was created (in 1991), its director had cabinet rank. The first director was Soledad Alvear.

2005 presidential campaign capitalized on these sentiments, and she promised that in her cabinet *"nadie se va a repitir el plato"* (no second helpings). This meant that she would appoint new people rather than those who had already served in past cabinets. She also committed herself to gender parity in cabinet, a promise that she achieved with her first cabinet. Although the conservative government of Sebastián Piñera, elected in 2010, did not continue with the parity standard, he nonetheless appointed women to more than 30% of portfolios. Piñera's appointments support Taylor-Robinson and Gleitz's argument that the development of norms about women's inclusion in cabinets makes it difficult for presidents not to meet expectations (chapter 3, this volume). In Chile, every initial cabinet since 2000 has included more than 30% women, indicating that a norm of gender inclusion (if not gender parity) is now well entrenched.

In sum, patterns of women's descriptive representation in Chile show that institutional factors, namely, formal and informal rules, matter more than cultural or socioeconomic factors (as argued in the introduction to this volume). Specifically, Chile's electoral rules produced informal practices, like coalition bargaining among an informal and closed network of political elites over nominations, which disadvantaged women. The new electoral law includes a mandatory quota and should, hopefully, eliminate these barriers. Women have fared better in appointed posts precisely because a norm about gender inclusion emerged and grew even stronger with the election of a female president. In the next section, I explore some of the broader policy consequences of women's presence in elected office.

THE CONSEQUENCES OF WOMEN'S DESCRIPTIVE REPRESENTATION: THE LINK BETWEEN PRESENCE AND POLICY

Women's presence in public office is consequential for a number of reasons. Elected women may pursue legislative and policy changes that promote gender equality. Some elected (or appointed) women enjoy their own appointment powers and can use that authority to further improve women's descriptive representation. Finally, women's presence can produce broader social changes such as reduced negative stereotypes about women, or increased women's political engagement. To what extent have such consequences occurred in Chile? Exploring the policy consequences of women's presence requires some discussion of the institutional context, including both the formal authorities and competencies enjoyed by each branch of government as well as the informal norms and practices that have developed in response to the political and institutional context.

Formal rules

Chile's constitution is often described as presidentialist, concentrating significant powers in the executive branch (Shugart and Carey 1992; Siavelis 2000). This means that women elected to the presidency, compared to those elected to congress, have greater opportunities to affect policy outcomes. Although both branches of government enjoy the formal right to introduce legislation, there are restrictions on the type of bills that members of congress may introduce, and the executive enjoys vast agenda-setting powers. Congress may not introduce bills that involve spending or that affect the budget, and the executive may declare "urgencies" that have the effect of fast tracking committee and full chamber discussion of a bill. The executive branch also possesses far greater resources in the legislative process, namely, access to congressional committees and greater human and technical resources. Liesl Haas's (2010) in-depth study of legislative policymaking on women's rights demonstrates the consequences of Chile's institutional design: Bills introduced by the executive branch are much more likely to succeed than bills introduced by members of congress.[6] However, if feminist legislators succeed in gaining executive support for their initiatives, their bills may also succeed. Haas writes that, "In addition to its greater formal powers, [the executive] has more resources and better technical assistance to write and lobby for bills. The superior staff available to the executive means that in the case of a bill that proposes sweeping legal reform, the executive is often able to write a more complete and technically more coherent bill" (2010, 58).

Informal rules

The vast powers that Chile's constitution concentrates in the executive branch are tempered in practice by a series of informal rules developed initially to maintain coalition unity and to reduce potential conflict that could threaten democratic stability. Peter Siavelis (2006) identifies the norm of "democracy by agreement," which refers to the practice of negotiating key policy issues before they are formally introduced in the legislative process. These negotiations would take place among the parties of the governing coalition but in some cases, would also occur between government and opposition. If the executive could not secure at least some support from the opposition, then the policy issue would be avoided. Siavelis explains, "reaching a pre-legislative *acuerdo* is an integral part of the Chilean informal political game, with consequences for violation" (2006, 50). This norm was particularly strong in the first decade or so following the transition to democracy, but appears to be weakening in recent years. Initially, fears of provoking instability or conflict produced fairly timid behavior among politicians, particularly on issues considered controversial. Of course, this meant that many issues related to women's rights—like abortion, birth control, and domestic violence—were either ignored entirely by the executive or addressed in a way that was tolerable to conservatives (in the governing coalition and the opposition).

How have these formal and informal rules shaped the policy impact of women's presence in politics? Because of the greater legislative resources of the executive branch relative to congress, women's policy interests have been pursued more effectively by Sernam than by elected women in congress. Until 2015, Sernam was housed within the Ministry of Planning, although its director had ministerial status. But in 2015, Bachelet created a Ministry of Women (*Ministerio de la Mujer*), which presumably wields more power within the state than did Sernam. Yet, even

---

6. Ten out of eleven executive bills were passed into law compared to nine out of fifty-three introduced by congress between 1990 and 2009, according to Haas' study (2010, 185–191).

though Sernam was not a stand-alone ministry, it was consistently well resourced, especially compared to women's policy agencies in neighboring countries, and its policymaking capacities grew over the years. Women's rights legislation was pursued through Sernam's well-staffed legal reform department, although for issues that were particularly controversial, like divorce and domestic violence, feminists were not always happy with the results (see Haas 2010). Sernam's directors rarely had ties to the women's movement, and in the early years of Chile's new democracy, Sernam was led by Christian Democrats, who took a fairly conservative view of women's rights. When Ricardo Lagos, a Socialist, became president in 2000, he appointed Adriana Delpiano, also a Socialist, to head Sernam. Under Delpiano's tenure, organizational changes occurred that increased Sernam's power in the state. More important, upon assuming the presidency, Bachelet increased Sernam's budget by 30%, with most of that increase earmarked for programs to address violence against women.

Despite having few resources and fewer opportunities for legislative success, many women elected to congress have nonetheless been tireless advocates for women's rights and equality. This is clear evidence that women's presence makes a difference in shaping policy agendas, even if their policy initiatives do not ultimately succeed (Franceschet and Piscopo 2008). Haas's study identifies fifty-three bills introduced by members of congress, and although she does not identify the sex of the bills' authors, my interviews with legislators between 1999 and 2008 indicate that women, rather than their male peers, have been the most active on women's policy issues. Female deputies have pursued legislation addressing domestic violence, reproductive rights, workplace equality, sexual harassment, and electoral quotas. Yet the informal rules of politics, particularly the norm of consensus seeking, have limited the scope of women's actions. A female legislator from the *Concertación* explained that legislators exercise quite a bit of self-censorship in an effort to avoid conflict in the coalition. She said that her colleagues take care "not to harm the political relationship" that exists among the parties of the coalition, and this was particularly true of issues like abortion that would provoke profound disagreement.[7]

Until the election of Chile's first female president, Michelle Bachelet, presidents, too, tended to avoid women's rights policies that might generate conflict. The domestic violence law adopted in 1994 prioritized family unity over women's safety, and family law reforms made the default marital property regime one in which husbands controlled marital property, unless couples chose otherwise at the time of their marriage (Htun 2003; Macaulay 2005). Bachelet, in contrast, has been far more willing than her predecessors to use executive power to challenge gender inequality (Franceschet 2010b; Stevenson 2012). During her first administration (2006–2010), Bachelet pursued a number of reforms that advanced women's rights and equality (Staab 2017). In some cases, like gender quotas, she did not initially succeed, but in other areas, like contraception and pensions, she got laws passed in congress that will have far-reaching consequences for women's lives.

Bachelet's policy achievements in the area of women's rights include pension reform, strengthening policy responses on domestic violence, expanding access to childcare, and universal access to emergency contraception (Waylen 2016). A pension reform introduced in 2006 provides a basic retirement income for poor women

---

7. Interview with female legislator from the Socialist party, November 21, 2006, Valparaíso, Chile.

who remained outside of the formal economy along with a bonus for each child born alive. Another policy expands access to public childcare and nursery schools, creating guaranteed spaces for poor women. The goal here is to increase women's ability to participate in the paid labor force, and to improve Chile's relatively low proportion of women in the workforce (Staab 2017). In the area of domestic violence, Bachelet expanded Sernam's budget by 30% in 2006, with the extra funds going to the creation of a network of government-funded refuges for women fleeing violence. Even more funding for shelters, victims' service centers, and public awareness campaigns were announced in 2008 (Franceschet 2010b).

Policy reforms in the area of pensions, childcare, and domestic violence were all popular and widely supported. But Bachelet demonstrated her willingness to pursue women's rights even when it generated opposition and controversy. In her first year in office, she took on religious conservatives in a battle to make emergency contraception (EC) available in public clinics. It is important to note that EC was already legally available for purchase in pharmacies. Bachelet wanted to make sure it would be available to those who could not afford to purchase it. Making it available (for free) to young women was also a way to combat Chile's remarkably high rates of teen pregnancy. Initially, Bachelet had her health minister promulgate a ministerial decree to require public clinics to distribute EC to anyone over fourteen that requested it. Conservatives pushed back, and eventually it was decided that the health minister did not have the authority to pursue this policy, leading Bachelet to issue a presidential decree of the same policy. This move provoked strong opposition from the right. Conservative mayors publicly refused to comply, ordering public clinics (which fall under municipal jurisdiction) to ignore the presidential decree. As such, the availability of emergency contraception depended on where one lived. Conservative legislators then petitioned the Constitutional Tribunal, which ultimately ruled that the policy violated the protection of life entrenched in Chile's constitution. Yet Bachelet persisted, introducing a new bill on fertility that included public access to all forms of contraception. She then used her executive prerogatives to fast track the bill through the legislative process, and it became law in January 2010 (Franceschet and Piscopo 2013).

The first year of Bachelet's second term provides further evidence of the difference that presidents can make. Although she pursued a gender quota law in her first term, the initiative did not have much support in congress and ultimately failed. In her second term, Bachelet incorporated a gender quota into the broader electoral reform bill that was approved by congress in January 2015. In her first term, Bachelet sidestepped the more controversial issue of abortion, and instead focused on reducing unwanted pregnancy by making emergency contraception more widely available. But in her second term, Bachelet took the historic step of introducing a bill to decriminalize abortion in three instances: when the fetus is not viable, when the mother's life is at risk, and when the pregnancy is the result of rape (Álvarez 2015). The move is historic because since the return of democracy, all of the legislative initiatives to liberalize Chile's strict abortion law were introduced by legislators, with no support of any kind from the executive. Bachelet's initiative was the first to come from the executive branch. The bill finally succeeded more than two years after being introduced, winning congressional approval in early August 2017, and a favorable ruling by the constitutional court later that month.

Finally, in March 2015, Sernam was replaced by the Ministry of Women, a goal that has long been promoted by feminists inside and outside the state. Because Sernam was not a ministry in its own right, but housed within another ministry, it could not implement programs on its own, but it could design policies and programs that would be put in place by other departments. But ministries and departments rarely give sufficient priority to issues that originate elsewhere and are not their own. Having a ministry for women should make policy implementation more effective. Symbolically, it demonstrates that gender equality and women's rights is a high priority for the state.

In an executive-dominated system like Chile's, the policy impact of a female president who is committed to gender equality cannot be overstated. Bachelet has succeeded in changing laws and policies in a host of areas that challenge women's inequality. But her very presence also emboldened legislators to take up women's issues. A sizable jump in legislative activity in the area of gender equality and women's issues occurred after her election in 2006. In the sixteen-year period between 1990 and 2005, a total of 169 bills were introduced to congress by either legislators or the executive in the area of gender equality and women's rights. Yet in the four years that Bachelet was president, 167 such bills were introduced. In fact, in 2007, gender equality and women's issue bills made up 20.6% of all bills introduced by members of congress (PNUD 2010, 174).

Beyond policy changes, presidents can have an impact by using their vast appointment powers to bring more women into arenas of power and decision making. This power was evident in Bachelet's highly visible appointment of a parity cabinet in 2006. Less attention was paid to Bachelet's tendency to appoint women in important, but less high profile, posts throughout the state. According to one of her former female ministers, people have been too preoccupied with Bachelet's failure to maintain strict parity (50-50) in her cabinet throughout her presidential term and insufficiently aware of just how many important positions elsewhere were given to women: "She opened doors [to women] in areas that would have been unthinkable in other moments."[8] The examples she gave included the Supreme Court, the defense council of the state, and the armed forces.

In sum, the institutional rules in Chile give the executive more resources to advance women's policy interests, making the president a more consequential actor than legislators for advancing women's rights. Yet there is also evidence that women's presence in legislatures matters. Women in congress are more likely than men to work on gender issues, even if they face difficulty in getting their policy initiatives passed.

CONTINUED CHALLENGES TO WOMEN'S EQUALITY IN POLITICS AND FUTURE QUESTIONS FOR RESEARCH

Women have made enormous progress since the return of democracy. Their presence is growing in all political arenas, albeit far too slowly, especially when compared to other countries in the region. Although the first few *Concertación* governments

8. Interview with former minister, August 11, 2014, Santiago, Chile.

were somewhat timid in addressing gender inequality, largely due to well-entrenched norms of conflict avoidance and consensus seeking, Bachelet's two governments have pushed back against conservative objections to policies that challenge traditional gender roles. Still, notable challenges remain. Probably the biggest challenge is for women to break the masculine dominance of elite party networks. Even if the quota law succeeds in compelling political parties to select more women as candidates, and even if more women are elected to congress, much of the power in Chilean politics remains in the hands of elites within the parties' inner circles.

Political parties play important gatekeeping roles and, as Morgan and Hinojosa note in chapter 5 of this volume, have often served as obstacles to women's equal representation. In Chile, with a few exceptions, women have rarely served as president of any of the major parties. In 2009, a man led each of Chile's five largest parties, and women comprised between 8% and 22% of party executives.[9] But even if women do occupy some of the top posts, like vice president or general secretary, the real power in political parties does not necessarily reside in those formal offices. Instead, the gatekeeping role that parties perform, such as selecting candidates for popular elections and preparing lists of recommendations for appointed posts in the executive, do not always occur through formal processes directed by individuals holding formal offices.[10] A former president of one of the parties of the *Concertación*, when discussing procedures for preparing lists of names for cabinet posts said, "there are some formal processes that carry less weight and others that are informal and carry more weight." Women's absence from elite party networks has important consequences for women's representation: they lack presence in those arenas where candidacies are determined and where suggestions for appointed office emerge. That is why it was so important that Bachelet insisted that parties include women's names on their lists of recommendations for appointed posts.

While elite party networks serve as an obstacle to women's access to and influence within political institutions, the overwhelming dominance of party elites in Chilean politics (*partidocracia*) has led to widespread dissatisfaction with parties and with the status quo in politics more generally. Parties remain strong and relatively stable, but there are signs of a crisis of representation in Chile, which, in turn, has created opportunities for women. Bachelet's success in 2006 and 2013 and congressional and public support for a gender quota are evidence of how public frustration with elite dominance in politics can create opportunities for women.

There are two gaps in existing research on women's representation in Chile that ought to be addressed in future research. First, perhaps because of Chile's status as a highly centralized political system, there has not been much research on the consequences of women's presence in local politics. While mayors have little financial and policy autonomy, there has been a considerable degree of decentralization, with local governments delivering a number of key services, particularly in the health sector. More research is needed on women's roles in municipal governments and whether their presence, particularly as mayors, can make a difference. A second area where more research is needed is on the broader societal consequences of women's

9. "Existencia de legislación de cuotas o paridad." GEPPAL, http://www.iadb.org/es/investiga-cion-y-datos/geppal/detalles-del-pais,17693.html?country=CHL.

10. Interviews with former party presidents, August 6, 2014 and August 18, 2014, Santiago, Chile.

presence in public office. Unlike other Latin American countries where increases in women's congressional presence have motivated research into whether women's presence changes public opinion or political behavior, Chile's political institutions have remained male-dominated, and hence, this kind of research has not been carried out. If the new quota law does indeed produce a jump in the number of women elected, perhaps Chile will be a good case study for testing the link between women's presence in congress and societal attitudes and political engagement.

9

Parity without Equality

Women's Political Representation in Costa Rica

JENNIFER M. PISCOPO ■

fragmented party system

Costa Rica ranks among Latin America's leaders in terms of women's political representation. Since 2002, women have held between 30 and 40% of elected posts at
the national and subnational level (IPU 2017; Zamora Chavarría 2012). Their presence in the cabinet and the presidency also has increased. This chapter attributes
this success to the nation's strong track record in applying affirmative action, beginning in the 1990s. The 2009 parity regime, which supplanted the 1996 quota law,
requires that parties must have 50% women on their candidate slates for *all* elected
offices; these include the national assembly and legislative and executive offices at
the subnational level. Quotas and then parity passed due to the lobbying efforts
of female party members and female legislators. A close analysis of this process
reveals a novel view of the causes and consequences of women's representation.
Rather than seeing causes and consequences as separate, I argue that they are intertwined and mutually reinforcing: as women ascend to positions of political power,
they insist upon statutes and regulations that would guarantee more women access
to this power.

The intertwining of the causes and consequences of women's representation
remains even as challenges persist. Costa Rica boasts the region's longest uninter-
rupted democracy. This chapter takes advantage of the opportunity to study how
women's representation evolved when democracy was *not* punctuated by authoritarian rule. This long view illuminates how Costa Rica's rates of women's representation
outpaced the Latin American average early on, though large advances only appeared
with the adoption of gender quotas in the 1990s. Yet recent structural changes in
Costa Rican politics have minimized quotas' effects. The entrance of more parties
means that more competitors divide the electoral spoils: since women are ranked
lower on party lists, their electoral chances fall relative to men once their party

I am grateful to Malena Ernani for her outstanding research assistance in preparing this chapter.
I also thank Leslie Schwindt-Bayer, the contributors to this volume, and Diana Z. O'Brien for
their helpful comments on earlier drafts.

begins losing seats. This analysis reveals that, while some challenges, such as gender bias in women's access to the best or more prestigious positions, are long-standing, others, such as party system fragmentation, are more recent.

In using historic and contemporary data to track women's representation, I offer the most in-depth portrait of gender and politics in Costa Rica to date. This chapter traces changing patterns in women's access to power before and after quotas' adoption and party system fragmentation. The crisis of representation has had gendered effects in not just the legislative branch, but the executive branch: Laura Chinchilla, the nation's first female president, endured a governability crisis that irreparably damaged her legacy. These challenges notwithstanding, I argue that Costa Rica's parity regime and the broader statutory protections for women's rights remain among the most progressive in the region.

ELECTIONS, REPRESENTATION, AND POLITICS IN COSTA RICA

Costa Rica is a small, unitary country of 4.8 million people.[1] The national government consists of a 57-member unicameral assembly, a president, and two vice-presidents. Legislators and executives are elected concurrently for four-year terms. Immediate reelection is prohibited. Legislators, known as *diputados* (deputies), are selected via closed-list proportional representation (PR) at the provincial level. The country's seven provinces play no further role, as the 1998 Municipal Code eliminated the provincial level of government.

Subnational governments with popularly elected officials exist at the *cantonal* (municipal) level and sub-*cantonal* (district) level. Costa Rica's 81 *cantones* have *alcaldes* (mayors) and municipal councilors seated on municipal councils. Below the *cantone*, 473 districts have *síndicos* (district chiefs) and district councils composed of four councilors plus the *síndico*.[2] Under the 1970 Municipal Code, municipal councilors and district chiefs were chosen via popular election, but mayors and district councilors were appointed. The 1998 Municipal Code provided for the direct election of all subnational offices beginning in 2002. Electoral decentralization notwithstanding, Costa Rica remains administratively and fiscally centralized. Cantons have authority over municipal development; they can collect additional taxes and establish budgets, and they can delegate functions to the districts, but the central government provides most financing and retains final say over policy. Political parties control nominations to all subnational offices, placing a premium on party service

1. Population data from World Bank, http://data.worldbank.org/indicator/SP.POP.TOTL (accessed 2 March 2015).

2. The number of districts changes over time. The 2010 elections involved 473 districts (TSE 2010). Additionally, Costa Rica has eight "small-scale municipalities" that, due to their geographical isolation, are neither full cantons nor separate districts (ICMA 2004, 5). These eight regions have popularly elected executives known as *intendentes* (akin to mayors) and popularly elected assemblies known as municipal-district councils.

and loyalty.[3] Legislators typically attain national office through prior party service and, following the 1998 reforms, through prior service in subnational posts.[4]

As will be shown below, Costa Rica's election of women to the district, cantonal, and national levels historically exceeded Latin America's regional average. The reasons for this exceptionalism can only be inferred indirectly. Costa Rica experienced a brief and relatively bloodless civil war in 1949, followed by a long period of political stability. Unlike neighboring El Salvador, Guatemala, Honduras, and Nicaragua, Costa Rica stayed democratic, economically successful, and free of armed conflict. Costa Ricans have expressed high levels of positive support for democracy and public trust since the 1950s (Lehoucq 2005; Seligson 2002). Women received the right to vote following the civil war, and their educational and occupational outcomes quickly rose to match those of the United States or Europe (Furlong and Riggs 1996, 636). By 1993, 75% of Costa Ricans believed a woman could be president (Furlong and Riggs 1996, 636–637). Political stability thus mixed with equality norms, creating a favorable environment for women's political participation: "The longer women have voted and been elected, the more experience they have gained and the more proficient they have become in winning seats and holding on to them" (Saint-Germain and Metoyer 2008, 87).

The 1949 constitution also contributed to political stability. Concurrent elections produced unified governments, and proportional representation combined with the 40% threshold for the presidency ensured leaders' opinions matched those of the median voter (Lehoucq 2005). Powers are distributed evenly across government branches, and autonomous agencies handle policymaking in contentious areas, such as pensions and healthcare (Lehoucq 2005). Political cooperation became further normalized as two parties emerged dominant by the 1980s: the left-leaning, social democratic *Partido Liberación Nacional* (National Liberation Party, or PLN), which dated back to the 1950s, and the right-leaning *Partido Unidad Social Cristiana* (National Social Christian Unity Party, or PUSC), whose precursor parties ran as *Unidad* in 1978 and formed the PUSC in 1986. Ideological labels notwithstanding, both parties operated as catch-all parties that drew support from multiclass constituencies (Clark 2001, 81–83). The parties' internal heterogeneity ensured their electoral dominance. To illustrate: the PLN and the PUSC together captured 98.6% of the popular vote in the 1990 presidential elections (United Nations 1991, 35). In the 1980s and in the early 1990s, the two parties governed through consensus and agreement (Rodríguez Echeverría 2006). Their pactmaking style was facilitated by their catch-all nature, responsiveness to public opinion, and delegation of policymaking authority to autonomous state agencies.

System stability began eroding in the mid-to-late 1990s (Booth 2007). The PLN and the PUSC, initially both supportive of neoliberal economic reforms, clashed once structural adjustment proved unsuccessful and unpopular, policymaking became less cooperative and more oppositional, and squabbling internal factions

3. Costa Rica's system of no immediate reelection has perverse effects on legislators' behavior. Presidents quickly become lame ducks, forcing career-minded deputies to coordinate their support not on the president, but on the party member they believe will become the next president (Wilson 1998).

4. Thank you to Michelle Taylor-Robinson for this point.

undercut party cohesion (Rodríguez Echeverría 2006). The 1998 elections marked a clear turning point: voters' dissatisfaction with economic progress, rising crime rates, and antisystemic attitudes led to historic levels of absenteeism as well as voter defection to minor or newer parties (Lehoucq 2005; Seligson 2002). In 1998 and in 2002, thirteen political parties contested the presidency, double the pre-1998 average (Wilson 1998; Wilson 2003). The PUSC won the executive both times, but with no legislative majority. Third parties—such as the *Partido Acción Ciudadana* (Citizens' Action Party, or PAC) and the *Movimiento Libertario* (Libertarian Movement, or ML)—gained power in the national legislature. Facing divided government, both PUSC administrations struggled to overcome corruption scandals, opposition to neoliberalism, and legislative inactivity (Wilson 2007).

Subsequent elections produced neither stability nor prosperity. With the PUSC discredited, the presidency returned to the PLN in 2006 and 2010, but with runoffs required each time. The assembly remained divided. The PLN could not boost economic performance; and public trust eroded even further (Frajman 2014; Wilson and Rodríguez-Cordero 2011). In the 2014 elections, the PAC, the ML, and another third party, the *Frente Amplio* (Broad Front, or FA), gained even more ground in the legislature. The PLN was trounced, just as the PUSC had been eight years earlier: the leftist PAC ended the two-party system by capturing the presidency with an overwhelming 80% of the second-round vote. Yet like its predecessors, the PAC would enter office without a majority in the assembly (Frajman 2014).

Table 9.1 shows the changing seat share in the national assembly. In 1998, the PLN and the PUSC together captured 50 of the 57 seats; by 2014, their combined dominance had fallen to 26 seats. No party has controlled the legislative assembly since 1998. These changes to the political and party system have gendered implications. On the one hand, the ascendancy of new parties signals disillusion with the current system of representation. The traditional parties' lack of ideological differentiation may have generated stability in an earlier era, but such heterogeneity ultimately leads to party system collapse (Morgan 2011). Representational crises may create an opening for female candidates, who are often associated with political renewal (Funk, Hinojosa, and Piscopo 2018; also highlighted by Schwindt-Bayer, chapter 1 and Reyes-Housholder and Thomas, chapter 2, this volume). On the other hand,

Table 9.1 PARTY SYSTEM FRAGMENTATION IN COSTA RICA (NUMBER OF SEATS WON IN THE NATIONAL ASSEMBLY, BY PARTY)

Party	Election				
	1998	2002	2006	2010	2014
PLN	23	17	25	23	18
PUSC	27	19	5	6	8
PAC	—	14	17	11	13
ML	1	6	6	9	4
FA	—		—	1	9
other	6	1	4	7	5
Total	57	57	57	57	57

SOURCES: Frajman (2014); Wilson (1998, 2003, 2007); Wilson and Rodríguez-Cordero (2011)

party system change, divided government, and legislative immobilism heightens inter- and intraparty competition. Male elites guard nominations more jealously when their party faces more electoral competition (Piscopo 2016b). In Costa Rica, as citizens became increasingly disenchanted with the traditional parties, leaders began adopting quota laws and courting female voters (Wilson 1998). At the same time, party magnitude—the number of seats a party wins per district—reduced women's probability of entering the legislature. The next sections examine how women's access to government evolved before and after this crisis of representation.

LOCAL SUCCESS, NATIONAL BARRIERS: ELECTING WOMEN BEFORE SYSTEM COLLAPSE

Costa Rica's electoral system presents a fair amount of complexity, especially at the subnational level. The 1998 Municipal Code provided for popular election of all subnational offices, with executives chosen from single-member plurality districts and legislators via closed-list proportional representation. Elections use a *propietario-suplente* candidate pairing for executive and legislative posts at the cantonal and district level.[5] This formula pairs a "primary" candidate (the *propietario*) with a "substitute" candidate (the *suplente*). Primary-substitute pairs are elected as units (hence the ability to speak of *alcaldes* and *síndicos* as occupying single-member districts). Generally, the substitutes have no independent authority, and only serve if the primary candidate resigns or becomes temporarily indisposed due to illness, travel, or other circumstance. For *alcaldes*, however, the substitutes served as vice-mayors in 2002 and 2006; in 2010, cantons began electing their executives via a four-name single ticket, consisting of one mayor and his or her substitute, and two vice-mayors without substitutes.

The *suplente* position offers parties a significant number of symbolic candidacies. This institutional design allows parties to cultivate support among female voters and members—without devolving actual policy authority. Table 9.2 shows the proportion of women elected at the subnational level before the quota law, when only municipal councilors and *síndicos* were popularly elected. The data begin in 1986, the earliest year available. Although the proportion of women elected increased across the three election periods, women clearly acceded to the substitute position more than the primary position. For example, women comprised 18.3% of *all* municipal councilors in 1994, but 22% of substitutes compared to 14.5% of titleholders. Nonetheless, these figures are much higher than the regional average between 1990 and 2000, which was 5% (Htun and Piscopo 2014). Women were especially successful at the district level, comprising 12.4% of primary *síndicas* in 1990 and 18.2% in 1994. Costa Rica thus outpaced Latin America early on.

During this period, women enjoyed high levels of participation in the PLN and PUSC, the dominant parties of the time. Women comprised 30% and 25% of national delegates to the PLN's and the PUSC's assemblies, respectively, and both parties had women's wings that organized women's participation at the national, cantonal, and district levels (United Nations 1991, 35–36).[6] These structures treated female

---

5. *Suplentes* do not accompany the eight *intendentes* chosen for the small-scale municipalities.

6. Matland and Taylor report a lower figure for women's presence in the PUSC's 1990 party assembly: 19.4% (1997, 189).

Table 9.2 WOMEN ELECTED AT THE SUBNATIONAL LEVEL, 1986–1994 (COUNT IN PARENTHESES INDICATES TOTAL NUMBER OF WOMEN ELECTED)

	Municipal Councilors (*Regidoras*)			District Chiefs (*Síndicas*)		
	All	**Primary**	**Substitute**	**All**	**Primary**	**Substitute**
1986	13.1% (114)	5.5% (24)	20.6% (90)	10.5% (88)	8.1% (34)	12.9% (54)
1990	14.1% (148)	12.0% (63)	16.2% (85)	13.8% (117)	12.4% (53)	15.1% (64)
1994	18.3% (199)	14.5% (79)	22.0% (120)	21.4% (183)	18.2% (78)	24.5% (105)

SOURCE: Zamora Chavarría (2012).

members as second-class citizens, relegating them to auxiliary roles such as door-to-door campaigning, organizing events (including preparing decorations, food, and drink), and implementing local government policies related to childcare and family health (Bustamante de Rivera 1995; Moreno 1995; Saint-Germain 1993; Zúñiga Quirós 1999). Nonetheless, these organizations may have increased women's political participation in cantons and districts. Women constituted 50% of party members at the district level by the 1990s (Moreno 1995, 115), and local-level women's wings drew in activists from the independent women's movement (Anonymous 2002. Author interview in San José, Costa Rica, January 24).

The situation at the national level appeared far less auspicious, confirming Escobar-Lemmon and Funk's findings (chapter 6, this volume) that women do not necessarily move steadily from local politics into national politics. Table 9.3 reports women's share of the national assembly over time. In 1953—the first election in which Costa Rican women exercised their political rights—the three women elected belonged to the PLN (García 1995). This pattern continued, as the PLN elected 22 female deputies between 1974 and 1994, compared to the PUSC, which elected 13. However, women comprised roughly 10% of both the PLN's and the PUSC's legislative delegations between 1974 and 1994.[7] These figures indicate that the PLN elects more women because it holds more overall seats in the assembly, not because it makes particular efforts to recruit women (Matland and Taylor 1997). Further, women's overall presence in the assembly remained low: women won 4 or 5 seats during elections between 1970 and 1982, 7 of 57 seats in the 1986 and 1990 elections, and 9 of 57 seats in the 1994 elections. These proportions—like those at the local level—were significantly above the Latin American average in the 1980s and the 1990s (Htun and Piscopo 2014). Yet these figures remained below the expectations of many educated, professional, and politically active women at the time (Bustamante de Rivera 1995; García 1995).

In the 1980s and early 1990s, party members and feminist activists perceived a clear bottleneck for women seeking to move from the local to the national level (Anonymous 2002. Author interview in San José, Costa Rica, January 24; Anonymous 2002. Author interview in San José, Costa Rica, January 24; Moreno

7. Data from the Costa Rican National Assembly, "Histórico de Diptuadas y Diputados por Fracción": http://www.asamblea.go.cr/Centro_de_informacion/Consultas_SIL/Pginas/Hist%C3%B3rico%20de%20diputadas%20y%20diputados%20por%20fracci%C3%B3n.aspx (accessed March 12, 2015). Data on the PUSC begins in 1978, when its precursor parties ran in an electoral alliance for the first time.

Table 9.3 WOMEN ELECTED TO THE NATIONAL ASSEMBLY,
1953–1994

| | | Women Nominated to |
Election	Women Elected	Winnable Seats
1953	6.7% (3 of 45)	
1958	3.5% (2 of 57)	
1962	1.8% (1 of 57)	
1966	5.3% (3 of 57)	
1970	7.0% (4 of 57)	
1974	7.0% (4 of 57)*	5.8% (4 of 69)
1978	8.8% (5 of 57)	8.6% (6 of 70)
1982	7.0% (4 of 57)	9.1% (6 of 66)
1986	12.3% (7 of 57)	14.5% (10 of 69)
1990	12.3% (7 of 57)	10.8% (7 of 65)
1994	15.8% (9 of 57)	14.7% (10 of 68)

(handwritten annotation: "Very low rep- resentation")

(handwritten annotation: "not in electable positions")

* Matland and Taylor report 3 women elected in 1974, but García
Quesada (2011, 30) and Zamora Chavarría (2012) report 4 women
elected.

SOURCE: García Quesada (2011), 1953–1970; Matland and Taylor
(1997), 1974–1994.

1995). Mobilization in the women's wings and at the subnational level relied on
traditional gender roles, reinforcing patriarchal norms within the parties. The
women's wing did not provide a pipeline to office, as women contesting national
assembly seats came from within the main party apparatus (Furlong and Riggs
1996, 637; Saint-Germain and Metoyer 2008, 189). The ornamental slots—the
nonelectable positions—on PR lists for the national assembly constituted a
ghetto for female candidates throughout the 1980s and 1990s (Anonymous 2002.
Author interview in San José, Costa Rica, January 24; Anonymous 2002. Author
interview in San José, Costa Rica, January 25). Indeed, as shown in Table 9.3,
women occupied just 5.8% of electable list positions in 1974, a proportion that
had increased to only 14.7% in 1994.[8] In both 1990 and 1994, only one woman
appeared in the top list position, and both times on a PUSC ballot (Alfaro
Redondo and Gómez Campos 2014, 6–7). Yet no overall pattern appears in the
PLN's versus the PUSC's likelihood to nominate women to winnable list positions. Neither the PLN nor the PUSC excelled at promoting women to choice
candidacies at the national level.

THE CRISIS OF REPRESENTATION: QUOTAS, PARITY, AND SYSTEM COLLAPSE

Women's inability to attain more than just symbolic or ornamental candidacies
compelled politically active women to seek solutions outside the political parties.

8. Data on list positions are not available prior to 1974.

Costa Rica adopted Latin America's second electoral quota law in 1996, five years after pathbreaking Argentina. The quota law passed at a moment when women held their highest number of seats in the assembly since democratization in 1953 (9 of 57). Several factors helped female deputies secure the quota law. First, the United Nations' world conferences on women, held between 1975 and 1995, drew national, regional, and global attention to women's underrepresentation in politics. Second, by the mid-1990s, the PLN and the PUSC faced eroding popular support. Costa Rican party leaders—like their counterparts elsewhere in Latin America—saw an electoral advantage in attracting women (Wilson 1998, 585).

Costa Rica's first-generation quota law, like initial quota statutes elsewhere in the region, contained more symbolism than substance (Piscopo 2015b). The 1996 electoral code imposed a 40% quota for all positions selected via popular election (except the president and the vice-presidents). However, the law did not specify where female candidates should be ranked on the PR lists used for legislative elections at the district, cantonal, and national levels. The law also failed to specify whether *suplente* candidates counted toward the quota. Further, the law imposed no sanctions on political parties for noncompliance.

Thus, as shown in Table 9.4, the 1998 elections yielded mixed results. Women gained only two additional seats in the national assembly: their numbers increased from 15.8% (9 seats) to 19.3% (11 seats). The quota appeared more effective at the subnational level, the last election held under the old municipal code. Women constituted 36.1% of the primary and substitute winners for municipal councilors, and 50.4% of primary and substitute winners for district chiefs. They won 33.3% of primary municipal council posts and 31.1% of primary district chief posts. These results continued the earlier trend wherein women attained better representation at the subnational level compared to the national level.

Yet women's election in 1998 fell universally short of 40%, prompting demands for stronger regulation. Mirroring a process that occurred throughout Latin America, female activists lobbied for additional rules that would enhance quotas' numerical effectiveness (Piscopo 2015b). In response, the TSE issued a 1999 decision that required parties to place female candidates in electable positions, as determined by each party's average results in the previous election.[9] The following year, the TSE added that the quota applied equally to primary and substitute candidacies.[10] These provisions governed women's election until 2009, when reforms to the electoral code raised the quota to parity with alternation (meaning that all candidate slates would alternate male candidates and female candidates down the list). The parity requirement applied to subnational elections beginning in 2010, and the national assembly beginning in 2014.

Table 9.4 shows that the TSE regulations, followed by parity, had notable but inconsistent effects. At the subnational level, affirmative action accompanied other institutional changes, including the direct election of mayors and district councilors beginning in 2002.[11] Women's representation in the municipal councils, the more

9. TSE resolution 1863/1999, September 23, 1999.

10. TSE resolution 804-E-2000, May 4, 2000. Noted by Zamora Chavarría (2009, 26).

11. The 2009 electoral reforms staggered subnational and national elections, which delayed cantonal and district elections from 2014 to 2016. Subnational officers elected in 2010 would serve a unique six-year term.

Table 9.4 WOMEN ELECTED UNDER QUOTAS AND PARITY, 1998–2014 (COUNT IN PARENTHESES INDICATES TOTAL NUMBER OF WOMEN ELECTED)

(handwritten annotation: "almost 40%")

	40% Quota			40% Quota (national) Parity (subnational)	Parity
	1998	2002	2006	2010	2014
Deputies	19.3% (11)	35.1% (20)	38.6% (22)	38.6% (22)	33.3% (19)
Municipal Councilors—all	36.1% (412)	50.1% (502)	43.4% (437)	42.8% (424)	—
Primary Councilors	33.8% (193)	46.3% (232)	40.8% (205)	38.6% (191)	—
Substitute Councilors	38.4% (219)	53.9% (270)	46.1% (232)	47.1% (233)	—
Mayors (*alcadesas*)		37.9% (92)	38.4% (93)	39.1% (95)	—
Primary Mayors		8.6% (7)	11.1% (9)	12.3% (10)	—
Secondary Mayors		52.5% (85)	52.2% (84)	52.5% (85)[1]	—
District Councilors—all		47.3% (1642)	49.0% (1777)	48.7% (1782)	—
Primary Councilors		47.8% (839)	46.7% (861)	48.2% (894)	—
Substitute Councilors		46.8% (803)	51.3% (916)	49.2% (888)	—
District Chiefs (*síndicas*)	50.4% (445)	51.7% (465)	51.8% (479)	49.7% (461)	—
Primary Chiefs	31.1% (138)	29.1% (132)	28.1% (132)	27.2% (128)	—
Secondary Chiefs	69.9% (307)	74.7% (333)	76.3% (347)	72.8% (333)	—

NOTE:

[1] In 2010, the substitute mayor position was replaced with a vice-mayor position; this figure refers to the female vice-mayors.

SOURCE: Zamora Chavarría (2012).

powerful of the two subnational branches, actually fell: women attained 46.3% of primary seats in 2002, 40.8% in 2006, and 38.6% in 2010. In the less powerful district councils, women's representation held steady well above 40%: women won 47.3% of primary council seats in 2002, 49.0% in 2006, and 48.7% in 2010. These figures far outpace the regional average of 21% (Escobar-Lemmon and Funk, chapter 6, this volume). At the same time, only the district councils approached the expectations set by the parity law. All parties complied with the requirement to nominate 50% women for the 2010 elections (TSE 2010), but women were clearly placed in winning districts more frequently for the district council elections. As Escobar-Lemmon and Funk (chapter 6, this volume) highlight for Latin America as a whole, the more powers an office gained under political decentralization, the less open to women.

Women's presence in subnational executives tells a similar story of exclusion from the best opportunities and higher posts. The number of female district chiefs elected actually decreased under quotas: whereas women held 31.1% of primary *síndica* posts in 1998, they won only 29.1% in 2002, 28.1% in 2006, and 27.2% in 2010. In the *cantones*, the outcomes proved even more disappointing. Women comprised nearly 40% of all mayors over these three elections, but their numbers as primary mayors increased marginally: women constituted 8.6% of *alcaldesas* in 2002, 11.1% in 2006, and 12.3% in 2010. These numbers are on par with the regional average of 12% (Escobar-Lemmon and Funk, chapter 6, this volume). Female mayors remained concentrated in the substitute posts, and women's access to primary executive posts remained well below parity. Overall, the use of a single-member plurality district to elect mayors and district chiefs gives parties the opportunity to violate the spirit, if not the letter, of the law: parties most likely run primary-male/female-substitute pairings in winning or competitive districts, and primary-female/male-substitute pairings in losing districts.

At the national level, affirmative action raised women's presence considerably, but without reaching or crossing the 40% threshold. Women's presence in the national assembly increased to 35.1% (20 seats) in 2002 and to 38.6% (22 seats) in 2006 and 2010. Left-leaning parties continued to elect more women than the PUSC, but again due to party magnitude rather than ideology: throughout the 2000s, the PUSC lost seats while the PLN held steady and the PAC gained (Picado León and Brenes Villalobos 2014, 399). Approximately 20 parties contested assembly seats over these three elections, resulting in scores of lists across the 7 districts—few of which placed women in the top position. Women headed just 21 lists in 2002 and 2006, and 14 lists in 2010 (Alfaro Redondo and Gómez Campos 2014, 6–7). Here, parties' tendency to exclude women from the choicest candidacies had extremely perverse effects, as parties were simultaneously becoming less likely to win multiple seats per province (Picado León and Brenes Villalobos 2014). Party system fragmentation, coupled with women's exclusion from the number one list position, explains why electoral results for the national assembly did not hit the quota target.

The negative effects stemming from citizens' disillusionment with the traditional political parties became even more evident in the 2014 national elections. Parity with alternation applied for the first time, but the proportion of female deputies elected fell to 33.3% (19 of 57 seats). Parties had named men to the first list positions nearly exclusively: out of approximately 100 lists contesting the assembly in 2014, women headed only 22, and largely in districts where parties had no chance of winning (Alfaro Redondo and Gómez Campos 2014, 6–7). The ordering of lists man-woman (rather than woman-man) meant that a party would need to win at least two seats per province to elect a woman. The results from San José, the capital district, prove illustrative. The province's 19 seats were won by 8 different parties, all of which ran lists headed by men. Only 3 of these 8 parties ultimately elected women (Picado León and Brenes Villalobos 2014, 407).

The broader crisis of representation thus reduced parity's effectiveness at the national level. Party system change—and the heightened competition that reserved the top seats for men—drove the proportion of women elected to disappointingly low levels. Costa Rica thus illustrates the broader regional trends in women's access to legislatures in Latin America, as described by Schwindt-Bayer and Alles (chapter 4, this volume). Quotas raise women's numeric representation considerably. Challenges to democratization, such as a rise in the effective number of parties, minimize quotas' effectiveness. Still, women's access to the legislature most likely remains higher with quotas than without.

WOMEN'S REPRESENTATION IN THE NATIONAL EXECUTIVE

The quota and parity laws that govern women's access to elected office have limited application to the national executive. Affirmative action does apply to the dual vice-presidency (discussed below), but cabinet posts and presidents are beyond the electoral code's reach. However, Costa Rica's quota and parity laws generated national-level discussions about the importance of women's access to political power, a dialogue that also influences women's recruitment and selection for executive office (Escobar-Lemmon and Taylor-Robinson 2005; Piscopo 2015b). Women's presence in the cabinet and the presidency is increasing, especially with the election of the first female president in 2010. Nonetheless, as with candidate nominations, women in the cabinet remain more likely to attain less prestigious posts.

The cabinet ←very important   Prestige low posts

Sources on female cabinet ministers in Costa Rica from the 1980s and 1990s differ in their exact estimations, but capture similar trends. Costa Rican women remain historically underrepresented in the cabinet. Women never held more than four ministerial posts in presidential administrations between 1953 and 1998, meaning that they constituted roughly zero to 20% of cabinet, depending on the administration (García Quesada 2003; United Nations 1991). Escobar-Lemmon and Taylor-Robinson report similarly low numbers: women comprised just 11.1% of all ministers (19 of 161) serving between 1980 and 2003 (2009, 688). Women also remained excluded from the most powerful cabinet posts (Escobar-Lemmon and Taylor-Robinson 2005, 2009; United Nations 1991). For instance, between 1978 and 1994, only two women were seated on what Costa Rica calls their "Security Council," which consists of the ministers of internal affairs, foreign affairs, justice, public security, and the presidency. Here, women held the posts of justice in the 1982–1986 and 1990–1994 administrations (United Nations 1991, 18).

More recent data confirms that these trends extend into the contemporary era. Table 9.5 presents cross-sectional data on presidents' initial cabinet appointments, including ministers with and without portfolios, for five administrations: Miguel

Table 9.5 FEMALE MINISTERS APPOINTED TO PRESIDENTS' INITIAL CABINETS

	1998–2002 Rodríguez PUSC	2002–2006 Pacheco PUSC	2006–2010 Árias PLN	2010–2014 Chinchilla PLN	2014–2018 Solís PAC
Female ministers–all	26.7% (4 of 15)	25% (4 of 16)	33.3% (5 of 15)	40.9% (9 of 22)	39.1% (8 of 21)
Female ministers–power posts	25% (1 of 5)	25% (1 of 5)	25% (1 of 5)	0% (0 of 4)[1]	25% (1 of 5)
Female ministers–social welfare posts	33.3% (2 of 6)	50% (3 of 6)	60% (3 of 5)[2]	50% (3 of 6)[3]	66.7% (4 of 6)

NOTES:

[1] Chinchilla did not appoint separate ministers of justice and public security.

[2] Árias did not appoint a minister of women.

[3] Chinchilla appointed a minister of social and family well-being, rather than a minister of women

SOURCE: Maria Escobar-Lemmon and Michelle-Taylor Robinson (1998, 2002, and 2006 administrations); Georgetown Political Database of the Americas (2010 administration, http://pdba.georgetown.edu/Executive/CostaRica/cabinet.html, accessed 2 March 2015), and for 2014–2018; CIA World Factbook (2014 administration, https://www.cia.gov/library/publications/world-leaders-1/CS.html, accessed 2 March 2015).

Ángel Rodríguez, PUSC (1998–2002); Abel Pacheco, PUSC (2002–2006); Oscar Árias Sánchez, PLN (2006–2010), Laura Chinchilla, PLN (2010–2014), and Luis Guillermo Solís, PAC (2014–2018).[12] The table reports numbers and percentages for all female ministers, and then examines just women occupying power posts (foreign affairs, finance, justice, the presidency, and public security) and women occupying social welfare posts (health, housing, education, labor and social security, culture, and women's issues).[13]

Table 9.5 corroborates that women's presence in the cabinet has increased over time, following the regional trend (Taylor-Robinson and Gleitz, chapter 3, this volume). Presidents appointed initial cabinets of approximately 25% women in the late 1990s and early 2000s, and 33% to 40% women beginning in the mid-2000s. This climb correlates with the factors identified by Taylor-Robinson and Gleitz (chapter 3, this volume) as facilitating women's access to cabinets in Latin America: the presence of leftist presidents (the PLN in 2006 and 2010 and the PAC in 2014); increases in women's legislative representation (the quota became more numerically effective

12. Data from the 1988, 2002, and 2006 administrations courtesy of Michelle Taylor-Robinson and Maria Escobar-Lemmon.

13. The categorization of social welfare ministries follows Escobar-Lemmon, Schwindt-Bayer, and Taylor-Robinson (2014). The categorization of power ministries follows Escobar-Lemmon and Taylor-Robinson (2005), though I differ by counting justice as a high prestige portfolio.

beginning in 2002); and the widespread acceptance of gender equality and gender balance norms. These figures thus lend preliminary evidence for the diffusion of women's representation across government branches, supporting the arguments made about the importance of political context in chapter 1.

As with other branches and levels, however, women's increased presence may not correlate with increased power, and women's participation may thus be more symbolic than substantive. The nation's first female president, Laura Chinchilla, appointed *no* women to inner cabinet positions. Other presidents named only one woman to the inner cabinet, continuing the historic practice of choosing women for the justice portfolio (female ministers of justice served under Rodríguez, Árias, and Solís). The Chinchilla and Solís administrations actually raised women's presence in cabinet by creating new portfolios for female ministers (e.g., appointing women to the new posts of science and technology, sport, and national planning). This strategy introduced more women while keeping the powerful posts for men. In Costa Rica—and elsewhere in Latin America (Escobar-Lemmon and Taylor-Robinson 2005, 2016; Taylor-Robinson and Gleitz, chapter 3, this volume)—women remain concentrated in the social welfare posts of culture, health, housing, and women's affairs. Thus, Costa Rican presidents comply with norms demanding more women's representation in cabinet by clustering women in the least valuable posts.

The presidency   *Symbolic Rep over Substantive*

In Costa Rica, the chief executive is elected from a three-candidate slate consisting of one presidential candidate and two vice-presidential candidates. TSE regulations issued in 1997 and 2001 that applied the then-40% quota to the chief executive ticket required at least one woman to appear on the three-candidate slate.[14] After the adoption of parity, the TSE added that, irrespective of the sex of the presidential candidate, the two vice-presidential candidates must contain one man and one woman, in either order.[15] This ruling came after the 2010 elections, in which the ultimately victorious PLN nominated two male vice-presidential candidates to accompany Laura Chinchilla on the presidential ticket. Thus, except for 2010, at least one female vice president has been elected since 1998 (Zamora Chavarría 2012).[16] Yet women's representation in one of the two vice president positions is again more symbolic than substantive, as the office wields little power or authority.

True executive authority resides with the president, and Costa Rica broke this glass ceiling by electing Laura Chinchilla in 2010. Chinchilla's path to power follows the route sketched by Reyes-Housholder and Thomas (chapter 2, this volume), wherein institutionalized party politics, the crisis of representation, and Latin America's left turn created a favorable political opportunity structure for a female candidate. A political insider and professional politician, Chinchilla rose through

14. TSE Acta de Sesión Ordinaria, March 25, 1997. Noted by Zamora Chavarría (2009, 21).

15. TSE resolution 3671-E8-2010, May 13, 2010. Noted by Zamora Chavarría (2014, 285).

16. In 1998, the victorious PUSC over-complied with the quota and chose two women as vice-presidents.

a series of prominent posts: she served as deputy minister and minister of public security, vice-minister of justice, and vice president under Oscar Árias. She became an attractive presidential candidate in 2010, as Costa Ricans continued to express frustration with neoliberal economic policies and elite, unrepresentative, and corrupt parties (Thomas 2014). As a woman, Chinchilla represented renewal, but as Árias' chosen successor, she represented continuity. Her campaign mixed masculine and feminine characteristics. Her slogan was "Laura, strong and honest." She won the first round of voting with 46.9% of the vote, 22 percentage points ahead of the second-place candidate, who was from the PAC (TSE 2014, 63).

Her popularity plummeted thereafter. Corruption scandals rocked her cabinet and the divided assembly remained immobile. Worse, Árias disagreed with her policy decisions and their mentor-mentee relationship soured in a dramatic and public fashion. His routine and public attacks undermined her support among the citizenry, her own party, and even her own cabinet (Jalalzai 2015, 105; Thomas 2014).

Gender was one of several factors that contributed to the meltdown of the Chinchilla administration. Árias reacted furiously when Chinchilla established her independence post-election (Jalalzai 2015, 118–119), perhaps because he expected that a female protégé would docilely continue his policies. Chinchilla also struggled to build her own faction within the PLN, perhaps because party elites remained uncomfortable with women's political authority (Thomas 2014). When Árias defected and Chinchilla had no loyalists to call her own, this gendered vulnerability made rallying party support even more difficult (Thomas 2014). But, Chinchilla also served during troubled times. Past governments had neither improved the economy nor mended citizens' distrust, the voter dissatisfaction that had upended the party system remained widespread, and previous presidents had departed under similar clouds of public anger.

The legacy of Chinchilla's presidency for women in thus mixed (Jalalzai 2015, 201–203). On the one hand, female officeholders had become commonplace by the time Chinchilla won the presidency, suggesting that Chinchilla rose and fell as an individual, not as a representative of her group (Jalalzai 2015, 201). On the other hand, even if nongendered political and economic factors contributed to Chinchilla's fall, dissociating her flawed administration from that of a *woman's* administration proves challenging. Chinchilla left office "with the unenviable distinction of being the most unpopular president in over 20 years" (Jalalzai 2015, 197). And, as Reyes-Housholder and Thomas show (chapter 2, this volume), female presidents in Latin America have endured harsher judgments relative to male presidents, even when controlling for performance.

The experience of Epsy Campbell Barr supports this pessimistic interpretation of Chinchilla's legacy.[17] Campbell is a prominent career politician and the third Afro-descendant woman ever elected to the national assembly.[18] Seeking the PAC's presidential nomination for the 2014 elections, Campbell reported widespread pushback

17. I am grateful to Gwynn Thomas for her recommendation to discuss the case of Campbell Barr.

18. Five Afro-descendent women have been elected to the national assembly since 1953, though Campbell is the only Afro-descendent woman elected twice, first in 2002 and again in 2014; see *Boletín de Consultas Resueltas*, http://www.tse.go.cr/pdf/ifed/diputados_afrodescendiente.pdf (accessed October 12, 2015).

from the political elite: "Many have said [to me] that, since the Chinchilla presidency has gone so poorly, there's no possibility that another woman could be elected."[19] Throughout her primary campaign, Campbell nonetheless insisted that "another woman has the capacity to lead this country."[20] Costa Rican citizens may have agreed, as a 2013 public opinion survey revealed that 76% of voters would choose another female president.[21] Yet the PAC clearly had their doubts. Despite reports that Campbell held a 20 percentage point lead against her male copartisans vying for the nomination, she finished a surprising third-place at the party's nominating convention.[22] She then obtained the second position on the PAC's legislative ballot for San José, only entering the national assembly because the PAC won more than one seat in the capital district. The PAC president elect, Solís, subsequently floated her name as a potential assembly president, but ultimately chose a man.[23] Women may be increasing their presence in party leadership posts (Morgan and Hinojosa, chapter 5, this volume), but Costa Rican voters seem more willing than party leaders to place women in important positions, especially ethnic minority women.

PROMOTING WOMEN'S EQUALITY FROM THE LEGISLATIVE AND EXECUTIVE ARENAS

Party system collapse and informal preferences for male candidates have exerted downward pressure on women's access to the top positions since the 1990s, but women in office have successfully drawn policy attention to women's rights and gender issues. Most changes have come from the national assembly, though the executive branch also plays a leadership role. Female deputies in Costa Rica are more likely than male deputies to individually sponsor bills on children and families, and female deputies cosponsor women's issues bills three times more often than male deputies (Schwindt-Bayer 2010, 95). Female deputies also participate more actively in floor debates, especially when the bills involve women's issues (Schwindt-Bayer 2010, 193). Furthermore, when female deputies do speak in the plenary, they invoke their gender identity and gender experiences more than men (Hinojosa, Carle, and

19. "Epsy Campbell: 'Otra mujer tiene la capacidad de liderar este país.'" *La Nación* July 21, 2013: http://www.nacion.com/nacional/politica/Epsy-Campbell-mujer-capacidad-liderar_0_1355064586.html (accessed August 25, 2017).

20. Ibid.

21. "Epsy precandidata." *Revista Poder* April 1, 2013: http://www.poder.cr/inicio/2013/01/epsy-precandidata/ (accessed October 5, 2015).

22. "Epsy Campbell tilda de sorpresivo e inesperado resultado de convención del PAC." *Monumental* July 21, 2013: http://www.monumental.co.cr/noticia/epsy-campbell-tilda-de-sorpresivo-e-inesperado-resultado-de-convencion-del-pac (accessed October 5, 2015).

23. "Ottón Solís y Epsy Campbell encabezerían lista de diputados PAC" *Semanario Universidad* September 26, 2013: http://semanariouniversidad.ucr.cr/sin-categoria/ottn-sols-y-epsy-campbell-encabezaran-lista-de-diputados-pac/ (accessed October 5, 2015); "Epsy Campbell aceptaría oferta de candidatura para presidir el Congreso" *El Financiero* March 13, 2014: http://www.elfinancierocr.com/economia-y-politica/elecciones_2014-segunda_ronda-primero_de_mayo-asamblea_legislativa-epsy_campbell_0_481151906.html (accessed October 5, 2015).

Woodall, forthcoming). Assemblywomen introduce gender equality legislation more than assemblymen, though no difference appears in female and male ministers on this measure (Escobar-Lemmon, Schwindt-Bayer, and Taylor-Robinson 2014). Executive officials may, however, lobby for gender equality legislation introduced by the president or by deputies.

The hallmark 1990 Law for the Promotion of Women's Social Equality exemplifies how female deputies and cabinet ministers work together on key legislation. The law was written by then-First Lady Margarita Penón and then-second vice president Victoria Garrón, in collaboration with current and former female ministers and vice ministers. President Oscar Árias introduced the law on International Women's Day (March 8) in 1988 (Saint-Germain and Morgan 1991). The law eliminated widespread discrimination across myriad policy areas, from education to sex abuse, and constituted "one of the most sweeping ideas for political reform introduced by a party in power since the 1949 Constitution" (Saint-Germain and Morgan 1991, 36–37). Penón, female ministers, feminist lawyers, and women's groups organized widespread displays of support, including marches, letter-writing and telegram campaigns, and public opinion polls (Saint-Germain and Morgan 1991). Only seven women held seats in the national assembly at the time, though they actively participated in revising the proposal as it moved through committee. The leadership of PLN deputy Hilda González as the chair of the Commission on Social Affairs proved especially critical during both revisions and the floor vote (Saint-Germain and Morgan 1991, 56–61).

The bill had proposed a 50% electoral quota and a 25% "budgeting quota" for parties' expenditures on cultivating women's political participation. Though these provisions were removed from the final version, the law did require parties to revise their statutes to include mechanisms that would increase women's nomination and access to posts within the public administration. These measures, though tepid by current standards, were pathbreaking for the time: Costa Rica became the first Latin American country to pass legislation enacting the positive action mandates in the 1979 United Nations' Convention on the Elimination of All Forms of Discrimination against Women (Hidalgo 2009, 65).

After the Social Equality Law passed, party women, in alliance with feminist lawyers and civil society activists, continued to demand more rights. Female deputies introduced the mandatory electoral quota in 1992 and again in 1996, when it was ultimately successful (García Quesada 2003; Sagot 2010). In 1998, the executive branch launched the Program for the Promotion of Women's Active Citizenship (PROCAM), which publicized women's political rights and organized trainings for female aspirants and female candidates (Estado de Costa Rica 2000, 35). In 1998, the legislative assembly chartered the national women's institute (the *Instituto Nacional de las Mujeres*, or INAMU). Female lawmakers then gained their own platform in 1999, winning the creation of a permanent legislative commission on women. Additional laws protecting women from domestic violence and sexual harassment, and promoting responsible paternity and breastfeeding, also passed during the late 1990s and early 2000s (Schwindt-Bayer 2010, 85).

Politically active women—including deputies, party members, feminist lawyers, and executive branch members—also played significant roles in ensuring affirmative action's effectiveness. Following the 1998 election's disappointing results, female politicians and the newly appointed head of INAMU successfully demanded that the TSE establish a placement mandate for filling the quota on PR lists (Zamora Chavarría 2009, 24). Female deputies then authored and introduced several bills that would establish both vertical parity (alternation of women's and men's names down the list) and horizontal parity (alternation of women as list-headers across all the party's lists) (Zamora Chavarría 2009). Concurrently, the constitutional court issued a series of rulings that affirmed not just the legality, but the desirability of affirmative action (Piscopo 2016b). The court's rulings, the TSE's support, and female deputies' pressure facilitated the inclusion of vertical parity in the 2009 electoral reforms. In the plenary debate, no deputies spoke against parity; all orators speaking in favor were women, including the now reelected PLN deputy Hilda González.[24] After the 2014 elections' disappointing results, female deputies introduced a bill demanding horizontal parity. The initiative passed the women's commission with unanimous approval. The assembly leadership, however, continued to stall the floor debate: over 2014 and early 2015, chamber leaders scheduled the item so far down the daily agenda that the discussion never occurred.[25]

The slow progress on horizontal parity notwithstanding, Costa Rica's quota law and parity regime are clearly causes *and* consequences of women's representation. Indeed, expanding or guaranteeing opportunities for women's access to political power constitutes one policy area where women, irrespective of their partisan, ideological, or other relevant differences, can agree to work together. While some scholars contend that Costa Rican women elected under quotas do not advance a feminist or social justice agenda (Sagot 2010), female deputies clearly work to protect women's rights, particularly their political rights. The women's commission in Congress has provided a platform for female legislators to work on issues of shared concern, especially the horizontal parity bill.

Advances that challenged traditional gender roles also appeared during the Chinchilla administration, even though Chinchilla herself explicitly rejected feminism. Her signature program, *Red de Cuido* (Network of Care), expanded elder and childcare centers throughout the country. Implemented through the executive branch in 2010, and ratified by congress in 2014, the *Red de Cuido* was advertised by Chinchilla as a pro-family and children-oriented program. However, the program also freed women from domestic work, enabling them to pursue employment and careers outside the home (Jalalzai 2015, 233–235). Chinchilla thus did not actively support women's rights—but neither did she actively obstruct them. Furthermore, Chinchilla did not veto laws that she opposed on religious grounds (Jalalzai 2015, 233–236). These included the Youth Law, which contained a provision that would legalize same-sex civil unions.[26] The parity law requiring gender balance for the directorates of civil society associations also passed during her term, marking Costa Rica as the only Latin American nation (and perhaps the globe) to extend parity rules to nongovernmental organizations.[27] Chinchilla's actions suggest feminists

24. Costa Rican Assembly, plenary transcript, August 10, 2009.

25. Conclusion based on tracking the scheduling of Bill 19010/Bill 19019 for debate on the *orden del día* (daily agenda) from March 2014 to March 2015.

26. The legal status of same-sex civil unions remains unresolved. As of February 2017, a challenge to the Youth Law's provision remained pending before the Constitutional Court.

27. Law 8901, November 3, 2010.

should not overlook the ability of female executives—or other politicians—to support progressive change even when they do not publicly embrace feminism.

CONCLUSION

Women have made enormous gains in conquering Costa Rica's legislative and executive branches, placing Costa Rica among the vanguard in Latin America and the globe. Yadira Calvo, a Costa Rican writer and feminist theorist, recalled asking her octogenarian mother to sign a petition supporting the 1990 equality law. Calvo's mother agreed, stating, "I sign so that women such as you will not have to live as I have lived" (Calvo 1995, 71). Her conviction was prescient. The 1990 Law for the Promotion of Women's Social Equality, itself pushed by female legislators and female activists, spurred important political reforms.

The most notable reform—the adoption of the electoral gender quota—caused women's political representation to increase significantly, and, as a consequence, female politicians demanded reforms that strengthened and broadened the quota's reach. Nonetheless, the unraveling of the traditional political party system has mitigated women's representation at the national level (as also shown by Schwindt-Bayer and Alles, chapter 4, this volume). Party leaders may generally associate female candidates with political renewal, but they still preserve the top list positions for men. Absent party system fragmentation, then, women would probably hold closer to 50% of all political offices in the country.

The Costa Rican experience thus underscores the importance of several trends throughout the region, as argued in this volume. First, formal and informal institutions predict patterns of women's representation. In Costa Rica, the *propietario-suplente* system (formal) and the allocation of the choicest or safest candidacies to men (informal) have reduced women's election, even under quotas and parity. Second, political factors also matter, but often in contradictory ways. The formal rules and informal norms of gender-equal representation have pushed parties to nominate women for both legislative and executive office at the national and subnational level. The Costa Rican case confirms that quotas remain a key cause for women's higher representation in legislatures at the national and subnational level (Schwindt-Bayer and Alles, chapter 4, and Escobar-Lemmon and Funk, chapter 6, this volume). At the same time, women face persistent gender discrimination in access to the best ballot positions, no matter the level or branch of government. Third, once in office, female legislators do promote women's issues more than men, often in collaboration with women in cabinet. Yet the stalled bill on horizontal parity illustrates how women's efforts alone cannot transform all the gendered aspects of political institutions.

The Costa Rican case also provides rich avenues for future research. Women's increased presence in all arenas of representation presents an opportunity to explore the consequences of their presence for society at large. Though Campbell Barr's experience suggests a connection between Chinchilla's disastrous presidency and reduced opportunities for women aspiring to political leadership, scant research has been conducted into how mass publics have responded to Costa Rican women's presence at the district, cantonal, and national level. Researchers have not explored whether Costa Rican women's participation in party life has evolved past their ghettoization in women's wings, though some parties like the PLN and PAC boast high proportions of women in their national executive (Morgan and Hinojosa, chapter 5, this volume). Little is also known about the policy consequences of women's election to the district and cantonal level, and whether the patterns of collaboration among female legislators and female ministers observed at the national level hold at the subnational level.

The parity law for civil society organizations also offers additional possibilities for future research. Whereas quotas and parity propel women into the traditionally masculine spaces of government, the parity law for nonprofit organizations is propelling men into the traditionally feminine spheres of charity and public service (Piscopo 2015b). With this law, Costa Rica has truly broken new ground. Although Costa Rican women face the same informal barriers to full equality as their peers in other countries, this small Central American nation still leads the way in developing a legal framework that seeks parity in men's and women's political representation.

Marginalization of Women and Male Privilege in Political Representation in Uruguay

NIKI JOHNSON ∎

2009 quotas in uruguay (handwritten)

Uruguay's record on women's political representation stands out in the region for both positive and negative reasons. On one hand, the first female suffrage bill was presented as early as 1907, and in December 1932 Uruguay became the first Latin American country to grant women equal and unrestricted political rights to vote and be elected.[1] The first female legislators were elected to parliament in 1942, and women continued to be successful at every election until the country's democratic regime was suspended in 1984 by an eleven-year-long civil-military dictatorship. On the other hand, not a single woman was elected to parliament in the 1984 elections that marked the return to democracy, and over the following twenty-five years, women's parliamentary representation rate never exceeded 12%. Women's rights campaigners within political parties and in the feminist movement espoused the cause of electoral gender quotas, with an early bill presented in 1988. However, it was not until 2009, long after most other South American countries had followed Argentina's lead, that quota legislation was finally passed; moreover, the law was restricted to a one-off application in 2014 and 2015 for posts at national and departmental levels. In contrast to its closest neighbors, none of Uruguay's three main political parties has ever fielded a female presidential candidate.

While feminists have construed the lack of women in top political posts as a threat to the representativeness of the country's democracy, Uruguay's political system has not suffered a crisis of representation in recent years to the same degree as most other Latin American countries (as also noted in Schwindt-Bayer, chapter 1, this volume). Within the region it presents the lowest rates of electoral volatility and the highest average levels of confidence in parliament and political parties over the

stable democracy (handwritten)

no female presidential candidate (handwritten, right margin)

1. Earlier legislation introduced in Ecuador (1929) and Chile (1931) established differential rights for men and women (IPU 1995).

period in which other countries' party and political systems suffered severe blows or directly broke down.[2] Undoubtedly Uruguay's resilience owes much to its long-standing, stable party system, as well as its highly institutionalized electoral system with strong electoral authorities that ensure clean and fair elections. These characteristics set Uruguay apart from many of its neighbors and have helped it to weather the different economic crises that have hit the region without the political system collapsing, although certain actors have fared worse than others.

However, it may also be that the very robustness of the political system—and hence lack of a pressing need for the political class to ask searching questions about its representativeness—acts as an obstacle to gender parity in political representation. Political debate on the issue of women's representation has tended to go no further than politically correct statements of intent that are conveniently forgotten when it comes to actually selecting electoral candidates or designating executive positions. Taking this context of relative institutional stability into account, this chapter discusses the causes and consequences of women's political representation in Uruguay. It does so using findings from previously published research by the author as well as new data from the 2014–2015 research project "Electoral Monitoring from a Gender Perspective," in partnership with the feminist NGO *Cotidiano Mujer* and funded by the Dutch Foreign Ministry's FLOW Program.

WOMEN'S DESCRIPTIVE REPRESENTATION IN URUGUAY IN THE POST-DICTATORSHIP PERIOD

The Uruguayan political system   *two chamber parliament*

Uruguay has a highly institutionalized unitary system of government. The executive branch at the national level comprises two elected posts—president and vice president—and 13 ministers and under-secretaries who are appointed (or removed) directly by the president. The national legislature is a two-chamber parliament: a 31-seat senate (30 members plus the vice president) and a 99-seat chamber of deputies. At the subnational level the executive head of each of the 19 departmental governments is the *intendente*, while the departmental legislative bodies—*juntas departamentales* (JDs)—each have 31 members (*ediles*). A second level of subnational government consists of 112 municipal councils (*concejos municipales*),[3] which have 5 members (*concejales*) each. In each municipality, the first-placed candidate on the ballot receiving the most votes holds the post of mayor (*alcalde*). Apart from *ediles* and *concejales*, all political posts are paid.

The 5-year electoral cycle comprises: (1) simultaneous presidential primaries and internal elections to party national and departmental conventions in June, (2) simultaneous presidential and parliamentary elections in October, and (3) departmental and municipal elections in May of the following year. In all elections a system of proportional representation is used, with closed and blocked electoral lists. *Intendentes*

2. See PNUD (2014) Figure 4.1, p. 148, and Tables 4.3, p. 172 and 4.4, p. 173.

3. This subnational level of government was created in 2009 with 89 municipal councils originally being contested in the 2010 elections.

and mayors may seek immediate reelection once, then they must sit out a period of government before running again; there is unrestricted reelection to parliament, JDs, and municipal councils. In all elections, except for president and vice president, ballot papers must include lists of *titulares* and *suplentes*. *Titular* candidates are those elected as primary seatholders; their *suplentes* occupy the seat on a temporary basis when the *titular* is on leave, on official duties elsewhere, or on a permanent basis if the *titular* resigns or dies while in office. Electoral law allows candidates to stand in the same election for multiple posts (for example, as *titular* and *suplente*, or to the senate and lower house), always within the same party.

The characteristics of the Uruguayan political system, and the particular attributes *hier-archy* of each arena of representation within it, create a clear hierarchy between the different levels of government, which is, moreover, highly gendered. The possibility of unlimited election to the senate and only temporary restrictions on reelection to *intendente* create a bottleneck where politicians who have reached these levels in their careers—the vast majority of whom are men—seek to perpetuate their stay in power, by moving from one sphere to the other and back, unless their party wins the presidential elections, which opens up the possibility of equally coveted, high-profile posts in the cabinet. *Staying in positions for whole lives*

At the other end of the pyramid, the fact that the post of *edil* is unpaid makes it less attractive, although for many—particularly women—it is their first rung on the political ladder. Since the post of *edil* requires practically full-time dedication, an informal "job-sharing" dynamic has emerged between *titulares* (mostly men) and their *suplentes* (more often women). This is usually a losing scenario for the latter, who share the workload, but do not enjoy the same status as the *titulares*. Moreover, they are often given the behind-the-scenes work, such as committee meetings and administrative tasks, while the *titulares* engage in activities that give them public exposure and therefore opportunities to consolidate their electoral base. *titulares can consolidate base*

Uruguay's party system

Uruguay has three main political parties: the liberal *Partido Colorado* (PC) and conservative *Partido Nacional* (PN), both founded in the 19th century, and the left-wing *Frente Amplio* (FA) coalition, founded in 1971. Although the PC dominated Uruguayan politics for much of the twentieth century, in the post-dictatorship period the FA gained ground, leading to a three-way split of the vote at the national level in 1999. Following the severe economic crisis of 2002, in 2004 the PC suffered a resounding defeat, bringing the left to power. The FA retained control over national government in two subsequent elections (2009 and 2014), with a small parliamentary majority in all three periods. Currently the FA accounts for around 50% of the vote, the PN just over 30%, and the PC under 15%.[4]

While all three parties have formal party-wide decision-making structures, they are comprised of numerous internal factions, each of which has its own structure and operative rules, which vary significantly even within parties. In elections, candidates

---

4. The remaining 5% of the vote was shared in 2014 between two other minor parties.

run, not on party lists, but rather on faction lists, and electors cast a "double simultaneous vote" for the party and, within the party, the faction of their choice. It is therefore at the faction level that candidate selection takes place, although factions may also forge intra-party alliances as a short-term electoral tactic or for long-term strategic reasons. Many factions are informal and highly personalistic elite groupings, clustered around strong leadership figures, which operate with the support of clientelistic "homosocial networks" (Bjarnegård 2013) at the sub-national level. The informal dynamics of these factions perpetuate "male power monopolies" (Hinojosa 2012) at both the national and subnational levels, generating barriers for women's entry to the different arenas of representation. A smaller number of factions have formal structures and follow bureaucratic rules at both the national and subnational levels, which allow for participation by party membership in internal decision-making processes.[5]

Thus in the three main parties, power is diffused among a large number of internal factions, which means that groups pursuing claims to greater representation rights must wage their campaign both at party and faction levels, and intra-party power struggles provide a constant subtext to all internal debates. This creates significant disadvantages for female newcomers. Furthermore, when the governing party assigns political posts at the start of a new term, the first and most important criterion is always what is known as the "political quota": distribution according to the party's internal balance of power, measured quantitatively in terms of the share of the votes won by each faction. The primacy of this party political criterion effectively blocks consideration of any other criteria, such as gender, that might be relevant for achieving balance in democratic representation.

Women's representation in national executive posts

Uruguay has never had a female president or vice president, nor have any of the major parties fielded female candidates for these posts since the 1996 constitutional reform that introduced open primaries to select parties' single presidential candidacies. Since then, only two women have contested the presidential nomination within any of the three main parties. Cristina Maeso stood for nomination in the PN primary in 2004, but lacked support from any major party faction, and did not manage to win backing among smaller factions. Her clear outsider status and defiant feminist discourse deterred conservative PN voters and Maeso won only 0.41% of votes (see Johnson 2005, 99–105).

In contrast, Constanza Moreira's bid for nomination as presidential candidate of the FA in 2014 against the clear favorite, ex-president Tabaré Vázquez, was considerably more effective, although ultimately unsuccessful. Like Maeso, Moreira did not receive the support of any major FA faction. However, her progressive ideological agenda combined a return to more "radical" left positions (which the FA had abandoned in its shift to win the electoral center) with support for the "new rights" agenda, including gender parity and LGBT rights. This and her increasingly independent

---

5. These tend to be less frequent and are to be found basically in the FA.

Table 10.1 FEMALE CABINET APPOINTMENTS, 1985–2015

Government		Total appointments		Most at any one time number (percentage)	
Period	Party	Ministers	Undersecretaries	Ministers	Undersecretaries
1985–1990	PC	1	0	1 (7.7%)	0 (0.0%)
1990–1995	PN	0	1	0 (0.0%)	1 (7.7%)
1995–2000	PC	2	1	2 (15.4%)	1 (7.7%)
2000–2005	PC	0	0	0 (0.0%)	0 (0.0%)
2005–2010	FA	5	3	4 (30.8%)	3 (23.1%)
2010–2015	FA	4	3	2 (15.4%)	2 (15.4%)
2015–	FA	5	2	5 (38.5%)	2 (15.4%)

SOURCE: Data from ONSC Guía de Autoridades and ministry websites.

profile within the FA;[6] won her backing from a number of smaller FA sectors and an eclectic group of unaligned FA supporters (including students, feminists, LGBT activists, and more traditional older generation *frenteamplistas*), who were opposed to Vázquez's renewed bid for the presidency. Despite campaigning on a shoestring budget, Moreira won 17.9% of votes in the FA's presidential primary and the lists that supported her jointly won more votes in Montevideo than any other FA faction; she subsequently ran successfully for the senate.

Until the first FA government, women's presence was also minimal among top designated positions—13 ministers and 13 undersecretaries—in the national executive arena. Table 10.1 shows the total number of cabinet posts held by women in each administration (not all appointments last for the whole period) and the maximum number serving at any one time. President Vázquez's first cabinet (2005–2010) included as many as four women ministers in office at the same time, and he appointed five women ministers at the start of his second term in office (2015–2020). However, the second FA administration, led by José Mujica (2010–2015), returned to a much more masculinized cabinet, with only two women holding ministerial portfolios at any one time. This supports Taylor-Robinson and Gleitz's observation in chapter 3 (this volume) that whether presidents who enjoy a strong institutional setting appoint more women is conditional on their interest in doing so.

Although a total of 27 ministerial or undersecretary posts have been held by women over the 30 years since the return to democracy, only 19 women have been appointed at this level, since several held posts more than once. Of these, just seven stayed in office for the full term. An analysis of ministerial appointments by sex from March 2010 to June 2013 shows that women ministers had a higher removal rate than their male counterparts (50% and 26.7% respectively) and lasted on average less than half the time that men did in these positions (14.8 versus 32.9 months) (Johnson 2013, 20).

6. During her first term in the senate (2010–2015), Moreira on several occasions publicly disputed the official FA position on issues relating to the armed forces' budget and to human rights abuses under the dictatorship, although she observed strict party discipline when voting.

Women's representation in the national legislature

Following the inauspicious return to democracy for women in 1985, the percentage of women in parliament rose slowly but steadily until 2005, when a glass ceiling appeared to have been reached, with two fewer female deputies and the same number of women senators elected as in the previous elections (see Figure 10.1 and full data in Table A10.1 in the appendix). In 2010 numbers rose again, with 19 women holding seats at the start of the legislature, while the application of the quota law in the 2014 elections resulted in 26 women—18 deputies and 8 senators—taking up seats in parliament in February 2015.

As Figure 10.1 shows, until the 2015 legislature following quota application, the senate consistently registered lower rates of female representation than the lower house, reflecting the gendered hierarchy between these posts. If data are disaggregated by party (Table 10.2), we see that since 1995 the FA has consistently elected the most women to parliament in absolute terms, and that number has increased steadily from one election to the next. In contrast, the PN and PC do not register a regular upward trend in their numbers of women legislators.

As far as legislative turnover is concerned, Altman and Chasquetti (2005, 250) found that, by the turn of the century, overall reelection rates for national legislators stood at 65%, with higher incumbent reelection (70%) in the growing FA,

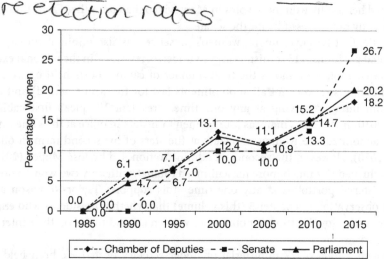

Figure 10.1 Percentage of Women *Titular* Legislators at Beginning of Each Legislature, 1985–2015
SOURCE: Data from the Uruguayan parliament.

Table 10.2 WOMEN ELECTED TO PARLIAMENT, BY PARTY, 1990–2015 (NUMBER)

Party	1990	1995	2000	2005	2010	2015
Frente Amplio	1	6	8	11	12	17
Partido Nacional	2	0	3	3	3	4
Partido Colorado	3	3	5	0	4	5

SOURCE: Data from the Uruguayan parliament.

compared to under 60% for the two traditional parties. Since women's representation rates remain so low, it is impossible to compare differences in reelection by sex at single points in time. However, if we consider the whole period during which women have been elected (1990–2015), their overall reelection rate (53%) is considerably lower than the global re-election rate identified by Altman and Chasquetti.

The composition of parliament is also socially homogeneous in other ways. Although around 8% of the population is afro-Uruguayan, the first male Afro-Uruguayan legislator (FA) took up a seat as *titular* in parliament in 2005,[7] while the first female Afro-Uruguayan *titular* candidate (PN) was successful in the 2014 elections. There is also a generational bias in top political posts, with the average age of members of the chamber of deputies ranging from 49–52 years and of senate and cabinet posts from 54–57 years, over the three terms from 2000–2015 (Serna et al. 2012, 60).

minority women = problem

Women in sub-national executives and legislatures

Not until 2010 were women elected as *titulares* to the post of *intendente*. In that year FA candidates Ana Olivera and Patricia Ayala won in Montevideo and Artigas respectively, and Adriana Peña (PN) won in Lavalleja, representing 15.8% of total *intendentes*. However, this did not signal the start of a consolidated presence for women in this highly prized arena of representation. In the 2015 departmental elections only 15 of the 122 candidates to *intendente* (12.3%) fielded by the three main parties were women, of whom only one was successful. Peña was reelected in Lavalleja, but Ayala failed to win again, while Olivera did not stand for a second term, bringing women's presence in this arena down to 5.3%.

Women's representation in other subnational elective posts (Table 10.3) is somewhat higher—and also higher than in parliament—as could be expected given that these are lower-status posts, and in the case of *ediles* and municipal councilors, honorary. In both subnational levels women's access to elective executive positions (*intendente* and *alcalde*) actually dropped in the last elections, despite the application of the quota. Although the institutional factors affecting the impact of the quota in these posts will be discussed below, the post of *intendente* is highly disputed within parties, and although subject to a two-term limit, generally favors election of the incumbent (Cardarello, Freigedo, and Cisneros 2016), who are normally men.

In contrast, the results of the 2010 municipal elections seem to contradict the general rule characterizing access to all arenas of representation in Uruguay—namely, that it is more difficult for women to reach high-status, paid, single-member posts. In the first municipal elections, the proportion of women elected as mayors (23.6%) was greater not only than female municipal councilors (18.3%), but also *edilas* (18.8%) in the upper level of subnational government. However, this relation was inverted five years later, even though the total number of posts in dispute rose from 89 to 112. As Pérez (2015) suggests, this may have to do with the fact that in 2010 there was little clarity regarding the functions and status these new posts would have in practice; by 2015 their attraction was clearer, as paid positions with close ties to the territory, thus constituting a potential platform from which to build an electoral base.

incumbent advantage

7. He was not reelected for a second term, but was appointed subsecretary for Industry in 2010.

Table 10.3 PERCENTAGE OF WOMEN IN SUBNATIONAL ELECTIVE
POSTS, 2010 AND 2015

Arena	Post	2010	2015	Difference
Departmental	*Intendentas*	15.3	5.3	−10.0
	Edilas	18.8	28.0	9.2
Municipal	Alcaldes	23.6	17.0	−6.6
	Councillors	18.3	23.9	5.6

SOURCE: Johnson (2005) and (2013); Pérez (2015).

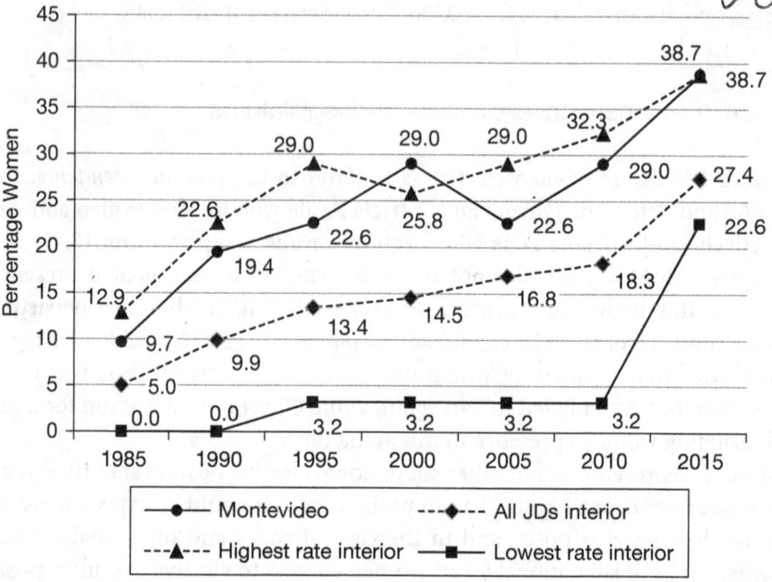

[handwritten annotation: Still not many women mayors]

Figure 10.2 Percentage of Women in *Juntas Departamentales* by Region, 1985–2015
SOURCE: Johnson (2005, 2013) and Pérez (2015).

If we look at the evolution of the percentage of women *edilas* by region since 1985
(Figure 10.2), we see that Montevideo shows consistently a greater female presence than
the 18 departments of the interior of the country taken together, although only in 2000
is it the department with the highest representation rate for women. While overall there
is an incremental trend in women's presence in this arena, in individual departments
gains in one election may be lost in the next (see Table A10.2 in the appendix). Since
1995 in all departments, at least one *edila* has been elected in each period, but the variation between departments is huge (a maximum of 29.1 percentage points in 2010).

If we compare average percentages of women in multi-member posts across the
different arenas of representation for the period 1990–2010 (Table 10.4),[8] there
appears to be little correlation between women's presence at national, departmental, and municipal levels. Some departments show similar rates—whether higher

---

8. Given the differential impact of the quota in 2014–2015, the data from 2010 provides a more
faithful picture of whether diffusion exists between the representative bodies and arenas.

Table 10.4 PERCENTAGE OF WOMEN ELECTED TO THE CHAMBER OF DEPUTIES,
JUNTAS DEPARTAMENTALES AND MUNICIPAL COUNCILS, 1990–2010*

Department	Chamber of deputies	Juntas departamentales	Municipal councils[†]
Treinta y Tres	30.0	23.9	40.0
Rocha	27.3	15.5	20.0
Tacuarembó	27.3	10.3	10.0
Río Negro	20.0	21.3	20.0
Lavalleja	20.0	18.1	0.0
Montevideo	15.5	24.5	25.0
Cerro Largo	9.1	20.0	30.0
Artigas	9.1	15.5	20.0
San José	8.3	10.3	10.0
Salto	7.1	6.5	13.3
Canelones	1.5	9.7	18.6
Flores	0.0	21.9	40.0
Durazno	0.0	18.1	10.0
Paysandú	0.0	16.1	53.3
Maldonado	0.0	16.1	12.5
Rivera	0.0	13.5	0.0
Florida	0.0	12.9	20.0
Soriano	0.0	7.1	10.0
Colonia	0.0	5.8	26.7

NOTES:

* For Chamber of Deputies and JDs, percentages are average over the whole period; for municipal councils, elected for the first time in 2010, percentages are for that year.
[†] Both types of post in the municipal councils—councilor (4) and mayor (1)—are included, as they are elected on the same list.

SOURCE: Data from Johnson (2013) and the Uruguayan parliament.

(e.g., Treinta y Tres, Río Negro, Montevideo) or lower (e.g., San José, Salto, Rivera, Soriano)—across all three arenas. Others show extreme variation with no female representation at all at one level and high representation rates in the other(s) (e.g., Lavalleja, Flores, Paysandú).

Political parties in Uruguay

The data presented thus far show the FA to be generally more open to electing and designating women across all arenas of representation. In this section, I look at whether this reflects a higher presence of women in the FA's internal structures compared to other parties (see Morgan and Hinojosa, chapter 5, this volume, for a regionwide perspective). Women have traditionally been absent from leadership posts in all parties. However, in 2012, women were elected to preside over both the PC and FA. In March 2012, Martha Montaner, deputy for Tacuarembó, was appointed Secretary-General of the PC, a post that since 2009 is elected annually by

Table 10.5 PERCENTAGE OF WOMEN *TITULARES* IN PARTY EXECUTIVE BODIES,
SEPTEMBER 2015

Party: Executive body	Total members	N° women	% women
Partido Nacional—Directorate	17*	6†	35.3
Partido Colorado—National Executive Committee	15	5	33.3
Frente Amplio—Political Board	19‡	4	21.1

executive bodies

* These include 15 members elected by the PN's national convention and two delegates elected by the PN's youth section.

† Although seven women were elected as *titulares*, Adriana Peña (*intendente* of Lavalleja) has been on permanent leave since the start of the term, and her *suplente* is a man.

‡ This excludes the four rotating delegates from grassroots membership.

SOURCE: Data from party websites and official sources.

the National Executive Committee (NEC) from among its members belonging to the dominant PC faction. In May of the same year, the socialist senator Mónica Xavier beat her three male opponents by a twenty-point margin in the first ever open elections to elect the FA's president. Accompanying her presidency were three appointed vice presidents, one of whom was a woman.

In the PC a 15-member National Executive Committee (NEC) and in the PN a 17-member Directorate run the party, whereas the FA's internal structures include a Plenary of around 175 members and a 23-member Political Board.[9] Table 10.5 shows the percentage of women *titulares* in the PN's Directorate and the PC's NEC, both of which are elected by their respective national conventions, and the 19 non-rotating members of the FA's Political Board. Since 2009, any second-grade elections to party executive bodies must apply the quota law. This has had a significant effect on women's presence in the PC and PN executives, which prior to that date had at the most one woman member. By contrast, the FA's Political Board's members are delegates, nominated directly by faction leadership or by grassroots structures at the regional level, and therefore it remains untouched by the quota.

CAUSES OF THE LOW LEVELS OF WOMEN'S POLITICAL REPRESENTATION IN URUGUAY

Why have levels of women's political representation remained so low over the post-dictatorship period? Supporting the arguments made in the introduction to this book, the principal obstacles to increased access for women to political posts in Uruguay are not socioeconomic or cultural factors. Rather it is the architecture of Uruguay's electoral system and highly gendered political institutions and practices that continue to impede equal representation for women.

highly gendered political inst.

9. The Political Board includes the FA president and three vice presidents, 15 delegates from the main FA factions, and 12 delegates from FA grassroots committees; of the latter four attend Board meetings on a rotating basis.

Socioeconomic and cultural factors

Since the late 1980s, women have gradually outstripped men in education levels: by 2012 women accounted for 64% of undergraduate matriculations, 66% of under-graduate graduations, and 62% of postgraduate students at the country's main uni-versity (Udelar 2014, 119, 137, 178). Similarly, over the post-dictatorship period, the percentage of women active in the workforce has risen 15 percentage points.[10] While important inequalities still persist in the labor market, such as horizontal and verti-cal segregation and wage gaps (Inmujeres 2010), over 75% of women aged 18–49 are economically active, with high participation rates (over 60%) even when they have three or more children, and the percentage of women employed as professionals is double that of men (Inmujeres 2013, 26, 30). In short, Uruguayan women do not lack what can be considered to be the principal unwritten qualifications for public office.

Cultural factors do not either provide a strong explanation for the trends in wom-en's political representation, since Uruguay is a secular country which shows high levels of public support for women in politics. The church and state were formally separated in 1917 and Uruguayan society now registers very low levels of religious belief and practice compared to most other countries in the region.[11]

Public opinion surveys show generally favorable attitudes to women's participation in the public sphere (see Table 10.6), although few deal with attitudes to women's political participation in any depth. However, a survey carried out at the end of 2007, when the quota law had not yet been passed, showed that a majority of Uruguayans were favorable toward a greater presence of women in politics and evaluated positively women's performance in office (see Table 10.7 and Table A10.3 in for full details).

The use of closed and blocked electoral lists makes it difficult to explore whether the actual behavior of the electorate reflects these positive attitudes toward women. Nonetheless, there is evidence indicating that being a woman is not a disadvantage for election. For example, Pérez (2005) analyzed female candidacies to *intendente* from 1984–2005[12] and found that the electorate expressed no clear preference for either sex. Similarly, although generally more conservative attitudes are to be found in the interior of the country,[13] women from all three parties have been elected at some point as deputies in nine departments of the interior. Given that in these small districts elections basically involve a runoff between list leaders, these results suggest that being a woman is not a disadvantage per se.

This finding is further endorsed by a series of recent cases of elections to single-member posts involving women candidates. One example was the election in 2010 of the three women *intendentes*, who all competed against strong male candidates from within their own parties, as well as from others. In that same year, Ana Lía Piñeyrúa

10. Instituto Nacional de Estadística, http://www.ine.gub.uy/socio-demograficos/socioeconomi-cos2008.asp

11. See World Values Survey, http://www.worldvaluessurvey.org/WVSOnline.jsp.

12. The study was designed controlling for differential party and faction weights, which could influence the results.

13. These are evident in public opinion surveys; also in interviews women from all parties elected in departments in the interior stress the more conservative views held by their constituents regarding women's participation in public life.

very supportive of women

Table 10.6 PUBLIC OPINION REGARDING WOMEN'S PARTICIPATION IN PUBLIC LIFE, 2011

	Agree	Disagree	N/A
A university education is more important for a boy than for a girl	9.2	86.1	4.7
When jobs are scarce, men should have more right to a job than women	26.2	66.3	7.5
On the whole, men make better business executives than women do	15.6	77.3	7.1
On the whole, men make better political leaders than women do	8.3	82.6	9.1

SOURCE: Questions V52, V45, V52, V51 of the 2011 World Values Survey; http://www.worldvaluessurvey.org/WVSOnline.jsp

Table 10.7 PUBLIC ATTITUDES TO WOMEN'S PARTICIPATION AND PERFORMANCE IN POLITICS, 2007

	% in agreement
There should be more women in parliament	59.8
There should be more women in the cabinet	55.0
Female ministers perform as well as or better than male ministers	80.0
It would be desirable for parties to include women in their presidential formulas at the next election	74.4

SOURCE: Data from the survey carried out in 2007 by the Politics, Gender and Diversity Area of the Institute of Political Science, Universidad de la República with funding from International IDEA.

won more than 60% of the PN vote in the elections to the *intendencia* of Montevideo,[14] and as has already been mentioned, in 2012 Xavier won the FA's presidency with a 20% lead. While Piñeyrúa and Xavier had the backing of strong party factions, other cases show that women can do well even when they are "outsider" candidates or compete in open primaries. I have already mentioned the case of Moreira's bid for the FA's presidential nomination and her subsequent successful candidacy to the senate. Another example is Verónica Alonso's (PN) successful campaign in the 2014 internal elections to the party convention, which resulted in her winning more votes in Montevideo than any other candidate from Alianza Nacional, one of the two main PN factions.

Institutional and political factors

As clarified in this book's introductory chapter, institutional and political factors are conceptually different. However, in Uruguay, they are so interwoven that it is

14. This represented 16% of overall votes, which is the highest percentage reached by a PN candidate in the capital in the post-dictatorship period.

impossible to separate out their relative effects on women's political representation. While the design of the party and electoral systems entrenches highly gendered institutional dynamics within and across the different arenas of representation, male privilege is also actively perpetuated in many cases by male power monopolies, which control crucial avenues of access to political posts, such as candidate selection processes, and actively resist institutional reforms designed to promote gender equality in political representation.

LOW DISTRICT AND PARTY MAGNITUDES

All electoral districts in the Uruguayan national and departmental legislatures are multimember; however, their size varies greatly. The senate is elected in a single, country-wide 30-member district, while the 19 districts in the chamber of deputies vary from just two to 41 seats. At the subnational level, the JDs are each elected in a 31-seat district, while municipal councils have just five seats. If we disaggregate women's representation rates at national and subnational levels by district magnitude (Figure 10.3) before the quota, we find that women generally had a greater presence in the larger districts—the Montevideo district in the chamber of deputies, the JDs, and the Senate. While the small districts are multimember, the limited number of seats in dispute means that only the first place on the list has any chance of success. In the 2004 elections, only 9% of lists presented in these districts were headed by female candidates, rising to 14.4% in 2009.

Canelones, the only medium-sized district, with between 14 and 15 seats since 2000, has a more patchy record. Women have only won seats there in the last two elections and before quota application it performed below the rate for the smallest chamber of deputies' districts (see Figure 10.3). This brings us to the second major institutional factor that represents an obstacle to the election of women: the use of the double simultaneous vote and the consequently low party magnitude. Even in larger electoral districts the tendency is for many lists to win

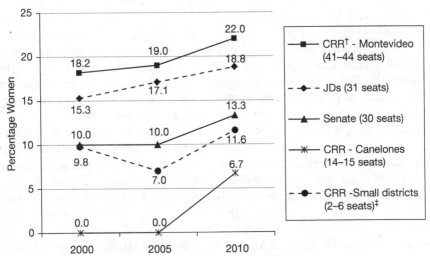

Figure 10.3 Women's Representation Rates by District Magnitude, 2000–2010
SOURCE: Data from the Electoral Court and Uruguayan parliament.
NOTE: Data are of women who took up seats as titulares at the beginning of the legislature.
[†] CRR = chamber of deputies. [‡] The 17 small districts total 41–44 seats.

few seats, which means that only the first one or two list positions are competitive. For example, in 2009 in Canelones, 15 seats were distributed between 11 lists, nine of which won only one seat; in 2014, they were shared between seven lists, only one of which won more than two seats. Similar scenarios can be found in Montevideo—in 2014, of 14 successful lists, nine won just one seat, while only one won more than four; and to a lesser degree in the Senate—in 2014, the 30 seats were shared out between ten lists, half of which won a single seat, and just one of which reached six seats.

However, small district size and low party magnitudes do not per se exclude women. What these institutional features do is reduce the number of competitive positions on faction lists. What decides women's low representation rates in parliamentary posts is the fact that women candidates generally do not appear in those safe positions. This means, therefore, that, as Morgan and Hinojosa argue in chapter 5 of this volume, the principal direct cause of women's exclusion should be sought in the procedures used by Uruguayan party factions to draw up their candidate lists.

MALE-BIASED CANDIDATE SELECTION

balance of faction alliances

The majority of Uruguayan party factions do not have formal rules governing candidate selection processes (see Johnson 2010), and these are heavily influenced by the very dynamics of party factions. Factions are seldom unitary structures; more often they are made up of diverse "groups" or "currents," although differences at this level are certainly more personalistic than programmatic or ideological. In addition, electoral law does not simply allow, but creates incentives for alliance building between factions. As a result, ensuring that candidate lists reflect a balance between intra-faction currents, or between inter-faction allies, outweighs any other possible criteria of political representation.

The dominant model for candidate selection in Uruguay is what Norris and Lovenduski (1995) call "recruitment by patronage." This model is based on "criteria of *acceptability*, [. . .] on informal, implicit and 'subjective' judgements [. . .] the key question by these criteria is whether the aspirant is 'one of us'" (Norris and Lovenduski 1995, 238, original emphasis). Under this system the power of decision lies, most informally, with the faction leader, sometimes accompanied by a select circle of associates, or more formally, with the faction's highest executive organ, which are in all cases exclusively or predominantly male. In this scenario just getting women *visible* as potential candidates is a challenge, since they are virtually absent from the inner circles of party power and clearly are not "one of us."

More recently a number of factions have decided to use primaries (the results of the June internal elections to party departmental conventions) to determine the candidates and their position on the faction list to the chamber of deputies in October. This decision is publicly defended by male leadership as being the most "democratic" method of selection. However, the specialist literature generally finds primaries detrimental to women (Baldez 2007; Hinojosa 2012; Jones 2010; Roza 2010) as they favor insiders and require access to sufficient resources to fund campaigning. In Uruguay, Verónica Alonso (PN) (see above) provides an atypical example of one female candidate who was able to beat the boys at their own game: despite being a newcomer to *Alianza Nacional* (AN) and having limited resources, Alonso's dual strategy of building a solid electoral base among constituency members with

using primaries

links to socially active religious groups and presenting multiple electoral lists gave her the edge over her male within-faction competitors. Not so fortunate were Beatriz Argimón and Sandra Etcheverry, both aspirants in AN's June 2009 primaries (Johnson and Pérez 2010, 81–85). They were both incumbents in the chamber of deputies and had long records of party militancy, and one also in public office, but lacked the funds to wage a successful campaign. Although they argued for other merits apart from vote-winning capacity to be taken into account, they could not persuade the male majority in the faction's local leadership. They also failed to win support from AN's national leader, who refused to "interfere" in the decisions taken by the Montevideo leadership.

The one notable exception is the *Partido Socialista* (FA), where women's access to electable candidacies is favored by the combined effect of a formal, decentralized nomination system, using closed party primaries, and a statutory norm establishing the use of a "mirror" quota[15] in all candidate selection processes. Since 2005, this has guaranteed almost equal numbers of male and female PS legislators in the large districts of the senate and the Montevideo district in the chamber of deputies, but the PS has never had a woman elected in any of the small lower-house districts.

Despite the unfavorable electoral structure in these districts, 11 of them have elected women (in total 21 instances) since the return to democracy. The first PS women elected in this period tended to have ties to prominent local political families, which acted as their passport to party structures and an electoral base. More recently other pathways to power have opened up for women in these districts, with several from the main FA faction winning candidacies on the basis of their performance in internal closed primaries, where their party record is visible to grassroots membership. These alternative pathways allow women aspirants to either successfully challenge or circumvent the local male power monopolies, which traditionally control selection in these districts. However, given the impenetrable male control over candidate selection in most cases and the absence of any sign that other factions would follow the PS's lead and adopt voluntary quotas, support for quotas steadily grew among political women during the 1990s and early 2000s.

GUARANTEEING WOMEN'S ACCESS? THE URUGUAYAN QUOTA LAW

The original bill, presented in 2006, proposed introducing a quota as a permanent measure designed, first, to guarantee and accelerate women's access to electable candidacies, and second, to act as a permanent fail-safe mechanism guaranteeing minimum levels of representation for both men and women. However, the fact that a special two-thirds majority was required to pass the bill was used by legislators opposed to the quota but who were conscious of the need to do something to improve Uruguay's image internationally.[16] As a result, during discussion the bill's scope was

15. The quota was adopted voluntarily by the PS in 1992 and establishes that all PS internal decision-making organs and electoral lists should include men and women in the same proportions as they are present among party membership.

16. While the bill was languishing at the committee stage in the lower house, having finally been passed in the senate in May 2008, Uruguay received the "Concluding observations" of the CEDAW Committee regarding the country's 2008 progress report. Among these, the CEDAW Committee urged Uruguay "to speed up adoption of draft laws on quotas" (6).

systematically reduced until finally the law passed, establishing the quota as a permanent mechanism only in internal elections while delaying its application in national and departmental elections to a single electoral cycle in 2014–2015. This move, orchestrated by PN legislators, was aided by the lack of conviction regarding the quota within some of the main FA factions. Rather than refusing to negotiate the terms of the law down to its minimum expression, unconvinced FA legislators argued that they had no choice but to accept the PN's conditions otherwise the bill would fail.[17]

The gender quota law passed in 2009 requires parties to include candidates of both sexes among every three consecutive positions on their lists of both *titulares* and *suplentes* and to field *titulares* of different sex in two-member districts. The law also establishes that lists that do not comply will not be registered by the electoral authorities. In theory, then, the law represented an institutional reform that included all the formal elements that, according to the literature (Archenti and Tula 2008a; Jones 2009; Krook 2009; Schwindt-Bayer 2009), should ensure an effective application (see also Schwindt-Bayer and Alles, chapter 4, this volume). However, analyses of the application of the quota in the 2009 internal elections (Johnson and Pérez 2010) and the 2014–2015 electoral cycle show how certain formal characteristics of the electoral and party systems—in particular low district and party magnitudes—interact with informal candidate selection procedures controlled by male power monopolies to limit the law's effectiveness.

Figure 10.4 compares percentages of female candidates in top list positions and women elected pre- and post-quota application by electoral district size. In all but the 17 small districts in the chamber of deputies the quota had a significant impact in terms of feminizing candidate lists, with increases of 10 to 23 percentage points. In the small districts, not only did the application of the quota have a minimal effect on the presence of women list leaders, but the same number of women (five) were elected, as in 2009. Low party magnitudes also limited the impact of the quota in two of the larger districts, with only two more women deputies elected in Montevideo and one more in Canelones.

In contrast, the quota had a significant effect on women's presence in all 19 JDs. As well as an overall increase of almost 10 percentage points, an unprecedented maximum of 38.7% women was achieved in two departments. In addition, the quota raised the minimum rate in any one JD from 3.2% to 22.6%, thus reducing the gap in women's representation rates across all departments to a maximum of 16 points. In the senate, too, the quota had a much greater impact, more than doubling the number of women elected, from four in 2009 to nine in 2014. This is because the relative exclusion of women from the senate in the past was not due to low party magnitudes (several lists regularly win more than three seats in the senate) but rather can be attributed to male resistance to ceding safe list positions for election to what are some of the most prized posts in the political system.

impact of quota → only on JDs

KEEPING WOMEN OUT

Male resistance is also reflected in the way in which the law was applied by party gatekeepers in the 2014 parliamentary elections. Analysis of how the quota was applied to electable positions on parties' winning lists to the senate and the two largest districts

male resistance to putting women in safe list pos.

17. See Johnson and Pérez (2011) for an account of how quotas were introduced and finally adopted in Uruguay.

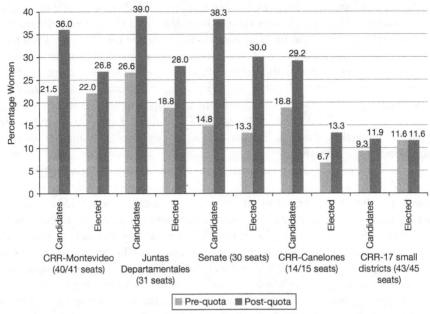

Figure 10.4 Women Candidates in Top List Positions and Women Elected Pre- and Post-Quota, by District Magnitude (*Frente Amplio, Partido Nacional* and *Partido Colorado*)
NOTE: "Top list positions" were defined according to the maximum number of seats won by a list in previous elections: CRR-Montevideo – 10 places; JDs – 10 places; Senate – 6 places; CRR-Canelones – 4 places; CRR small districts – 1st place. "Women elected" refers to the women candidates proclaimed seat winners by the Electoral Court on completion of the vote count. For all districts, pre-quota is 2009, except for the JDs, where pre-quota data was unavailable for 2010 and comes from 2005. For all districts, post-quota data is from 2014/2015.
SOURCE: Own elaboration from Johnson (2005), Pérez (2015), and data from the Uruguayan Electoral Court.

putting female in last of each three list position

in the chamber of deputies reveals a majority tendency in all parties to apply the quota in a minimalist fashion, that is, placing a single female candidate in the last of each three list positions. Four of the PC's five successful lists in these districts followed this pattern, as did 62.5% of the PN's eight winning lists. In both parties, their remaining lists also included just one woman in every three places, albeit not in the third position. Half of the FA's winning lists were also all minimalist in their application of the quota, 10% included the minimum legal number of women positioned in higher places, while the remaining 40% exceeded the law's minimum requirements. However, the FA's better performance in comparison with the two traditional parties is basically due to the presence of a couple of parity lists rather than to better performance across left factions as a whole. These exceptions are, on the one hand, the PS's lists, where the party's voluntary quota exceeds the stipulations of the quota law and the lists supporting Constanza Moreira's candidacy to the senate.[18]

18. Gender parity in political representation was one of Moreira's central policy proposals and a recurrent theme in her campaign discourse and it was a standard that she strongly encouraged the groups that supported her to adopt (Schenck 2015).

Apart from doing the minimum possible to comply with the quota law, the strength of resistance to the quota within the PN is evident from the use of more underhanded tactics to evade the quota without contravening the law. These involved taking advantage of loopholes offered by two apparently minor details of the electoral system: the use of *suplencias* and the possibility of candidates standing for multiple posts in the same election. In 2009, in the first quota-regulated elections to the PN's Directorate, one of the newly elected women directors resigned her seat in the first session and was replaced by her male *suplente*. Given that her *suplente* was in fact the leader of her faction, it is clear that hers was a "puppet" candidacy and her resignation agreed upon beforehand.[19]

In the 2014 parliamentary elections a more sophisticated version of this tactic involved a former FA member, Graciela Bianchi, who a year before the elections defected to the PN's majority faction. She was subsequently placed third on the faction's lists to both the senate and the chamber of deputies in Montevideo, and in both cases her *suplente* was a man. Since it was clear that she was certain to be elected to both posts, it is hard to interpret this move as anything other than a premeditated tactic to bypass the quota law. And in effect, shortly before the new parliament convened, Bianchi resigned her seat in the senate. However, this was not simply a case of male party gatekeepers bringing pressure to bear: Bianchi publicly admitted that she had herself offered to fill both places on the lists in order to facilitate the way into the senate for the faction leader's right-hand man. Bianchi, then, appears as an accomplice in the manipulation of the formal institutions of political representation to serve the ends of male elites and safeguard the status quo.

Finally, it is true that there have also been cases of male candidates running simultaneously for the senate and the chamber of deputies. Moreover, some of these have actually paved the way for women's entry into parliament: since 2005, six women originally fielded as *suplentes* subsequently took up seats as *titulares* in the chamber of deputies when the male seatholders were also elected to the senate. However, in four of these cases the repeated male candidacy was in fact a fail-safe mechanism, since it was dubious whether the candidate would be successful in his bid to the senate. By contrast, the use of repeated female candidacies in an electoral context with quota application clearly has other implications, in that it allows parties to not increase their supply of female candidates, without actually contravening the law. In other words, the repetition of candidates (whether male or female) combined with the *suplente* system configure a highly gendered institution that is basically used to guarantee the election of male candidates.

CONSEQUENCES OF WOMEN'S REPRESENTATION

Notwithstanding the generally low levels of women's descriptive representation in Uruguay, many of the few women elected to parliament have proven active and successful in promoting bills on women's rights and gender issues. In particular, Uruguay's cross-party women's caucus made important legislative gains in the first decade of

19. In the same year a similar scandal, but on a much larger scale, occurred in Mexico, when eight women federal deputies stood down in favor of their male *suplentes* (Piscopo 2011b).

[handwritten: normalising women]

the new century. Women's designation in cabinet posts, on the other hand, has had more limited consequences for women's political representation. Undoubtedly, the increased number of women appointed as ministers by Vázquez during his first term (2005–2010) helped to "normalize" women as legitimate political leaders. Moreover, his designation of women to the Defense and Interior portfolios deconstructed the traditional image of "hard" politics as "men's business." Nonetheless, only one female cabinet member in the first two FA administrations had a history of sustained gender activism. The socialist Daisy Tourné, Minister for the Interior from 2007–2009, laid the ground for important institutional reforms within the ministry and the police for dealing with domestic violence crimes. In contrast, María Julia Muñoz, health minister in the first FA government, shared Vázquez's opposition to the legalization of abortion and in 2008 cosigned his executive veto overthrowing the decriminalization law passed by parliament.

[handwritten: women in cabinet / domestic violence crimes]

Women promoting gender legislation in parliament

To combat their small numbers, one extremely successful strategy adopted by Uruguayan women legislators to promote gender issues in parliament was the creation in 2000 of the *bancada femenina* (BF), a cross-party women's caucus (see Johnson 2014). The founding of the BF resulted from a window of opportunity created by the simultaneous election of three deputies from the three main political parties, who already had a long history of cross-party articulation in other arenas of political representation.[20] For the next ten years they managed to maintain an effective cross-party dynamic around a shared agenda, coordinating both internally with male allies in parliament and externally with the women's movement and with women occupying posts in other political arenas. As a result, between 2000 and 2012 major laws were passed on domestic violence, sexual and reproductive rights (including the decriminalization of abortion), sexual harassment at work and in educational centers, labor rights for domestic workers, extensions to maternity and paternity leave, quotas for women's political participation, and legal recognition of unmarried couples, among others. Prior to 2000, bills on these issues tended to languish at the committee stage before finally being shelved at the end of the legislature.

However, despite a slight increase in the number of women in parliament from 2010, the BF lost vitality and started to function more erratically and less effectively than in previous legislatures. Several factors can be seen to have contributed to this result. First, by 2010 none of the three founding members—who had informally acted as the BF's leading figures even though formally it was a horizontal organization—were still present in parliament. Second, the original balance between government and opposition legislators was strongly skewed toward a large FA majority. And third, many of the new women legislators did not have a record of gender-based activism or previous experience of cross-party organizing. In this scenario of

20. They first worked across party lines in the JD in Montevideo from 1990–1995, and in 1992 founded the *Red de Mujeres Políticas*, a multiparty network of women politicians that aims to prepare women for political leadership and encourages them to incorporate a gender equality perspective in their political practice.

a weakened commitment to gender activism and a more complex balance of party political divisions, the survival of the BF depended on whether the new legislators entering parliament perceived that belonging to the BF was something that would strengthen their own political standing in some way. While many first generation BF members had already paid the personal and political price for campaigning on gender issues and confronting the male power monopolies in their parties, the newer generations of women legislators appeared less willing to pay the same price. Thus, in the BF's third term (2010–2015), joint actions were limited almost exclusively to the issue of domestic violence, one that all women legislators agree on.

THE CHALLENGES THAT REMAIN FOR CONSOLIDATING WOMEN'S POLITICAL POWER IN URUGUAY

Existing research on women's political representation in Uruguay reveals that if women are to break through the glass ceiling and access posts in greater numbers, one of the key areas that must be transformed is the party system. Across the ideological spectrum—notwithstanding a couple of exceptional factions in the FA—parties' hierarchical structures and political practices remain tied to male privilege, directly excluding women from positions of power and also from acquiring the political capital vital for advancing along the pathways to power. The recent incursion of women with high profiles and clear party or electoral support into previously male-only realms of power—such as party leadership positions, the cabinet, the presidential nomination contest, or subnational executives—gives the impression that the spread of women's presence throughout the different arenas of political power is unstoppable. However, experience shows that this is not necessarily the case and that what has been gained can just as easily be lost. Male dominance is not only perpetuated by the fact that men still comprise the majority of gatekeepers, but also by how male privilege has been institutionalized in both the formal structures and informal practices of Uruguay's system of representative democracy.

The one-off application of the quota law in national and departmental elections and the minimalist fashion in which it was applied by the vast majority of factions across all parties makes it reasonable to expect a return to "business as usual" in the next elections, with women once more being excluded from competitive positions on lists. The one chance that this may not happen is provided by the law itself, which establishes that the 2015–2020 legislature must "evaluate its application and possible modifications to apply in future elections" (Law 18.476, Art. 5). The challenge here is how far those modifications might go, whether simply extending the law for another cycle or more, or correcting its flaws and closing the loopholes that allowed parties to bypass it, or even raising the stakes to gender parity. In both personal and public interviews a majority of female legislators have stated that they are in favor of extending the law for at least two more electoral cycles and a significant number have also expressed support for parity. However, given that women still represent only a 20% minority of parliament members, they will need to forge alliances with male colleagues in order to reach the special majority required to make any of these changes to the law.

need to join forces with male deputies

CONCLUSIONS

From this review of the situation of women's political representation in Uruguay it is possible to identify areas for future research that could shed further light on how informal and formal institutions in the Uruguayan party and electoral systems inter-act not only to keep women out, but also to keep men in power. First, more needs to be understood about how parties select candidates, in particular exploring the differences in these processes at national and departmental levels and identifying the conditions and resources that favor women's success. This leads to the need for a broader look at how parties function internally, and in particular, how male monop-olies maintain their hold on power within and through parties, and whether and how women are excluded from accessing political capital within party structures that may be crucial for developing their political careers. Linked to this, more research is needed to identify similarities and differences in women's and men's political career paths. Another area that merits future study is the post-quota scenario: how will the influx of more women into parliament affect the BF and the legislative agenda? Will gender equality champions manage to negotiate the majority support they need to review the quota law? Finally, studies are needed to explore the impact of women's political representation on the electorate's attitudes regarding the representativeness of the system and the gendered constructions of political leadership.

11

Women's Conditioned Access to Political Office in Mexico

PÄR ZETTERBERG ∎

When the Institutional Revolutionary Party (PRI) lost the presidency to the National Action Party (PAN) in 2000, a more than seven-decade-long dominant-party regime ended and Mexico became one of the last countries in Latin America to democratize. Although Mexico was a federal state, the PRI had created a political system that was extremely hierarchical and centralized, where the president exercised strong control over politics and policy at all levels of government. In the post-democratization period, the federal structure of Mexico has resurfaced and revitalized state-level and local-level politics (Rosas and Langston 2011). At the same time, political institutions have in many ways been stable. For instance, the two-chamber legislature and mixed electoral system have remained, and the three political parties that were the main actors during the transition period—the PRI and the two opposition parties, the PAN and the Party of the Democratic Revolution (PRD)—have continued to be the major forces in Mexican party politics.

The clientelist structures and corrupt practices that were parts of the PRI-era's legacy had generated a large degree of mistrust among the electorate toward politicians and political institutions. As a consequence, calls to open up the political system for new groups even predated the democratic transition (Rodríguez 2003) and have continued in the post-transition period (see, e.g., Baldez 2007). However, whereas the attempts that have been made to create more inclusive legislative institutions have been quite extensively researched (see, e.g., Baldez 2007; Bruhn 2003), we know less about how receptive the democratized Mexican political system at large is to newcomers and thus how accessible different arenas of representation, at various levels of government, are to previously politically marginalized groups.

Financial support was provided by the Swedish Research Council [grant no 2015-00955]. The author thanks participants at the Women and Leadership in Latin America conference at Rice University (Houston, TX, April 10–11, 2015), for constructive comments on an earlier draft of this chapter. A special thanks to Leslie Schwindt-Bayer for organizing the conference and for all feedback and support.

This chapter addresses these issues by examining the gendered nature of Mexican politics, and more specifically, developments for women in various arenas of representation before and after the transition to democracy: from the early 1990s to 2014. First, it presents unique descriptive statistics over time on the number of women in legislative institutions at the federal and state level; in executive bodies at the federal, state, and local level; and in political party leaderships. I show that women are substantially better represented in legislative institutions, and to some extent within party leaderships, than in executive bodies. Second, attempting to understand the causes of the distinct gendered nature of various arenas of representation, the chapter pays specific attention to the development of electoral gender quotas for intraparty and legislative positions, and how women's cross-party collaboration has paved the way for these reforms. Third, exploring the consequences of an increased number of women in the Mexican legislature, I identify a gendered division of labor in the policymaking process and in the allocation of leadership positions within the executive and the legislature. Fourth, discussing the challenges that remain for women in Mexican politics, I highlight persistent gender segregation and argue for the need to re-gender arenas of representation. Finally, I conclude by summarizing the main argument of the chapter: Mexican women's advances in politics during the transition and post-transition period have been conditioned by men's continued dominance and control over key areas of Mexican politics. Thus the exclusive and informal nature of Mexican politics persists even where formal rules are changed to open up the political system to previously excluded groups.

WOMEN'S PRESENCE AND ABSENCE IN ARENAS OF REPRESENTATION

In the early 1990s, Mexican women were largely unrepresented in politics. About half a century after they were given the right to stand for election, women held less than 10% of the seats in the Chamber of Deputies. In 2012, after various "waves" of gender quota policy adoption, the number of women in the Chamber of Deputies was about four times higher, 37%, than in the early 1990s. The dramatic increase of women in the Chamber of Deputies puts Mexico in a top-20 position in the world (as of January 1, 2015), with an equivalent number of women in parliament as progressive countries such as Denmark and the Netherlands (IPU 2015). In the Senate, women's representation reached 33% after the 2012 election. For a country that has been portrayed as a typical *machista* society (Baldez 2004), and in which women for decades were largely left out of formal decision making, it is quite a remarkable achievement.

To understand the implications of the positive development for women in the Mexican federal legislature, a crucial question is whether the increased presence of women in congress has been accompanied by an influx of women also in other bodies of political decision making. The idea here is that a greater presence of women legislators may very well spill over to other bodies, enlarging the pool of potential cabinet ministers, governors, mayors, etc. After compiling data from various sources, I address this question by focusing on the number of women (in percentages) over time in a number of federal and subnational political institutions (see Figure 11.1).

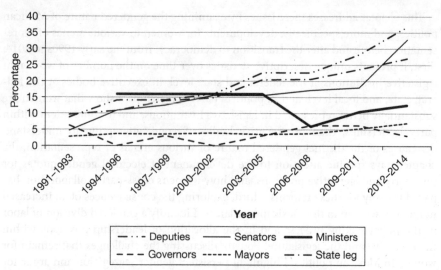

Figure 11.1 Women's Representation in Executive and Legislative Institutions, 1991–2014
SOURCE: Author's elaboration based on the following information: Deputies and
senators: IPU 2015. Ministers: Medina Espino (2010); Jalalzai and Tremblay (2011);
UNDP (2013). Governors: Medina Espino (2010); CEAMEG (2014). Mayors: Vázquez
García (2010); UNDP (2013). State legislators: Reynoso and D'Angelo (2006); Zaremberg
(2009); UNDP (2013); CEAMEG (2014).

Perhaps most strikingly, Figure 11.1 shows that women are substantially more
represented in the legislative arena than in the executive (see also Barnes and Jones,
chapter 7, this volume). The number of women in the 32 state legislatures (the Federal
District included) has increased dramatically in the last 20 years, from about 10% in
1991 to approximately 27% in 2014. However, there is no such trend in the executive
arena, from which women are still relatively absent. For instance, not only has there
been no female Mexican president and barely any female presidential candidates
(only once has one of the three major parties had a female presidential candidate:
PAN's Josefina Vazquez Mota in 2012); the cabinet ministers are mainly men. As
for women in cabinet, Mexico has, if anything, had a small negative trend since the
early 1990s, including a record low 6% in 2006 that (temporarily) put the country
at the bottom of the list of female cabinet ministers in Latin America (Jalalzai and
Tremblay 2011). Even in 2014, women's percentage of the cabinet was only 12.5%.
Thus, male presidents appear to select mostly cabinet ministers of their own sex.
The situation is similarly bad for subnational executive offices: the number of female
governors has been within a range from 0% to 6% (or 0 to 2 governors) during the
last 20 years, and no clear trend can be identified. The situation for mayors is similar,
ranging from 3% to 7% women from 1991 forward. However, in this case the trend
is positive: the amount has more than doubled since the early 1990s, although from
a very low level.

Figure 11.1 also shows that the male dominance in politics is, on average, bigger at
subnational levels than at the federal level, regardless of whether focus is on the legislative or executive arena (see also Escobar-Lemmon and Funk, chapter 6, this volume).
Of course there are exceptions: in February 2014, the states of Tabasco, Chihuahua, and

Chiapas all had 39% women or more in their state legislatures, thereby surpassing the female presence in the Chamber of Deputies (CEAMEG 2014).

Various features of the Mexican political system interact to explain the continuously low numbers of women in the executive arena. As elsewhere in the world, executive positions in Mexico are prestigious and powerful posts that are highly attractive among ambitious politicians (Beer and Camp 2016). As a consequence, competition for these positions is strong. Additionally, very strict term limits in Mexico are likely to have further increased the competition for executive positions at various levels of government: Up until the 2015 elections, Mexican politicians were prohibited from running for a second consecutive term.[1] The long tradition of prohibiting immediate reelection, and thus the lack of incumbency advantages in Mexican politics, has interacted with the federal structure to create a system where ambitious office-seeking politicians have strong incentives to move between levels in the federal system (e.g., from subnational levels to the federal level or vice versa) as well as between the executive and legislative arena (see, e.g., Kerevel 2015; Rosas and Langston 2011). In this "rotation system," the strong hierarchies within Mexican political parties (not least the PRI) play a key role: Mexican politicians' constant search for new positions make them very dependent on a few party gatekeepers for their political careers (Piscopo 2016a). As a consequence, having the right contacts and networks becomes crucial. Thus, "insiders" are benefited, whereas new groups of politicians, such as women, have a harder time accessing these networks. When much is at stake and a single candidate is to be selected (as governor, mayor, etc.), party gatekeepers are likely to select among those in the parties' inner circles—traditionally, men.[2] Thus, informal practices within political parties can interact with formal (electoral) rules to restrict women's access to executive positions.

Looking closer at intraparty positions, women in Mexico have historically had a hard time accessing party leadership positions. For instance, when demands for gender quotas were initiated in the early 1990s, no woman had been president of any of the major parties. As a consequence, the demands for quotas were not only demands for increased female representation in legislative bodies but also for greater presence of women in formal party decision-making posts. The resulting party quotas within the PRI and the PRD were responses to such demands from party leadership.[3] During the last two decades, however, slightly more than a handful of women in the three biggest Mexican political parties (the PRI, the PAN, and the PRD) have been able to work their way through the different levels of the party organizations and up to the party presidency. Having had 35 male party presidents from 1929 forward, the PRI elected María de los Ángeles Moreno

---

1. After a reform of the constitution, reelection is now possible for deputies, senators, and subnational legislators, starting with those who were elected in the 2015 elections.

2. When selecting candidates to legislative institutions, on the other hand, party gatekeepers have the possibility to include a mix of candidates—both men and women—on candidate lists to multimember districts. Such electoral rules have been held to be beneficial for women (see, e.g., Paxton, Hughes, and Painter 2010; Rule 1987; but see Schwindt-Bayer and Alles in chapter 4, this volume).

3. The PAN has a recommendation of parity in its statutes (Fernández Poncela 2011).

in 1994 to become the first female president of the party. She ran the party in 1994–1995 (PRI 2015). After her, Dulce María Sauri Riancho (1999–2002) and Beatriz Paredes Rangel (2007–2011) followed suit and occupied the presidency of the party (Fernández Poncela 2011). In addition, Cristina Díaz Salazar was deputy party president two times, in 2011 and in 2012. In the PRD, Amalia García Medina (1999–2002) and Rosario Robles Berlanga (2002–2003) were party presidents (Fernández Poncela 2011), and in the PAN, Cecilia Romero Castillo was deputy party president for a short period in 2014, becoming the first woman to run the party (PAN 2014).

Figure 11.2 presents the gender composition in each of the three largest parties' national executive committees over time (1990–2009). It shows a positive trend similar to that for party presidencies: women's representation in the party leadership has increased significantly in all three parties during the time period, especially after 1999. The PRI had the largest increase but the smallest number of women: it doubled the number of women, from 12.5% to 25%, during the time period. After a dramatic decrease in 1999, the PRD recovered quickly and, in 2009, had the largest number of women in the party executive: 33%. In general, women's presence in party leadership positions is slightly smaller than their representation in the federal legislature; however, women are significantly more represented in political parties than in executive bodies. For various reasons, it is important to continue the upward trend in women's representation in the formal party leadership. For instance, research has shown that when women reach gatekeeping positions within their parties, the number of women candidates to legislative institutions increases (Cheng and Tavits 2011).

To summarize this section, the increased presence of women in congress has been accompanied by an influx of women in other arenas of representation only to a limited extent. In particular, there is overrepresentation of men among heads of various political bodies, especially within the executive (as presidents of the republic,

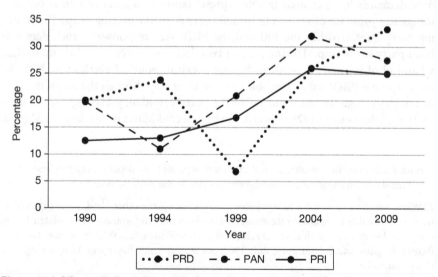

Figure 11.2 Women in Party Executive Committees, 1990–2009
SOURCE: Author's elaboration based on information in Fernández Poncela (2011).

governors, mayors, etc.). In addition, there appear to be more obstacles for women at the subnational level than at the federal level, particularly in the executive but also in the legislative arena to some extent.

Understanding representation: From party quotas to parity reform

To understand gendered patterns of representation over time and in various arenas in Mexico, I make the argument that a much researched formal institutional factor (e.g., Baldez 2007; Piscopo 2016a; Reynoso and D'Angelo 2006; Vidal Correa 2014; Zetterberg 2008)—gender quotas—provide a key account for the variation (see also Escobar-Lemmon and Funk, chapter 6, this volume; Schwindt-Bayer, chapter 1, this volume; and Schwindt-Bayer and Alles, chapter 4, this volume). As Figure 11.1 and Figure 11.2 show, women are today clearly most present in those arenas of representation where quotas apply: federal and subnational legislatures as well as formal party leadership positions. In the early 1990s, before the first quotas were adopted, there were no clear differences between party and legislative positions on the one hand and executive positions on the other. Also when moving beyond mere descriptive statistics and taking advantage of the federal structure's subnational variation in socioeconomic development and institutional design (e.g., electoral laws), research has shown that quotas—and specific quota provisions—are an important predictor of Mexican women's political representation (Reynoso and D'Angelo 2006).

Developing this argument, I draw on previous work to suggest that effective quota policies, and thus women's advances in the party and legislative arenas, are mainly the result of women's cross-partisan mobilization for increased inclusion in politics. During a reform process that lasted for approximately twenty years (from the first intraparty quotas adopted by the PRD in the beginning of the 1990s, to a series of gender quota policy adoptions and revisions, to the parity law adopted in 2014), women from all the major political parties worked strategically together in informal alliances to push reluctant male-dominated party leaderships to advance the issue of women's underrepresentation (for a detailed analysis of the reform process, see Piscopo 2016a). The outcome of the reform process can, in a sense, be regarded as a success story: women's exclusion from political decision making has been put on the political agenda, gender equality in political representation has been perceived as such an important value that it merits constitutional protection, and women's representation in the legislature and within party leaderships has increased substantially.

The key events of the reform process initially took place within political parties. In 1991, the PRD adopted a quota for its internal decision-making structures (Piscopo 2011b). In 1993, the party became the first Mexican political party to adopt a 20% gender quota for candidate in public elections (Bruhn 2003; Piscopo 2011b). The PRD had been founded just a few years earlier, in 1989, by defectors from the left wing of the governing PRI. As electoral competition increased in the late 1980s and early 1990s, the PRI's initial response was to exclude women from party lists: they were considered to pose too much of an electoral risk for the party (Rodríguez 2003). As a consequence, women activists within the party started to build alliances with potential presidential candidates in order to secure more positions in the future. In

1996, the party assembly accepted a proposition from a PRI women's forum to revise the party statutes and adopt a 30% quota for the proportional representation candidate lists (Bruhn 2003).

The same year, a gender quota was for the first time included in Mexico's federal electoral law (COFIPE). The law included a recommendation to political parties to field no more than 70% of candidates of the same sex on their candidate lists. The quota law replaced previous wording, from 1993, which established that political parties should promote an increased proportion of women in decision-making posts. However, it was not as strict as the first quota laws that were adopted at the subnational level, in the state of Chihuahua in 1994 (which *required* parties to field no less than 30% women) and in Sonora in 1995 (which included sanctions for noncompliance) (Zetterberg 2011).

The first quota law at the federal level proved to be largely toothless. Political parties' discourses on gender equality in political representation reached further than their actions: Women were commonly put as alternates (*suplentes*) on the candidate lists, at the bottom of the lists for the PR seats, or as candidates in district that the parties were unlikely to win (Rodríguez 2003). As a consequence, the number of women elected to the Chamber of Deputies increased only 2 percentage points (or from 14% to 16%, see also Figure 11.1) from 1994 to 2000.[4]

The lack of compliance with the spirit of the quota law (i.e., to get more women elected) points at a general problem during the reform process: (male) party gatekeepers' resistance to quotas and thus the lack of political will to make them effective (see, e.g., Baldez 2007). For instance, the party holding the presidency from 2000 to 2012—the PAN—was initially against the use of quotas, on the grounds that they were at odds with the party's liberal ideology as well as with its democratic candidate selection procedures (i.e., party primaries). In 2001, the party filed an action of unconstitutionality of the quota law; however, it lost in the Supreme Court.

As a consequence of quota resistance, advocates of quotas started to push for revisions of the law. Using some of the Mexican states' (e.g., Chihuahua, Oaxaca, and the Federal District) quota laws as examples (Zetterberg 2011), a cross-partisan mobilization for a stricter federal quota law succeeded in revising COFIPE in 2002. The modified quota policy established that political parties were *required* to field no less than 30% women as primary candidates (*propietario*). In addition, the law included both rank order requirements and sanctions for parties that do not comply with the requirements. However, it also included an escape clause: parties that selected their single-member district (SMD) candidates via "direct vote" were exempted from fulfilling the quota (Baldez 2004).

In 2008, women from all the major political parties successfully mobilized to revise the COFIPE again and increase the quota to 40%. After a successful 2003 election, in which there was a 50% (or 8 percentage point) increase in the number of women in the Chamber of Deputies to an all-time high of 23%; there was no change in the number of female deputies in the 2006 elections. Women in political parties argued that parties used the escape clause as an excuse to avoid complying with the

4. For the Senate, there was a continuous increase in women's political representation in the 1990s, from 5% in 1991 to 16% in 2000 (see also Figure 11.1).

quota for the SMD seats. Officially, the parties claimed that they had used direct election (i.e., primary elections) to select their candidates. However, women from the different parties claimed that party gatekeepers *de facto* used more informal ways to select candidates, thereby excluding women (Piscopo 2016a).

The reform process also points at the potential role of the judiciary in making quotas effective and thus in advancing women's political representation. When meeting resistance in the legislature to eliminate the loopholes of the quota law, the cross-partisan coalition of women successfully approached the Electoral Tribunal of the Federal Judiciary (TEPJF). In 2011, the TEPJF established that *propietario* and *suplente* candidates should be of the same sex, thereby marking an end to the *Juanita* cases where elected female *propietario* candidates stepped down and were replaced by their male *suplentes* (Vidal Correa 2014). Then in 2012, before the elections, the TEPJF decided that parties under no circumstances were exempted from fulfilling the quota. In other words, they removed the escape clause (Piscopo 2016a). Consequently, the 2012 elections resulted in a large increase in the number of women in the Chamber of Deputies: from 28% in 2009 to 37% in 2012 (see Figure 11.1).

The final steps to parity were taken in late 2013 and in 2014. Emboldened by the electoral tribunal's resolutions and by the large number of women deputies, quota advocates intensified their efforts to go from a 40% quota to parity. In 2013, the new PRI government initiated a constitutional reform process. Women from all three major parties pushed for the inclusion of parity in the revised constitution. They requested that women should participate on equal terms with men in politics. Again, the cross-partisan coalition was successful. Parity was included in the revised constitution in early 2014 as well as in the new Law of Political Parties. Importantly, in contrast to previous quota laws, where the federal structure of Mexico enabled the states to make their own decisions about gender quotas, the parity law established that candidate lists for both federal and subnational legislatures must be composed of an equal number of men and women (Lovera 2014; Peña Molina 2015).

The quota reform process illustrates well the importance of cross-partisan advocacy coalitions for leveling out gender inequalities in politics. However, another important lesson from the quota reform process concerns party gatekeepers' reluctant compliance: it demonstrates that opening up various arenas of representation to new groups has not been a top priority for male-dominated party leaderships (see also Morgan and Hinojosa in chapter 5, this volume). Reluctance to comply with quotas has been observed in various parts of the world and is thus not unique to Mexico (Bjarnegård and Zetterberg 2016; Hinojosa 2012). However, where the de facto control over candidate selection is placed in the hands of a few party gatekeepers, and where informal networks are strong, it becomes particularly challenging to make the selection process more inclusive. In addition, and to reiterate, "insiders'" constant search for new positions—due to the no-reelection clause and thus to the "rotation system" it has created—might reinforce these challenges and thus make it difficult for newcomers to catch party gatekeepers' attention. Although these suggestions need to be confirmed by empirical analyses, it is possible that such challenges are relatively big for women aspiring for an executive post: it is likely that male leaders' strategic concerns (to distribute posts to people within their existing networks) trump other concerns especially when there are few positions to fill. This suggestion is in line with research on Mexican subnational legislative institutions, which shows

that when women aspire to a seat in the single-member districts they are less successful than when they aspire to a PR seat (Reynoso and D'Angelo 2006). This challenge
may be particularly big at the subnational level, for instance for women with aspira-
tions to become governor or mayor: being further away from the national spotlight,
local politicians may get less pressure to promote women (e.g., Krook 2009) and be
more able to keep a strategic focus on maintaining their informal and clientelist networks (Bjarnegård 2013; Danielson, Eisenstadt, and Yelle 2013). In regards to other
commonly suggested explanatory factors for women's representation (see Schwindt-
Bayer, chapter 1, this volume), the few within-country analyses that have been conducted provide no empirical evidence that cultural (Danielson, Eisenstadt, and Yelle
2013) or socioeconomic (Reynoso and D'Angelo 2006) factors should play a major
role in the Mexican case. Although *machista* attitudes in Mexican politics and society are likely to be obstacles to women in politics, they do not explain why women
are better represented in some arenas of representation than in others.

THE CONSEQUENCES OF MEXICAN WOMEN'S POLITICAL REPRESENTATION

From a feminist institutionalist perspective, gender dynamics are not only shaped by
the interaction between formal (e.g., gender quotas) and informal (e.g., intraparty
norms) institutions but can have consequences for how politics and political institutions operate (Krook and Mackay 2011). Bringing these insights to the Mexican context, a relatively small but growing body of literature has focused mostly on whether
the influx of women into legislative institutions has left an imprint, first, on politics
and policy, and second, on citizens' political attitudes.

A gendered division of labor

In general, large-scale analyses of policymaking in Mexico have rarely had a gender
perspective. Rather, their emphasis has been mainly on the congress, more precisely
on the role of institutional features (election law, party competition, federalism,
intraparty factors, etc.) in shaping legislator behavior. For instance, research on the
Mexican legislature has shown that party discipline is generally strong because office-
seeking legislators are primarily beholden to party leaders for their future careers
(Piscopo 2014b). However, instances of legislators not toeing the party line have
become somewhat more common as party competition has increased (see, e.g., Díaz
Rebolledo 2005). In addition, research has shown that there are also some important
variations in legislator behavior among elected representatives. For instance, those
who are elected through the first-past-the-post system in single-member districts
appear to engage more in constituency service than legislators who sit in a PR seat
(Kerevel 2015), and governors have been found to impact the voting behavior of
legislators from their own party and state (Rosas and Langston 2011). A reason for
this behavior is that the state level is a good option for ambitious politicians who
seek new employment after finishing their term in congress (Kerevel 2015; Rosas and
Langston 2011). Thus, national party leaders are not the only ones who hold the key
to politicians' future careers.

Yet, the scholarly literature on legislative politics in Mexico has not paid much attention to the question of whether women and men respond differently to these incentive structures or to the issue of potential differences in political ambition between male and female politicians. Under the condition that women in Mexican politics are as ambitious and thus as office-seeking as their male colleagues, however, they face a dilemma or "double bind" (e.g., Miguel 2012) that male politicians do not face: whether they should mainly be loyal to the party or to women as a group (e.g., Zetterberg 2013). On the one hand, female legislators in Mexico need to be loyal to party gatekeepers (and thus consistently toe the party line) to further their political careers. On the other hand, they may perceive a mandate to represent women and are thus likely to lose support among groups of constituents if they do not give priority to "women's interests" (see also Franceschet and Piscopo 2008; Miguel 2012).

Although research has not shed much light on the potential for women in Mexican politics to reconcile an identity as a "party loyalist" with an identity as a "group delegate" for women (e.g., Siavelis and Morgenstern 2008), empirical work has shown that Mexican women—especially those elected from PR lists—indeed conceive of women as a constituency (Piscopo 2014b; see also Zetterberg 2008). In a large-scale analysis of the Chamber of Deputies (1997–2012), Piscopo (2014b) shows that such a perceived mandate to represent women is also manifested in action. By analyzing bill introduction in the area of gender equality issues, she finds that an increase in female legislators has been accompanied by an increase in bills addressing women's concerns (see also Kerevel and Atkeson 2013). Whereas only 5% of male deputies authored a bill on gender equality issues during the period, 31% of the women did. Thus, consistent with previous work on women's substantive representation in Latin America (e.g., Franceschet and Piscopo 2008; Schwindt-Bayer 2010), Piscopo concludes that electing women to the Mexican congress has re-gendered the legislature by diversifying the legislative agenda. Unsurprisingly, party also matters for bill introduction on gender equality issues: deputies representing the rightest PAN were found to author fewer bills on the topic than their colleagues in the PRI and the PRD. Interestingly, however, there was also a gender difference within the PAN: *panista* women were more likely to write proposals concerning progressive gender roles than their male party colleagues. Thus both women and leftists seem to be required for initiating processes of progressive policy change within the area of gender equality (Piscopo 2014b).

Bringing new issues onto the political agenda is of course much easier than to adopt new legislation (e.g., Franceschet and Piscopo 2008). Of the 360 gender equality bills analyzed by Piscopo (2014b), only 22 (or 6%) succeeded. At first glance, this number appears to be low. Yet, in their analysis of the Mexican Chamber of Deputies from 2000 to 2009, Kerevel and Atkeson (2013) show that bills related to women's interests have had a higher passage rate than other bills. The bills introduced by women that have been successful span over different areas within gender equality issues, such as legal frameworks (or infrastructure) for gender equality (e.g., the creation of the federal executive agency InMujeres—the National Institute for Women), children's rights (e.g., enhanced penalties for pedophiles and child pornographers), violence against women (e.g., the creation of a national response system), health (e.g., the creation of programs that assist women with AIDS), and education (e.g., the training of teachers about gender equity in the classroom) (Piscopo 2011b, 2014b).

In order to get a fuller understanding of the imprint women have had on Mexican politics, it is important to broaden the perspective and also look beyond the pursuit of gender equality issues. Women are not and should not be exclusively concerned with gender equality issues. As a consequence, I next look at the policy areas in which women are involved. One way of measuring that is to examine female cabinet ministers' portfolios, similar to Taylor-Robinson and Gleitz (chapter 3, this volume).

In Figure 11.3, I present the portfolios of each of the women who have been cabinet ministers in Mexico, from 1980 (when Rosa Luz Alegria Escanilla became the first female Mexican cabinet minister) to 2014. The figure shows that the most common portfolio for women (four times) is tourism and social development *(desarrollo social)*, followed by natural resources/environment and foreign affairs (twice). Once a woman had the portfolios of education, energy, labor, agrarian reform *(reforma agraria)* and *función pública* (equivalent to an office of audit and control), and health, respectively. There are also a number of portfolios that only have been assigned to men: defense (navy included), public security, economy and finance, transport, and interior.

The results of the descriptive analysis are largely consistent with other work in Latin America that has emphasized a division of labor between men and women in the cabinet: women are more commonly assigned to "soft" portfolios, or "social welfare" portfolios (e.g., social development, health, and education), than to "hard" portfolios (e.g., defense and economy), which can be divided into "central" and "economics" portfolios (see Taylor-Robinson and Gleitz, chapter 3, this volume). Escobar-Lemmon and Taylor-Robinson (2005) divide the ministries into low-, medium-, and high-prestige ministries, based on national policy prestige and budget size. Using their classification, Mexican women's access to high-prestige portfolios has been restricted to one of five: foreign affairs (defense, public security, interior, and economy and finance being the others).

A gendered division of labor is not restricted to the executive arena or policy. Analyzing the committees in the Chamber of Deputies and in the Senate that were headed by a woman in 2014, a similar pattern emerges as for the cabinet: None of the high prestige committees in the lower house was headed by a woman. In the Senate,

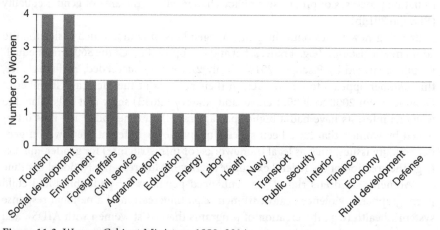

Figure 11.3 Women Cabinet Ministers, 1980–2014
SOURCE: Author's elaboration based on information in CEAMEG (2014).

the picture is somewhat more qualified: women were presidents of two of the high prestige committees (interior and foreign affairs) in 2014 (CEAMEG 2014).[5]

Taken together, the entry of women into Mexican decision-making bodies seems to have generated an amplified legislative agenda and, to some extent, new pieces of legislation. However, while being protagonists in the area of gender equality, and presiding also over committees and ministries that deal with other (mostly "soft") issues, women have had a harder time breaking into the cabinet's and congress's inner circle. There are at least two crucial policy areas—security issues and finance—to which access to a leadership position is virtually restricted to men. Attempting to understand this gendered division of labor, where men more commonly preside over prestigious policy areas than women, it is suggested to be at least partly a result of deeply rooted perceptions about "male" and "female" qualifications or character traits: women are seen as having more compassion and empathy than men, whereas men are perceived as tougher and more aggressive than women (e.g., Dolan 2005). When assigning portfolios and committee chairmanships to men and women, (predominantly male) gatekeepers may (intentionally or unintentionally) play to these stereotypes to reproduce male dominance and condition women's access to positions of power.

An increased diversity of women—and somewhat reduced gender stereotypes

Within the framework of symbolic representation, scholars have argued that an increased number of women legislators has positive consequences on the links between representatives and the citizenry—for instance, by making citizens more sympathetic to (women) politicians (see e.g., Franceschet, Krook, and Piscopo 2012, for an overview). The idea is that more gender-equal political institutions signal greater inclusiveness in the political system, and a large influx of women legislators sends cues to citizens that politics is not only a male domain.

To address these issues, a relevant first question concerns the extent to which women's increased inclusion in legislative institutions has diversified politics more broadly by bringing in women with different backgrounds. It could be argued that the exclusive nature of Mexican politics results in the election of women from a small elite, with few ties to large segments of society. The few analyses that have had such an intersectional perspective on descriptive representation point in somewhat different directions. On the one hand, an analysis of indigenous women finds that there are only three of them in the Mexican congress (as of 2013), comprising 0.6% of the congress (Htun 2016). On the other hand, an analysis of approximately 500 senators from 1964 to 2012 shows that after gender quota adoption the number of women senators from working class families increased substantially. Thus a more diverse group of women has entered the Senate as the number of women senators has increased. At the same time, an analysis of the senators' educational and political background shows that there is no tradeoff between increased diversity and

---

5. However, if we broaden the scope of the analysis to include also memberships, women are as likely as men to be assigned to high-prestige committees (Kerevel and Atkeson 2013).

legislator quality: women senators are not less qualified than their male colleagues (Beer and Camp 2016).

Looking at the links between elite politicians and citizens in Mexico, it should first be mentioned that such analyses are very rare. A good exception is Kerevel and Atkeson's (2015) analysis of women mayors and whether their presence is associated with a re-gendering of an informal institution: gender norms about politicians. Analyzing approximately 1,500 constituents in 110 Mexican municipalities, they find that being currently governed by a female mayor reduces gender stereotypes about political leadership among males; however, having past experiences of a woman mayor is not associated with men's greater approval of women as political leaders. As a consequence, the authors conclude that male citizens' frequent and repeated encounters with women in executive positions are needed to produce long-term change in gender stereotypes about political leadership.

In addition to Kerevel and Atkeson's (2015) analysis, there are also a limited number of analyses of a more descriptive character, where conclusions are at best tentative (see, e.g., Zetterberg 2012). Looking at other aspects of symbolic representation, such as the relationship between an increased number of women legislators and citizens' political interest and trust in political parties as well as in congress, no such correlation is found (e.g., Schwindt-Bayer 2010). However, in order to get a fuller picture of the symbolic effects of women's descriptive representation, more research is needed.

CHALLENGES: RE-GENDERING ARENAS OF REPRESENTATION IN MEXICO

While women in various respects have been successful in increasing their presence in Mexican politics during the last twenty years, there are important challenges remaining in order to make politics in Mexico more inclusive. Most importantly, there is a need for re-gendering arenas of representation in Mexico. The descriptive statistics presented in this chapter (Figure 11.1 and Figure 11.3) clearly show how politics in Mexico is gendered and how gender segregation persists in at least two ways: Vertically, most political bodies are still being *headed* by a man (e.g., mayors, governors, etc.), although women's *representation* in various bodies has increased substantially. In other words, women have had relatively few opportunities to govern. And horizontally, some of the most prestigious issue areas (e.g., economy, defense, etc.) keep being under the control of men; thus women have sometimes been given the power over some issue areas but not over others.

In order to re-gender politics in Mexico, it is crucial to understand why gender segregation persists even decades after women's political inclusion was put on the legislative agenda. In this chapter, I have suggested that attention should be put on the ways in which informal norms and practices keep setting the conditions for women in politics after formal policy change (i.e., gender quotas and parity reforms) has taken place. First, traditional cultural norms and sex stereotypes among gatekeepers (and possibly voters) place men and women in different domains and thus put restrictions on what is seen as appropriate "male behavior" and "female behavior" (see also Huddy and Terkildsen 1993; Shair-Rosenfield and Hinojosa 2014). Second, although centralized candidate selection procedures may increase the number of women elected to political office in Mexico (see, for example, Hinojosa 2012), such a concentration of power to (male) party bosses at various levels may be harmful for women's political careers. In a "rotation system" where incumbency advantage has been absent, a few gatekeepers are able to maintain control over politicians' careers by supporting some politicians and sidelining others. As long as women continue not to crack the inner circles of the parties and move to not only formal but also informal leadership positions, male leaders are likely to have both rational (e.g., economic benefits) and emotional motives for mainly selecting other men (e.g., Bjarnegård 2013; Cheng and Tavits 2011).

These constraining factors are certainly part of Mexican women's reality, and they put women politicians in delicate situations, not least those who run for executive offices (governor, etc.). First, they will have to decide whether they should play to sex stereotypes or not in their campaigns. They may have good short-term motives for doing so; however, such behavior may work to cement a distinction between 'male' and 'female' issues and inhibit Mexican women from breaking into traditionally male domains (e.g., Dolan 2005). Second, because of the power that gatekeepers still exercise, Mexican women's "double bind" (Miguel 2012) may force them to try to strike a balance between loyalty with the party leadership and with their constituents (including women). Too much emphasis on the former may create disillusionment within the citizenry; too much focus on the latter may endanger women's political careers.

More broadly, I suggest that a re-gendering of political institutions requires a democratization and greater inclusiveness of Mexican (party) politics. There are certain authoritarian features remaining in Mexico, which quota adoption and women's influx into the legislature has not changed. Most importantly, informal practices of clientelism in candidate selection processes and election campaigns, along with corruption scandals and allegations of electoral fraud, make it difficult for Mexican women as a group to change the way politics is made. The (informal) rules are already set.

In relation to these challenges, I suggest a few societal and legal processes that should be analyzed from a gender perspective: For instance, the removal of the prohibition of immediate reelection (after the 2015 elections) may have important gendered consequences with respect to men's and women's possibilities to be reselected and reelected: they give politicians the chance to build their own power platform which may have consequences for intraparty power structures. In addition, the gendered consequences of "*narcotráfico*" and organized crime on the political system and on intraparty politics merit attention. It is possible that these features of society reproduce and reinforce the masculinized nature of Mexican politics.

CONCLUSION: MEXICAN WOMEN'S CONDITIONED ACCESS TO POLITICAL OFFICE

This chapter has shown that, in various respects, the last twenty years have been a success story for women in Mexican politics. Women have successfully claimed their space in legislatures and in political parties' decision-making bodies, and they have been able to put new issues onto the legislative agenda and, at least to some extent, adopt new policies, by pushing for issues that are of particular relevance for women as a group. However, the main argument of this chapter is that these advances have been conditioned by men's maintained dominance and continued control over key areas of Mexican politics: the executive (the presidency, etc.) and some of the most prestigious issue areas (e.g., economy, defense, etc.). In a Latin American perspective, Mexico stands out as one of those (relatively few) countries that never has had a female president or minister of finance and rarely had a female presidential contender.

From such a perspective, it is evident that Mexico's long track record of quota iterations, culminating in a parity reform, has not been enough to break glass ceilings, re-gender politics, and fully include women into all arenas of representation. In this sense, the legislature has not successfully served as a breeding ground for other offices. As a consequence, future research should seek to explain the continued male dominance in executive positions as well as in other top leadership positions (as committee chairs, presidential candidates, etc.). Such analyses require an increased focus on men in Mexican politics—especially those in (party) gatekeeping positions—and how they make use of formal and informal institutions to resist change and maintain the status quo. This is particularly necessary in a situation where formal rules are changed to open up the political system to previously excluded groups.

12

Women, Power, and Policy in Brazil

CLARA ARAÚJO, ANNA CALASANTI, AND MALA HTUN ■

Brazil is one of the few countries in the world to have elected a woman as president. In 2010, Brazilian voters authorized Dilma Rousseff of the Workers' Party to assume the Presidency and reelected her in 2014. Then, in 2016, Rousseff became the first woman president to be impeached by Congress. Many of her accusers and denouncers were themselves the subject of criminal investigations for personal enrichment and other corruption-related crimes. Brazil's national parliament has one of the lowest levels of women's participation in the region and the world, especially in the Chamber of Deputies, where women's share of seats has never exceeded 8 to 10% of the total. Women's low numbers in the legislature are puzzling, since the country adopted a gender quota law in 1996 and reformed it significantly in 2009. In the 2014 national elections, for the first time since the law's approval, the number of women candidates came close to the quota level of 30%, and even surpassed this in some races (see Figure 12.1). Large numbers of both the male and female candidates were nonwhite. However, the dramatic growth in the number of women candidates did not lead to the election of more women.[1]

How could Brazilians elect a woman as president, but not elect more women to the national legislature and to state legislatures? Why has the quota law not produced the big jumps in women's presence in elected office that we have seen in other countries, particularly those in this volume? How could the number of women in some chambers decline, as was the case in some state legislatures? Did having a woman as president help, or hurt, the prospects for women candidates? Why is there such a big gap between the number of women candidates and the number of women elected? The 2014 election results, in particular, call for an explanation of women's low presence in legislative offices, analysis of when and why quota laws help to elect more women, and an exploration of the consequences of women's low presence in power for advocacy of women's rights issues.

---

1. See the next chapter on Colombia for a similar phenomenon.

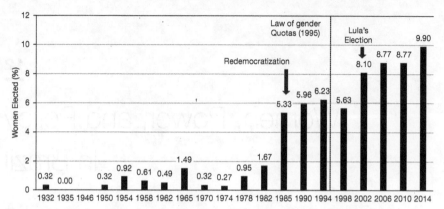

Figure 12.1 Women Elected to the Chamber of Deputies, As a Share of the Total, 1932 to 2014
SOURCE: TSE/Repository of electoral data. Date of generation: July 27, 2015.
Tabulation: NUDERG.

To explain the scarcity of women in power, scholars often focus on voter attitudes, underlying social conditions, and the effects of institutions (Araújo and Alves 2011; Htun 2003; Piatti-Crocker 2011). Research conducted during the last decade, however, has found that Brazilian voters are not against electing women (Alves, Pinto, and Jordão 2012; Fundaçao Perseu Abramo 2010). What is more, the position of women in Brazilian society has advanced significantly, while the numbers of women in elected office have not. In this chapter, as in the others in this volume, we focus on the effects of institutions. As we will see, features of Brazilian political institutions and electoral context—including the candidate-centered and personalist electoral system, decentralized nomination procedures in parties, the role of money, and the interaction of incumbency and TV time—constitute major obstacles to the election of a greater number of women, as well as for the success of the gender candidate quotas.

WOMEN'S PRESENCE IN GOVERNMENT

Figure 12.1 shows that the number of women in the federal Chamber of Deputies (lower house of parliament) has grown since 1932, when women were able to run for office for the first time. The return to democracy in 1985 triggered a significant increase (though only to 5% of the total); there was another bump following the election of Lula in 2002 (to 8%). But women's numbers remain low relative to their participation in the economy and society, as well in comparison with levels of legislative representation in other Latin American countries.

Figure 12.2, Panel A depicts the growing discrepancy between the share of candidates who are women and women's share of elected officials in the federal Chamber of Deputies between 1998 and 2014. It shows that the number of women candidates has grown steadily over time, with huge increases between 2006 and 2010, and again between 2010 and 2014. A similar pattern holds in state legislatures and municipal councils. In the former, women's presence among candidates grew from 7% in 1994 to 21% and 29% in the 2010 and 2014 elections, respectively. In municipal council races, the share of candidates who were women was historically higher than in federal and state legislative elections: women made up some 17% of candidates as early as 1996. This figure grew to 22% in 2008, and in the 2012 elections, women constituted a whopping 32% of municipal council candidates (municipal elections are held on a different cycle than state and federal ones). All three chambers are elected with open-list proportional representation, though district sizes vary.

Quota reforms adopted in 2009 are largely responsible for the sharp increases in the numbers of women contesting legislative elections after 2010. These reforms closed a loophole in the original quota law, dating from 1996. The 1996 law stated that parties needed to *reserve* 30% of candidate positions for women but did not require that those positions actually be *filled*. In other words, parties could not run men in the reserved candidate positions, but they didn't have to run women either. What is more, since parties were allowed to postulate 50% more candidates than positions in dispute (in other

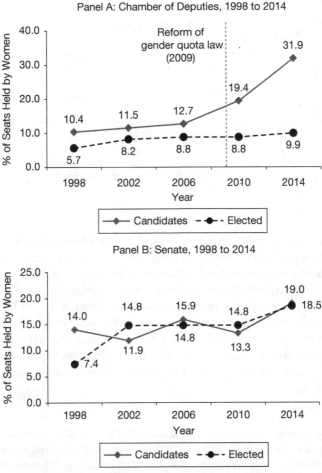

Figure 12.2 Women's Share of Candidates and Elected Officials for Various Arenas
SOURCE: All data from TSE/Repository of electoral data. Date of generation: July 27, 2015.
Tabulation: NUDERG.

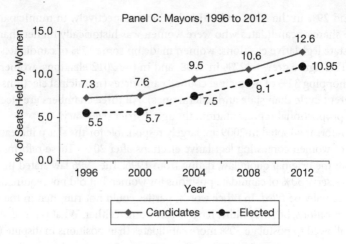

Panel C: Mayors, 1996 to 2012

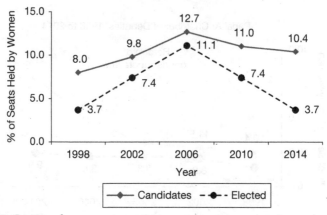

Panel D: Governors, 1998 to 2014

Figure 12.2 Continued

words, a party had the right to postulate 15 candidates in a 10-seat district, while reserving five of those positions for women), a party could theoretically field a full slate of candidates without a single woman and still comply with the letter of the law (Htun 2005).

The 2009 reforms prevented parties from simply reserving candidacies for women. The reforms also required that parties dedicate a minimum of 10% of their free television time to women, and that parties assign a minimum of 5% of their budgets to programs to promote women's participation.[2] As a result, in the 2016 municipal elections, the electoral courts rejected several parties' applications to contest elections on the ground that the parties had failed to postulate slates in which women made up 30% of candidates.

2. Art. 93-A states that "the Superior Electoral Court (TSE), in the period between March 1 and June 30 of election years, in time equal to the provisions of art. 93 of this law, can promote institutional advertising on radio and television, to encourage gender equality and women's participation in politics." The launch of the campaign "Women in Politics" in March 2014, by the TSE, with the support of Congress, seems to have had considerable results. These mechanisms were kept in the 2015 electoral reform.

Yet in spite of the massive growth in number of women candidates, especially after 2010, the number of women actually elected remained low at all legislative levels. In the federal Chamber of Deputies, women's share of seats barely rose, to 10% of the total in 2014 (51 women were elected, compared to 45, or 9%, of the total in 2010) (see the dotted line in Figure 12.2, Panel A).[3] In state legislatures, the number of women elected stayed roughly the same (12% of the total in 2006, 13% in 2010, and 11% in 2014), even as the number of women candidates spiked. The same pattern held for municipal councils: though women made up 33% of candidates in 2012, they accounted for merely 13% of those actually elected. The share of municipal council seats held by women registered only slight growth over time, from 11% in 1996 to 13% in 2012.[4]

The 2014 elections were notable for another reason. For the first time in Brazilian history, the Electoral Court gathered information on the race/color of candidates. This marked the first time that any Latin American country had collected such data. Politicians declaring their color to be "black" or "brown" constituted 44% of candidates for federal deputy, and 47% of candidates for state assemblies (compared to their 52% share of the population overall). Whereas men slightly outnumbered women among whites, women slightly outnumbered men among "black" and "brown" candidates. However, as was the case with women, nonwhites did not get elected in proportion to their share of candidacies. In 2014, the number of politicians elected to the lower house who self-declared their race/color as black or brown to the Electoral Court was 103, or 21%, of the total (Locatelli 2014).[5] In state assemblies, around one-quarter of elected deputies declared themselves to be black or brown. As this suggests, the vast majority of deputies at the federal and state levels continued to be white.

Women's numbers are low in parties across the spectrum, with the exception of the *Brazilian Communist Party* (PC do B, where women made up four of ten deputies after the 2014 elections). The PC do B is also the most diverse party by race/color, as six of the deputies self-identified as *preto* or *pardo*. Women tended to be elected in greater numbers in parties classified as Left or Center-Left (including the *Partido dos Trabalhadores–PT*, the *Partido Socialista Brasileiro–PSB*, the *Partido Democrático Trabalhista–PDT*, and the PC do B) and Center (*Partido da Social Democracia Brasileira–PSDB*, *Partido do Movimento Democrático Brasileiro–PMDB*) than in parties classified as Right (*Democratas–DEM*, *Partido Popular–PP*, *Partido Trabalhista*

3. Of the 51 women elected, 29 were newcomers to the Chamber (though many had been elected to public office before), and 20 had been reelected (12 women running for reelection were defeated).

4. Note that the exact numbers of women in elected office vary between elections as some resign, others are appointed to different positions, and so forth.

5. In the Congress elected in 2010, self-declared Afrodescendants (who are not the same group as those declaring themselves to be *preto* or *pardo*) numbered only 44, or 9% of the total (Htun 2016). It is important to note that longitudinal data on race/color in Congress were collected using different methods, and by different organizations, and are therefore not comparable. The 2014 data refer to people who self-classified as *"preto"* or *"pardo"* (which the Brazilian government considers to form the "black population"), while the 2010 data come from UOL's *Congresso em Foco*, which gave a list of self-declared *"Afrodescendentes."*

Brasileiro–PTB) (Power and Zucco 2012).[6] It is notable that a few of the largest parties (PSD, PP, PTB, DEM), which are all on the Right end of the spectrum, elected either no or very few women.

Elections held under different rules—such as for the federal Senate, state governors, and mayors—conform to different trends. Elections to the federal Senate, for example, are held under plurality rules. Each state elects three senators to serve alternating eight-year terms. Over-time trends in Senate elections show a close correspondence between numbers of women candidates and number of women elected (Figure 12.2, Panel B). This suggests that once a party or coalition decides to postulate a woman as candidate for Senate, they put their full support behind her. The same holds for mayoral races. There is a persistent, but relatively small, gap between numbers of women candidates and numbers of women elected (See Figure 12.2, Panel C).

Governors' races show a different pattern. Figure 12.2, Panel D depicts the non-linear trend in women's presence among governors. Numbers of women candidates for governor and numbers of women elected increased slowly and peaked in 2006, when women made up 13% of candidates and 11% of elected governors. Since 2006, the number of women candidates decreased slightly, but numbers of women elected dropped even more steeply.

Nonelected positions

Women's presence among Brazilian cabinet ministers has tended to be lower than in other Latin American countries, even under a woman president (see Taylor-Robinson and Gleitz, chapter 3, this volume, for regionwide data). There were 11 women in the cabinet when Dilma Rousseff's first term started, and six when the term ended. In her second presidential term, Rousseff reshuffled the cabinet entirely, reducing the number of ministries from 39 to 31 and merging what used to be three separate departments into a single Ministry of Women, Racial Equality, and Human Rights. In this new cabinet, only four of the cabinet members were women. After Rousseff was compelled to leave office in May of 2016, the cabinet of 22 ministers appointed by her former Vice President, Michel Temer, contained not a single woman or a single Afrodescendant.

Women have tended to preside over ministries of lower status and power. Among the ten ministries considered to be important in terms of political and economic impact, women led only two, and only in Rousseff's first term. Women have never led some of the more high-profile ministries, such as the Justice Ministry, the Ministry of Health, and the Foreign Affairs Ministry. The same applies to other positions of high status, such as the Central Bank (Duran, Simão, and Luciano 2015). It is rare to see women in leadership positions in important state companies such as Petrobras, Electrobras, and Furnas (though Rousseff herself had been CEO of Petrobras).[7]

---

6. Not all Left parties elected higher numbers of women; women made up only 1 of 19 deputies in the PDT block.

7. State companies are an important pillar of the indirect administration of the Brazilian state. In 2013, for example, there were a total of 143 state-owned enterprises (Berta "Estatais dependentes e inchadas," newspaper *O Globo*, p. 33, 09/20/2015).

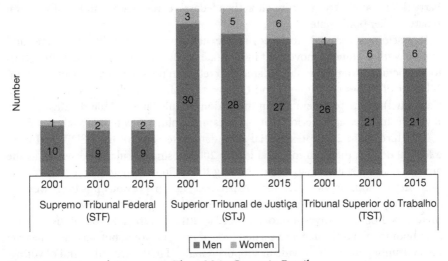

Figure 12.3 Women's Presence in Three Main Courts in Brazil
SOURCE: TSE/Repository of electoral data. Date of generation: July 27, 2015.
Tabulation: NUDERG.

Preliminary surveys of the gender composition of parliamentary offices, ministries, and DAS (Higher Education Advisory Positions) show that low turnover rates keep women's numbers low (e.g., Schwindt-Bayer 2005).

The presence of women in the judiciary has improved since the adoption of public procurement rules in the 1988 Constitution. However, as shown in Figure 12.3, women's presence in the country's three highest courts remains low, though it has increased gradually over time. Between January 2011 and June 2015, of the total of 16 judges Rousseff appointed to the Supreme Federal Court (STF) and the Superior Court of Justice (STJ), only three were women.

Women are scarce in the higher ranks of union federations, as well as other national organizations with political clout, such as the Order of Lawyers of Brazil (OAB) (Araújo and Guedes 2010). Occupying positions in these organizations helps ambitious individuals gain networks and build political capital. Low numbers of women in these organizations therefore reinforces their low presence in political office.

THE 2010 AND 2014 PRESIDENTIAL ELECTIONS

Brazil, with Argentina and Chile, is one of a handful of Latin American countries to have not only elected a woman to the presidency, but to have successfully reelected the same woman. Dilma Rousseff's gender was a crucial element in both elections, although this played out in subtle and counterintuitive ways.

In 2010, the first round of presidential elections saw nine candidates for the office, two women and seven men. The two female candidates were Dilma Rousseff and Marina Silva, both of whom had a history of struggle against the military dictatorship. Silva was active in social justice organizations as an environmentalist linked to movements of rubber workers. She belonged to the PT and later joined the Green

Party (PV), was elected city councilor, then federal representative, and finally federal senator in her home state of Acre.

Rousseff was arrested, tortured, and exiled during the military regime, and worked with a women's movement in the state of Rio Grande do Sul after the return to democracy. From there, she became a secretary in the state government, a federal Minister of Mines and Energy, and then was appointed as chief of staff (Chefe da Casa Civil) in the presidential administration of Luis Ignacio Lula da Silva (Lula). It was during this latter period that she became a politician with national presence.

The third main 2010 presidential candidate, José Serra of the PSDB, had been a federal deputy, then ran for President in 2002 (losing to Lula), and served as the governor of the state of São Paolo. Among the main candidates, Rousseff was the only one without previous electoral experience, as her previous positions were all appointed offices. At the time, survey data revealed a gender gap, with more men preferring Rousseff (Alves, Pinto, and Jordão 2012). In the election, Rousseff won over both men and women and earned 56% of the total votes, but was more heavily favored among men. This divide in support remained in the second round of voting, when Rousseff squared off against Serra.

As some authors suggest, the fact that Rousseff is a woman had very little to do with her victory. There is no evidence that women voted for her in greater numbers; on the contrary, she held a greater share of male support. Yet gender still mattered in the election. During the campaign, political elites and the media held Rousseff to a different standard than men. In particular, her opponents raised fears that, if elected, she would promote the liberalization of Brazil's strict laws on abortion. (In the past, though not during the presidential campaign, Rousseff had spoken our in favor of abortion law reform.) In order to keep the coalition together, she announced on national television that she was "pro life," and met privately with religious leaders to assure them that she would not take action on abortion if elected.

Ironically, however, it was not Rousseff but her opponent José Serra who had in the past taken action on abortion against the wishes of religious groups. As Minister of Health under the government of Fernando Henrique Cardoso (1994–2002), Serra had approved important reforms to the regulation of abortion in Brazil. At the same time that legislation on the issue was stalled in Congress, he instituted a technical norm that required all public hospitals in the country to attend to those abortions permitted by law (in the event of rape or a threat to the mother's life). The rule responded to demands long made by feminist movements, but was fiercely opposed by the Roman Catholic and evangelical churches. The fact that Rousseff, but not Serra, was taken to task for past action on abortion reveals a gendered double standard in electoral politics.

The 2014 election was marked by tragedy, as the PSB candidate Eduardo Campos was killed midway through the election, and replaced by Marina Silva. After Silva entered the race, various sources indicated a reversal in the polls. In the first round, there were eleven candidates, three of whom were women. These three women were among those five candidates who got more than 1% of the vote, including 42% for Rousseff, 21% for Silva, and 2% for Luciana Genro, totaling 64% of all first-round votes. Rousseff and Aécio Neves, the top two vote getters, entered the second round. Several polls suggested that Rousseff had a greater share of the women's vote than Aécio Neves, as well as greater support from nonwhite voters (Agência Patrícia Galvão 2015; Datafolha Instituto de Pesquisa 2016).

As this suggests, there was a clear change in the basis of Rousseff's support between the two election periods. In 2010, abortion dominated the agenda, and Rousseff had to work hard not to lose religious votes. In 2014, this issue was not as prominent. Rather, the economy and corruption were the focus, and there were concerns about the potential for economic decline, which subsequently bore fruit.

Feminists were dismayed about public discourse on gender issues during the campaign, including on sexual and reproductive rights, public policies to support domestic work and family life, and violence against women (Agência Patrícia Galvão 2015). Although the Rousseff campaign supported social programs that benefitted women, such as the *Bolsa Familia* (family grant program), the program My Home My Life, and PRONAF—a support program for small rural farms—they were not feminist in orientation. Most policies were based on a traditional understanding of women's gender roles. At the same time, however, the campaign also emphasized women's empowerment and affirmative action.[8]

In the second round, Rousseff was reelected in the closest presidential race in decades. She squeaked by with 51.6% of the vote over Neves's 48.4%. By gaining a stronger showing of support among women voters than she had enjoyed in the 2010 election, Rousseff was able to win reelection. This could have reflected growing confidence in women's capacity to govern, since not only did Rousseff get reelected but women overall got the majority of votes in earlier rounds of voting.

However, at the beginning of her second mandate, Rousseff lost support among political elites and the general population. In April 2015, less than three months after she formed her second administration, only 13% of the population considered their government *very good*, while 44% considered it *poor* or *very poor*. The trend of disapproval persisted. In April 2016, only 13% of people surveyed considered the government *very good*, while 63% considered it *poor* or *very poor*. There were few gender differences (Datafolha Instituto de Pesquisa 2016). Combined with the economic crisis and other factors, this lack of support gave fuel to the campaign for the president's impeachment during 2015.

WHY DO SO FEW WOMEN GET ELECTED?

Several mutually reinforcing factors set Brazil apart from other countries and help to account for the low numbers of women elected to the national legislature. These include the candidate-centered electoral system, decentralized legislative recruitment, the importance of money, and the interaction between incumbency and television.

First, Brazil has an extreme version of a candidate-centered electoral system, which tends to incentivize and reward individualistic behavior. Though the system allocates seats to parties by means of proportional representation (seats accrue to parties in direct proportion to their share of the popular vote), parties allocate seats to candidates in accordance with the number of individual preference votes they

---

8. In this regard, there is little consensus, since some studies and feminist groups point to maternalist, traditional policies, while others highlight the positive effect on the empowerment of women in the family sphere and on employment and income generation.

receive. In Chamber of Deputies elections, voters can cast a vote for a party or for an individual candidate, although most vote for individuals. This system creates strong incentives for candidates to stress their personal attributes, resources, and political capital rather than the party's program and generates competition among co-partisans (Ames 1995; Mainwaring 1999; Samuels 1999).

Comparative research shows that women tend to get elected in lower numbers in candidate-centered electoral systems than in party-centered systems (Matland and Studlar 1996; Norris 2004; Thames and Williams 2010), but also that these effects hold mostly in established democracies where institutions are more stable (Moser and Scheiner 2012). Scholars argue that women do better when parties exercise greater control over the ballot, such as in closed-list PR systems. In these contexts, parties can rank-order candidates on party lists, alternating women and men. In addition, more bureaucratic parties sustain more transparent rules, more organized structures, and more consistent leadership for advocates of women's presence to lobby (Lovenduski and Norris, 1993).

Why do women fare poorly in candidate-centered systems? Such systems encourage a free-for-all contest, in which success turns on the ability of individual candidates to develop relationships with individual voters. In this context, the personal resources of politicians and their ability to project a presence throughout the district are decisive. Social inequalities, hierarchies, and historical patterns of discrimination affect the ability of different social groups to acquire financial resources and amass political capital. Women were historically excluded from elite power networks out of which leaders emerged and were recruited. They are also less present among business elites, millionaires, and billionaires, and have a subordinate but growing presence in the media. Women's lower social position means they are less likely to self-nominate as candidates and have less access to the resources needed to finance successful electoral campaigns. In party-centered systems, by contrast, success depends on the relationship between individual candidates and party leaders. Partisan institutions and ideologies are more important.

The second factor to take into account is the decentralized legislative recruitment characteristic of Brazilian parties. State party conventions put together party lists for elections, but neither national nor state-level party leaders are in control. Instead, people tend to self-select as nominees for party and coalition lists (Samuels 2008). Few rules govern who may run for the legislature (just residence in the state and one-year membership in the party), except for the PT, which requires candidates to demonstrate support from within the party by producing signatures from officials and party members.[9]

Comparative research suggests that systems of self-nomination favor men, as women are less likely to nominate themselves for legislative office (Hinojosa 2012). Women are less likely, relative to men, voluntarily to seek out political candidacies due to a lack of resources, social norms, and other barriers (such as work-family conflicts). As mentioned above, women are less likely to participate in the power

9. The PT requires candidates to obtain signatures from a third of the members of the state party's executive committee, 5% of municipal councils in the state, and 1% of all party affiliates, or else approval from a sectoral meeting. In addition, candidates must receive approval votes from at least 20% of party members at the convention (Samuels 2008).

monopolies or networks that assist in fund-raising, dealmaking, and projecting influence. Power networks shape a politician's access to power as well as their ability to wield power *after* obtaining elected office. Historically dominated by men, power networks tend to exclude women in *practice*, even if not in *principle*. For example, communication in the network often occurs in places frequented by men (such as clubs and golf courses), where women may be unwelcome or just uncomfortable. Finally, at the mass level, women tend to belong to different types of social organizations and groups (those more oriented toward private and community life) than do men (whose membership patterns tilt toward more public and politically oriented organizations) (Sacchet 2009b).

Parties with exclusive and centralized nomination procedures tend to neutralize these gendered barriers. Candidates are hand picked by party leaders (rather than self-nominated) and power networks are less influential. Analyzing variation across parties in Chile, Hinojosa (2012) has shown that paradoxically, women tend to get elected in greater numbers when nomination is more centralized (or authoritarian) than decentralized (or democratic). Among Brazilian parties, the PT has the most bureaucratic nomination procedures, and tends to elect more women than other parties.

The extreme fragmentation of the Brazilian party system contributes to decentralized nomination procedures.[10] Politicians are constantly creating, merging, and dissolving parties. In 2014, there were 32 officially registered parties that competed in elections at different levels. Twenty-eight parties postulated candidates for Chamber of Deputies elections, and 22 won seats. By the second half of 2015, the number of registered parties increased to 35, including a new party called the Party of Brazilian Women (*Partido da Mulher Brasileira*—PMB). Yet only 2 of the PMB's 20 deputies were women. Leaders emphasized that the party was *not* feminist; in fact, it lacked any ideology or program.[11]

Another factor impeding the institutionalization of the party system and, by extension, more formal nomination procedures in parties, is the salience of family ties. In 2014, there were 211 elected deputies who were spouses, children, or siblings of other politicians, including 185 men and 26 women (making up a total of 40% of all male deputies and 51% of women deputies) (Departamento Intersindical de Assessoria Parlamentar 2014). Though family ties may help to get women into politics, they may also reduce these women's ability to exercise autonomous, effective leadership and to be seen by others as legitimate politicians.

The third feature of Brazilian politics that keeps women out is the importance of money. Money matters more in personalist than in programmatic politics, and is arguably the biggest problem in Brazil's political system. Politicians seek money to develop their reputations, broadcast their images, and differentiate themselves from

---

10. In 2017 the Brazilian Congress began to discuss a new political reform for the 2018 elections. Elements of the proposed changes include raising the threshold of representation in the Chamber of Deputies, increasing public financing of political parties, and most controversially, modifying electoral rules from proportional representation to a special type of majoritarian system, called "*Distritão*."

11. Deborah Melo, "A que veio o Partido da Mulher Brasileira?" *Carta Capital*. February 23, 2016. Available at: http://www.cartacapital.com.br/politica/a-que-veio-o-partido-da-mulher-brasileira.

other candidates (Samuels 2002). There is a strong association between access to campaign finance and electoral performance, especially for women. Money matters more for women than for male candidates because it enables them to overcome disadvantages posed by their gender position and their lower numbers among incumbents (Speck and Mancuso 2014).

Women have less access to money than men do. There are fewer women in executive positions in state and local governments, positions that enable aspiring politicians to develop connections to the owners of firms contracting with the government.[12] As mentioned earlier, women are less present in the business and industry networks where money is raised. These factors combine to lower the numbers of women who are willing to run for office. What is more, women who seek election but suffer defeat cite financial difficulties as the main reason they are unwilling to run again (Araújo and Borges 2012). Political parties tend to allocate fewer resources to women candidates than to male ones. The *Folha de São Paulo's* study of the 2010 elections showed that the 14 biggest parties gave women only 8% of their funds, even though they made up 20% of candidates (Ramos et al. 2014). Male candidates tend to get more resources from legal entities, while women's support tends to come from individual donations and in smaller volumes (Araújo and Borges 2012).

Figure 12.4 compares the campaign expenditures of candidates and elected officials for the Chamber of Deputies in the 2014 elections. It shows that both successful and unsuccessful male candidates outspent women candidates, in the latter case, by around 85,000 *reais*. In the 2010 elections as well, male candidates for federal deputy raised, on average, 48% more money than women candidates (Speck and Mancuso 2014, 46). Yet data also suggest that when women do spend as much money as men do, their chances of getting high vote shares increase dramatically, and even exceed men's (Ibid., 53).

During debates over political reform, many politicians and civic groups raised the question of how financial resources affect electoral success. The volume of money donated, primarily from private corporations (*pessoas jurídicas*), has grown from election to election. As a result, many actors have proposed limiting or even prohibiting corporate donations.

Finally, it is important to consider the importance of incumbency and the way it interacts with television time. In Brazil, incumbents have an automatic right to stand for reelection. Studies have emphasized the importance of incumbency for electoral success in any position (Araújo and Alves 2011). When a candidate is up for reelection, their chances of being reelected are greater than if they were running for the first time. What is more, when an incumbent candidate occupies a position of party leadership or leadership in a congressional committee, they are more likely to be elected (Araújo and Alves 2007, 2011; Araújo and Borges 2012). Such positions provide candidates with media exposure, and this visibility leads to invitations to give speeches and other appearances.

12. However, those women that do get elected in Brazil tend to have similar profiles compared to the men elected. For example, the 2014 elections produced several women deputies who were family members of male politicians, along with women who had served as mayor, state deputy, city councilor, and in the executive branch of state governments. But there are fewer women overall who have served in these positions, which generate access to power networks and are stepping stones to a national career (and then back to a local one) (e.g., Samuels 2003).

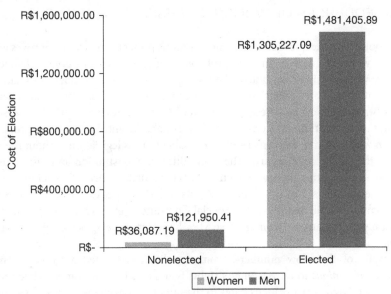

Figure 12.4 Average Candidate Cost of the Election Campaign by Sex and Result of Campaign, Chamber of Deputies, Brazil, 2014
SOURCE: TSE/Repository of electoral data. Date of generation: July 27, 2015.
Tabulation: NUDERG.

A recently conducted survey (UNDP 2013) showed that very few women are nominated to serve on congressional committees. When women are nominated to committees, they tend to occupy lower-status roles and rarely fill leadership positions. In this respect, Brazil conforms to regional and global trends (Heath, Schwindt-Bayer, and Taylor-Robinson 2005). Analysis of committee composition in the Senate and the Chamber of Deputies in 2015 showed that men occupied the vast majority of seats on important committees such as Economic Affairs, Science and Technology, and the Constitution and Justice, while the few women serving were found in Social Affairs and Education.

Another crucial determinant of success is television time. Brazilian law distributes Free Electoral Political Advertising Time (HGPE, or *Horario Gratuito de Propaganda Eleitoral*) to parties; two-thirds of that time is allocated according to their presence in the Chamber of Deputies (2/3) and one-third is allocated equally across parties. Parties, in turn, distribute the time among candidates as they wish, but they generally do so according to their perception of the candidate's ability to earn votes. Multiparty coalitions have become adept at engineering increased access to airtime, sometimes doubling or tripling allotments for the candidate representing the coalition, and maximizing exposure through alternating advertisements at the national and state levels. Women tend to be scarcer among incumbents and therefore tend to be given less time on air (Romero, Figueiredo, and Araújo 2012). Studies find that the vast majority of Brazilians watch all or at least some of the HGPE. Around half of those surveyed claim that the ads they see on the HGPE have some effect on their vote, while the other half claim that the ads have no effect at all (Panke and Tesseroli 2014, 17–19).

CONSEQUENCES OF WOMEN'S PRESENCE IN POWER

This book raises the question of whether women's presence in power improves advocacy of women's interests and the probability of legislative and policy changes to advance women's rights. Although the mere presence of women does not guarantee a commitment to an egalitarian agenda, it can operate as a catalyst for such action. Yet in Brazil, women's low presence in power overall carries over into a low presence on legislative committees. Even when they are able to introduce policy proposals, women who advocate women's rights are unable to pass legislation without the support of their male counterparts. The Committee on Constitution and Justice in the Chamber of Deputies, through which all bills pass, had, in early 2015, 43 men and 3 women as members, while the Human Rights and Minorities Committee had 13 men and 3 women as full members. The Special Committee set up to discuss the status of the family, an initiative of Conservative MPs, had 22 members, including 17 men and 5 women.

In spite of their low numbers, women politicians formed a women's caucus (*bancada femenina*) to raise women's rights issues and to give women's civic groups a voice in Congress. The caucus dates to the mid-1980s, when women delegates created the "lipstick lobby" in the constituent convention charged with writing a new constitution (enacted in 1988). The "lipstick lobby" (*bancada do batom*) succeeded in that the final text endorsed the principle of gender equality and a range of other women's rights (Pitanguy 1996). Since then, the caucus has met regularly and, assisted by the feminist lobbying organization CFEMEA, introduced numerous issues to the legislative agenda.

Legislative surveys[13] have revealed that women tend to be more involved with pro-equality initiatives than men. Women have raised and supported issues such as workplace equality, violence against women, and social policies that, from a feminist perspective, have been perceived to reinforce traditional gender roles such as the Family Grant (*Bolsa Familia*). Women united to support the Maria da Penha Law on gender violence in 2006, a fund to assist survivors/victims of violence, a parliamentary commission of inquiry to investigate gender violence, and a 2013 constitutional amendment proposal to grant domestic workers full labor rights.[14]

There is less consensual action among women on explicitly feminist issues such as abortion and reproductive health. Especially during the administration of Dilma Rousseff, programs emphasizing sexual rights and women's bodily autonomy were absent entirely or were blocked by political opposition. Women agree about the need to fight gender violence but not about what to do with one of the consequences of violence—namely, unintended pregnancy as the result of rape.[15]

13. Analysis of bills presented from 1995 to 2012 (UNDP 2013) and survey for the period 2013–2015.

14. Fourteen percent of working women are domestic workers, the third ranked category of women's work.

15. For example, the special rapporteur on women's rights, Elcione Barbalho (PMDB/PA), manifested her opposition to abortion in cases of rape because of religious beliefs (http://www2. camara.leg.br, accessed 31 October 2015).

Although having suffered rape exempts a woman from the criminal penalties usually incurred by illegal abortion, it is difficult to find a legal provider, even in these circumstances.

To a certain extent, this pattern of uneven congressional action on women's rights reflects public opinion. Surveys show high support for the participation of women in politics (Cavenaghi and Alves 2012; Matos and Pinheiro 2012). At the same time, the surveys reveal a high degree of conservatism on abortion, sexuality, same-sex marriage, and legalization of drugs, among other issues (Matos and Pinheiro 2012; Fundaçao Perseu Abramo 2011).

The severe gender imbalance in Congress contributes to a hostile institutional climate. There are explicit and open manifestations of "machismo" and even misogyny among male parliamentarians, some of whom have verbally insulted and assaulted their women colleagues. In general, this behavior is associated with parliamentarians belonging to more conservative parties and addressed to MPs seen as more feminist, defenders of human rights, or from Left parties. Men have called women "ugly" and "fat," and one male legislator told his female colleague that she was so ugly that she did not "deserve" to be raped. The next day, the same deputy repeated the claim in a newspaper interview, stating that the woman is not "worth raping; she is very ugly."[16]

The Congress elected in 2014 was considered the most conservative since the return to democracy, and the size of the evangelical caucus (*bancada evangélica*) grew significantly (Datafolha Instituto de Pesquisa 2016). In one of his first statements after being elected speaker of the Chamber of Deputies, Eduardo Cunha declared that he would not put on the agenda any rights pertaining to "gays, potheads, and abortionists."[17] As a result, and in spite of the political and economic crisis, Congress has focused a great deal of its attention on rolling back reproductive rights and LGBT rights. The evangelical caucus has proposed bills to impose a strict definition of family, restrict benefits for families of same-sex couples, and to criminalize abortions performed when the pregnancy results from rape, among other initiatives. Women legislators are divided vis-à-vis the socially conservative legislative agenda that gained force in 2015. For example, the Special Commission on the Status of the Family, created by legislators from the evangelical caucus, approved a bill that defines the family as a heterosexual partnership and denies various rights to nonconforming partnerships. Both the pro- and the antigay coalitions included women. What is more, though the legislators who most openly defend reproductive rights and LGBT rights tend to come from parties of the Left, pro- and antisocially conservative positions do not generally conform to Left-Right distinctions.

16. "Brazilian Congressman Ordered To Pay Compensation over Rape Remark." *The Guardian*. September 18, 2015. Other conflicts include clashes between then Congresswoman Cida Diogo (PT) and the then deputy Clodovil Hernandes (PTB) in 2007 and between Roberto Freire and Jandira Feghali in 2015.

17. Cunha was removed from the presidency of the Chamber of Deputies in May of 2016 for allegedly intimidating lawmakers and impeding an investigation alleging that he embezzled millions of dollars and stashed them in illicit Swiss and other foreign bank accounts. In June the ethics committee voted to remove him from Congress altogether.

CONCLUSION

It is puzzling that Brazil would elect a woman president for two consecutive terms, but preside over one of the lowest levels of women's parliamentary presence in the Western hemisphere. When we consider the organization of Brazil's political institutions and the inequalities in the rest of society, these outcomes need no longer surprise us. The candidate-centered electoral system that governs access to the Chamber of Deputies directly transmits societal inequalities to political races. Competition among candidates for legislative election is a free-for-all contest in which people with the most political and social capital—the richest and most famous—prevail. In a country with deeply entrenched inequalities, these people tend to be fair-skinned men.

We argue that Brazil's electoral institutions impede women's access to elected office. The personalist, candidate-centered system and associated features—such as the high cost of running for office—tend to put men at an advantage. Political reforms enacted in 2015 were aimed to mitigate some of these obstacles. They included a ban on private donations to campaigns, and a reduction in the period of free TV time from 45 to 30 days prior to the election. However, both of these reforms also increase competition for available public funds and for the remaining TV time, which is especially important given the fact that the open-list system has not been changed.

Other electoral regimes, such as closed-list proportional representation or even single-member district (SMD) systems, enable parties to intervene in the selection and election of candidates to promote greater diversity. For example, in a closed-list system, party leaders can alternate men with women candidates on the list, which increases the number of women elected. Vote-pooling in such systems aligns the collective interests of the party with the interests of individual politicians (Shugart 2013). During the campaign, every party member works to get more women candidates elected as this increases the party's share of seats overall. Women get elected to office in greater numbers in these countries not necessarily because the societies are more egalitarian, but because parties in these countries have used the institutional means available to help get more women elected. The result is that the polity seems more gender egalitarian than it is in actuality. In Brazil's open-list system, by contrast, candidates from the same party compete with one another for preference votes, and no individual has an incentive to work for the election of greater numbers of women. In these circumstances, low numbers of women in power are a more direct reflection of enduring gender subordination.

At the time that this chapter went to press, the outlook for women and gender equality was grim. The political crisis created by investigations of corruption involving the majority of elected officials, and especially the impeachment of Dilma Rousseff, revealed considerable bias against women in politics on the part of the media and the political class. The mere image of male legislators, the vast majority of whom were under investigation for illicit personal enrichment and other crimes, voting to impeach a woman president in May of 2016 signaled a major setback. One legislator even dedicated his vote to her former torturers in the military government. To make matters worse, the cabinet appointed by the interim president, Michel

Temer, contained not a single woman (nor did it contain anyone nonwhite).[18] In the process of reshuffling the executive, Temer demoted the secretariats of gender and racial equality from their former ministerial status.[19] The exclusion of women from the cabinet triggered immediate outcry both at home and abroad, demonstrating that in the eyes of the world, Brazil had taken a big step backward.

18. What is more, three of the newly appointed ministers resigned due to corruption charges.

19. Temer's nominee for the sub-secretariat for women (within the Ministry of Justice) is a former deputy from his party linked to the evangelical caucus who in 2012 declared her opposition to abortion in the event of rape. As of the time of this writing, she had not assumed the position due to accusations of corruption in her home state.

Female Representation in Colombia

A Historical Analysis (1962–2014)

MÓNICA PACHÓN AND SANTIAGO E. LACOUTURE ∎

In contrast to other Latin American countries, Colombia was an electoral democracy through almost all of the twentieth century and was one of the last countries in the region to grant women political rights. In 1954, the military government of Rojas Pinilla promoted the writing of a new constitution, which would allow his permanence in power. The need for support for the dictatorship allowed the emergence of a women suffragist movement, which, under the leadership of women like Esmeralda Arboleda,[1] created a petition signed by thousands of men and women to the National Constituent Assembly to include women's suffrage into the constitutional agenda. On August 25, 1954, the assembly approved women's right to vote and be elected.[2]

Part of the electoral analysis presented in this chapter was first published in an article of the journal *Latin American Politics and Society*. We would like to thank them for their permission to use part of the results here. We would also like to thank Leslie Schwindt-Bayer for all of her suggestions in every step of this chapter, as well as Maria Paula Aroca in earlier stages of this project.

1. Esmeralda Arboleda, born January 22, 1921, was one of the first female professionals and in 1945 became the first women lawyer to receive a degree from Universidad del Cauca. She was the daughter of Fernando Arboleda López, a Liberal Party politician, from whom she inherited her liberal political convictions (*El Espectador* 2011).

2. Nevertheless, when Rojas Pinilla was removed from office in 1957, the constitutional reform required ratification, which was achieved through the 1957 plebiscite, wherein the citizenry approved a 14-point plan, which included the alternation of power between the Liberal and Conservative Parties (known as the National Front) and women's suffrage. The passage of this plebiscite allowed women to become full Colombian citizens: they were given an identification card—*cédula*—(a process that had already begun in 1954) with which they could exercise their right to vote.

Yet, only recently have women's representation and women's rights become an issue in Colombian politics. It is only since 2006 that female legislators have formally organized themselves as a caucus in Congress. As Guzmán, Molano, and Uprimny (2015) report, there is still a considerable gap between legal changes and the reality that Colombian women face under conditions of exclusion, discrimination, and violence.

This chapter describes the incremental growth of women's representation in Colombian arenas of government since 1960 and shows the impact of institutional changes in the percentage of women nominated and elected at different levels of government.[3] Empirically, we show that during the last five decades, there has been great path dependence in the historically low numbers of women in political office. At regional and local levels, existing data show directly elected offices with majority rules are the toughest for women's election, whereas political contexts with more proportional rules produce more success. Only in exceptional circumstances do women become mayors or governors. We also evaluate which institutional reforms have had a positive impact in increasing women's representation, finding a significant effect of electoral quotas. Finally, we argue that these slow changes have had an impact on substantive representation in the Colombian Congress by increasing the introduction of women's issue bills.

FEMALE DESCRIPTIVE REPRESENTATION IN THE EXECUTIVE BRANCH

Throughout Colombia's history, no woman has won election to the Presidency of the Republic, although four women have run since 1998: Noemí Sanín in 1998, 2002, and 2010; Ingrid Betancourt in 2002; and Marta Lucía Ramírez and Clara López in 2014.[4] Likewise, no woman has ever held the position of Vice President, reestablished with

---

3. Many institutional changes came with and after 1991 Constitution. The electoral system was modified both in 1991 and 2003. Significant effort was also made in 2011 with Statutory Act 1475 which establishes "lists where 5 or more seats are chosen for corporations of popular election or those which are subject to consultation must comply by at least 30% of one gender" (Article 28 Statutory Act 1475), but parties can decide whether their lists will be open or closed. It also states that "5% of total state funding for parties would be equally distributed to the parties and movements in proportion to the number of elected women in their lists (Article 17 [6] Statutory Act 1475). Lists that do not meet the legal requirements, including the gender quota, will be rejected (Article 32 Statutory Act 1475)."

4. The first female presidential candidate in the country was María Eugenia Rojas Moreno-Díaz (daughter of former General and President Gustavo Rojas Pinilla), who ran for the presidency in 1974. However, it was not until 1998 that a second woman ran. Since then, women have participated in each contest, with the exception of 2006 when Álvaro Uribe was reelected by a wide margin. Regina Betancourt de Liska began a presidential campaign in 1998 but was kidnapped. Also, Ingrid Betancourt's campaign in 2002 could not continue because she was kidnapped by the FARC. For 2014 elections, the nominations of Aída Avella and Clara López were unified due to the alliance between their parties—López ran as the alliance's presidential candidate and Avella as vice president.

the 1991 Constitution.[5] This office has had eleven female candidates, however: María Emma Mejía in 1998; Vera Grabe Loewenherz and Clara Rojas[6] in 2002; Patricia Lara Salive and María Isabel Patiño in 2006; Elsa Noguera, Clara López, Ana María Cabal, and Olga Lucía Taborda in 2010; and Aída Avella and Isabel Segovia in 2014.

Table 13.1 displays the electoral results of the previously mentioned female candidates. If we look at the percentage of the margin of defeat compared to the winning candidate in the first round, except for the 2010 elections, the difference is more than 40%, which shows no woman has come close to winning a presidential election. However, as vice-presidential candidates, women have performed better, particularly when they have been on a ticket with a popular male candidate. This was the case for María Emma Mejía, who was almost elected in 1998 with Horacio Serpa. They won the largest vote share in the first round but lost in the second round. In 2006, Patricia Lara placed second as vice-presidential candidate in the first round, running with Carlos Gaviria.

At the subnational level, women's participation has been very low, especially for popularly elected mayors and governors. Before 1986, and as a result of a highly centralized political regime, presidents appointed governors who in turn appointed mayors. Since 1992, the percentage of female mayors, as well as the average percentage of female candidates at the municipal level, has not seen a significant increase (see Table 13.2). Female representation in these offices remains low, between 4% and 7%, although the percentage of candidates has almost doubled since 1992 (from 4.37% in 1992 to 8.07% in 2011). Likewise, Table 13.3 shows low representation of women at the departmental level (governor) and the small variation in this over time (women's representation as candidates for governor and as governor varies only from 0% to 7%).

In 1991, with the enactment of the Constitution, legally mandated representation of women in administrative roles began. The last clause of Article 40 of the Constitution states that "authorities shall guarantee the adequate and effective participation of women at the decision-making levels of public administration" (León and Holguín 2005). What that would look like in specific numeric terms, however, was not clear. Between 1992 and 1999, eight bills were introduced that sought to specify how that constitutional mandate should be enacted (Quintero 2005). Finally, Statutory Law 581 of May 2000 established that at least 30% of high-level positions and other decision-making offices within the government were to be held by women.[7] Figure 13.1 illustrates two things. First, there has been at least one female minister in office in every year since 1990. Second, incrementally more women have been appointed each year, although this trend stabilized around the 30% quota mandate in 2006.

Beyond overall gender imbalance in cabinets, the portfolios to which women and men get appointed reveal gender bias. Figure 13.2 shows the percentage of specific cabinet posts that were held by women compared to men before the quota reform

---

5. The office of the Vice President existed throughout most of the nineteenth century until its elimination in the 1910 constitutional reform and was reestablished by the 1991 Constitution.

6. Clara Rojas also was kidnapped while campaigning with Ingrid Betancourt in 2002.

7. This became known as the administrative quota law.

Table 13.1 WOMEN'S PARTICIPATION IN PRESIDENTIAL ELECTIONS

Presidential Candidate	Vice Presidential Candidate	Political Party	Total Votes	Vote Share	Margin of Defeat
Presidential Election 2014. First Round					
Martha Lucía Ramírez	Camilo Gómez	*Partido Conservador*	1,997,980	15.52%	−13.73%
Clara López	Aída Avella	*Polo Democrático - Unión Patriótica*	1,958,518	15.21%	−14.04%
Enrique Peñalosa	Isabel Segovia	*Partido Verde*	1,064,758	8.27%	−20.98%
Presidential Election 2010. First Round					
German Vargas Lleras	Elsa Noguera	*Partido Cambio Radical*	1,473,627	10.11%	−36.56%
Gustavo Petro	Clara López	*Polo Democrático*	1,331,267	9.13%	−37.54%
Noemí Sanín	Luis Ernesto Mejía	*Partido Conservador*	893,819	6.13%	−40.54%
Robinson Devia Gonzalez	Olga Lucía Taborda	*Movimiento La Voz de la Conciencia*	31,338	0.21%	−46.46%
Jaime Araujo Rentería	Ana María Cabal	*Alianza Social Afrocolombiana*	14,847	0.10%	−46.57%
Presidential Election 2006					
Carlos Gaviria Díaz	Patricia Lara Salive	*Polo Democrático Alternativo*	2,613,157	22.02%	−40.33%
Antanas Mockus	María Isabel Patiño	*Alianza Social Indígena*	146,583	1.23%	−61.12%
Presidential Election 2002					
Noemí Sanín	Fabio Villegas Ramírez	*Movimiento Sí, Colombia*	641,884	5.96%	−48.55%
Luis Eduardo Garzón	Vera Grabe Lewenberg	*Polo Democrático*	680,245	6.32%	−48.19%
Íngrid Betancourt	Clara Rojas	*Partido Verde*	53,922	0.48%	−54.05%
Presidential Election 1998. Second Round					
Horacio Serpa Uribe	María Emma Mejía	*Partido Liberal Colombiano*	5,658,518	46.53%	−3.86%
Presidential Election 1998. First Round					
Horacio Serpa Uribe	María Emma Mejía	*Partido Liberal Colombiano*	3,647,007	34.59%	+0.32%
Noemí Sanín	Antanas Mockus Sivickas	*Sí, Colombia*	2,825,706	26.88%	−7.71%

SOURCE: Registraduría Nacional del Estado Civil de Colombia.

Table 13.2 FEMALE REPRESENTATION IN THE EXECUTIVE
(LOCAL LEVEL [I.E., MAYORS])

Year	Percentage Female Mayors	Mean Percentage of Nominated Women
1992	4.11	4.37
1994	3.98	4.34
1997	6.11	6.18
2000	7.13	5.61
2003	4.44	5.24
2007	5.38	7.47
2011	5.37	8.02

SOURCE: Pachón and Sánchez (2014).

Table 13.3 FEMALE REPRESENTATION IN THE EXECUTIVE
(REGIONAL LEVEL [I.E., GOVERNORS])

Year	Percentage Female Governors	Mean Percentage of Nominated Women
1991	4.16	4.01
1994	3.23	1.67
1997	0	5.1
2000	3.33	6.03
2003	3.45	4.32
2007	3.13	5.71
2011	6.25	6.82

SOURCE: Pachón and Sánchez (2014).

in 2000 (Panel A) and after (Panel B). Average female representation in cabinets was 8% during the 1970–2000 period, and as can be observed, women did not dominate any ministry (less than 20% of the time a woman served in the office of National Education or Foreign Affairs).

After the enactment of the quota, average female representation in the cabinet increased to 30.5%, with a change in the pattern in which women became associated with certain public policy areas, such as culture or education. This pattern became similar to what Taylor-Robinson and Gleitz (chapter 3, this volume) found regionwide. Women were rarely appointed to National Defense[8] or Finance ministries. Gender balance was best in the National Education, Foreign Affairs, and Environment ministries, but still, women held those posts well less than 50% of the time, whereas men held them more than 50% of the time.

The quota law has only been effective in high-visibility posts such as cabinet ministries, whereas it has been largely ignored for other administrative positions

8. In fact, the only woman to lead this ministry was future presidential candidate Marta Lucía Ramírez between August 7, 2002 and November 10, 2003.

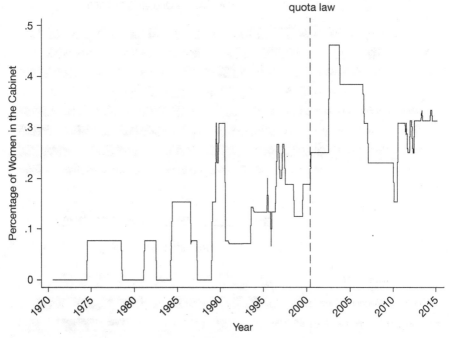

Figure 13.1 Percentage of Cabinet that is Female
NOTE: Data are plotted monthly. Thus, 1970 refers to January of 1970, 1975 refers to
January of 1975, and so on.
SOURCE: Elaborated by the authors.

and at local and regional levels (León and Holguín 2005). According to the Mesa
de Género, a coordinating body for international cooperation efforts in Colombia
that supports all gender related initiatives (2011), at the local and regional levels,
only 6 out of 32 departments and 18 of the 60 largest municipalities complied
with the quota law between 2004 and 2010. They argue that poor compliance is
explained by the lack of effective sanctions and insufficient attention from surveillance and enforcement bodies.[9] Aware of these constraints, women legislators
have introduced bills aiming to tackle the law's weaknesses, increasing the mandated appointment percentage from 30% to 50% and improving the enforcement
capacity and/or the punishment.[10] Unfortunately, all bills were archived before
the second debate, showing the difficulty of making substantial changes to the
status quo.

9. Indeed, the noncompliance to this law is grounds for malfeasance, punishable by a suspension
from office for up to thirty days or dismissal in case of further transgressions (Article 4, Law 581
of 2000). The surveillance and enforcement bodies—namely, the Office of the Inspector General
and the Ombudsman's Office—have never dismissed an official for non-compliance.

10. In chronological order, the bills were Senate Bill 130 of 2006, Senate Bill 03 of 2007, and House
Bill 171 of 2014. Two other bills sought to extend the quota to the private sector. Also, there have
been attempts to modify articles of the Constitution to make the quota more enforceable.

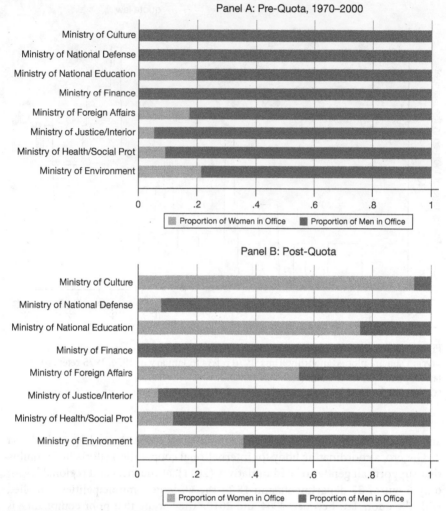

Figure 13.2 Proportion of Time in Office across Different Ministries, by Gender
SOURCE: Elaborated by the authors.

WHAT EXPLAINS THE LOWER LEVELS OF FEMALE REPRESENTATION IN COLOMBIA?

According to Wills (2005), the perception of women's role in Colombian society has dramatically transformed in the last century from being confined to the private sphere at the beginning of the 20th century to being accepted as participants in the public sphere.

Nonetheless, one of the most common explanations found in the literature to illustrate poor female political representation is the existence of a patriarchal culture. Supporters of this hypothesis argue that these values have negatively influenced public perception of women as participants in politics, particularly during the first half of the twentieth century.

Gutiérrez de Pineda (1988), who chronicles the weakening of the patriarchal family structure in Colombia, attributes this change to the persistent political assassination of men in rural Colombia, which resulted in the opportunity for women to become heads of household and migrate to cities. Gutiérrez de Pineda confirmed with evidence from the 1963 census, that Colombia was predominantly rural, with an agrarian economy and a high proportion of men to women in the countryside. The 1985 Census, on the contrary, showed an urbanized country with an economy focused on industry and services and where the number of women surpassed that of men in cities. For Gutiérrez de Pineda, it is this demographic change (an increase in the number of economically active women by 168.1% between 1970 and 1990), which in turn catalyzed female civic participation. In her argument, socioeconomic development is crucial for breaking down barriers imposed by a culture that limits women's political involvement.

Additionally, other authors suggest how family connections explained the early political careers of women in Colombia. Political dynasties, instead of women's empowerment, led to the election and appointment of women to Colombian political arenas. In his piece about women's opinions regarding their roles in Colombian society, Schmidt (1975) argues that social class affected political ambition among women. The author finds that women in political positions by 1972 were members of the ruling class and, in many cases, the daughters, sisters and wives of prominent political figures. The author concludes that the presence of women in political positions before 1975 should not be interpreted as the result of a cultural shift in Colombian society regarding their views of gender roles, but rather as a product of the existence of class access points. However, these historical analyses are unable to explain change, and also how it is that societies with strikingly similar cultures have such differences in female representation.

Thus, more recent comparative analyses have argued in favor of formal institutions, particularly norms of individual selection and electoral rules, to explain recent changes in female representation across the world. As explained by Schwindt-Bayer (chapter 1, this volume), women who decide to pursue a political career will encounter rules of the game that, by shaping political behavior, erect barriers to their entrance and permanence. In the case of Colombia, electoral reforms, the change from a centralized to a decentralized political system, as well as the use of quotas have been identified as significant stepping-stones explaining changes in women's representation.

Wills and Bernal Olarte (2002), for example, suggest that decentralization and the explicit intent to promote women's participation in the 1991 constitution explain the higher rate of women's inclusion in appointed positions and in elected offices. The authors argue that the existence of more opportunities and the opening of the political system incentivized political involvement of women at the national level. Bernal Olarte (2006) has argued that the changes to the electoral system in the 1991 constitution and the constitutional reform of 2003[11] had mixed impact on the success of

---

11. After the 2003 electoral reform, which introduced changes such as the requirement of one list per party, the use of the D'Hondt method of seat assignment, the establishment of thresholds, and the introduction of the preferential vote, researchers had the opportunity to carry out comparative studies of the two electoral systems.

women candidates in national elections.[12] The author argues that the 2003 electoral reform—by raising entry barriers when compared to the previous, more personalized electoral system—reinforced discrimination toward women as parties took control of the ballot.[13] Bernal Olarte also highlights how the phenomenon of "electoral micro-enterprises"[14] and the extreme political fragmentation before 2003, "were perhaps the only chances that women [. . .] or citizens from outside political parties had at obtaining public office" (Bernal Olarte 2006, 12). Finally, it also emphasized the relevance of district size for women's election in Colombia, since larger districts almost always elect at least one woman (Bernal Olarte 2008).

Nonetheless no study to date has attempted to cover the entire democratic period in which women have had the right to vote and get elected in all levels of government. Thus, the following section is an attempt to fill this gap, using all election data available, which allows us to observe the long-term trends of women's representation across the country.

Assessing the differential impact of institutional reforms

During the last six decades a number of institutional reforms have occurred which could potentially affect women's representation in politics. The first period (1962–1990) coincides with the return to democracy after a brief dictatorship from 1953–1957, in a period called "National Front." During this time, Colombia had a closed-list proportional representation system, which in practice behaved as a single nontransferable vote system because there was no limit on the number of lists per party. As a result, political party leaders did not have real control over the number of candidates or lists, generating high intraparty competition. Nonetheless, a highly centralized state where the president named all governors and those named all mayors in the country counteracted the centrifugal forces in place via the electoral system. Local elections (councils and assemblies) occurred every two years, and national elections every four. The Senate and the House of Representatives (elected every four years since 1974) had the same departmental constituencies.

As mentioned earlier, the first institutional departure from the political institutions established in the earlier 20th century was the 1991 constitution. Although the reform did not change the electoral rules themselves, it did change various aspects, which affected the ways in which candidates and politicians behaved within the electoral system. First, the political and fiscal decentralization meant

12. For Bernal Olarte (2006) female participants in politics face three barriers: 1) starting barriers: differences in necessary skills for the political game, which come as a result of educational disparities, 2) entry barriers: stereotypes derived from culture, 3) permanence barriers: once in politics, women do not identify themselves with the dynamics found inside politics.

13. Between the 2002 and 2006 elections, a significant decrease in the percentage of elected women both at the Senate and at the House occurred. This led many authors to blame the electoral reform as the main cause for this negative change.

14. These enterprises resulted from party multiplication (i.e., the exponential growth of the number of parties in the political system) because of the seat designation formula, which benefited small parties. For further information, we recommend consulting Pachón and Shugart (2010).

a significant diminution of the president's capacity to "keep the party together," as mayors and governors could be elected independently from the political forces of the center. Second, public campaign funding (regulated finally in 1994) was directed toward the lists instead of the party organizations. This meant, in practice, not only high intraparty fragmentation but a very significant increase in the number of parties and independent candidates competing in elections. Third, the Senate became a 100-seat national constituency, which allowed for extreme proportionality and rebalancing urban representation in Congress. And finally, coinciding with all of this, Colombia changed from a party-sponsored ballot to one administered by the National Registrar's Office. This meant that party machines were no longer needed for the party ballot distribution, a major constraint for all candidates. These reforms were meant to favor minority representation, and thus provided an opportunity for female representation to rise as party organizations became less and less important in pre-electoral settings. In 2002, over 72 political parties had a seat in the legislature (Shugart, Moreno, and Fajardo 2007).

The electoral reform of 2003 was a response to that extreme situation, where it had become increasingly difficult to identify party dividing lines across legislators. The reform aimed to change a system filled with representation flaws to one that encouraged more preelectoral coordination and would hopefully create the conditions for more programmatic negotiation between the president and the both houses of Congress. Thus, the 2003 electoral reform established that parties could only introduce one list per party (with optional open or closed list); established an electoral threshold of 2% (3% from 2014 onwards) for national elections and 50% of the Hare quota within districts; and finally, changed the electoral formula from Hare to D'Hondt (Pachón and Shugart 2010). Then, in 2011, Congress approved a female legislative quota of 30% in candidacies in all districts larger than four seats, effective for all levels of government. This was the result of a long debate about promoting women's political representation and included the support of many civil society organizations and the Congress' women's caucus.

Did these electoral reforms have an impact on women's representation in municipal councils, departmental assemblies, and the bicameral congress? We assess the relative importance of institutional reforms on women's electoral performance (Pachón and Sánchez 2014). The dataset we use contains the election results for each candidate in every elected legislative position from 1962 to 2014 at the municipal level, council data at the candidate level from 1994 onwards, local assembly data from 1962–2007, and Senate and House data from 1962–2014. This type of analysis allows us to measure the differential impact of each institutional context, depending on the type of election. In Figure 13.3, we present the average percentages per year of female candidates and female elected representatives, focusing on how they changed across the different electoral reforms.[15]

15. Although averages are informative, they could be misleading in the presence of high variation across observations. Thus the analysis presented here is complemented with the results of a more detailed statistical analysis (see appendix Table A13.1). The fixed effects model and a comparison within district is a better methodological strategy to evaluate the average impact of the reform within district, without being misled by the high variance in our dependent variable.

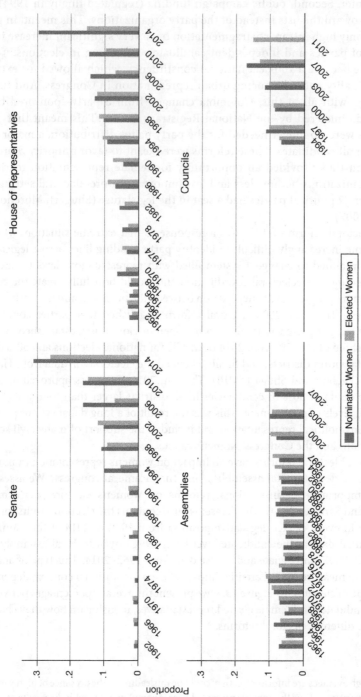

Figure 13.3 Evolution of Nominated and Elected Women by Type of Office

SOURCE: Data by Pachón and Sánchez (2014) and elaborated by the authors.

For local councils, we only have information from 1994–2011. Consequently, we can only assess the difference between representation after the 1991 reform and the 2003 and 2011 reforms. At the municipality level, women's nomination as candidates grew after the 2003 electoral reform, from an average of 18% (1994–2002) to 23% (2003–2010). After the quota reform of 2011, women's nomination went up to 36%. Nevertheless, the average percentage of elected women increased at a lower pace. After 2003, the average percentage of elected women increased from 5.4% to 8.5%, and only got close to 15%, on average, after the 2011 reform. Descriptive data coincides with the statistical analysis (see appendix Table A13.1), which found that the 2003 and 2011 reforms had a positive but modest impact on women's representation.

Assembly data exists from 1962–2007. Revealing a different trend that exists for the other arenas of representation, women's representation in assemblies barely changed over four decades. The average percentage of elected women is 4.91% with no real changes across six decades within district. The statistical analysis shows a negative and significant effect of the 2003 reform on the average percentage of nominated women within each district, but it reveals no effect for the 1991 constitutional reform.[16] Thus, in this case, reforms had very limited impact on the nomination of women departmental assemblies. The 1991 and 2003 reform show some impact on average elected women for assemblies.

At the national level, the percentage of elected women between 1960 and 1990 was the smallest of all the samples used, with 1.84% in the Senate and 8.23% in the House.[17] This figure rose after the enactment of the 1991 constitution to almost 10% of the seats in the Senate and in the House. In the period between 1991 and 2010, women obtained 8.2% of the seats in the Senate and 11.46% in the House. This average was affected by a drop in elected women in the 2006 and 2010 elections, the first elections after the 2003 reform. The statistical analysis shows that on average, reforms have had a significant effect within districts in nominated women, but they only had a significant and positive effect in elected women with the 2011 reform.

The greatest change can be clearly attributed to the 2011 reform (30% quota for legislative elections in districts larger than four seats).[18] In the House, the average of elected women went up to 16%, almost 8 percentage points below the Senate. The 2014 Senate represents a clear outlier as the percentage of women elected went to 24.69% of the seats. This was due to the closed list of the Centro Democrático, a right-wing civic movement led by former president Álvaro Uribe Vélez.

---

16. We cannot estimate the effect of the 2011 reform because we do not have data from any post-reform elections.

17. The Senate is not included in the statistical analysis because after 1991 our dependent variable has only one observation per election.

18. Law 1475, 2011: Establishes that in lists submitted for the election of 5 or more seats, at least 30% of candidates must be women (Article 28), but political parties can decide for themselves whether their lists will be open or closed. It also states that 5% of the total state funding for the political parties will be equally distributed to political parties and movements in proportion to the number of women representatives elected from their lists into publicly elected offices (Article 17[6]). Candidate lists that do not comply with the legal requirements, including the gender quota requirement, shall be rejected (Article 32).

Thus some conclusions emerge. It is clear that the highly personalized environment of political representation in Colombia is an adverse context in which it is difficult for women to compete and actually win. Even if some progress has been made, this is well below the region-wide average, as Schwindt-Bayer and Alles pointed out in chapter 4, this volume. Consequently, at the national level we observe reforms having a modest impact, increasing the number of women getting nominated to ballots but not necessarily increasing the number of women getting elected.

Also, institutional reforms have different effects, depending on the level of government. Further research is needed to understand exactly how women are recruited at the party level, and where (locally, regionally, or nationally) this recruitment occurs. The effects of the 2011 reform coincide with recent findings that suggest that quotas have a clear impact on nomination decisions for parties but a limited impact on women's elections. Nonetheless, more election cycles need to happen before any conclusions can be derived. More work needs to be done to determine if women included on lists are actively campaigning, have political backgrounds, or are instead family members, friends, or just party employees that lend their names to fulfill the legal requirement.

CONSEQUENCES OF WOMEN'S REPRESENTATION: THE PATH TOWARD SUBSTANTIVE REPRESENTATION

Despite slow progress, the growing number of women participating in different spheres of politics may lead one to believe that female interests are better represented by Colombian decision makers. As mentioned in the book's introduction, there are several different ways in which substantive representation of women can be accomplished. Few studies exist, however, that analyze the potential implications of this in the Colombian case.

Wills (2007, 2011) states that, to achieve substantive female representation, a critical mass[19] of those women representing their gender interests need to coordinate and consolidate a "feminist agenda" that responds to those concerns. By analyzing two decades of female representation following the 1991 constitution, Wills concluded that, in Colombia, the rise of female legislators had not translated into substantive representation. On the other hand, Rodríguez Valero (2013), by analyzing systematically legislative output of female legislators, agreed with Schwindt-Bayer (2010), suggesting that an increase in descriptive representation had made a difference for substantive representation. The creation of the congressional Women's Caucus and the adoption of a quota law are two of those main achievements.

Due to the lack of consensus relating to the impact women have on the representation of their interests when participating in politics in Colombia, we examine bill introductions related to women's issues here. Considering the percentage of congressional bills whose main topic is "women" as a percentage of total legislation in each legislative period, we see variation across time periods. Just over 2% of bills included

19. There is a wide literature on the issue of the existence of a critical mass to achieve representation; see Peña Molina (2005) or Wängnerud (2009).

women as a primary topic in 2010–2014 compared to less than 0.5% in 2002–2006 and 2006–2010 (just under 1% of bills focused on women in 1998–2002).

We statistically estimate the effect of being a congresswoman on the probability of proposing a bill related to women, controlling for a series of covariates that can directly affect this behavior. Controls include congressional committee, upper or lower house, legislative period, political party, previous experience as a legislator, and educational level of the member of congress (see appendix 13.2 for more details on variables and data analysis methods). Table 13.4 shows the results of this analysis.

Although the net effect of being a woman on the introduction of bills referencing women (shown in the first row) changes in each model, this effect has a low variance and is statistically very significant, demonstrating its robustness. On average, the probability that a woman introduces a bill that favors her gender is more than 200% of that of men. The other two persistent results across all models are the positive association between legislative experience (terms in office) and the overall number of bills introduced per individual.

Controls such as committees do not matter much when explaining women-related bills, except for the fourth (budget and fiscal control) and third (tax and monetary issues) committees where there is less probability of women-related legislation being introduced. Also, party effects are not significant and do not affect the probability that a legislator introduces more women-related bills.

To conclude, this analysis corroborates Rodríguez's and Schwindt-Bayer's theses, since women sponsor more women-focused bills than do men, which could possibly result in more substantive representation of women's issues. However, Wills's argument cannot be refuted because the introduction of a bill does not imply the approval of it. Therefore, it could be that a consolidation of a female "critical mass" may be required for these projects to gain approval.

CONCLUSION: CHALLENGES TO FEMALE REPRESENTATION IN COLOMBIA

This chapter began showing the historical trends and the current state of descriptive female representation in every arena of representation in the country. We discussed the causes for these historical trends, emphasizing the effect of the changes in rules that could potentially influence women's representation. Indeed, we found that although reforms have moved in the direction of incentivizing parties to recruit more women to legislative and executive offices (both elected and appointed), the gap between female and male descriptive representation remains. We illustrated in detail what has happened in the cabinet, showing how the quota established in 2000 for appointed executive posts has had a positive and significant effect on the percentage of women, with a new trend of specialization in certain policy areas such as culture and education. Nonetheless, as has been illustrated in other cases, the 30% can become both the minimum and the maximum for female representation.

At the departmental and national levels, female representation remains relatively low despite the increases in the percentage of female nomination. More research, similar to that of Morgan and Hinojosa in chapter 5 of this volume, is required to understand what goes on within party organizations in Colombia and how the quota established in 2011 has changed women's recruitment processes across offices. In

Table 13.4 Determinants of Women's Issue Bill Introduction

VARIABLES	Model 1	Model 2	Model 3	Model 4	Model 5	Model 6	Model 7
Women	2.725***	2.788***	2.645***	2.709***	2.398***	2.328***	2.271***
	(0.188)	(0.196)	(0.179)	(0.188)	(0.245)	(0.258)	(0.249)
First Committee	-0.196	0.0386	-0.0220	0.0913	-0.176	-0.0907	0.0773
	(0.262)	(0.267)	(0.247)	(0.245)	(0.263)	(0.286)	(0.270)
Second Committee	-0.270	0.272	-0.278	0.220	-0.313	-0.0284	-0.0724
	(0.324)	(0.310)	(0.296)	(0.282)	(0.328)	(0.344)	(0.317)
Third Committee	-0.596*	-0.219	-0.535	-0.255	-0.609*	-0.735*	-0.661*
	(0.339)	(0.339)	(0.326)	(0.326)	(0.340)	(0.393)	(0.380)
Fourth Committee	-0.857**	-0.523	-0.830**	-0.482	-0.829**	-0.650*	-0.657*
	(0.387)	(0.382)	(0.369)	(0.364)	(0.386)	(0.393)	(0.377)
Fifth Committee	0.0287	0.262	0.0525	0.193	0.0379	0.153	0.191
	(0.288)	(0.284)	(0.270)	(0.261)	(0.290)	(0.308)	(0.291)
Sixth Committee	-0.640*	-0.216	-0.382	-0.146	-0.615*	-0.601	-0.363
	(0.360)	(0.338)	(0.334)	(0.320)	(0.359)	(0.380)	(0.353)
Senate	0.0241	0.0831	0.149	0.0890	-0.454	-0.377	-0.229
	(0.194)	(0.186)	(0.184)	(0.173)	(0.315)	(0.319)	(0.311)
Incumbency	0.0989	0.0307	-0.220	-0.202	0.109	0.0200	-0.283
	(0.206)	(0.198)	(0.193)	(0.188)	(0.208)	(0.224)	(0.214)
Replacement	-1.057***	-0.794***	-0.909***	-0.599**	-1.050***	-0.381	-0.387
	(0.274)	(0.274)	(0.268)	(0.272)	(0.274)	(0.285)	(0.278)
Total Bills	0.0344***	0.0413***	0.0235***	0.0359***	0.0349***	0.0334***	0.0239***
	(0.00545)	(0.00667)	(0.00455)	(0.00628)	(0.00537)	(0.00582)	(0.00511)

	(1)	(2)	(3)	(4)	(5)	(6)	(7)
Party Effects		YES (non-sig)		YES (non-sig)			
2002–2006			0.790**	0.594*			0.678*
			(0.340)	(0.361)			(0.351)
2006–2010			1.475***	1.005***			1.234***
			(0.324)	(0.344)			(0.331)
2010–2014			1.612***	1.319***			1.314***
			(0.324)	(0.350)			(0.329)
Women*Senate					0.767**	0.595	0.513
					(0.384)	(0.404)	(0.386)
Undergraduate Studies						0.0165	-0.241
						(0.655)	(0.623)
Graduate Studies						-0.0695	-0.304
						(0.657)	(0.624)
Constant	-3.396***	-14.69	-4.331***	-16.57	-3.232***	-3.179***	-3.691***
	(0.267)	(1,084)	(0.363)	(1,978)	(0.273)	(0.660)	(0.655)
Observations	1,824	1,824	1,824	1,824	1,824	1,288	1,288

Standard errors in parentheses.
*** $p < 0.01$, ** $p < 0.05$, * $p < 0.1$.

local mayoral and gubernatorial elections, women's representation is rare. Only after the 2011 election have women accounted for more than 5% of all mayors and governors in the country.

In terms of legislative output, we show that female legislators in Colombia are interested in representing their gender-related interests through bill sponsorship. Nonetheless, there is a long way to go between bills getting introduced and enacted, and not enough legislators are willing to engage in this type of agenda. More research is needed to understand how the judicialization of many of these core topics may in fact create an alternative avenue that proves more efficient in the short term and favorable to political minorities' battles.

Conclusion

The Gendered Nature of Democratic Representation in Latin America

LESLIE A. SCHWINDT-BAYER ■

Since the Latin American transitions to democracy in the 1980's, significant increases in women's representation in political arenas have occurred. Six countries have had female presidents and the percentage of cabinets, national and subnational legislatures, and political party leadership posts that are female now average around 25% regionwide. Yet, gender parity in representation has not been achieved, and the regionwide average obscures the wide variation that exists across countries and arenas of government. This book draws on the expertise of gender and representation scholars in Latin America to describe the nature of gender equality in five Latin American arenas of representation and seven country cases, explain why it looks as it does, and evaluate the consequences of the inclusion of women for different arenas, for citizen attitudes toward and participation in Latin American democracies, and for representative democracy.

In this concluding chapter, I summarize what we have learned about gender and representation in Latin America, highlighting generalizable conclusions about the causes and consequences of gender representation in the region and pointing out where patterns diverge across countries and arenas. Specifically, I present overarching findings about 1) what representation of women and men in Latin America looks like in the five arenas studied here, 2) what explains variation in representation of women across arenas, countries, and time, 3) what the consequences of strong and weak gender balance in representation are for the five arenas of representation, and 4) what the consequences of women's inclusion in politics are for democracy and society in Latin America. I conclude by highlighting the holes that have emerged in existing research and offering suggestions for future research on gender and representation in Latin America.

WOMEN IN LATIN AMERICAN ARENAS OF REPRESENTATION

This book has presented extensive and new data on women's representation in the presidency, cabinets, national legislatures, political parties, and subnational governments to

presidency = gendered

document the state of gender equality in representational arenas today and how it has changed over time. In some chapters, authors provide statistics on elected representatives as well as candidates for political office. What the data show, as a whole, is that in nearly every arena of representation and every country of Latin America, gender equality in numerical representation has yet to be achieved and sustained. Women have broken the highest glass ceiling by getting elected president (in six countries), gender parity cabinets have been appointed (twice), and numerical gender equality has been reached in legislatures (in Bolivia), but these have been exceptions rather than the norm in the countries and arenas where they occurred. Instead, the chapters show wide variation in gender equality in all five arenas. They also show just how gendered the institutions are not just in terms of an imbalance in the election of women and men but in the types of offices that women and men get elected or appointed to.

In the presidency, for example, Reyes-Housholder and Thomas (chapter 2, this volume) point out that, by 2015, six Latin American countries had elected female presidents a total of nine times (three women were reelected), and more than half of the countries in the region (13 of 18) have had competitive female candidates for president. However, this also means that 13 countries have never had a female president, and the overall percentage of presidencies that have been held by women in the region is small. Their chapter and the chapters on countries with female presidents show that gender has been an important factor in elections both disadvantaging and advantaging women. The presidency itself is a gendered institution, and women have had to carefully negotiate gender stereotypes and gendered expectations on their path to power and once in office. At the same time, being female helped several of the women who became president as political crises and democratic challenges led parties and voters to look for leaders outside the traditional male elite.

A similar pattern of gender inequality exists in cabinets. Today, women's representation in Latin American cabinets averages 25%, up from 15% around 2000 and only 5% in 1980 (Taylor-Robinson and Gleitz, chapter 3, this volume). Across countries, however, women's cabinet representation varies widely, as demonstrated by both the Taylor-Robinson and Gleitz chapter and the seven country chapters. Although women have done reasonably well numerically, Taylor-Robinson and Gleitz point out that they have not been appointed to the most prestigious and powerful cabinet portfolios, such as the economy. Piscopo (chapter 9, this volume) agrees, pointing out that in Costa Rica "women in the cabinet remain more likely to attain less prestigious posts" (166) and are more likely to be in social welfare posts than more prestigious posts. Pachón and Lacouture (chapter 13, this volume) also highlight the gendered nature of cabinet portfolio appointments in Colombia, and Johnson (chapter 10, this volume) identifies another challenge for women in cabinets, which is that, in Uruguay, women have served shorter cabinet terms than men and have higher removal rates.[1]

cabinet positions

In national legislatures, political parties, and subnational governments, numerical gender disparities remain strong today, as well. The regional average for legislatures and party leaderships is approximately 25% but wide variation exists across

---

1. The extent to which this applies to other countries in the region is not clear because it was not consistently analyzed in this volume. Escobar-Lemmon and Taylor-Robinson (2016) found that in five countries the patterns are more similar for women and men. More research is needed to assess the generalizability of Johnson's finding.

countries. In legislatures, some of the countries we studied have done well at increasing gender equality (e.g., Argentina, Costa Rica, Mexico), but others have done poorly (Chile, Uruguay, Brazil, Colombia). Morgan and Hinojosa (chapter 5, this volume) and the country chapters show that some political parties have surpassed parity whereas others have had no women in party leadership. In Uruguay, a woman was elected for the first time to the top post in the FA and PC, the two largest parties, only in 2012 (Johnson, chapter 10, this volume). Subnational governments include a larger range of offices (executive and legislative at the local and intermediate levels), but reveal similar patterns. Escobar-Lemmon and Funk (chapter 6, this volume) identify a large gap that exists between women's representation in subnational executives and subnational legislatures. At the local level, women hold only 12% of executive offices but 26% of local assemblies. At the intermediate level, the statistics are 7% and 21%, respectively. Individual country statistics, however, vary widely around these averages.

Patterns of gender representation across arenas and within countries show that gender equality in political representation has increased in most political arenas (least in subnational governments), but it is still far from parity, on average, and varies widely across countries and over time. Women also have not attained access to the same kinds of offices as men have within arenas. Thus the chapters in this book clearly demonstrate the gendered nature of representation in Latin American governments, which most often advantages women. *Why* this is the case is the next question this book answers.

EVALUATING CAUSES: EXPLANATIONS FOR GENDER IMBALANCE IN REPRESENTATION IN LATIN AMERICA

This book shows that the explanations for varying progress in numerical gender equality are not cultural and socioeconomic changes or differences across countries, but instead, they are institutional and political factors. Formal and informal institutions have both helped and hurt women's entry into Latin American arenas of representation. Longstanding obstacles to legislative arenas posed by parties' candidate selection rules, for example, continue to hinder women's progress even in light of the adoption of gender quotas, a mechanism designed specifically to re-gender the electoral process in a way that would level the playing field for women and men. Quotas have helped women in some countries, but in others, parties and male elites continue to find loopholes that weaken the power of quotas or have failed to adopt quotas or implement them effectively. The political climate of party system fragmentation, corruption, and citizen distrust of political elites has played a similarly important role for explaining differences in women's representation across countries. On one hand, political crises have helped women get elected president because of frustration with traditional male elites. On the other hand, disillusionment resulting from overinflated expectations about a newly elected woman's ability to solve a country's problems has significantly obstructed her term in office and legacy, perhaps having negative consequences for future female leaders. Below, I highlight three of the main findings regarding the weakness of culture and socioeconomics as a cause of women's representation, the ways institutions matter, and the role of the Latin American political context for women's representation.

The weakness of cultural and socioeconomic factors

Much as I theorized in the introductory chapter, the cultural and socioeconomic environment within countries has little direct influence on gender equality in Latin American political representation today. The vast majority of Latin Americans do not believe that men make better political leaders than women and generally support gender equality, and voter discrimination is not an explanation for women not getting elected to political offices. Many chapters in the volume highlight the ways in which societal gender equality has improved in Latin America. Barnes and Jones (chapter 7) point out that Argentine culture is much more open to women as candidates today, and Taylor-Robinson and Gleitz (chapter 3) link international diffusion of gender equality norms to a new norm of appointing at least some women to cabinets (see Franceschet, chapter 8, this volume, for a discussion of this in Chile). The legislatures chapter (Schwindt-Bayer and Alles, chapter 4) points out that women are well represented in the candidate pool, having significantly increased their representation in the paid labor force, and in some countries, outnumber men in their presence in higher education. These cultural and societal improvements in gender equality do not necessarily correlate with increased women's representation in arenas or countries, however.[2]

The strong role for formal and informal institutions

This book shows that formal and informal institutions are critically important for explaining gender imbalance in Latin American political arenas. Both the arena-focused and country-focused chapters provide extensive evidence to support this, and they support a core set of institutions that matter consistently across countries and arenas of representation—party rules and norms about candidate selection, gender quotas, electoral and appointment rules, power and prestige norms, and incumbency norms.

CANDIDATE SELECTION RULES AND NORMS

A key explanation for gender representativeness in Latin America is who selects candidates for election or appoints political leaders to nonelected posts and how they do it. Chapter after chapter identified a major role for parties, specifically party elites and the rules and norms they use to select candidates and appoint leaders, for explaining gender disparities in levels of representation. Authors identified centralized candidate selection processes as facilitating women's access to candidacies and political appointments, following Hinojosa (2012). For example, Barnes and Jones argue in chapter 7 that centralized candidate selection norms in the PJ were important for getting Cristina Fernández de Kirchner elected president after her husband served one term. Franceschet (chapter 8) points out that, in Chile, women have done much better getting into appointed posts than elected positions, and she argues that a key reason for women's success in cabinets, specifically, is the fact that cabinet

who selects candidates

2. See, however, Escobar-Lemmon and Funk (chapter 6, this volume), who find that labor force participation and fertility rates do matter for subnational legislatures.

[handwritten: appointments in hands of one person = better for women]

appointments are in the hands of one person—the president—rather than in the hands of myriad party and coalition leaders, as is the case for selecting candidates for legislative elections in Chile. Araújo, Calasanti, and Htun (chapter 12, this volume) argue that one reason why women do poorly in Brazilian legislative elections is that nomination is highly decentralized. This creates weak party leaders and the need for candidates to self-nominate, which women are less likely to do. Politicians also must rely on traditional political networks to get into or stay in both elected and appointed office, which women historically have had less access to.

Informal party norms, however, can moderate the effect of centralized candidate selection or directly work to limit women's access to arenas of representation.[3] Barnes and Jones (chapter 7) suggest that women's *absence* from party leadership results from "political factors and the informal and behind-the-scenes selection procedures that give rise to party leaders" in Argentina (131). Similarly, Johnson (chapter 10) suggests that the lack of formal selection rules in most parties in Uruguay creates informal norms that are "male biased." Candidate selection is centralized, at the level of faction leaders, but factions have to informally negotiate who gets on the party ballot. This produces disadvantages for women because it leads to "recruitment by patronage," and women are often absent from patronage networks. The norms of proportionality used to allocate faction candidates to party ballots leave little room for other criteria, such as gender.

[handwritten: Self-nom + trad. pol networks = very bad for Gen Rep]

GENDER QUOTAS

Many parties and governments have adopted rules that are gendered in a way to help women—gender quotas. Quotas have been a successful mechanism for increasing women's representation in legislatures, subnational governments, and political parties. Schwindt-Bayer and Alles (chapter 4) show that national legislatures with quotas have, on average, 10 percentage points more women than national legislatures without quotas, and well-designed quotas with large sizes, placement mandates, and enforcement mechanisms do much better than poorly designed quotas. Subnational legislatures with quotas also have more women in them than those without quotas (Escobar-Lemmon and Funk, chapter 6), and quotas explain some of the differences in women's representation in party leadership positions (Morgan and Hinojosa, chapter 5).[4] Pär Zetterberg's analysis of Mexico (chapter 11) shows clearly that the 2009 quota reform was critical to increasing women's representation in the Mexican congress in recent years.

Quotas are not a guaranteed solution to political gender inequality, however. As several chapters in this book point out, where parties have wanted to subvert quota rules, they have been able to do so either by adopting weak and ineffective quotas or finding loopholes in existing laws. Mexican parties used primaries as a way to

[handwritten right margin: Quotas are imp for Gender Rep]

---

3. New research by Bjarnegård and Zetterberg (2016) may contribute to future analyses by considering not just the centralization of selection rules but their bureaucratization.

4. Interestingly, Morgan and Hinojosa (chapter 5, this volume) find that neither quotas nor party ideology directly correlate with party-level variation in gender representation on party ballots. They report that parties without quotas sometimes have high representation of women whereas those with them do not. Similarly, leftist and rightist parties alternately demonstrate high and low representation of women on party ballots.

bypass the 2000 quota law up until its reform in 2009 (Zetterberg, chapter 11, this volume). In Uruguay, a quota was only adopted in 2009 and was to be implemented in only one election in 2014. Its implementation led to only approximately 20% of the congress being female, however, because small district and party magnitudes reduced the effectiveness of the quota (Johnson, chapter 10, this volume). In Brazil, the quota passed in 1996 worked with the electoral law in such a way that parties did not actually have to fill quota positions (Araújo, Calasanti, and Htun, chapter 12, this volume). That loophole was closed with the 2009 quota reform, but women's legislative representation still has not improved dramatically.[5]

Even in contexts where quotas were well designed and have been effective, party elites often do not apply gender parity rules to the head of the ballot. In Uruguay, women were poorly represented in top ballot positions in small magnitude districts leading to no more women getting elected than were elected in 2009, prior to the quota (Johnson, chapter 10, this volume). Piscopo (chapter 9) shows that, in Costa Rica, women's representation underwent a significant increase after the implementation of a much stronger quota in 2002, but improvements have been inconsistent since then, even with the adoption of a zipper quota (i.e., a quota requiring alternation of women and men on the ballot). She argues that a key explanation for subsequent weak improvement is that women were less likely to be represented at the head of party legislative ballots. Similarly, in Costa Rican mayoral races, parties simply ran women as mayoral candidates in the districts they thought they were less likely to win.

Quotas are a primary explanation for increased women's representation in Latin American arenas of representation. However, they only work when parties and male elites rally behind the quotas' spirit of gender equality.

ELECTORAL AND APPOINTMENT RULES

Despite existing research that has identified electoral rules as a key explanation for women's underrepresentation in politics, electoral rules emerge in this book as less important than the candidate selection process that takes place in parties prior to the elections themselves. That said, several chapters still point out important ways that electoral rules continue to influence gender representation and how they interact with gender quotas to exacerbate those effects. Schwindt-Bayer and Alles (chapter 4) find no regionwide statistical role for proportional representation or district magnitude when quotas are taken into account (i.e., quotas matter more than electoral rules), but several chapters do identify nuanced ways that these rules matter in some arenas and some countries. Franceschet (chapter 8) highlights the challenge of small districts in Chile. Chile's district magnitude of 2 in every electoral district, combined with a rule requiring a party to win twice as many votes as the second-place party in a district to win both seats, is a major obstacle to increasing women's representation in the Chilean congress.[6] This coupled with coalition norms that require parties within a coalition to negotiate over the candidates to put on the ballot significantly

---

5. Women's candidacies, however, did increase in 2014 to record numbers.

6. Elections at the end of 2017 will occur under revised electoral rules that may significantly increase the number of women elected to the Chilean congress.

limits the number of female candidates and members of congress. Chile is also a case where women have done better getting appointed to political posts than elected.

Zetterberg (chapter 11) shows that, in Mexico, the use of a mixed electoral system where one tier uses proportional representation with a large district magnitude (M = 40) has been key to women's success getting elected to the national congress, particularly once combined with a strong gender quota. Johnson (chapter 10) argues that, in Uruguay, more women were elected in larger magnitude districts at both national and subnational legislatures before the quota election in 2014, and that once the quota was implemented, it led to more women getting elected in large M districts but not in small M ones.

District magnitude is also identified as an obstacle to women in executive elections. A district magnitude of 1 for presidents, governors, and mayors makes these elections a zero-sum game, and it then becomes difficult to include gender as a criterion for candidate selection. Piscopo (chapter 9, this volume) highlights this as a challenge for women in mayoral elections in Costa Rica.

Other electoral rules highlighted in the chapters include the candidate or party-centered nature of the party system and the use of *suplente* (substitute) systems that require parties to nominate primary candidates along with substitutes to a party ballot. Brazil and Colombia illustrate the disadvantages for women of open-list proportional representation and the candidate-centered election norms that result from it. For example, Araújo, Calasanti, and Htun (chapter 12, this volume) point out that Brazil's candidate-centered system has hurt women's election because those types of systems create contests where personal resources and political capital are critical to winning. Women have less of both of these in Brazil. Pachón and Lacouture (chapter 13, this volume) highlight the personalistic nature of electoral rules (and the broader political context) in Colombia as a key obstacle to women's election and appointment to political offices.

Uruguay, Colombia, and Costa Rica (subnational) use *suplente* systems, and Johnson (chapter 10, this volume) and Piscopo (chapter 9, this volume) argue that this system has been detrimental to women's election in Uruguay and Costa Rica because it allows party leaders to put women in secondary, less important positions and still claim gender representation. As Johnson noted, *suplentes* often do the majority of the grunt work and do not reap the benefits needed to build a political career. Interestingly, these findings differ from those of Hinojosa and Gurdián (2012) who find no negative effects of the *suplente* system on women's legislative election in Nicaragua.

ARENA RULES AND NORMS

The rules and norms that exist within arenas are also important for shaping numerical gender equality. Norms of power and office prestige, for example, appeared in several chapters as explanations for why women have not been elected or appointed to some arenas. In general, the more prestigious and powerful the office, the fewer women represented in it (Schwindt-Bayer and Squire 2014). This is evident for Latin American cabinets, where women's representation has increased but women still do not get access to the powerful economy post very often (Taylor-Robinson and Gleitz, chapter 3, this volume). It also is evident in party leadership positions, where the posts that women get appointed to most often are not those that are the most powerful and prestigious or have control over candidate selection (Morgan and Hinojosa, chapter 5, this volume). Escobar-Lemmon and Funk (chapter 6) demonstrate the importance of powerful executive offices for limiting women's representation by showing that where more fiscal decentralization has taken place, and thus local executives have greater economic powers, fewer women have been elected mayor. Piscopo's findings (chapter 9) also provide direct support for this, showing a clear decline in women's municipal representation in Costa Rica after 1988 when mayors began to be elected, fiscal decentralization occurred, and mayoral posts became more valuable for parties and career politicians.

Prestige also appears to explain some of the differences in women's representation across legislative and executive offices and between national and subnational level representation. Where executive posts are powerful (e.g., governors and mayors in Argentina, Brazil, and Mexico), fewer women hold office.

Incumbency and term limits are additional institutional norms and rules that can help or hurt women. Low incumbency norms in general in the region should increase women's numeric representation (Schwindt-Bayer 2005) because they help level the playing field for men and women. Only a couple of chapters in this volume address incumbency and term limits, but those that do support the argument that high levels of incumbency hurt women's selection and election chances when men are the majority of incumbents. Women not being incumbents means they are excluded from the advantages that incumbency brings to political elites. Johnson (chapter 10) argues that high incumbency rates of 60%–70% across parties in Uruguay may be part of the reason why it has been so hard for women to enter the legislative arena. Araújo, Calasanti, and Htun (chapter 12) argue that incumbency is a major obstacle to women being elected in Brazil. The small numbers of women in office in Brazil means that women do not benefit from electoral advantages, such as television advertising time. In Brazil, television time is allocated more to incumbents than challengers, and since women are less likely to be incumbents, they are disadvantaged in advertising their campaigns. Thus at least in some countries, incumbency norms are gendered, disadvantaging women while advantaging men.[7]

The positive and negative effects of political context

Considering gender and representation in the context of the political challenges that Latin American countries face today reveals that political context is another explanation for differences in gender equality in political representation. Interestingly, the democratic challenges of leftist populists, economic instability, crime and violence, party system fragmentation, corrupt and clientelistic politics, and growing citizen distrust in government both help and hurt women's representation. Many of these problems have had negative effects on women's appointment and election to office, but paradoxically, some actually increase opportunities for women's election

---

7. An additional cause addressed in several chapters is cross-arena diffusion. Women's representation in one arena can lead to greater women's representation in another. Yet the chapters that raised this phenomenon found that diffusion does not always occur in the standard pattern of politicians starting at local levels and working their way up to the highest political office. Instead, it occurs in a much more irregular pattern that is often country-specific. We leave deeper analysis of this pattern and the reasons why it occurs to future research.

or appointment and provide potential advantages. Political context is particularly important for the executive arena.

incumbency

POLITICAL CRISES

Although political crises are challenges for Latin American democracy, they have proven to be surprising opportunities for women. They have spurred political parties and voters to look for candidates who are outside the traditional class of political elites in order to break with incumbents who voters blame for poor political, economic, and social performance. Reyes-Housholder and Thomas (chapter 2, this volume) point out that intraparty turmoil and crises helped Latin American female presidents get elected because women represent both "continuity and change," although as Barnes and Jones (chapter 7) point out, this was less the case for Fernández de Kirchner in Argentina, who actually benefited from her insider status as the wife of the incumbent president. Michelle Bachelet in Chile, however, benefited from being considered outside the core group of disparaged party elites in the Concertación coalition in 2006 (see Franceschet, chapter 8, this volume). Piscopo (chapter 9) emphasized that Laura Chinchilla in Costa Rica fit the pattern because she provided "continuity" by being former President Arias's choice for successor but also "renewal" by being a woman. *continuity and change*

The negative side of this phenomenon, however, is that when women are elected in contexts of party or democratic crisis, they get elected into environments where they are most likely to fail (i.e., the "glass cliff" theory), which can have negative consequences for both women and political representation in the region (Bruckmüller and Branscombe 2010; Ryan and Haslam 2005). Araújo, Calasanti, and Htun (chapter 12, this volume) show this in the case of Dilma Rousseff in Brazil, who was impeached before the end of her term, and Piscopo (chapter 9, this volume) raises it as a potential problem for women running for office in the post-Chinchilla period. Although political crises can be beneficial for the election and appointment of women, particularly in the presidency, they create gendered consequences for women at the same time.

IDEOLOGY AND THE "RISE OF THE LEFT" *impact of left*

The rise of the left in Latin America, which started with the election of Hugo Chavez in Venezuela in 1998, also was a boost for women in the region. This volume's chapters show that leftist parties have selected more women to ballots and elected more women to legislatures than rightist parties (see Brazil (chapter 12), Costa Rica (chapter 9), and Uruguay (chapter 10) for specific discussions of this). Five of the six elected female presidents in Latin America won office after the left turn began, and four of them were elected from left or left-of-center parties (Reyes-Housholder and Thomas, chapter 2, this volume). Populist, leftist presidents were also more likely to appoint women to cabinets (see Piscopo, chapter 9 of this volume, for an example of this in Costa Rica).[8] This is evident for party leaderships too. Morgan and Hinojosa

8. Taylor-Robinson and Gleitz (chapter 3, this volume) found only a marginally significant effect for gender of the president. The small number of female presidents in Latin America makes generalizing about the impact of women on cabinet appointments more difficult. More research will be needed as more women win presidencies.

(chapter 5) show that in Costa Rica, for example, the center-left PLN had parity whereas the center-right PUSC had only 25% of its party leadership being female.

PARTY SYSTEM FRAGMENTATION

This volume also highlights the challenge that increased fragmentation of party systems has created for gender equality in representational arenas. Even countries that have had two or three main political parties for the better part of the last century have experienced reduced seat and vote shares for those parties in recent elections and the emergence of new parties into the party system. This fragmentation has been an obstacle to women's representation. Schwindt-Bayer and Alles (chapter 4) provide statistical evidence that party system fragmentation reduces the number of women elected to national legislatures and limits the effectiveness of gender quotas. Piscopo (chapter 9) explicitly identifies party system fragmentation as a major challenge in Costa Rica. Costa Rica has had one of the longest-running democracies in Latin America, and until recently, one of the highest quality democracies. But corruption scandals, ineffective governance, and reduced citizen trust in parties has led to the decline of the traditional two-party system. As politics has fragmented, women's election gains have stagnated. Even with quotas, if women are not represented at the top of the ballot or in the "choicest candidacies," as Piscopo refers to them, increased representation of women is unlikely.

EVALUATING CONSEQUENCES: THE EFFECTS OF FEMALE REPRESENTATION INSIDE ARENAS

This volume suggests several important conclusions about the consequences of women's representation and how gender shapes representational arenas in Latin America. First, the chapters reveal that, in general, women in Latin America are promoting women's issue and gender equity policies more than men are, although to varying degrees across arenas and countries. It occurs more often in legislative arenas than executive arenas and more often in those countries where more women have been elected or appointed to office.

Second, in contrast to women's efforts to promote women's issues and gender equality policies, they have not been as successful working in the areas of the economy or bringing about broader political improvements in Latin America. They do, however, play a significant role in social policy in many countries, which could be important for improving citizen satisfaction with democracy since citizens tend to respond positively to service delivery. Women also have not gained access to full political power to the extent that men have. This is particularly evident in legislatures, where several chapters showed that women do not get into chamber leadership as often as men or gain access to leadership on all types of committees. But it also appears in cabinet appointments where women are relegated to less powerful and prestigious cabinet portfolios.

Finally, women's presence in political arenas has not brought about significant transformation of the gendered arenas in which politics takes place, their agendas, or their institutions. Other than gender quotas, few rules and norms have been changed to incorporate women's voices or facilitate better interactions between men and women, and women have not achieved more equal power inside the arenas. In some countries, political arenas still present hostile climates to women.

Promoting women's issues

The chapters of this volume present evidence that women in office promote women's issues and gender equality policies and do so more than men. Reyes-Housholder and Thomas (chapter 2) highlight the ways in which Michelle Bachelet has brought women's issues to the forefront of her policy agenda as president of Chile. Schwindt-Bayer and Alles (chapter 4) show that in addition to existing research's findings about women promoting women's issues through bill sponsorship and cosponsorship, speaking on the floor of the legislature, participating in committees, and interacting with female constituents, female legislators have more positive attitudes toward gender equality, abortion rights, and divorce rights than male legislators do. Escobar-Lemmon and Funk (chapter 6) demonstrate that women in office focus more on these issues at the subnational level as well. Finally, the country chapter authors provide numerous examples of ways in which women have rallied behind women's issues from the formation of cross-party *bancadas femininas* (women's caucuses) in Uruguay and Brazil to comprehensive policy programs aimed at gender equality, such as the 1990 Law for the Promotion of Women's Social Equality and the creation of a special women's issues committee in 1999 in Costa Rica. Pachón and Lacouture (chapter 13) use statistical models to show that women are more likely to sponsor women's issue bills than men in the national congress.

The extent to which women representing women occurs, however, varies across the arenas of representation, as suggested in the theoretical framework of the introductory chapter (chapter 1). First, women promoting women's issues occurs only minimally in executive offices, such as the presidency and cabinets. Reyes-Housholder and Thomas (chapter 2) and Taylor-Robinson and Gleitz (chapter 3) highlight that female presidents and women in cabinets have been much less likely to promote a women's policy agenda than women in legislatures. Aside from Bachelet, female presidents have not been active promoters of women's rights. Araújo, Calasanti, and Htun (chapter 12), Barnes and Jones (chapter 7), and Piscopo (chapter 9) argue this for Dilma Rousseff, Cristina Fernández de Kirchner, and Laura Chinchilla, respectively. Female presidents do have to navigate their gender carefully to maintain political support, but they have not always pushed for more gender equal policies or programs (Reyes-Housholder and Thomas, chapter 2, this volume). For cabinets, portfolios have narrow policy purviews, women are often appointed to cabinet posts with limited resources, and cabinet ministers are beholden to presidential agendas such that promoting women's rights is rarely feasible (Taylor-Robinson and Funk, chapter 3, this volume). Female ministers serving in ministries specifically for women have made the most progress in these areas (see Franceschet, chapter 8, this volume, for more on Sernam, the women's ministry, in Chile).

Second, women in political parties have had only minimal opportunity to bring women's issues to the party agenda. Morgan and Hinojosa (chapter 5) demonstrate that parties have not warmed to women's issues. Parties do not prioritize them, women are not well-represented in party leadership positions, and women do not strongly identify with Latin American political parties. As Morgan and Hinojosa note, women have "little substantive voice in the region's parties" (84). The near-absence of discussion of parties representing women's rights in the country chapters may be a reflection of this.

Third, women in legislatures have been much more likely than women in other arenas to take liberal policy attitudes toward gender equality, bring women's and gender equality issues to the legislative agenda, and work to pass legislation in these areas (Schwindt-Bayer and Alles, chapter 4, this volume). The country chapters on Argentina, Colombia, Costa Rica, Mexico, Uruguay, and Brazil demonstrate this well. In the first three, it has happened through bill sponsorship, committee assignments, and legislative speeches. In the latter two, it has occurred most directly through the *bancadas femininas*. One explanation for the different ways in which promoting women's rights takes place inside legislatures may be the overall representation of women. Where women are present, (Argentina, Costa Rica, and Mexico), the power of women's numbers within parties may provide sufficient impetus for working through regular legislative channels to promote women's rights. Where women are largely absent (Uruguay and Brazil), cross-party organizations are necessary to have sufficient power to bring women's issues to the agenda. Franceschet (chapter 8, this volume) argues in Chile that the small numbers of women in office combined with institutional norms that place significant power in the hands of the president means that most women's issue policies have emerged from Sernam, the bureaucratic entity responsible for women's rights. Women in congress raise these issues but rarely have the power to push them through to policy passage.

women = absent, need crossparty boundaries

Promoting social, economic, and political outcomes

In addition to women's rights and gender equality, women in many Latin American political arenas have worked to improve social policy in Latin America. Women have had less impact, however, on improving economic policy and easing the political challenges that Latin American countries face. Female presidents have not always trumpeted gender equality directly (Araújo, Calasanti, and Htun, chapter 12, this volume; Reyes-Housholder and Thomas, chapter 2, this volume), but they have worked on social issues, such as antipoverty programs (e.g., Cristina Fernández de Kirchner in Argentina). As noted previously, women have been more likely to be appointed to social cabinet portfolios and as *ministras de la mujer* where women's ministries exist (e.g., Costa Rica and Chile) than to economic portfolios. Additionally, female legislators have been better represented on social committees than they have been on economic committees, particularly when it comes to leadership of those committees (e.g., Argentina, Mexico, and see Schwindt-Bayer and Alles, chapter 4, this volume).

In terms of working inside political arenas to address political challenges in Latin America, the chapters provide little evidence to suggest that women have improved the political context more than men. Despite the influx of women, corruption is no lower today than it was ten years ago, and it is still, if not more, rampant within many political arenas. Female presidents Laura Chinchilla, Dilma Rousseff and Cristina Fernández de Kirchner ended their presidencies with their countries facing worse

economic conditions than when they entered office.[9] Female legislators see the democratic and political challenges that their countries face as more problematic than
do their male counterparts, but little evidence suggests they have more successfully
combated these challenges through policy (see Schwindt-Bayer and Alles, chapter 4,
this volume). And women's limited power with parties has made it difficult for them
to work to improve the challenges that political parties themselves face, which continues to result in fragmentation of the party system. Thus increased gender equality
has not been a panacea for the ills that face Latin American democracies.

Transforming arenas

Increased gender equality inside of Latin America's arenas of representation also
has not led to significant transformation of the gendered nature of the arenas. The
increased numbers of women in political arenas, particularly the presidency, sets
high expectations for women breaking the glass ceiling and gaining access to full
political power. But nearly all of the chapters show that even where women's numbers in the arenas have increased, women's presence has not been equally distributed
across all types of offices within those arenas. If women are not appointed to "hard"
cabinet portfolios or economic and defense legislative committees, then power is not
equally distributed within the arenas and women have less ability to transform the
arena. Brazil illustrates a frustratingly hostile environment for women that may only
get worse as a result of the impeachment of Dilma Rousseff.

Even female presidents, who would appear to have extensive abilities to transform
politics in a way to make it less gendered toward men and masculine values and
power, have done little in this regard. Reyes-Housholder and Thomas (chapter 2, this
volume) point out that the women elected president thus far in Latin America have
not done much to re-gender the presidency and instead have simply conformed to
the masculine norms of the office. As Piscopo (chapter 9) argues, "women's efforts
alone cannot transform all the gendered aspects of political institutions" (173).[10]
In sum, the gendered formal and informal institutions that structure all five arenas
of representation have not changed significantly with increased gender equality in
Latin America.

EVALUATING CONSEQUENCES: THE EFFECTS OF FEMALE
REPRESENTATION OUTSIDE ARENAS

The second question that this volume asks about the consequences of women's representation is how it affects democracy and women and men in society. Focusing
specifically on two categories of consequences—those related to societal attitudes
about gender equality in politics and those related to attitudes toward democracy,

9. In part, this is explained by worsening economic conditions regionwide.

10. See Escobar-Lemmon and Funk (chapter 6, this volume) for some examples of positive
impacts women have had in subnational arenas.

political engagement, and political participation—the chapters in this volume show that women's representation in Latin America does have effects on both categories of societal attitudes, but the effects vary across arenas of representation, as was theorized in the introductory chapter.

Consequences for gender equality in politics

Women's presence in executive and legislative offices improves societal attitudes toward gender equality. Schwindt-Bayer and Alles (chapter 4, this volume) found that having more women in Latin American legislatures correlates with higher support for female political leaders among both women and men, with a stronger effect for women. Reyes-Housholder and Thomas (chapter 2, this volume) draw on existing research to suggest similarly that female presidents in Latin America may be linked to greater support for women in politics. Zetterberg (chapter 11, this volume) highlights a study from Mexico that having female mayors reduces gender stereotyping among men (Kerevel and Atkeson 2015). Thus women's presence in both legislatures and executives can have positive effects on society's views of gender equality in politics.

The chapters also sound a cautionary note, however, that poor performance by female presidents could have negative effects on attitudes toward women as political leaders. Piscopo (chapter 9) gives the example of Epsy Campbell-Barr failing to get her party's presidential nomination in the 2014 Costa Rican election because of doubts about nominating a woman in the aftermath of Laura Chinchilla's highly criticized presidency. Araújo, Calasanti, and Htun (chapter 12) make a similar point about possible negative symbolic consequences of Dilma Rousseff's impeachment.

Consequences for democracy, engagement, and participation

impact of women in legislatures

Similarly, consequences for society's attitudes toward democracy and its political engagement and participation come from both women's presence in legislatures and in executives. Reyes-Housholder and Thomas (chapter 2, this volume) report results from recent studies that show the presence of female presidents leads to more campaigning, the intention to vote, and a higher probability of attending local meetings among women. Schwindt-Bayer and Alles (chapter 4, this volume) show that more women in national legislatures leads to greater political engagement and participation and more positive feelings toward democracy in the region. In political parties, Morgan and Hinojosa (chapter 5, this volume) note that *not* incorporating women, or more specifically women's issues, leads to women feeling disconnected from parties and less likely to identify with any particular party. It is too soon to know the impacts of Dilma Rousseff's impeachment in August 2016, but much work needs to be done on the gendered nature of the impeachment process and its consequences for democracy and society. At the subnational level, effects are less clear and vary across arenas. Barnes and Jones (chapter 7, this volume) show that, in Argentina, having more women in provincial legislatures increases trust in government but having more women in provincial cabinets does not. The reverse is true when examining the extent to which citizens seek help from elected officials as a form of political engagement.

FUTURE RESEARCH AGENDA

Each chapter of this volume identified specific research areas where new research on gender and political representation in Latin America is needed in specific arenas or countries. Here I highlight several more general suggestions for a future research agenda on gender and representation in Latin America. First, this book makes clear that we know much more about the causes of women's representation in Latin America than we do the consequences of it, and this is particularly true for the ways in which greater gender equality in Latin America's arenas of representation affects democracy and society. Most chapters focused much more on explaining why women's levels of representation look as they do than they did on consequences. Part of the reason for this is the challenge of conducting research on gender and representation inside of political arenas. Exploration of questions of how rules and norms are gendered and the ways in which women are kept out of political power inside political arenas deals with issues that are difficult to observe and measure. Data collection for this relies on fieldwork, participant observation, interviews, archival and website research, and elite surveys which are much more difficult to collect and analyze, especially for cross-national comparison, than are numbers of male and female elected officials. Yet we need more research on the consequences of women's presence in arenas for understanding elite gender relations, governing, and the functioning of democracy.

Even on causes, however, there are areas of research where holes exist. One of those is a cause that this book identified as being one of the most important—parties and how candidate selection operates and helps/hurts gender balance in elections. This book largely confirms Hinojosa's (2012) argument that centralized selection processes help women, but some chapters in this volume suggested that centralization may not always be beneficial for women's candidacies and appointment. How and when does it help and how and when does it hurt? To ascertain this, we need more information on political parties, the role of women in them, their candidate selection rules and norms, and political aspirants and candidates for parties. Again, the challenges of this kind of data collection have been an obstacle to research in this area, but to understand more about the ways in which parties are obstacles to gender equality—something this volume has made very clear is the case in Latin America— we need to begin collecting and analyzing these kinds of data.

In terms of consequences for society, we need more research on exactly where and why women's presence has positive (or negative) effects and when women in elected and appointed office can represent women's interests or work on programs and policies that try to address societal frustrations with government. This means moving beyond establishing statistical correlations between numbers of women and societal attitudes as measured in mass surveys, which has been a common research method in this area. It means focusing more specifically on individual democratic consequences and analyzing explanations with more attention to the causal pathways by which women's presence has effects on democracy. For example, as mentioned at the end of the "challenges" section, we need answers to questions such as how do other elites and citizens evaluate men's and women's performance in office in gendered ways?

What positive or negative effects might this have for potential candidates or future elite behavior? Exploring this through survey experiments designed specifically for the purpose of answering these questions or conducting interviews with elites and citizens may provide better methods for answering these types of questions.

In this book, we have tried to address "gender" and not just "women" in our analysis of representation in Latin America. Yet, at times, we continue to prioritize women over men in research or discuss women with men as the implicit "other." Explicitly examining both women and men is important for future research. Additionally, it is important to push the envelope to understand better how women *and* men shape and are shaped by existing arenas, institutions, and social and cultural environments in ways that prioritize one over the other (i.e., how they are "gendered"). We have tried to do that in this volume but more work taking this approach is needed.

Another dimension of gender and representation that we touched on only minimally in this volume was how gender intersects with other identities in Latin America, such as Afro-descendants and indigenous Americans. Research on "intersectionality" is growing but has not made large inroads into work on gender and representation in Latin America (see, however, Htun 2016). Zetterberg (chapter 11, this volume); Araújo, Calasanti, and Htun (chapter 12, this volume); and Johnson (chapter 10, this volume) highlighted the very small numbers of female minorities represented in Mexico, Brazil, and Uruguay in their chapters, but questions about how gender and minority status work together to create obstacles for getting elected and access to power within arenas once elected were not addressed. Future research could make significant contributions in this area.

Social movements were an important part of the story of gender and representation during Latin America's transitions to democracy and the adoption of gender quotas in some countries. Yet their role in politics today has received less attention than that of gender and representation. Social movements should be reincorporated into the story of gender and representation. They matter for helping women get elected, for interacting with policymakers to shape policy, and their very nature may be influenced by gender representation in the political system. We did not study social movements specifically in this book but future work on the interplay of women's movements and gender representation is needed.

Finally, although this book brought together a large number of arenas of representation and countries, we still left out several important ones, such as bureaucracies, the judiciary, the poorer countries of Central America, and some Andean countries.[11] Research is needed on gender and representation in these arenas and countries too, particularly as the Left begins to fade from power in many of these countries, economies slow, and political challenges continue to obstruct democracy.

CONCLUSION

Significant research exists on Latin American political institutions and the democratic and representational crises that currently face many Latin American countries.

---

11. Not, of course, because they are unimportant but because space constraints required us to choose only five arenas.

Yet, it rarely addresses gender. At the same time, research on gender politics and women's representation has flourished worldwide, with some of it studying gender and women's representation in Latin America. Yet this research has not often been integrated into the Latin American democracy and institutions literature. This book has aimed to bring these literatures together by exploring important questions about and offering a holistic analysis of gender and representation in Latin American democracies that highlights the significant role played by institutions and the Latin American political context in explaining the nature of gender representation in Latin America today.

This book shows that gender equality in representation has made progress but is still lacking in many arenas and countries. It argues that Latin American arenas of representation are gendered in ways that prioritize incumbent male elites over female newcomers, even though we have seen record numbers of women as presidents, in cabinets, in legislatures, in parties, and in subnational governments in recent years. The book shows that even rules that aim to re-gender arenas, such as gender quotas, can sometimes fail to perform in ways that bring greater gender equality to politics, and that both formal and informal political institutions and the broader political challenges Latin American countries are facing interact with gender to shape equality in Latin American political arenas. It also highlights that, although women's numbers have increased in many arenas, the rules and norms of those arenas continue to obstruct equal access to political power for women and men in ways that create unequal and unrepresentative democracies. The arenas themselves are gendered to disadvantage women in politics and obstruct the ability of women to pursue traditionally masculine agendas where their contributions could help to strengthen democracies. Gender equality in Latin American arenas of representation is moving in the right direction but challenges remain. Overcoming those is the next step.

APPENDICES

CHAPTER 4 APPENDIX

Table A4.1 DESCRIPTIVE STATISTICS (PERCENTAGE OF LEGISLATURE THAT IS FEMALE ANALYSES)

Variables	Valid Obs.	Mean (or %)	SD	Median	Min	Max
Dependent Variable						
Women in the Legislative Body (%)	242	13.65	10.67	10.78	0	53.08
Socioeconomic Factors						
GDP Per Capita, Logged	244	8.10	0.62	8.13	6.69	9.19
Women Workforce, up to 2007	193	45.98	11.28	44.53	26.44	69.10
Women Workforce, 1990 on	171	37.34	4.00	37.45	27.94	45.01
Political Institutions						
Level of Democracy	241	2.56	0.93	2.50	1	6.5
Gender Quota	244	34.02%		0	0	1
Quota Size	244	10.85	15.87	0	0	50
Placement Mandate	244	0.58	0.85	0	0	2
Enforcement Mechanisms	244	0.93	1.34	0	0	3
Quota Index	244	52.47	84.68	0	0	300
PR Rules (% of seats)	243	0.73	0.42	1	0	1
District Magnitude, Logged	243	1.99	1.33	1.67	0	5.30
Informal Institutions and Quality of Government						
Retention	95	26.67	22.32	26.13	0	73.61
Quality of Government	199	4.62	1.35	4.72	1.11	7.78
Clientelism	23	22.81	8.44	24.71	8.66	33.17
Disproportionality	216	7.53	6.03	5.80	0.39	40.84
ENPP	242	3.50	1.82	2.96	1.06	13.22
Decade Dummies						
1980 Decade	244	19.26%				
1990 Decade	244	30.74%				
2000 Decade	244	29.51%				
2010 Decade	244	15.16%				

Table A4.2 STATISTICAL MODELS OF SOCIOECONOMIC AND INSTITUTIONAL INFLUENCES ON THE PERCENTAGE OF A LEGISLATIVE CHAMBER THAT IS FEMALE

	(1) Main Model	(2) Quota Design—all countries	(3) Quota Design— quota countries only	(4) Quota Index — quota countries
GDP Per Capita, Logged	1.46 (0.89)	1.73* (0.82)	5.23** (1.75)	5.29** (1.76)
Level of Democracy	0.55 (0.57)	0.67 (0.52)	3.89* (1.62)	4.26* (1.65)
Quota	9.65*** (1.21)	.	.	.
Quota Size	.	0.25*** (0.08)	0.66*** (0.15)	.
Placement Mandate	.	8.27*** (2.21)	7.19* (2.97)	.
Enforcement Mechanisms	.	−3.95** (1.45)	2.93 (2.49)	.
Quota Index	.	.	.	0.09*** (0.02)
PR—Percentage Seats	0.67 (1.31)	0.71 (1.22)	−2.08 (2.76)	−1.15 (2.70)
District Magnitude, Logged	−0.28 (0.40)	−0.22 (0.37)	−1.55 (0.86)	−2.00* (0.85)
1980 Decade	1.73 (2.26)	1.68 (2.07)	.	.
1990 Decade	3.40 (2.23)	3.20 (2.03)	.	.
2000 Decade	9.06*** (2.30)	8.07*** (2.10)	6.48* (2.65)	6.73* (2.68)
2010 Decade	12.92*** (2.56)	10.81*** (2.37)	6.41* (3.13)	8.34** (3.03)
Constant	−8.79 (8.10)	−11.34 (7.46)	−70.77*** (18.48)	−45.11* (17.36)
N	239	239	80	80
Adjusted R^2	0.54	0.62	0.48	0.47

NOTE: Table reports OLS estimates with standard errors in parentheses. The excluded decade is the 1970s in models 1 and 2 and the 1990s in models 3 and 4.
* $p<0.05$; ** $p<0.01$; *** $p<0.001$

Table A4.3 Informal Institutions and Quality of Government

	(1)	(2)	(3)	(4)	(5)	(6)	(7)
	Retention	Quality of Govt	Programmatic Parties	Disproportionality	ENPP	ENPP (quotas)	ENPP (no quotas)
GDP Per Capita, Logged	3.75**	1.86	-1.65	1.28	1.96*	5.76**	-0.15
	(1.37)	(1.03)	(6.94)	(0.88)	(0.85)	(2.03)	(0.63)
Level of Democracy	-0.64	0.55	1.05	0.17	0.61	1.98	0.10
	(0.91)	(0.60)	(3.86)	(0.59)	(0.54)	(1.84)	(0.32)
Quota	7.85***	9.61***	16.06*	7.81***	9.35***		
	(1.76)	(1.17)	(5.47)	(1.23)	(1.15)		
PR - Percentage Seats	0.56	1.48	-3.41	0.94	1.87	-1.96	1.17
	(2.02)	(1.31)	(6.52)	(1.45)	(1.26)	(3.17)	(0.90)
District Magnitude, Logged	0.03	0.12	-0.03	0.19	-0.32	-1.81	0.36
	(0.60)	(0.40)	(2.16)	(0.42)	(0.38)	(0.97)	(0.26)
Retention	-0.01						
	(0.03)						
Quality of Government		0.78					
		(0.48)					
Clientelism			0.38				
			(0.35)				
Disproportionality				0.08			
				(0.10)			
ENPP					-1.30***	-1.90***	-0.63***
					(0.25)	(0.56)	(0.19)

	(1)	(2)	(3)	(4)	(5)	(6)	(7)
1980 Decade	3.48	.	.	1.68	2.24	.	1.72
	(3.15)			(2.12)	(2.15)		(1.15)
1990 Decade	5.76	0.62	.	3.87	4.92*	.	4.98***
	(3.15)	(1.42)		(2.09)	(2.13)		(1.16)
2000 Decade	11.73***	6.49***	.	9.12**	10.95***	9.49***	9.59***
	(3.36)	(1.55)		(2.18)	(2.21)	(3.00)	(1.24)
2010 Decade	.	11.13***	0.70	14.24***	15.02***	13.20***	13.48***
		(2.23)	(5.11)	(2.66)	(2.47)	(3.35)	(1.64)
Constant	−26.40*	−14.47	17.33	−8.17	−10.69	−25.06	5.05
	(12.31)	(7.98)	(68.28)	(7.96)	(7.68)	(19.35)	(5.53)
N	95	197	22	214	238	79	159
R^2	0.48	0.54	0.22	0.52	0.58	0.30	0.46

NOTE: Table reports OLS estimates with standard errors in parentheses. The excluded decade is the 1970s or decade with no estimates in the table prior to the one with estimates.

* $p<0.05$; ** $p<0.01$; *** $p<0.001$

Table A4.4 DESCRIPTIVE STATISTICS (PELA SURVEY)

Variables	Valid Obs.	Mean (or %)	SD	Median	Min	Max
Gendered policy issues						
Gender Inequality	240	5.28	2.47	5	1	10
Divorce	2704	6.49	3.22	7	1	10
Abortion	2690	4.78	3.41	5	1	10
Threats to democracy						
Democratic Instability	4619	28.86%			0	1
Economic Crisis	4653	74.55%			0	1
Terrorism and Violence	4644	44.62%			0	1
Drug Trafficking	4641	66.62%			0	1
Citizen Insecurity	4648	75.11%			0	1
Labor Conflicts	4636	40.85%			0	1
Citizen Disinterest	4632	54.94%			0	1
Exec-Legis Relations	4624	38.19%			0	1
Legislators' characteristics						
Female Legislator	5240	17.52%			0	1
Age	5185	47.66	9.84	47	22	86
No Prior Office	4665	65.34%			0	1
Ideology	4589	4.93	2.01	5	1	10
Education	4538	4.97	0.96	5	1	6
Married	4656	78.74%			0	1
No Longer Married	4656	11.08%			0	1

NOTE: Percentage instead of mean is reported for dummy variables. For the "threats to democracy" variables, we collapse the PELA 4-point response scales into dichotomous variables. For democratic instability, we used a question on views of democratic stability and collapsed those who responded "not stable" and "a little stable" into one category and inverted the PELA scale to make those our "1" category. For the remaining issues, we used a PELA question on legislator views of how much a threat each issue is to democratic consolidation, and we created a score of "1" for those who "strongly" or "somewhat" agree that the issue is a threat. "Married" comprises both domestic partners and married legislators. "No longer married" includes widows/widowers and divorced legislators.

Table A4.5 LEGISLATOR ATTITUDES TOWARD DIVORCE AND
ABORTION LAW

	(1)	(2)	(3)
	Gender Inequality	**Divorce**	**Abortion**
Sex	1.46***	0.27	0.40*
	(0.41)	(0.16)	(0.17)
Age	−0.02	−0.01	0.02*
	(0.02)	(0.01)	(0.01)
No Prior Office	0.10	0.40**	−0.47***
	(0.32)	(0.13)	(0.14)
Ideology	−0.36***	−0.23***	−0.38***
	(0.08)	(0.03)	(0.03)
Education	−0.13	0.30***	0.25***
	(0.16)	(0.06)	(0.07)
Married	−0.55	−0.92***	−0.52*
	(0.53)	(0.19)	(0.21)
No Longer Married	−1.11	0.65**	0.11
	(0.69)	(0.25)	(0.27)
Constant	7.80***	7.55**	5.10**
	(1.43)	(0.58)	(0.64)
N	235	2611	2600
R^2	0.24	0.19	0.14

NOTE: Table reports OLS estimates with standard errors in parentheses.
Country dummies are not presented.
* $p<0.05$; ** $p<0.01$; *** $p<0.001$

Table A4.6 Legislator Perceptions of Threats to Democracy

	(1) Democratic Instability	(2) Economic Crisis	(3) Terrorism and Violence	(4) Drug Trafficking	(5) Citizen Insecurity	(6) Labor Conflicts	(7) Citizen Disinterest	(8) Exec-Legis Relations
Sex	0.30**	0.30**	0.46***	0.48***	0.41***	0.38***	0.26**	0.38***
	(0.11)	(0.11)	(0.09)	(0.10)	(0.11)	(0.09)	(0.09)	(0.09)
Age	−0.004	0.01**	0.01**	0.02***	0.02***	−0.002	0.002	−0.004
	(0.004)	(0.004)	(0.004)	(0.004)	(0.004)	(0.004)	(0.004)	(0.004)
No Prior Office	0.01	−0.05	−0.08	−0.09	−0.06	−0.27***	−0.08	−0.14
	(0.09)	(0.09)	(0.08)	(0.08)	(0.08)	(0.07)	(0.07)	(0.08)
Ideology	−0.14***	−0.12***	0.13***	0.05*	0.03	0.04*	−0.01	0.03*
	(0.02)	(0.02)	(0.02)	(0.02)	(0.02)	(0.02)	(0.02)	(0.02)
Education	−0.07	0.08	0.002	−0.08	−0.05	−0.06	−0.01	0.07
	(0.04)	(0.04)	(0.04)	(0.04)	(0.04)	(0.03)	(0.03)	(0.04)
Married	−0.20	−0.09	0.03	−0.13	0.01	0.01	−0.18	0.12
	(0.13)	(0.14)	(0.12)	(0.13)	(0.13)	(0.11)	(0.11)	(0.11)
No Longer Married	−0.03	−0.07	−0.14	−0.20	−0.09	−0.01	−0.13	0.22
	(0.17)	(0.18)	(0.15)	(0.16)	(0.16)	(0.14)	(0.14)	(0.15)
Democratic Instability	.	0.89***	0.45***	0.40***	0.43***	0.40***	0.24**	0.57***
	.	(0.11)	(0.08)	(0.09)	(0.10)	(0.08)	(0.08)	(0.08)
Constant	−1.83***	0.06	−2.25***	−1.38***	−0.38	−0.24	0.55	−1.20***
	(0.42)	(0.39)	(0.34)	(0.36)	(0.37)	(0.32)	(0.32)	(0.34)
N	4,303	4,280	4,271	4,267	4,274	4,265	4,258	4,251
Log Likelihood	−2,044.04	−2,034.34	−2,556.41	−2,333.55	−2,227.33	−2,809.69	−2,817.52	−2,617.92

NOTE: Table reports logit estimates with standard errors in parentheses. Models include country dummies for 18 countries, but the table does not present them.

* $p<0.05$; ** $p<0.01$; *** $p<0.001$

Table A4.7 DESCRIPTIVE STATISTICS (LAPOP ANALYSES)

Variables	Valid Obs.	Mean (or %)	SD	Median	Min	Max
Dependent Variables						
Support Female Leaders	51627	72.76%			0	1
Political Interest	118039	30.02%			0	1
Persuading Others	132696	16.93%			0	1
Government Assistance	134156	19.87%			0	1
Campaigning	129554	10.41%			0	1
Follow Politics in News	60513	62.88%			0	1
Support for Democracy	129561	3.94	1.79	4	1	7
Satisfaction with Democracy	119211	54.48%			0	1
Trust in Legislature	130958	3.62	1.82	4	1	7
Corruption Perceptions	132551	3.56	1.90	4	1	7
Respondent Characteristics						
Sex (1 = female)	137550	51.53%			0	1
Age	137228	38.89	15.83	36	16	99
Education	135771	2.91	1.19	3	1	5
Wealth	124981	3.87	1.75	4	0	7
Ideology (6 = right)	108557	3.50	1.43	3	1	6
Country Characteristics						
Women in Legislature	137551	19.16	9.33	16.7	5.5	40.2
Gender Quota	137552	63.12%			0	1
GDP Per Capita, Logged	137552	8.36	0.73	8.36	6.86	9.63
Disproportionality	137551	6.74	3.62	6.34	1.1	17.54

NOTE: All variables coded in order of increasing value (increasing support for democracy, trust in legislature; more corruption; more educated, wealthier) or if the respondent said they supported an idea or participated in an activity (e.g., 1 = support female leaders).

Table A4.8 LAPOP ANALYSES OF RELATIONSHIP BETWEEN WOMEN IN LEGISLATURE AND SUPPORT FOR FEMALE LEADERS AND POLITICAL ENGAGEMENT

	(1) Support Female Leaders	(2) Political Interest	(3) Persuading Others	(4) Seeking Government Assistance	(5) Helping with Campaign	(6) Following Politics in News
Women in Legislature	0.009**	0.008**	0.007*	0.011**	0.012**	0.005*
	(0.002)	(0.003)	(0.003)	(0.003)	(0.004)	(0.002)
Sex	0.639**	-0.378**	-0.377**	-0.026	-0.412**	-0.074
	(0.059)	(0.036)	(0.043)	(0.041)	(0.055)	(0.049)
Women Legislature * Sex	0.005	0.004**	0.004*	0.002	0.004	-0.005*
	(0.003)	(0.002)	(0.002)	(0.002)	(0.003)	(0.002)
Age	-0.001	0.006**	0.008**	0.009**	0.010**	0.021**
	(0.001)	(0.001)	(0.001)	(0.001)	(0.001)	(0.001)
Education	0.196**	0.289**	0.158**	0.075**	0.241**	0.259**
	(0.013)	(0.009)	(0.010)	(0.009)	(0.012)	(0.012)
Wealth	0.003	0.034**	0.014	-0.109**	-0.046**	0.112**
	(0.009)	(0.006)	(0.008)	(0.007)	(0.008)	(0.009)
Ideology	-0.061**	-0.009	-0.029**	-0.011	0.016	0.019*
	(0.008)	(0.006)	(0.008)	(0.007)	(0.009)	(0.008)
Gender Quota	0.008	-0.169*	0.166	-0.322**	0.106	-0.020
	(0.036)	(0.077)	(0.109)	(0.095)	(0.113)	(0.038)
GDP Per Capita, Logged	0.033	0.033	-0.117	-0.218	-0.367*	-0.026
	(0.029)	(0.123)	(0.155)	(0.130)	(0.161)	(0.028)
Disproportionality	-0.050**	-0.002	0.011	0.015	-0.020	0.010
	(0.005)	(0.008)	(0.010)	(0.009)	(0.013)	(0.005)
Constant	-0.008	-2.019	-1.876	-0.061	-0.121	-1.142**
	(0.251)	(1.089)	(1.347)	(1.120)	(1.408)	(0.238)
N	41326	92035	93761	94643	91333	48155

NOTES: Table reports logit estimates with standard errors in parentheses. Survey weights are included in the models. Although not shown, all models except models 1 and 6 include country fixed effects. All models also include time fixed effects with 2004 as the excluded year, except for models 1 and 6 which have only two time points and exclude 2008 and 2010, respectively.

Table A4.9 LAPOP ANALYSES OF EFFECT OF WOMEN IN LEGISLATURE ON VIEWS OF LATIN AMERICAN DEMOCRACY

	(1) Support for Democracy	(2) Satisfaction with Democracy	(3) Trust in Legislature	(4) Corruption Perceptions
Women in Legislature	0.02**	0.00**	0.02**	0.01**
	(0.00)	(0.00)	(0.00)	(0.00)
Sex	−0.05**	−0.02**	0.05**	−0.01
	(0.01)	(0.00)	(0.01)	(0.01)
Age	0.00**	0.00	0.00	−0.00
	(0.00)	(0.00)	(0.00)	(0.00)
Education	−0.03**	−0.03**	−0.06**	−0.09**
	(0.01)	(0.00)	(0.01)	(0.01)
Wealth	−0.02**	−0.01**	−0.05**	−0.05**
	(0.01)	(0.00)	(0.01)	(0.01)
Ideology	0.03**	0.02**	0.08**	0.03**
	(0.01)	(0.00)	(0.01)	(0.01)
Gender Quota	−0.14	−0.00	−0.01	−0.08
	(0.07)	(0.03)	(0.07)	(0.07)
GDP Per Capita, Logged	−0.41**	−0.13**	−0.07	−0.83**
	(0.11)	(0.05)	(0.11)	(0.11)
Disproportionality	−0.02**	−0.01**	−0.01	−0.02**
	(0.01)	(0.00)	(0.01)	(0.01)
Constant	7.37**	3.46**	4.37**	10.47**
	(0.94)	(0.42)	(0.95)	(0.98)
N	93699	84635	94334	95078
R^2	0.08	0.05	0.08	0.08

NOTE: Table reports OLS estimates with standard errors in parentheses. Models include country dummies for 18 countries and time dummies for 5 years, but the table does not present them.

* $p<0.05$; ** $p<0.01$

CHAPTER 6 APPENDIX

Table A6.1 What Determines Women's Representation in Local Governments?

	Model 1: Women in City Councils, Percentage	Model 2: Woman Mayors, Percentage
Fixed Components		
Female Labor Force Participation	0.226*	0.082
	(0.098)	(0.079)
Fertility Rates	−5.150**	−1.165
	(1.744)	(1.398)
Urban Population	−0.166	0.119
	(0.111)	(0.085)
Federal Country	−2.702	−0.250
	(3.473)	(2.514)
Local Quota	2.956**	1.927*
	(1.030)	(0.878)
Fiscal Decentralization	−0.815	−2.539**
	(1.347)	(0.966)
Years Since 1st Local Elections	0.139**	−0.041
	(0.052)	(0.040)
% Women Legislators	0.228**	0.065
	(0.068)	(0.058)
Woman President	−0.411	1.852#
	(1.143)	(0.981)
% Woman Mayors	0.037	
	(0.075)	
% Woman City Councilors		0.030
		(0.055)
Level-1 (Country-Year) Intercept	27.787*	−0.029
	(12.039)	(9.477)
Variance Components		
Level-2 (Country) Intercept	16.835	8.229
N Country-Years	239	239
N Countries	18	18

NOTES: *$p<0.05$, **$p<0.01$. Estimates obtained from hierarchical linear regression models using the mixed command in Stata 13. Level 1 is the country-year and level 2 is the country. Standard errors in parentheses. Cases included: Bolivia (1999–2013), Brazil (1998–2013), Chile (1998–2013), Colombia (1999–2013), Costa Rica (2002–2013), Cuba (2004–2013), Dominican Republic (1998–2013), Ecuador (1998–2001, 2003–2013), El Salvador (2000–2012), Guatemala (1998–2010), Honduras (1998–2012), Mexico (2004–2011), Nicaragua (2005–2011), Panama (2000–2013), Paraguay (1999–2013), Peru (1998–1999, 2001–2013), Uruguay (1998–2013), Venezuela (1998–2006).

CHAPTER 7 APPENDIX

Table A7.1 DESCRIPTION AND MEASUREMENT OF VARIABLES INCLUDED
IN SYMBOLIC REPRESENTATION ANALYSIS

Variable	Description and Measure
Dependent Variables	
Trust in Local Government	Trust in Local Governments ranges from 0 (not at all) to 7 (a lot). This is taken from LAPOP B3: "To what extent do you trust the local or municipal government?"
Contact Local Government	Contact with Local Governments is coded 1 when respondents report having had contact with local officials in the past year and 0 otherwise. This is taken from LAPOP CAP4A: "Now, moving on to a different subject, sometimes people and communities have problems that they cannot solve by themselves, and so in order to solve them they request help from a government official or agency. In order to solve your problems have you ever requested help or cooperation from a local public official or local government for example, a mayor, municipal council, councilman, provincial official, civil governor or governor?"
Level 1 Variables	
Female	Female is coded 1 when the respondent is female and 0 when the respondent is male.
Urban	Urban is coded as 1 when the respondent lives in an urban area and 0 if the respondent lives in a rural area. This is taken from LAPOP (UR).
Children	Children is coded as 1 if the respondent has children and 0 otherwise. This information is taken from LAPOP Q12: "Do you have children?"
Education	Education is measured as the number of years of schooling the respondent completed. This is taken from the LAPOP question (ED): "How many years of schooling have you completed?"
Church Attendance	Church attendance ranges from 1 to 5 and is measured using LAPOP Q5A: "How often do you attend religious services? (1) More than once per week (2) Once per week (3) Once a month (4) Once or twice a year (5) Never or almost never."
Political Interest	A measure of political interest that ranges from 1 to 4. We use POL1 from LAPOP which asks: "How much interest do you have in politics: (1) A lot (2) Some (3) Little (4) None"
Level 2 Variables	
Percent Women in Legislature	Women's descriptive representation in the legislature is measured as the percentage of the lower chamber/unicameral chamber occupied by women in the year before the survey was fielded.
Percent Women in Cabinet	Women's descriptive representation in the cabinet is measured as the percentage of the cabinet occupied by women in the year before the survey was fielded.
Development	Development is measured using the human development index.
Gender Inequality	Gender Inequality is measured using the gender development index.
Income Inequality	Income inequality is measured using the GINI coefficient.
Presidential Election Year	Presidential Election Year is coded 1 if the survey was fielded during a presidential election year and 0 otherwise.

Table A7.2 SYMBOLIC CONSEQUENCES OF WOMEN'S REPRESENTATION
IN SUBNATIONAL GOVERNMENTS

	(1) Trust in Local Government	(2) Contact Local Government
Female	−0.45^	−0.95*
	(0.27)	(0.46)
Percent Women in Legislature	0.02*	−0.02
	(0.01)	(0.02)
Female* % Women in Legislature	0.01	0.03^
	(0.01)	(0.01)
Percent Women in Cabinet	−0.01	−0.02
	(0.01)	(0.01)
Female* % Women in Cabinet	0.01*	0.03*
	(0.01)	(0.01)
Development	−9.69**	−6.19
	(3.55)	(5.50)
Gender Inequality	11.51**	5.14
	(3.94)	(6.12)
Income Inequality	0.01	0.05
	(0.03)	(0.04)
Rural	0.15^	0.71***
	(0.08)	(0.12)
Age	−0.02**	0.05**
	(0.01)	(0.02)
Age^2	0.00**	−0.00***
	(0.00)	(0.00)
Children	0.01	0.16
	(0.06)	(0.11)
Education	−0.01	−0.05***
	(0.01)	(0.01)
Church Attendance	−0.10***	−0.21***
	(0.02)	(0.04)
Political Interest	−0.10***	−0.32***
	(0.03)	(0.04)
Presidential Election Year	0.46***	0.19
	(0.11)	(0.18)
Respondents	5249	5355
Province-Years	70	70

Coefficients from multilevel models with a random intercept for the province-year.
Model 1 is a multilevel mixed-effects ordered logistic regression. Model 2 is a multilevel
mixed-effects logistic regression. Standard errors in parentheses.

^ $p<0.10$, * $p<0.05$, ** $p<0.01$, *** $p<0.001$

CHAPTER 10 APPENDIX

Table A10.1 WOMEN *TITULAR* LEGISLATORS AT BEGINNING OF EACH LEGISLATURE, 1985–2015

Year	Chamber of deputies		Senate		Parliament	
	Number	Percentage	Number	Percentage	Number	Percentage
1985	0	0.0	0	0.0	0	0.0
1990	6	6.1	0	0.0	6	4.7
1995	7	7.1	2	6.7	9	7.0
2000	13	13.1	3	10.0	16	12.4
2005	11	11.1	3	10.0	14	10.9
2010	15	15.2	4	13.3	19	14.7
2015	18	18.2	8	26.7	26	20.2

SOURCE: Data from the Uruguayan parliament.

Table A10.2 PERCENTAGE OF WOMEN IN *JUNTAS DEPARTAMENTALES*, BY DEPARTMENT, 1985–2015

Department	1985	1990	1995	2000	2005	2010	2015
Artigas	6.5	9.7	19.4	19.4	16.1	12.9	29.0
Canelones	0.0	0.0	6.5	19.4	129	9.7	22.6
Cerro Largo	3.2	12.9	16.1	25.8	22.6	22.6	29.0
Colonia	6.5	6.5	3.2	6.5	3.2	9.7	25.8
Durazno	12.9	12.9	12.9	12.9	29.0	22.6	29.0
Flores	6.5	9.7	16.1	25.8	25.8	32.3	35.5
Florida	0.0	6.5	12.9	16.1	12.9	16.1	38.7
Lavalleja	6.5	22.6	25.8	12.9	9.7	19.4	29.0
Maldonado	0.0	6.5	12.9	16.1	16.1	29.0	22.6
Montevideo	9.7	19.4	22.6	29.0	22.6	29.0	38.7
Paysandú	9.7	19.4	16.1	12.9	19.4	12.9	22.6
Río Negro	9.7	16.1	29.0	22.6	19.4	19.4	22.6
Rivera	6.5	9.7	12.9	12.9	9.7	22.6	25.8
Rocha	3.2	3.2	6.5	6.5	29.0	32.3	35.5
Salto	3.2	3.2	3.2	3.2	3.2	19.4	25.8
San José	0.0	6.5	9.7	16.1	16.1	3.2	25.8
Soriano	6.5	0.0	6.5	6.5	9.7	12.9	29.0
Tacuarembó	3.2	16.1	6.5	3.2	19.4	6.5	22.6
Treinta Tres	6.5	16.1	25.8	22.6	29.0	25.8	22.6

SOURCE: Johnson (2005, 2013) and Pérez (2015).

Table A10.3 PUBLIC ATTITUDES TO WOMEN'S PARTICIPATION AND
PERFORMANCE IN POLITICS, 2007

	% in agreement
Opinion on number of women in parliament	
The current number is okay	14.2
There should be more women	59.8
There should be fewer women	3.4
The sex of members of parliament is irrelevant	14
Don't know	8.6
Opinion on number of women cabinet ministers	
The current number is okay	12.4
There should be more women	55
There should be fewer women	3.9
The sex of cabinet members is irrelevant	21.9
Don't know	6.8
Opinion on female ministers' performance	
Perform as well as or better than male ministers	80
Perform worse than male ministers	6.5
Don't know	13.5
Opinion on minimum gender quotas for cabinet posts	
In favor	50.6
Against	28.5
Don't know	20.8
Opinion on inclusion of women in presidential formulas at the next election	
It would be desirable	74.4
It would not be desirable	3.9
It is irrelevant	14.2
Don't know	7.4
Opinion on quota law	
In favor	49.2
Against	15.5
Don't know	35.4

SOURCE: Data from the survey carried out in 2007 by the Politics, Gender and Diversity Area of the Institute of Political Science, Universidad de la República with funding from International IDEA.

CHAPTER 13 APPENDIX

APPENDIX 13.1: CAUSES OF FEMALE REPRESENTATION IN COLOMBIA

We constructed two dependent variables from the available electoral data (Pachón and Sánchez, 2014): the percentage of female candidates per district and the percentage of elected women per district. Our unit of analysis is the department (municipality) / election. We tested the hypotheses in different types of elections: councils (1994–2007), assemblies (1970–2007), and the House of Representatives (1960–2014). We coded each woman in the sample by using her first name. Although there is some room for inaccuracies, we went over the data through several rounds to ensure that most names were accounted for. Ultimately, our file of names accounted for approximately 11,000 different names for more than 50,000 candidates in the dataset. To capture the impact of institutional changes introduced by the 1991 Constitution, the political reform of 2003, and the 2011 quota law, dummy variables are included. To account for the "path dependent" nature of the data, we include the lagged percentage of elected women as an independent variable.

Thus, the full model is explained in the following equation,

$$Percentage\ of\ nominated\ /elected\ women_{i,t}$$
$$= \beta_0 + \beta_2 * district_{mag_{i,t}} + \gamma * Reform_{k,i} + \%Elected\ Women_{i,t-1} + e_{i,t} \qquad (1)$$

where i denotes the district, t the year when an election took place, and k the reform (1991, 2003, or 2011). We use fixed effects models[1] in an unbalanced panel because our sample differs given the historical change in the units of analysis. Also, the number of observations varies depending on the type of election and levels of data aggregation.[2] Table A13.1 presents the results.

1. Results of both random effects (RE) and fixed effects (FE) models are presented only when the Haussman specification test indicated systematic differences on estimated parameters.

2. We could have used a probit or logit model to observe the impact on the probability of a women being elected, but since we do not have variables measuring individual characteristics, we decided to aggregate the data by district.

Table A13.1 RELATIVE IMPORTANCE OF FUNDAMENTAL CAUSES OF FEMALE REPRESENTATION ACROSS LEGISLATIVE BODIES IN COLOMBIA

	Municipal Councils		Departmental Assemblies		House of Representatives	
Average Percentage of Women	Nominated (1)	Elected (2)	Nominated (3)	Elected (4)	Nominated (5)	Elected (6)
1991 Constitution	—	—	-0.0096	0.0214**	0.0406***	0.0342
			(0.0071)	(0.0089)	(0.0097)	(0.0306)
2003 Reform	0.0498***	0.0271***	-0.0131*	0.0362**	0.0836***	0.0112
	(0.0021)	(0.0030)	(0.0067)	(0.0139)	(0.0136)	(0.0225)
2011 Reform	0.1391***	0.0623***	—	—	0.3305***	0.1107**
	(0.0025)	(0.0042)			(0.0182)	(0.0494)
District Magnitude	-0.0085***	0.0039**	-0.0024**	0.0001	-0.0017	-0.0046
	(0.0006)	(0.0018)	(0.0010)	(0.0013)	(0.0019)	(0.0028)
L_Elected	-0.0345***	-0.0662***	0.0829	0.1961**	0.0690**	0.1449*
	(0.0105)	(0.0141)	(0.0497)	(0.0802)	(0.0285)	(0.0727)
Constant	0.1859***	0.0544***	0.1314***	0.0491*	0.0746***	0.0830***
	(0.006)	(0.0194)	(0.0190)	(0.0264)	(0.0162)	(0.0284)
Observations	6,234	6,098	495	494	389	384
R-squared	0.3728	0.0647	0.0182	0.0893	0.4126	0.0819
Number of muni_code	1.100	1.099				
Number of dpto_code			32	32	33	33

Robust standard errors in parentheses, * $p<0.1$, ** $p<0.05$, *** $p<0.01$

APPENDIX 13.2: DETERMINANTS OF WOMEN'S ISSUE BILL SPONSORSHIP IN COLOMBIA

To analyze the influence of female descriptive representation (Table 13.4), we built a model using the count of bills sponsored that had women as the main topic per legislator as the dependent variable.[3] Data was available for four periods: 1998–2002 (Pastrana's administration), 2002–2006 (first presidential term of Álvaro Uribe), 2006–2010 (second term of Uribe's administration) and 2010–2014 (Santos's first term as president).

The independent variables account for the characteristics of the legislator that could influence the introduction of women's issue bills. The main explanatory variable (sex) is a binary variable that takes a value of 1 when the legislator is female. Since the incumbency status of a legislator could positively relate to the introduction of this type of bill, a dummy variable that indicates whether the legislator is an incumbent or not is included as an explanatory variable.

A control for committee is also necessary since bills related to women's issues are more likely to be introduced by legislators that belong to the 7th committee because that committee focuses on social issues and is more likely to study women's issue bills. Also, we include controls for which chamber the legislator belongs to ("1" = Senate), whether the legislator was originally elected ("1") or is a replacement ("0"), and the overall number of bills introduced by the legislator. Note that the inclusion of the total number of bills introduced as a control variable means that the effect (model coefficient) should be interpreted as the tendency to introduce bills related to women's issues, holding constant overall legislative activity.

We use a negative binomial regression model, which is a model developed for the analysis of over-dispersed count outcome variables.[4] Table 13.4's first model's specification follows this formula:

$$Count\ of\ women's\ issue\ bills_i$$
$$= \beta_0 + \beta_1 * women_i + \beta_2 * Committe\ Dummies_i + \beta_3 * Senate_i$$
$$+ \beta_4 * Incumbency_i + \beta_5 * Replacement_i + \beta_6 * Total\ Bills_i + e_i \quad (2)$$

Six additional models with different specifications were run to verify the robustness of the results. In model 2 of Table 13.4, party dummies were included since membership in a party and thus a different ideology of the legislator could differentially affect the types of bills sponsored. Model 3 includes a control for the legislative period, since the topics that each administration is interested in are different.[5] Both

---

3. Women's issue bills are those that affect women in a direct way (for example, Bill 160/13 of the Senate, the Women's Integral Protection Law, or Bill 202/14 of the Senate that proposed creation of a Commission for Gender Equality in Municipal Councils and Departmental Assemblies). This coding does not include issues that have been traditionally related to women's concerns like children, education, and family.

4. Poisson and zero-inflated negative binomial distributions models were also tried, but AIC and BIC criteria suggested the negative binomial distribution was a better fit for the data.

5. Because some of the legislators can repeat periods, the assumption of independence of the observations may be violated. We ran the regression for each legislative period separately, and the results were robust.

party and legislative period effects are included in model 4. Since female senators have a "national" scope, they could be more likely to promote legislation in favor of women, therefore an interaction between women and senate is included as a control in model 5. In addition, education can influence this decision because men with more education may sponsor more bills in favor of women, which is why model 6 includes dummies for educational level[6] alongside of the interaction between women and senate. Model 7 is just like the previous one but adding period effects, which were previously significant.

The results of each of the seven models show the robustness of the effect that a woman has on the number of women's issue bills sponsored. The chapter analyzes this and other results in greater detail.

---

6. In the dataset, education is a categorical variable. Therefore, dummy variables indicating the educational level were constructed: basic education, undergraduate education, and graduate education. When using this variable, the model has fewer observations because some legislators lack educational information in the dataset.

REFERENCES

Adams, Melinda, and Gwynn Thomas. 2010. "Breaking the Final Glass Ceiling: The Influence of Gender in the Elections of Ellen Johnson-Sirleaf and Michelle Bachelet." *Journal of Women, Politics & Policy* 31, no. 2: 105–131.

Agência Patrícia Galvão. 2015. "Gênero e raça nas eleições." In *Eleição presidencial de 2014: a força das mulheres.* São Paulo, Brazil: Instituto Patricia Galvao.

Alcántara Sáez, Manuel. 2008a. *Politicians and Politics in Latin America.* Boulder, CO: Lynne Rienner.

Alcántara Sáez, Manuel. 2008b. *Sistemas políticas de América Latina.* Vol. 1, *América del Sur.* 4th ed. Madrid: Editorial Tecnos.

Alcántara Sáez, Manuel. 2013. *Sistemas políticas de América Latina.* Vol. 2, *México, América Central y el Caribe.* 3rd ed. Madrid: Editorial Tecnos.

Alcántara Sáez, Manuel, dir. 2017. *Proyecto de elites parlamentarias Latinoamericanas (PELA).* Salamanca: Universidad de Salamanca.

Alexander, Amy C. 2012. "Change in Women's Descriptive Representation and the Belief in Women's Ability to Govern: A Virtuous Cycle." *Politics and Gender* 8, no. 4: 437–464.

Alfaro Redondo, Ronald, and Steffan Gómez Campos. 2014. "Análisis electoral y de partidos políticos en Costa Rica." San José, Costa Rica: Programa Estado de la Nación, Defensoría de los Habitantes. http://estadonacion.or.cr/files/biblioteca_virtual/020/politica/Alfaro&Gomez2014.pdf

Alles, Santiago. 2007. "¿Hacia la consolidación política? Cambios en la 'Estructura de oportunidades electorales' de las mujeres en Argentina." *América Latina Hoy* 47: 123–154.

Alles, Santiago. 2008. "Efectos del sistema electoral sobre la representación de mujeres: Argumentos y evidencia a partir del caso Argentino (1983–2005)." *Revista SAAP* 3, no. 2: 313–352.

Alles, Santiago. 2009. Elección de mujeres, sistema electoral y cuotas de género en las provincias argentinas. *XXVIII International Congress*, LASA, Río de Janeiro: June 11–14.

Alles, Santiago. 2014. "Ideología partidaria, competencia electoral y elección de legisladoras en cinco democracias Latinoamericanas: Argentina, Brasil, Chile, Perú y Uruguay, 1980–2013." *América Latina, Hoy* 66: 69–94.

Alles, Santiago, and Leslie A. Schwindt-Bayer. 2015. "An Integrated PELA Dataset." Rice University.

Altman, David, and Chasquetti, Daniel. 2005. "Re-Election and Political Career Paths in the Uruguayan Congress, 1985–99." *The Journal of Legislative Studies* 11, no. 2: 235–253.

Álvarez, Rosario. 2015. "Presidenta Bachelet presenta proyecto sobre despenalización del aborto terapéutico hasta las 12 semanas de gestación." *La Tercera*, January 31, 2015. http://www.latercera.com/noticia/politica/2015/01/674-615019-9-presidenta-bachelet-presenta-proyecto-sobre-despenalizacion-del-aborto.shtml Accessed March 11, 2015.

Alves, José Eustáquio Diniz, Céli Regina Jardim Pinto, and Fátima Jordão, eds. 2012. *Mulheres nas eleições 2010*. 1st ed. São Paulo, Brazil: ABCP/SPM.

Ames, Barry. 1995. "Electoral Strategy under Open-List Proportional Representation." *American Journal of Political Science* 39, no. 2: 406–433.

Ames, Barry. 2001. *The Deadlock of Democracy in Brazil*. Ann Arbor: University of Michigan Press.

Amorim Neto, Octavio. 2006. "The Presidential Calculus: Executive Policy Making and Cabinet Formation in the Americas." *Comparative Political Studies* 39, no. 4: 415–440.

Andeweg, Rudy B. 2000. "Ministers as Double Agents? The Delegation Process between Cabinets And Ministers." *European Journal of Political Research* 37, no. 3: 377–395.

Annesley, Claire, and Francesca Gains. 2010. "The Core Executive: Gender Power and Change." *Political Studies* 58, no. 5: 909–929.

Annesley, Claire, Susan Franceschet, Karen Beckwith and Isabelle Engeli. 2014. "Gender and the Executive Branch: Defining a New Research Agenda." Paper presented at the ECPR Joint Sessions. Salamanca, Spain. April 10–15.

Anria, Santiago. 2016. "Democratizing Democracy? Civil Society and Party Organization in Bolivia." *Comparative Politics* 48, no. 4: 459–478.

Araújo, Clara. 2008. "Mujeres y elecciones legislativas en Brasil: Las cuotas y su (in) eficacia." In *Mujeres y política en América Latina: Sistemas electorales y cuotas de género*, edited by Nélida Archenti and María Inés Tula, 87–106. Buenos Aires, Argentina: Heliasta.

Araújo, Clara, and José Eustáquio Diniz Alves. 2007. "Impactos de indicadores sociais e do sistema eleitoral sobre as chances das mulheres nas eleições e suas interações com as quotas." *Dados* 50, no. 3: 535–577.

Araújo, Clara, and José Eustáquio Diniz Alves. 2011. "Participation of Women in the Elections of 2002, 2006 and 2010: The Quota Policy and the Brazilian Electoral System." In *Diffusion of Gender Quotas in Latin America and Beyond: Advances and Setbacks in the Last Two Decades*, edited by Adriana Piatti-Crocker, 70–97. New York: Peter Lang.

Araújo, Clara, and Doriam Borges. 2012. "O gênero, os elegíveis e os não-elegíveis: Uma análise das candidaturas para a Câmara Federal em 2010." In *Mulheres nas eleições 2010*, edited by José Eustáquio Diniz Alves, Céli Regina Jardim Pinto, and Fátima Jordão, 337–385. Rio de Janeiro, Brazil: ABCP\SPM.

Araújo, Clara, and Ana Isabel García. 2006. "Latin America: The Experience and the Impact of Quotas in Latin America." In *Women, Quotas, and Politics*, edited by Drude Dahlerup, 83–111. New York: Routledge.

Araújo, Clara, and Moema Guedes. 2010. "Igualdade de oportunidades no Mercado de Trabalho." *Revista do Observatório Brasil da Igualdade de Gênero*. Dezembro: 50–66.

Archenti, Nélida, and Laura Albaine. 2012. "Las mujeres en los gobiernos locales: Argentina, 2007–2011." *Revista SAAP* 6, no. 2: 227–247.

Archenti, Nélida, and Niki Johnson. 2006. "Engendering the Legislative Agenda With and Without the Quota: A Comparative Study of Argentina and Uruguay." *Sociologia, Problemas e Práticas* 52: 133–153.

Archenti, Nélida, and María Inés Tula. 2007. "Cuotas de género y tipo de lista en América Latina." *Opinião Pública* 13, no. 1: 185–218.

Archenti, Nélida, and María Inés Tula, eds. 2008a. *Mujeres y política en América Latina: Sistemas electorales y cuotas de género*. Buenos Aires: Heliasta.

Archenti, Nélida, and María Inés Tula. 2008b. "La ley de cuotas en la Argentina: Un balance sobre lagros y obstáculos." In *Mujeres y política en América Latina: Sistemas electorales y cuotas de género*, edited by Nélida Archenti and María Inés Tula, 31–52. Buenos Aires: Heliasta.

Archenti, Nélida, and María Inés Tula. 2011. "Candidate Selection as Political Barriers for Gender Quotas: The Case of Argentina at Subnational Levels." In *Diffusion of Gender Quotas in Latin America and Beyond*, edited by Adriana Piatti-Crocker, 18–35. New York: Peter Lang.

Baker, Andy, and Kenneth F. Greene. 2011. "The Latin American Left's Mandate: Free-Market Policies and Issue Voting in New Democracies." *World Politics* 63, no. 1: 43–77.

Baker, Andy, Barry Ames, Anand E. Sokhey, and Lucio R. Renno. 2016. "The Dynamics of Partisan Identification when Party Brands Change: The Case of the Worker's Party in Brazil." *Journal of Politics* 78, no. 1: 197–213.

Baldez, Lisa. 2002. *Why Women Protest: Women's Movements in Chile*. New York: Cambridge University Press.

Baldez, Lisa. 2003. "Women's Movements and Democratic Transition in Chile, Brazil, East Germany, and Poland." *Comparative Politics* 35, no. 3: 253–272.

Baldez, Lisa. 2004. "Elected Bodies: The Gender Quota Law for Legislative Candidates in Mexico." *Legislative Studies Quarterly* 29, no. 2: 231–258.

Baldez, Lisa. 2007. "Primaries vs. Quotas: Gender and Candidate Nominations in Mexico, 2003." *Latin America Politics and Society* 49, no. 3: 69–96.

Barnes, Tiffany D. 2012a. "Gender and Legislative Preferences: Evidence from the Argentine Provinces." *Politics & Gender* 8, no. 4: 483–507.

Barnes, Tiffany D. 2012b. "Gender Quotas and the Representation of Women: Empowerment, Decision-making, and Public Policy." PhD diss., Rice University, Houston.

Barnes, Tiffany D. 2014. "Women's Representation and Legislative Committee Appointments: The Case of the Argentine Provinces." *Revista Uruguaya de Ciencia Politica* 23: 135–163.

Barnes, Tiffany D. 2016. *Gendering Legislative Behavior: Institutional Constraints and Collaboration*. New York: Cambridge University Press.

Barnes, Tiffany D., and Emily Beaulieu. 2014. "Gender Stereotypes and Corruption: How Candidates Affect Perceptions of Election Fraud." *Politics and Gender* 10, no. 3: 365–391.

Barnes, Tiffany D., and Stephanie M. Burchard. 2013. "'Engendering' Politics: The Impact of Descriptive Representation on Women's Political Engagement in Sub-Saharan Africa." *Comparative Political Studies* 46, no. 7: 767–790.

Barnes, Tiffany D., and Abby Córdova. 2016. "Making Space for Women: Explaining Citizen Support for Legislative Gender Quotas in Latin America." *Journal of Politics* 78, no. 3: 670–686.

Barnes, Tiffany D., and Mark P. Jones. 2011. "Latin America." In *Women in Executive Power: A Global Overview*, edited by Gretchen Bauer and Manon Tremblay, 105–121. New York: Routledge.

Barnes, Tiffany D., and Diana Z. O'Brien. Forthcoming. "Defending the Realm: The Appointment of Female Defense Ministers Worldwide." *American Journal of Political Science.*

Barnes, Tiffany D., and Michelle Taylor-Robinson. 2018. "Women Cabinet Ministers and Empowerment of Women: Are the Two Related?" In *Measuring Women's Political Empowerment Across the Globe: Strategies, Challenges, and Future Research,* edited by Amy Alexander, Catherine Bolzendahl, Farida Jalalzai. New York: Palgrave MacMillan.

Barrera Bassols, Dalia, and Alejandra Massolo. 1998. *Mujeres que gobiernan municipios: experiencias, aportes y retos.* Mexico: Colegio de México, Programa Interdisciplinario de Estudios de la Mujer.

Bayard de Volo, Lorraine. 2001. *Mothers of Heroes and Martyrs: Gender Identity Politics in Nicaragua, 1979–1999.* Baltimore: Johns Hopkins University Press.

Beer, Caroline C., and Roderic Ai Camp. 2016. "Democracy, Gender Quotas, and Political Recruitment in Mexico." *Politics, Groups, and Identities* 4, no. 2: 179–195.

Bernal Olarte, Angélica. 2006. "Colombia: balance crítico de la participación política de las mujeres en la elección para el Congreso 2006–2010." *Friedrich Ebert Stiftung en Colombia.* http://www.bogota.gov.co/galeria/analisiselecciones.pdf

Bernal Olarte, Angélica. 2008. "Paridad política en los cargos de representación." Paper presented at the 1st Congreso de Ciencia Política. Bogotá, Colombia: Universidad de los Andes.

Birnir, Jóhanna Kristín. 2007. *Ethnicity and Electoral Politics.* New York: Cambridge University Press.

Bjarnegård, Elin. 2013. *Gender, Informal Institutions and Political Recruitment: Explaining Male Dominance in Parliamentary Representation.* Basingstoke, UK: Palgrave Macmillan.

Bjarnegård, Elin, and Pär Zetterberg. 2016. "Political Parties and Gender Quota Implementation: The Role of Bureaucratized Candidate Selection Procedures." *Comparative Politics* 48, no. 3: 393–417.

Blake, Charles H., and Stephen D. Morris, eds. 2009. *Corruption and Democracy in Latin America.* Pittsburgh: University of Pittsburgh Press.

Blay, Eva Alterman, and Susan A. Soeiro. 1979. "The Political Participation of Women in Brazil: Female Mayors." *Signs* 5, no. 1:42–59.

Blofield, Merike. 2006. *The Politics of Moral Sin: Abortion and Divorce in Spain, Chile and Argentina.* New York: Routledge.

Bonder, Gloria, and Marcela Nari. 1995. "The 30 Percent Quota Law: A Turning Point for Women's Political Participation in Argentina." In *A Rising Public Voice: Women in Politics Worldwide,* edited by Alida Brill, 183–193. New York: The Feminist Press at The City University of New York Press.

Booth, John A. 2007. "Political Parties in Costa Rica: Democratic Stability and Party System Change in a Latin American Context." In *Party Politics in New Democracies,* edited by Paul Webb and Steve White, 305–345. New York: Oxford University Press.

Borrelli, MaryAnne. 2002. *The President's Cabinet: Gender, Power and Representation.* Boulder, CO: Lynne Rienner.

Borzutzky, Silvia, and Gregory B. Weeks. 2010. *The Bachelet Government: Conflict and Consensus in Post-Pinochet Chile.* Gainsville: University Press of Florida.

Brinks, Daniel, Marcelo Leiras, and Scott Mainwaring. 2014. *Reflections on Uneven Democracies.* Baltimore: Johns Hopkins University Press.

Bruckmüller, Susanne, and Nyla R. Branscombe. 2010. "The Glass Cliff: When and Why Women Are Selected As Leaders in Crisis Contexts." *British Journal of Social Psychology* 49, no. 3: 433–451.

Bruhn, Kathleen. 2003. "Whores and Lesbians: Political Activism, Party Strategies, and Gender Quotas in Mexico." *Electoral Studies* 22, no. 1: 101–119.

Burki, Shahid Javed, Guillermo E. Perry, and Willian R. Dillinger. 1999. *Beyond the Center: Decentralizing the State*. Washington, DC: World Bank.

Bustamante de Rivera, Tirza. 1995. "La trascendencia del voto para las mujeres." In *Elegir y no ser elegidas: El significado político del voto femenino*, edited by Centro Nacional para el Desarrollo de la Mujer y Familia and Fundación Friedrich Ebert, 13–16. San José, Costa Rica: CMF.

Calvo, Yadira. 1995. Las claves del a cuestión. In *¿Feminismo en Costa Rica? Testimonios, reflexiones, y ensayos*, edited by Lorena Aguilar Revelo et al., 67–80. San José, Costa Rica: Editorial Mujeres.

Camerlo, Marcelo, and Aníbal Pérez-Liñán. 2015. "The Politics of Minister Retention in Presidential Systems: Technocrats, Partisans, and Government Approval." *Comparative Politics* 47, no. 3: 315–333.

Caminotti, Mariana. 2009. "En el nombre de la democracia: La invención del cupo femenino y la difusión subnacional de las cuotas en Argentina." PhD diss., Escuela de Política y Gobierno de la Universidad Nacional de San Martín, San Martín, Argentina.

Camp, Roderic Ai. 1998. "Women and Men, Men and Women: Gender Patterns in Mexican Politics." In *Women's Participation in Mexican Political Life*, edited by Victoria E. Rodríguez, 167–178. Boulder, CO: Westview.

Cardarello, Antonio, Martín Freigedo, and Isaac Cisneros. 2016. "No tan fuerte, pero muy cerca. Las elecciones departamentales y el ciclo electoral." In *Permanencias, transiciones y rupturas: Elecciones en Uruguay 2014/15*, edited by Adolfo Garcé and Niki Johnson, 299–320. Montevideo, Uruguay: Fin de Siglo, ICP-FCS-Udelar.

Carey, John M. 1996. *Term Limits and Legislative Representation*. New York: Cambridge University Press.

Carey, John M. 2009. *Legislative Voting and Accountability*. New York: Cambridge University Press.

Carey, John M., and Matthew Soberg Shugart, eds. 1998. *Executive Decree Authority*. Cambridge, UK: Cambridge University Press.

Carlin, Ryan E. 2014. "What's Not to Trust? Rubrics of Political Party Trustworthiness in Chile and Argentina." *Party Politics* 20, no. 1: 63–77.

Carranza, Mario E. 2005. "Poster Child or Victim of Imperialist Globalization? Explaining Argentina's December 2001 Political Crisis and Economic Collapse." *Latin American Perspectives* 32, no. 6: 65–89.

Carroll, Susan J. 1984. "The Recruitment of Women for Cabinet-Level Posts in State Government: A Social Control Perspective." *Social Science Journal* 21, no. 1: 91–107.

Castañeda, Jorge G. 2016. "Latin Americans Stand Up to Corruption: The Silver Lining in a Spate of Scandals." *Foreign Affairs* 95, no. 1: 145–152.

Castro, Rocío. 2014. "Gênero e participação cidadã para o desenvolvimento local: Os conselhos municipais de Salvador-Bahia." *Organizações & Sociedade* 6, no. 16: 129–151.

Catalano, Ana. 2009. "Women Acting for Women? An Analysis of Gender and Debate Participation in the British House of Commons 2005–2007." *Politics & Gender* 5, no. 1: 45–68.

Catterberg, Gabriela, and Valeria Palanza. 2012. "Argentina: Dispersión de la oposición y el auge de Cristina Fernández de Kirchner." *Revista de Ciencia Política* 32, no. 1: 3–30.

Cavenaghi, Suzana, and José Eustáquio Diniz Alves. 2012. "Quem vota em quem: um retrato das intenções de voto nas eleições para presidente em setembro de 2010." In: *Mulheres nas eleições 2010*, edited by José Eustáquio Diniz Alves, Céli Regina Jardim Pinto, and Fátima Jordão, 91–133. 1st Edition. São Paulo, Brazil: ABCP/SPM.

CEAMEG. 2014. "La reforma hacia la paridad: Cerrando la brecha y promoviendo el liderazgo político de las mujeres." Mexico City.

Chaney, Elsa. 1979. Supermadre: *Women in Politics in Latin America*. Austin: University of Texas Press.

Cheibub, Jose Antonio, Zachary Elkins, and Tom Ginsburg. 2011. "Latin American Presidentialism in Comparative and Historical Perspective." *Texas Law Review* 89, no. 7: 1707–1739.

Cheng, Christine, and Margit Tavits. 2011. "Informal Influences in Selecting Female Political Candidates." *Political Research Quarterly* 64, no. 2: 460–471.

Childs, Sarah. 2008. *Women and British Party Politics: Descriptive, Substantive, and Symbolic Representation*. London: Routledge.

Clark, Mary A. 2001. "Costa Rica: Portrait of an Established Democracy." In *Citizen Views of Democracy in Latin America*, edited by Roderic Ai Camp, 73–89. Pittsburgh: University of Pittsburgh Press.

Collier, Ruth B., and David Collier. 1991. *Shaping the Political Arena: Critical Junctures, the Labor Movement, and Regime Dynamics in Latin America*. Princeton, NJ: Princeton University Press.

Collier, Simon. 1967. *Ideas and Politics of Chilean Independence, 1808–1833*. Cambridge, UK: Cambridge University Press.

Conniff, Michael L. 1999. "Introduction." In *Populism in Latin America*, by Michael L. Conniff, 1–22. Tuscaloosa: University of Alabama Press.

Correa, Fernanda Vidal. 2014. "Federalism and Gender Quotas in Mexico: Analysing *Propietario* and *Suplente* Nominations." *Representation* 50, no. 3: 321–335.

Costa Benavides, Jimena. 2003. "Women's Political Participation in Bolivia: Progress and Obstacles." Paper read at International IDEA Workshop on The Implementation of Quotas: Latin American Experiences. February 23–24, 2003, at Lima, Peru.

Cox, Gary, and Scott Morgenstern. 2002. "Epilogue: Latin America's Reactive Assemblies and Proactive Presidents." In *Legislative Politics in Latin America*, edited by Scott Morgenstern and Benito Nacif, 446–468. Cambridge, UK: Cambridge University Press.

Craske, Nikki. 1999. *Women and Politics in Latin America*. New Brunswick, NJ: Rutgers University Press.

Dahlberg, Stefan, Sören Holmberg, Bo Rothstein, Felix Hartmann, and Richard Svensson. 2015. *The Quality of Government Basic Dataset, version Jan 15*. University of Gothenburg: The Quality of Government Institute. Available from http://www.qogdata.pol.gu.se/dataarchive/qog_bas_jan15.pdf

Danielson, Michael Stephen, Todd Alan Eisenstadt, and Jennifer Yelle. 2013. "Ethnic Identity, Informal Institutions, and the Failure to Elect Women in Indigenous Southern Mexico." *Journal of Politics in Latin America* 5, no. 3: 3–33.

Datafolha Instituto de Pesquisa. 2016. "Avaliação da Presidente Dilma." http://media.folha.uol.com.br/datafolha/2016/04/11/avaliacao-presidente-dilma.pdf

Daughters, Robert, and Leslie Harper. 2007. "Fiscal and Political Decentralization Reforms." In *The State of State Reform in Latin America*, edited by Educardo Lora, 213–261. Washington, DC: World Bank.

Davis, Rebecca Howard. 1997. *Women and Power in Parliamentary Democracies: Cabinet Appointments in Western Europe, 1968–1992.* Lincoln: University of Nebraska Press.

del Campo, Esther. 2005. "Women and Politics in Latin America." *Social Forces* 83, no. 4: 1697–1725.

del Campo, Esther, and Evelyn Magdaleno. 2008. "Avances legislativos de acción positiva en Bolivia, Ecuador, y Perú." In *Mujeres y escenarios ciudadanos*, edited by Mercedes Prieto, 275–297. Quito: FLACSO, Sede Ecuador.

De Luca, Miguel. 2008. "Political Recruitment and Candidate Selection in Argentina: Presidents and Governors, 1983 to 2006." In *Pathways to Power: Political Recruitment and Candidate Selection in Latin America*, edited by Peter M. Siavelis and Scott Morgenstern, 189–218. University Park, PA: The Pennsylvania State University Press.

Departamento Intersindical de Assessoria Parlamentar. 2014. Radiografia do Novo Congresso: Legislatura 2015–2019. Brasília: DIAP. http://www.diap.org.br/index.php/publicacoes/viewcategory/41-radiografia-do-novo-congresso

Desposato, Scott W., and Barbara Norrander. 2009. "The Gender Gap in Latin America: Contextual and Individual Influences on Gender and Political Participation." *British Journal of Political Science* 39, no. 1: 141–162.

Díaz Rebolledo, Jerónimo. 2005. "Los determinantes de la indisciplina partidaria. Apuntes sobre la conexión electoral en el Congreso mexicano." *Política y Gobierno* 12, no. 2: 313–330.

Dolan, Kathleen. 2005. "Do Women Candidates Play to Gender Stereotypes? Do Men Candidates Play to Women? Candidate Sex and Issues Priorities on Campaign Websites." *Political Research Quarterly* 58, no. 1: 31–44.

Domínguez, Jorge I. 1997. "Latin America's Crisis of Representation." *Foreign Affairs* 76: 100–113.

Domínguez, Jorge I., and James A. McCann. 1995. "Shaping Mexico's Electoral Arena: The Construction of Partisan Cleavages in the 1988 and 1991 National Elections." *American Political Science Review* 89, no. 1: 34–48.

Dore, Elizabeth. 2000. "One Step Forward, Two Steps Back: Gender and the State in the Long Nineteenth Century." In *Hidden Histories of Gender and the State in Latin America,* edited by Elizabeth Dore and Maxine Molyneux, 3–32. Durham, NC: Duke University Press.

Dore, Elizabeth, and Maxine Molyneux, eds. 2000. *Hidden Histories of Gender and the State in Latin America.* Durham, NC: Duke University Press.

Drew, Eileen. 2000. "Career Trajectories: Convergence or Divergence?" In *Gendering Elites: Economic and Political Leadership in 27 Industrialised Societies,* edited by Mino Vianello and Gwen Moore, 50–65. London: Macmillan.

Duerst-Lahti, Georgia. 2008. "'Seeing What Has Always Been': Opening Study of the Presidency." *PS, Political Science & Politics* 41, no. 4: 733–737.

Duke, James T. 1976. *Conflict and Power in Social Life.* Provo, UT: Brigham Young University Press.

Duran, Camila, Barnara Simão, and Maria Luciano. 2015. "Qual é a representatividade da mulher no Brasil?" *Carta Capital,* August 3, 2015. www.cartacapital.com.br/politica/qual-e-a-representatividade-da-mulher-no-brasil-8635.html

Eaton, Kent. 2012. "Decentralization and Federalism." In *Routledge Handbook of Latin American Politics*, edited by Peter Kingstone and Deborah J. Yashar, 33–48. New York, NY: Routledge.

Edwards, George C., III. 2001. "Why Not the Best? The Loyalty-Competence Trade-Off in Presidential Appointments." In *Innocent Until Nominated: The Breakdown of the Presidential Appointments Process*, edited by G. Calvin Mackenzie, 81–106. Washington, DC: Brookings Institution Press.

Escobar-Lemmon, Maria C., and Ashley D. Ross. 2014. "Does Decentralization Improve Perceptions of Accountability? Attitudinal Evidence from Colombia." *American Journal of Political Science* 58, no. 1: 175–188.

Escobar-Lemmon, Maria C., Leslie A. Schwindt-Bayer, and Michelle M. Taylor-Robinson. 2014. "Representing Women: Empirical insights from Legislatures and Cabinets in Latin America." In *Representation: The Case of Women*, edited by Maria C. Escobar-Lemmon and Michelle M. Taylor-Robinson, 205–224. New York: Oxford University Press.

Escobar-Lemmon, Maria C., and Michelle M. Taylor-Robinson. 2005. "Women Ministers in Latin American Government: When, Where, and Why?" *American Journal of Political Science* 49, no. 4: 829–844.

Escobar-Lemmon, Maria C., and Michelle M. Taylor-Robinson. 2008. "How Do Candidate Recruitment and Selection Processes Affect Representation of Women?" In *Pathways to Power: Political Recruitment and Candidate Selection in Latin America*, edited by Peter M. Siavelis and Scott Morgenstern, 345–368. University Park: Pennsylvania State University Press.

Escobar-Lemmon, Maria C., and Michelle M. Taylor-Robinson. 2009. "Getting to the Top: Career Paths of Women in Latin American Cabinets." *Political Research Quarterly* 62, no. 4: 685–699.

Escobar-Lemmon, Maria C., and Michelle M. Taylor-Robinson. 2014. "Dilemmas in the Meaning and Measurement of Representation." In *Representation: The Case of Women*, edited by Maria C. Escobar-Lemmon and Michelle M. Taylor-Robinson, 1–16. New York: Oxford University Press.

Escobar-Lemmon, Maria C., and Michelle M. Taylor-Robinson. 2016. *Women in Presidential Cabinets: Power Players or Abundant Tokens?* New York: Oxford University Press.

El Espectador. 2011. "Una mujer que hizo historia." *El Espectador.com,* January 22, 2011. http://www.elespectador.com/noticias/nacional/una-mujer-hizo-historia-articulo-246521

Espinal, Rosario, and Shanyang Zhao. 2015. "Gender Gaps in Civic and Political Participation in Latin America." *Latin American Politics and Society* 57, no. 1: 123–138.

Estado de Costa Rica. 2000. "Plataforma de Acción de Beijing: Cinco Anos Después. Avances, Experiencias Innovadoras, Lecciones Aprendidas. Costa Rica 1995–1999." Response to Questionnaire on the Implementation of the Beijing Platform for Action. Division of the Advancement of Women, United Nations. http://www.un.org/womenwatch/daw/followup/responses/costarica.pdf

Ewig, Cristina. 1999. "The Strengths and Limits of the NGO Women's Movement Model." *Latin American Research Review* 34, no. 3: 75–102.

Falleti, Tulia G. 2005. "A Sequential Theory of Decentralization: Latin American Cases in Comparative Perspective." *American Political Science Review* 99, no. 3: 327–346.

Falleti, Tulia G. 2010. *Decentralization and Subnational Politics in Latin America.* New York: Cambridge University Press.

Farah, Marta Ferreira Santos. 2004. "Gênero e políticas públicas." *Estudos Feministas* 12, no. 1: 47–71.

Farah, Marta Ferreira Santos. 2014. "Gênero e políticas públicas na esfera local de governo." *Organizações & Sociedade* 6, no. 14: 65–104.

Felstiner, Mary Lowenthal. 1983. "Family Metaphors: The Language of an Independence Revolution." *Comparative Studies in Society and History* 25, no. 1:154–180.

Fernández Poncela, Anna María. 2011. "Las cuotas de género y la representación política femenina en México y América Latina." *Argumentos* 24, no. 66: 247–275.

Foweraker, Joe. 1998. "Institutional Design, Party Systems and Governability— Differentiating the Presidential Regimes of Latin America." *British Journal of Political Science.* 28, no. 4: 651–676.

Frajman, Eduardo. 2014. "The General Election in Costa Rica: February/April 2014." *Electoral Studies* 35, no. 3: 61–66.

Franceschet, Susan. 2005. *Women and Politics in Chile.* Boulder, CO: Lynne Rienner.

Franceschet, Susan. 2010a. "Explaining Domestic Violence Policy Outcomes in Chile and Argentina." *Latin American Politics and Society* 52, no. 3: 1–29.

Franceschet, Susan. 2010b. "Continuity or Change? Gender Policy in the Bachelet Administration." In *The Bachelet Government: Conflict and Consensus in Post-Pinochet Chile,* edited by Silvia Borzutzky and Gregory Weeks, 158–180. Gainesville FL: University of Florida Press.

Franceschet, Susan. 2011. "Gender Policy and State Architecture in Latin America." *Politics and Gender* 7, no. 2: 273–279.

Franceschet, Susan. 2016. "Disrupting Informal Institutions? Cabinet Formation in Chile in 2006 and 2014." In *Gender, Institutions and Change in Bachelet's Chile,* edited by Georgina Waylen, 67–94. New York: Palgrave Macmillan.

Franceschet, Susan, Mona Lena Krook, and Jennifer M. Piscopo, eds. 2012. *The Impact of Gender Quotas.* New York: Oxford University Press.

Franceschet, Susan, and Jennifer M. Piscopo. 2008. "Gender Quotas and Women's Substantive Representation: Lessons from Argentina." *Politics & Gender* 4, no. 3: 393–425.

Franceschet, Susan, and Jennifer M. Piscopo. 2013. "Federalism, Decentralization, and Reproductive Rights in Argentina and Chile." *Publius: The Journal of Federalism* 43, no. 1: 129–150.

Franceschet, Susan and Jennifer M. Piscopo. 2014. "Sustaining Gendered Practices? Power, Parties, and Elite Political Networks in Argentina." *Comparative Political Studies* 47, no. 1(1): 85–110.

Franceschet, Susan, Jennifer M. Piscopo, and Gwynn Thomas. 2016. "*Supermadres,* Maternal Legacies and Women's Political Participation in Contemporary Latin America." *Journal of Latin American Studies* 48, no. 1: 1–32.

Franceschet, Susan, and Gwynn Thomas. 2010. "Renegotiating Political Leadership: Michelle Bachelet's Rise to the Chilean Presidency." In *Cracking the Highest Glass Ceiling: A Global Comparison of Women's Campaigns for Executive Office,* edited by Rainbow Murrary, 177–195. Santa Barbara, Praeger.

Franceschet, Susan, and Gwynn Thomas. 2015. "Resisting Parity? Gender and Cabinet Appointments in Chile and Spain." *Politics & Gender* 11, no. 4: 643–664.

Friedman, Elisabeth J. 2000. *Unfinished Transitions: Women and the Gendered Development of Democracy in Venezuela, 1936–1996.* University Park: Penn State University Press.

Friedman, Elisabeth Jay. 2009. "Re(gion)alizing Women's Human Rights in Latin America." *Politics & Gender* 5, no. 3: 349–375.

Fundação Perseu Abramo. 2010. *Mulheres brasileiras e gênero nos espaços público e privado*. São Paulo, Brazil: Perseu Abramo. http://www.apublica.org/wp-content/uploads/2013/03/www.fpa_.org_.br_sites_default_files_pesquisaintegra.pdf

Funk, Kendall D. 2015. "Gendered Governing? Women's Leadership Styles and Participatory Institutions in Brazil." *Political Research Quarterly* 68, no. 3: 564–578.

Funk, Kendall D. 2017. *The Causes and Consequences of Women's Representation in Local Governments*. Ph.D. Diss., Texas A&M University, College Station, TX.

Funk, Kendall D., Magda Hinojosa, and Jennifer M. Piscopo. 2018. "Stil Left Behind? Gender, Political Parties, and Latin America's Pink Tide." *Social Politics* (Winter): in press.

Funk, Kendall D., Thiago Nascimento da Silva, and Maria Escobar-Lemmon. 2017. "Leading Toward Equality: The Effect of Women Mayors on Gender Equality in Local Bureaucracies." *Politics, Groups, and Identities*. Forthcoming.

Furlong, Marlea, and Kimberly Riggs. 1996. "Women's Participation in National-Level Politics and Government: The Case of Costa Rica." *Women's Studies International Forum* 19, no. 6: 633–643.

Gamson, William A. 1968. *Power and Discontent*. Homewood, IL: The Dorsey Press.

Gandrud, Christopher. 2015. Gallagher Electoral Disproportionality Data: 121 Countries, 1945–2014, version 2. March 20, 2015. http://christophergandrud.github.io/Disproportionality_Data/

García, Ceclia. 1995. "Derechos políticos: ¿Mito o realidad?" In *Elegir y no ser elegidas: El significado político del voto femenino*, edited by Centro Nacional para el Desarrollo de la Mujer y Familia and Fundación Friedrich Ebert, 20–24. San José, Costa Rica: CMF.

García Quesada, Ana Isabel. 2003. "Putting the Mandate into Practice: Legal Reform in Costa Rica." Paper Presented at the International IDEA Workshop. Lima, Peru. February 23–24.

García Quesada, Ana Isabel. 2011. "From Temporary Measures to the Parity Principle: The Case of Costa Rica." In *Diffusion of Gender Quotas in Latin America and Beyond*, edited by Adriana Piatti-Crocker, 114–129. New York: Peter Lang.

GEPPAL. 2014. "Género y partidos políticos en América Latina." https://publications.iadb.org/handle/11319/708. Accessed October 2014.

Gibson, Edward L. 1996. *Class and Conservative Parties: Argentina in Comparative Perspective*. Baltimore: Johns Hopkins University Press.

Gilardi, Fabrizio. 2015. "The Temporary Importance of Role Models for Women's Political Representation." *American Journal of Political Science* 59, no. 4: 957–970.

Gingerich, Daniel W. 2013. *Political Institutions and Party-Directed Corruption in South America: Stealing for the Team*. New York: Cambridge University Press.

Granara, Aixa. 2014. "Representación legislativa de las mujeres en las provincias Argentinas, 1989–2011." *América Latina Hoy* 66: 115–143.

Grindle, Merilee S. 2000. *Audacious Reforms: Institutional Invention and Democracy in Latin America*. Baltimore: Johns Hopkins University Press.

Gutiérrez de Pineda, Virginia. 1988. *Honor familia y sociedad en la estructura patriarcal: El caso de Santander*. Bogotá, Colombia: Empresa Editorial de la Universidad Nacional.

Guzmán, Diana Esther, Paola Molano, and Rodrigo Uprimny. 2015. *¿Camino a la igualdad?: Derechos de las mujeres a partir de la Constitución de 1991*. Bogotá: ONU Mujeres Colombia.

Haas, Liesl. 2001. "Changing the System from Within? Feminist Participation in the Brazilian Workers' Party." In *Radical Women in Latin America: Left and Right*, edited by Victoria Gonzalez and Karen Kampwirth, 249–271. University Park: Pennsylvania State University Press.

Haas, Liesl. 2010. *Feminist Policymaking in Chile*. University Park: Pennsylvania State University Press.

Hagopian, Frances. 1998. "Democracy and Political Representation in Latin America in the 1990s: Pause, Reorganization, or Decline?" In *Fault Lines of Democracy in Post-Transition Latin America*, edited by Felipe Agüero and Jeffrey Stark, 99–143. Coral Gables, FL: North-South Center Press at the University of Miami.

Hagopian, Frances. 2016. "Brazil's Accountability Paradox." *Journal of Democracy* 27, no. 3: 119–128.

Hagopian, Frances, and Scott P. Mainwaring. 2005. *The Third Wave of Democratization in Latin America: Advances and Setbacks*. New York: Cambridge University Press.

Heath, Roseanna M., Leslie A. Schwindt-Bayer, and Michelle M. Taylor-Robinson. 2005. "Women on the Sidelines: Women's Representation on Committees in Latin American Legislatures." *American Journal of Political Science* 49, no. 2: 420–436.

Helmke, Gretchen, and Steven Levitsky. 2004. "Informal Institutions and Comparative Politics: A Research Agenda." *Perspectives on Politics* 2, no. 4: 725–740.

Hidalgo, Ana. 2009. "Impacto de la Ley de Promoción de la igualdad social de la mujer de Costa Rica." In *La legislación para la igualdad entre mujeres y hombres en América Latina*. By Instituto Interamericano de Derechos Humanos, 61–162. San José, Costa Rica: Instituto Interamericano de Derechos Humanos.

Hinojosa, Magda. 2009. "Whatever the Party Asks of Me: Women's Political Representation in Chile's Unión Demócrata Independiente." *Politics & Gender* 5, no. 3: 377–407.

Hinojosa, Magda. 2010. "She's Not My Type of Blonde: Media Coverage of Irene Sáez's Presidential Bid." In *Cracking the Highest Glass Ceiling: A Global Comparison of Women's Campaigns for Executive Office*, edited by Rainbow. Murray, 31–47. Santa Barbara, CA: Praeger.

Hinojosa, Magda. 2012. *Selecting Women, Electing Women: Political Representation and Candidate Selection in Latin America*. Philadelphia: Temple University Press.

Hinojosa, Magda, Jill Carle, and Gina Woodall. Forthcoming. "Speaking as a Woman: Descriptive Presentation and Representation in Costa Rica's Legislative Assembly." *Journal of Women, Politics, and Policy*.

Hinojosa, Magda, and Susan Franceschet. 2012. "Separate but Not Equal: The Effects of Municipal Electoral Reform on Female Representation in Chile." *Political Research Quarterly* 65, no. 4: 758–770.

Hinojosa, Magda, and Ana Vijil Gurdián. 2012. "Alternate Paths to Power? Women's Political Representation in Nicaragua." *Latin American Politics and Society* 54, no. 4: 61–88.

Hinojosa, Magda, and Jennifer M. Piscopo. 2013. "Promoción del derecho de las mujeres a ser elegidas: veinticinco años de cuotas en América Latina." In *Cuotas de género: visión comparada*, edited by José Alejandro Luna Ramos, 55–107. Mexico City, Mexico: Electoral Tribunal of the Federal Judicial Power.

Hipsher, Patricia. 2001. "Right and Left-Wing Women in Post-Revolutionary El Salvador: Feminist Autonomy and Cross-Political Alliance Building for Gender Equality." In *Radical Women in Latin America: Left and Right*, edited by Victoria Gonzalez and Karen Kampwirth, 133–164. University Park: Pennsylvania State University Press.

Htun, Mala. 2003. *Sex and the State: Abortion, Divorce, and the Family under Latin American Dictatorships and Democracies*. New York: Cambridge University Press.

Htun, Mala. 2005. "Case Study: Latin America: Women, Political Parties and Electoral Systems in Latin America." In *Women in Parliament: Beyond Numbers*, edited by Julie Ballington and Azza Karam, 112–121. Revised ed. Stockholm: International IDEA.

Htun, Mala. 2016. *Inclusion Without Representation in Latin America: Gender Quotas and Ethnic Reservations*. New York: Cambridge University Press.

Htun, Mala N., and Mark P. Jones. 2002. "Engendering the Right to Participate in Decision-Making: Electoral Quotas and Women's Leadership in Latin America." In *Gender and the Politics of Rights and Democracy in Latin America*, edited by Nikki Craske and Maxine Molyneux, 32–56. New York: Palgrave.

Htun, Mala, Marina Lacalle, and Juan Pablo Micozzi. 2013. "Does Women's Presence Change Legislative Behavior? Evidence from Argentina, 1983–2007." *Journal of Politics in Latin America* 5, no. 1: 95–125.

Htun, Mala, and Juan Pablo Ossa. 2013. "Political Inclusion of Marginalized Groups: Indigenous Reservations and Gender Parity in Bolivia." *Politics, Groups and Identities* 1, no. 1: 4–25.

Htun, Mala, and Jennifer Piscopo. 2014. "Women in Politics and Policy in Latin America and the Caribbean." New York: Social Sciences Research Council, Conflict Prevention and Peace Forum Working Papers on Women in Politics, No. 2.

Htun, Mala, and Timothy J. Power. 2006. "Gender, Parties, and Support for Equal Rights in the Brazilian Congress." *Latin America Politics and Society* 48, no. 4: 83–104.

Htun, Mala, and S. Laurel Weldon. 2012. "The Civic Origins of Progressive Policy Change: Combating Violence against Women in Global Perspective, 1975–2005." *The American Political Science Review* 106, no. 3: 548–569.

Huber, John, and Cecilia Martínez-Gallardo. 2008. "Replacing Cabinet Ministers: Patterns of Ministerial Stability in Parliamentary Democracies." *American Political Science Review* 102, no. 2: 169–180.

Huddy, L., and N. Terkildsen. 1993. "The Consequences of Gender Stereotypes for Women Candidates at Different Levels and Types of Office." *Political Research Quarterly* 46, no. 3: 503–525.

IDEA. 2003. *The Implementation of Quotas: Latin American Experiences*. Lima, Peru: IDEA.

Indridason, Indridi, and Christopher Kam. 2008. "Cabinet Reshuffles and Ministerial Drift." *British Journal of Political Science* 38, no. 4: 621–656.

Inglehart, Ronald, and Pippa Norris. 2003. *Rising Tide: Gender Equality and Cultural Change around the World*. New York: Cambridge University Press.

Inmujeres. 2010. *Desigualdades en los Ingresos: ¿Qué es de la Autonomía Económica de las Mujeres?* Montevideo, Uruguay: MIDES-Instituto Nacional de las Mujeres, Cuadernos del Sistema de Información de Género, nº 2.

Inmujeres. 2013. *Estadísticas de Género 2013. Evolución de los Indicadores de Género en el Período 2009–2013*. Montevideo, Uruguay: MIDES-Instituto Nacional de las Mujeres.

International City/County Management Association (ICMA). 2004. "Costa Rica Country Report: Trends in Decentralization, Municipal Strengthening, and Citizen Participation in Central America, 1995–2003." Prepared by the U.S. Agency for International Development.

IPU. 1995. *Women in Parliaments, 1945–1995: A World Statistical Survey*. Geneva: Inter-Parliamentary Union. http://www.ipu.org/PDF/publications/women45-95_en.pdf

IPU. 2015. *Women in National Parliaments*. http://www.ipu.org/wmn-e/classif.htm. Accessed January 15, 2015.

IPU. 2016. *Women in Parliaments: World and Regional Averages*. Inter-Parliamentary Union. http://www.ipu.org/wmn-e/world.htm. Accessed August 5, 2016.

IPU. 2017. *Women in National Parliaments, as of July 1, 2017*. Inter-Parliamentary Union. http://www.ipu.org/wmn-e/arc/classif010717.htm. Accessed September 9, 2017.

Jacob, Suraj, John A. Scherpereel and Melinda Adams. 2014. "Gender Norms and Women's Political Representation: A Global Analysis of Cabinets, 1979–2009." *Governance* 27, no. 2: 321–345.

Jalalzai, Farida. 2004. "Women Political Leaders: Past and Present." *Women & Politics* 26, nos. 3–4: 85–108.

Jalalzai, Farida. 2008. "Women Rule: Shattering the Executive Glass Ceiling." *Politics & Gender* 4, no. 2: 205–231.

Jalalzai, Farida. 2013. *Shattered, Cracked or Firmly Intact? Women and the Executive Glass Ceiling Worldwide*. Oxford: Oxford University Press.

Jalalzai, Farida. 2015. *Women Presidents of Latin America: Beyond Family Ties?* New York: Routledge.

Jalalzai, Farida, and Pedro G. dos Santos. 2015. "The Dilma Effect? Women's Representation under Dilma Rousseff's Presidency." *Politics & Gender* 11, no. 1: 117–145.

Jalalzai, Farida, and Mona Lena Krook. 2010. "Beyond Hillary and Benazir: Women's Leadership Worldwide." *International Political Science Review* 31, no. 1: 5–23.

Jalalzai, Farida, and M. Tremblay. 2011. "North America." In *Women in Executive Power: A Global Overview*, edited by G. Bauer and M. Tremblay, 122–140. New York: Routledge.

Jaquette, Jane. 1976. "Female Political Participation in Latin America." In *Sex and Class in Latin America*, edited by June Nash and Helen I. Safa, 221–244. New York: Praeger.

Jaquette, Jane S., ed. 1994. *The Women's Movement in Latin America: Participation and Democracy*. 2nd ed. Boulder, CO: Westview.

Jara, Camila. 2014. "Democratic Legitimacy Under Strain? Declining Political Support and Mass Demonstrations in Chile." *European Review of Latin American and Caribbean Studies* 97:25–50.

Jiménez Polanco, Jacqueline. 2011. "Women's Quotas in the Dominican Republic: Advances and Detractions." In *Diffusion of Gender Quotas in Latin America and Beyond*, edited by Adriana Piatti-Crocker, 130–151. New York: Peter Lang.

Johnson, Niki. 2005. *La política de la ausencia: Las elecciones Uruguayas (2004–2005), las mujeres, y la equidad de género*. Montevideo, Uruguay: CNS Mujeres, ICP-FCS-Udelar.

Johnson, Niki. 2010. "Destapando la "caja negra": representación de género y procesos de selección de candidaturas, Uruguay 2009." In *Del Cambio a la Continuidad: Ciclo Electoral 2009–2010 en Uruguay*, edited by Daniel Buquet and Niki Johnson, 71–100. Montevideo: Fin del Siglo, CLACSO, ICP-FCS-Udelar.

Johnson, Niki. 2013. *Mujeres en cifras: El acceso de las mujeres a espacios de poder en Uruguay*. Montevideo, Uruguay: Cotidiano Mujer.

Johnson, Niki. 2014. "La bancada femenina en Uruguay: Un 'actor crítico' para la representación sustantiva de las mujeres en el parlamento." *América Latina Hoy* 66: 145–165.

Johnson, Niki, and Verónica Pérez. 2010. *Representación (S)electiva: Una mirada feminista a las elecciones Uruguayas 2009*. Montevideo, Uruguay: Cotidiano Mujer, ICP-FCS-Udelar, UNIFEM.

Johnson, Niki, and Verónica Pérez. 2011. "From Vanguard to Straggler: Women's Political Representation and Gender Quotas in Uruguay." In *Diffusion of Gender Quotas in Latin America and Beyond: Advances and Setbacks in the Last Two Decades*, edited by Adriana Piatti-Crocker, 151–172. New York: Peter Lang.

Jones, Mark P. 1996. "Increasing Women's Representation via Gender Quotas: The Argentine *Ley de Cupos*." *Women & Politics* 16, no. 4: 75–96.

Jones, Mark P. 1997. "Legislator Gender and Legislator Policy Priorities in the Argentine Chamber of Deputies and the United States House of Representatives." *Policy Studies Journal* 25, no. 4: 613–629.

Jones, Mark P. 1998. "Gender Quotas, Electoral Laws, and the Election of Women Lessons from the Argentine Provinces." *Comparative Political Studies* 31, no. 1: 3–21.

Jones, Mark P. 2004. "Quota Legislation and the Election of Women: Learning from the Costa Rican Experience." *Journal of Politics* 66, no. 4: 1203–1223.

Jones, Mark P. 2008. "The Recruitment and Selection of Legislative Candidates in Argentina." In *Pathways to Power: Political Recruitment and Candidate Selection in Latin America*, edited by Peter M. Siavelis and Scott Morgenstern, 41–75. University Park: The Pennsylvania State University Press.

Jones, Mark P. 2009. "Gender Quotas, Electoral Laws, and the Election of Women: Evidence from the Latin American Vanguard." *Comparative Political Studies* 42, no. 1: 56–81.

Jones, Mark P. 2010. "La representación de las mujeres en la Asamblea Nacional de Panamá: diagnóstico, buenas prácticas y propuestas de reforma." In *Las reformas electorales en Panamá: Claves de desarrollo humano para la toma de decisiones*, edited by Harry Brown Araúz, 275–316. Panamá: PNUD.

Jones, Mark P., Santiago Alles, and Carolina Tchintian. 2012. "Cuotas de género, leyes electorales y elección de legisladoras en América Latina." *Revista de Ciencia Política* 32, no. 2: 331–357.

Jones, Mark P., and Scott Mainwaring. 2003. "The Nationalization of Parties and Party Systems: An Empirical Measure and an Application to the Americas." *Party Politics* 9, no. 2: 139–166.

Jones, Mark P., and Juan Pablo Micozzi. 2013. "The Argentine Congress under the Kirchners: Unrepresentative and Ineffective." In *Representativeness and Effectiveness in Latin American Democracies: Congress, Judiciary and Civil Society*, edited by Moira MacKinnon and Ludovico Feoli, 40–74. New York: Routledge.

Jones, Mark P., and Patricio Navia. 1999. "Assessing the Effectiveness of Gender Quotas in Open-List Proportional Representation Electoral Systems." *Social Science Quarterly* 80, no. 2: 341–355.

Kampwirth, Karen. 1996. "The Mother of the Nicaraguans: Doña Violeta and the UNO's Gender Agenda." *Latin American Perspectives* 23, no. 1: 67–86.

Kampwirth, Karen. 2010. *Gender and Populism in Latin America: Passionate Politics*. University Park: Pennsylvania State University Press.

Kanter, Rosabeth M. 1977. "Some Effects of Proportion on Group Life: Skewed Sex Ratios and Response to Token Women." *American Journal of Sociology* 82, no. 5: 965–990.

Keman, Hans. 1991. "Ministers and Ministries." In *The Profession of Government Minister in Western Europe*, edited by Jean Blondel and Jean-Louis Thiébault, 99–118. London: Macmillan.

Kerevel, Yann. P. 2015. "Pork-Barreling without Reelection? Evidence from the Mexican Congress." *Legislative Studies Quarterly* 40, no. 1: 137–166.

Kerevel, Yann P., and Lonna Rae Atkeson. 2013. "Explaining the Marginalization of Women in Legislative Institutions." *The Journal of Politics* 75, no. 4: 980–992.

Kerevel, Yann P., and Lonna Rae Atkeson. 2015. "Reducing Stereotypes of Female Political Leaders in Mexico." *Political Research Quarterly* 68, no. 4: 732–744.

King, Anthony. 1994. "Ministerial Autonomy in Britain." In *Cabinet Ministers and Parliamentary Government*, edited by Michael Laver and Kenneth A. Shepsle, 203–225. Cambridge, UK: Cambridge University Press.

Kitschelt, Herbert, and Steven I. Wilkinson. 2007. "Citizen-Politician Linkages: An Introduction." In *Patrons, Clients, and Policies: Patterns of Democratic Accountability and Political Competition*, edited by Herbert Kitschelt and Steven I. Wilkinson, 1–49. New York: Cambridge University Press.

Kitschelt, Herbert, Kirk A. Hawkins, Juan Pablo Luna, Guillermo Rosas, and Elizabeth J. Zechmeister. 2010. *Latin American Party Systems*. New York: Cambridge University Press.

Kitschelt, Herbert. 2014. Democratic Accountability and Linkages Project (DALP). Dataset. https://sites.duke.edu/democracylinkage/

Kittilson, Miki Caul. 2008. "Representing Women: The Adoption of Family Leave in Comparative Perspective." *Journal of Politics* 70, no. 2: 323–334.

Klein, Ethel. 1984. *Gender Politics: From Consciousness to Mass Politics*. Cambridge, MA: Harvard University Press.

Krook, Mona Lena. 2009. *Quotas for Women in Politics: Gender and Candidate Selection Reform Worldwide*. Oxford: Oxford University Press.

Krook, Mona Lena, and Fiona Mackay, eds. 2011. *Gender, Politics, and Institutions: Towards a Feminist Institutionalism*. Basingstoke, UK: Palgrave Macmillan.

Krook, Mona Lena, and Diana O'Brien. 2012. "All the President's Men? The Appointment of Female Cabinet Ministers Worldwide." *Journal of Politics* 74, no. 3: 840–855.

Krook, Mona Lena, and Jacqui True. 2012. "Rethinking the Lifecycles of International Norms: The United Nations and the Global Promotion of Gender Equality." *European Journal of International Relations* 18, no. 1: 103–127.

Lagos, Marta. 2001. "Between Stability and Crisis in Latin America." *Journal of Democracy* 12, no. 1: 137–145.

Lagos, Marta. 2014. "The End of Barriers." Baker Institute for Public Policy, Houston, TX. https://bakerinstitute.org/files/8552/

Latinobarómetro. 2004. *Informe Resumen: Una Década de Mediciones*. Santiago de Chile: Corporación Latinobarómetro.

Lavrín, Asunción. 1995. *Women, Feminism, and Social Change in Argentina, Chile, and Uruguay, 1890–1949*. Lincoln: University of Nebraska Press.

Lehoucq, Fabrice Edouard. 2005. "Costa Rica: Paradise in Doubt." *Journal of Democracy* 16, no. 3: 140–154.

León, Magdalena, and Jimena Holguín. 2005. "La cuota sola no basta: El caso de Colombia." In *Nadando contra la corriente: Mujeres y coutas políticas en los Países Andinos*. Edited by Magdalena León, 41–89. Bogotá: Universidad Nacional de Colombia/Unifem.

Levine, Daniel H., and Jose E. Molina, eds. 2011. *The Quality of Democracy in Latin America*. Boulder, CO: Lynne Rienner.

Levitsky, Steven. 2003. *Transforming Labor-Based Parties in Latin America: Argentine Peronism in Comparative Perspective*. New York: Cambridge University Press.

Levitsky, Steven, and Kenneth M. Roberts, eds. 2011. *The Resurgence of the Latin American Left*. Baltimore: Johns Hopkins University Press.

Lewis, David E. 2008. *The Politics of Presidential Appointments: Political Control and Bureaucratic Performance*. Princeton, NJ: Princeton University Press.

Linz, Juan J. 1994. "Presidential or Parliamentary Democracy: Does it Make a Difference." *The Failure of Presidential Democracy: The Case of Latin America*, edited by Juan J. Linz and Arturo Valenzuela, 3–87. Baltimore: Johns Hopkins University Press.

Linz, Juan, and Arturo Valenzuela, eds. 1994. *The Failure of Presidential Democracy*. Baltimore: Johns Hopkins University Press.

Lissardy, Gerardo. 2016. "¿Hay machismo, sexismo o misoginia contra Dilma Rousseff, la suspendida presidenta de Brasil?" BBC Mundo, May 12, 2016. http://www.bbc.com/mundo/noticias/2016/04/160420_brasil_dilma_rousseff_machismo_gl

Locatelli, Piero. 2014. "Brancos serão quase 80% da Câmara dos Deputados." *Carta Capital*. August 10, https://www.cartacapital.com.br/politica/brancos-serao-quase-80-da-camara-dos-deputados-3603.html

Lopreite, Debora. 2012. "Travelling Ideas and Domestic Policy Change: The Transnational Politics of Reproductive Rights/Health in Argentina." *Global Social Policy* 12, no. 2: 109–128.

Lopreite, Debora. 2014. "Explaining Policy Outcomes in Federal Contexts: The Politics of Reproductive Rights in Argentina and Mexico." *Bulletin of Latin American Research* 33, no. 4: 389–404.

Lopreite, Debora. 2015. "Gender Policies in Argentina after Neoliberalism: Opportunities and Obstacles for Women's Rights." *Latin American Perspectives* 42, no. 1: 64–73.

Lopreite, Debora, and Laura Macdonald. 2014. "Gender and Latin American Welfare Regimes: Early Childhood Education and Care Policies in Argentina and Mexico." *Social Politics: International Studies in Gender, State & Society* 21, no. 1: 80–102.

Lovenduski, Joni, and Pippa Norris. 1993. *Gender and Party Politics*. Thousand Oaks, CA: SAGE.

Lovera, Sara. 2014. "México: Aprobada paridad electoral." *Vocero*, January 13, 2014. http://www.vocero.com.mx/mexico-aprobada-paridad-electoral/. Accessed March 10, 2015.

Lukes, Steven. 1974. *Power: A Radical View*. New York: Macmillan.

Luna, Elba, Vivian Roza, and Gabriela Vega. 2008. "El camino hacia el poder: Ministras Latinoamericanas 1950–2007." Interamerican Development Bank, Programa de Apoyo al Liderazgo y la Representación de la Mujer (PROLID). http://www.iadb.org/document.cfm?id=1415084. Accessed March 17, 2014.

Luna, Juan Pablo. 2014. *Segmented Representation: Political Party Strategies in Unequal Democracies*. New York: Oxford University Press.

Luna, Juan Pablo. 2016. "Chile's Crisis of Representation." *Journal of Democracy* 27, no. 3: 129–138.

Luna, Juan Pablo, and David Altman. 2011. "Uprooted but Stable: Chilean Parties and the Concept of Party System Institutionalization." *Latin American Politics and Society* 53, no. 2: 1–28.

Luna, Juan Pablo, and Rodrigo Mardones. 2010. "Chile: Are the Parties Over?" *Journal of Democracy* 21, no. 3: 107–121.

Lupu, Noam. 2015. "Partisanship in Latin America." In *The Latin American Voter*, edited by Ryan E. Carlin, Matthew M. Singer, and Elizabeth J. Zechmeister, 226–245. Ann Arbor: University of Michigan Press.

Lynch, J. 1986. *The Spanish American Revolutions, 1808–1826*. New York: W.W. Norton.

Macaulay, Fiona. 2005. "Judicialising and (de)Criminalising Domestic Violence in Latin America." *Social Policy and Society* 5, no. 1: 103–114.

Macaulay, Fiona. 2006. *Gender Politics in Brazil and Chile: The Role of Parties in National and Local Policymaking*. New York: Palgrave Macmillan.

Mainwaring, Scott. 1990. "Presidentialism in Latin America." *Latin American Research Review* 25, no. 1: 157–179.

Mainwaring, Scott. 1993. "Presidentialism, Multipartism, and Democracy: The Difficult Combination." *Comparative Political Studies* 26, no. 2: 198–228.

Mainwaring, Scott. 1999. *Rethinking Party Systems in the Third Wave of Democratization: The Case of Brazil.* Stanford, CA: Stanford University Press.

Mainwaring, Scott. 2006. "The Crisis of Representation in the Andes." *Journal of Democracy* 17, no. 3: 13–27.

Mainwaring, Scott, Ana Maria Bejarano, and Eduardo Pizarro Leongómez. 2006. *The Crisis of Democratic Representation in the Andes.* Stanford, CA: Stanford University Press.

Mainwaring, Scott, and Aníbal Pérez-Liñán. 2015. "Cross-Currents in Latin America." *Journal of Democracy* 26, no. 1: 114–127.

Mainwaring, Scott, and Timothy R. Scully, eds. 1995. *Building Democratic Institutions: Party Systems in Latin America.* Stanford, CA: Stanford University Press.

Mainwaring, Scott, and Matthew Soberg Shugart, eds. 1997. *Presidentialism and Democracy in Latin America.* New York: Cambridge University Press.

Mainwaring, Scott, Matthew Soberg Shugart, and J. Linz. 1997. "Presidentialism, and Democracy: A Critical Appraisal." *Comparative Politics* 29, no. 4: 449–471.

Mallon, Florencia E. 1995. *Peasant and Nation: The Making of Postcolonial Mexico and Peru.* Berkeley: University of California Press.

Manza, Jeff, and Clem Brooks. 1998. "The Gender Gap in U.S. Presidential Elections: When? Why? Implications?" *American Journal of Sociology* 103, no. 5: 1235–1266.

Marx, Jutta, Jutta Borner, and Mariana Caminotti. 2007. *Las legisladoras: Cupos de género y política en Argentina y Brasil.* Buenos Aires: Siglo XXI Editora Iberoamericana.

Marx, Jutta, Jutta Borner, and Mariana Caminotti. 2009. "Gender Quotas, Candidate Selection, and Electoral Campaigns." In *Feminist Agendas and Democracy in Latin America,* edited by Jane S. Jaquette, 45–64. Durham, NC: Duke University Press.

Matland, Richard E., and Donley T. Studlar. 1996. "The Contagion of Women Candidates in Single-Member District and Proportional Representation Electoral Systems: Canada and Norway." *Journal of Politics* 58, no. 3: 707–733.

Matland, Richard E., and Michelle M. Taylor. 1997. "Electoral System Effects on Women's Representation." *Comparative Political Studies* 30, no. 2: 186–210.

Matos, Marlise, and Marina Brito Pinheiro. 2012. "Dilemas do conservadorismopolítico e do tradicionalismo de gênero no processoeleitoral de 2010: O eleitorado brasileiro e suas percepções." In *Mulheres nas eleições 2010,* edited by José Eustáquio Diniz Alves, Céli Regina Jardim Pinto, and Fátima Jordão, 47–90. 1st edition. São Paulo: ABCP/SPM.

Medina Espino, Adriana. 2010. *La participación política de las mujeres: De las cuotas de género a la paridad.* Mexico City: CEAMEG.

Medina Vidal, D. Xavier, Antonio Ugues, Jr., Shaun Bowler, and Jonathan Hiskey. 2010. "Partisan Attachment and Democracy in Mexico: Some Cautionary Observations." *Latin American Politics and Society* 52, no. 1: 63–87.

Meier, Kenneth J., and Kendall D. Funk. 2017. "Women and Public Administration in a Comparative Perspective: The Case of Representation in Brazilian Local Governments." *Administration & Society* 49, no. 1: 121–142.

Mesa de Género. 2011. *Balance de la aplicación de la ley 581 de 2000.* Bogotá: Agencia Española de Cooperación Internacional para el Desarrollo.

Mezey, Michael L. 1979. *Comparative Legislatures.* Durham, NC: Duke University Press.

Miguel, Luis Felipe. 2008. "Political Representation and Gender in Brazil: Qutoas for Women and their Impact." *Bulletin of Latin American Research* 27 (2): 197–214.

Miguel, Luis Felipe. 2012. "Policy Priorities and Women's Double Bind in Brazil." In *The Impact of Gender Quotas*, edited by Susan Franceschet, Mona Lena Krook, and Jennifer M Piscopo, 103–118. New York: Oxford University Press.

Miguel, Luis Felipe, and Cristina Monteiro de Queiroz. 2006. "Diferenças regionais e o êxito relativo de mulheres em eleições municipais no Brasil." *Revista Estudos Feministas* 14, no. 2: 363–386.

Mills, C. Wright. 1957. *The Power Elite*. New York: Oxford University Press.

Mitchell, Michael N. 2012. *Interpreting and Visualizing Regression Models using Stata*. College Station, TX: Stata Press.

Montero, Alfred, and David J. Samuels. 2004. *Decentralization and Democracy in Latin America*. Notre Dame, IN: University of Notre Dame Press.

Moore, Laura M., and Reeve Vanneman. 2003. "Context Matters: Effects of the Proportion of Fundamentalists on Gender Attitudes." *Social Forces* 82, no. 1: 115–139.

Morales, Mauricio. 2008. "La primera mujer presidenta de Chile: ¿Qué explicó el triunfo de Michelle Bachelet en las Elecciones de 2005–2006?" *Latin American Research Review* 43, no. 1: 7–32.

Moreno, Elsa. 1995. *Mujeres y política en Costa Rica*. San José: FLACSO.

Morgan, Jana. 2007. "Partisanship during the Collapse of Venezuela's Party System." *Latin American Research Review* 42, no. 1: 78–98.

Morgan, Jana. 2011. *Bankrupt Representation and Party System Collapse*. University Park: Penn State Press.

Morgan, Jana. 2015. "Gender and the Latin American Voter." In *The Latin American Voter*, edited by Ryan E. Carlin, Matthew M. Singer, and Elizabeth J. Zechmeister, 143–167. Ann Arbor: University of Michigan Press.

Morgan, Jana, and Melissa Buice. 2013. "Latin American Attitudes toward Women in Politics: The Influence of Elite Cues, Female Advancement, and Individual Characteristics." *American Political Science Review* 107, no. 4: 644–662.

Morgenstern, Scott, and Benito Nacif, eds. 2002. *Legislative Politics in Latin America*. New York: Cambridge University Press.

Morris, Stephen D., and Charles H. Blake, eds. 2010. *Corruption and Politics in Latin America: National and Regional Dynamics*. Boulder, CO: Lynne Rienner.

Moser, Robert G., and Ethan Scheiner. 2012. *Electoral Systems and Political Context: How the Effects of Rules Vary across New and Established Democracies*. New York: Cambridge University Press.

Murray, Rainbow. 2010. *Cracking the Highest Glass Ceiling: A Global Comparison of Women's Campaigns for Executive Office*. Santa Barbara, CA: ABC-CLIO Press.

Navia, Patricio. 2008. "Legislative Candidate Selection in Chile." In *Pathways to Power: Political Recruitment and Candidate Selection in Latin America*, edited by Peter M. Siavelis and Scott Morgenstern, 92–118. University Park: The Pennsylvania State University Press.

Nickson, R. Andrew. 1995. *Local Government in Latin America*. Boulder, CO: Lynne Rienner.

Norris, Pippa. 2004. "Electoral Engineering: Voting Rules and Political Behavior." Cambridge, UK: Cambridge University Press.

Norris, Pippa, and Joni Lovenduski. 1995. *Political Recruitment: Gender, Race and Class in the British Parliament*. Cambridge, UK: Cambridge University Press.

Osborn, Tracy L. 2012. *How Women Represent Women: Political Parties, Gender and Representation in State Legislatures*. New York: Oxford University Press.

Pachón, Mónica, and Matthew S. Shugart. 2010. "Electoral Reform and the Mirror Image of Inter-Party and Intra-Party Competition: The Adoption of Party Lists in Colombia." *Electoral Studies* 29, no. 4: 648–660.

Pachón, Mónica, and Fabio Sánchez. 2014. "Base de datos sobre resultados electorales CEDE, 1958–2011." *CEDE*. https://economia.uniandes.edu.co/components/com_ booklibrary/ebooks/dcede2014-29.pdf

PAN. 2014. Ratifica CEN a Cecilia Romero como Presidenta Nacional del PAN. *Sepuede*. https://www.pan.org.mx/blog/ratifica-cen-a-cecilia-romero-como-presidenta-nacional-del-pan/. Accessed March 5, 2015.

Panke, Luciana, and Ricardo Tesseroli. 2014. "HGPE en Brasil: Historia e características." Paper presented at Quinto Congreso Uruguayo de Ciencia Política, "¿Qué ciencia política para qué democracia?" Asociación Uruguaya de Ciencia Política. October 7–10, 2014.

Paxton, Pamela, Melanie M. Hughes, and Matthew A. Painter II. 2010. "Growth in women's Political Representation: A Longitudinal Exploration of Democracy, Electoral System and Gender Quotas." *European Journal of Political Research* 49, no. 1: 25–52.

Payne, Mark J. 2007. *Democracies in Development: Politics and Reform in Latin America*. Washington, DC: Inter-American Development Bank.

Peña Molina, Blanca Olivia. 2005. "Sistema de cuota y masa crítica en los gobiernos subnacionales de México." *Otras Miradas* 5, no. 1. http://www.redalyc.org/articulo. oa?id=18350103

Peña Molina, Blanca Olivia. 2015. "Paridad de género en México: anverso y reverse." *Condistintosacentos*. http://www.condistintosacentos.com/paridad-de-genero-en-mexico-anverso-y-reverso/. Accessed March 10, 2015.

Pereira, Carlos, and Marcus André Melo. 2012. "The Surprising Success of Multiparty Presidentialism." *Journal of Democracy* 23, no. 3: 156–170.

Pérez, Verónica. 2005. "Algunos cambios pero no tantos: La presencia femenina en cargos ejecutivos en Uruguay." In *Las Claves del Cambio. Ciclo Electoral y Nuevo Gobierno 2004/2005*, edited by Daniel Buquet, 205–223. Montevideo, Uruguay: EBO, ICP-FCS-Udelar.

Pérez, Verónica. 2015. *La participación política de las mujeres en el nivel sub-nacional en Uruguay: Elecciones departamentales y municipales 2015*. Montevideo, Uruguay: Cotidiano Mujer, CIRE, UN Women.

Pérez-Liñán, Aníbal. 2002. "Television News and Political Partisanship in Latin America." *Political Research Quarterly* 55, no. 3: 571–588.

Piatti-Crocker, Adriana, ed. 2011. *Diffusion of Gender Quotas in Latin America and Beyond: Advances and Setbacks in the Last Two Decades*. New York: Peter Lang.

Picado León, Hugo, and Luis Diego Brenes Villalobos. 2014. "Evaluando la paridad y la alternancia." *Revista Derecho Electoral/Tribunal Supremo de Elecciones* 18: 384–414.

Piscopo, Jennifer. M. 2010. "Primera Dama, Prima Donna? Media Constructions of Cristina Fernández De Kirchner in Argentina." In *Cracking the Highest Glass Ceiling: A Global Comparison of Women's Campaigns for Executive Office*, edited by Rainbow Murray, 197–219. Santa Barbara, Praeger.

Piscopo, Jennifer M. 2011a. "Rethinking Descriptive Representation: Rendering Women in Legislative Debates." *Parliamentary Affairs* 64, no. 3: 448–472.

Piscopo, Jennifer M. 2011b. "Gender Quotas and Equity Promotion in Mexico." In *Diffusion of Gender Quotas in Latin America and Beyond*, edited by A. Piatti-Crocker, 36–53. New York: Peter Lang.

Piscopo, Jennifer M. 2014a. "Female Leadership and Sexual Health Policy in Argentina." *Latin American Research Review* 49, no. 1: 104–127

Piscopo, Jennifer M. 2014b. "Beyond Hearth and Home: Female Legislators, Feminist Policy Change, and Substantive Representation in Mexico." *Revista Uruguaya de Ciencia Política* 23, no. 2: 87–110.

Piscopo, Jennifer M. 2015a. "Democracy as Gender Balance: the Shift from Quotas to Parity in Latin America." *Politics, Groups, and Identities* 4, no. 2: 214–230.

Piscopo, Jennifer M. 2015b. "States as Gender Equality Activists: The Evolution of Quota Laws in Latin America." *Latin American Politics and Society* 57, no. 3: 27–49.

Piscopo, Jennifer M. 2016a. "When Informality Advantages Women: Quota Networks, Electoral Rules, and Candidate Selection in Mexico." *Government & Opposition* 51, no. 3: 487–512.

Piscopo, Jennifer M. 2016b. "Gender Balance as Democracy: The Shift from Quotas to Parity in Latin America." *Politics, Groups, and Identities* 4, no. 2: 214–230.

Piscopo, Jennifer M. 2016c. "Quota Laws for Gender Equality." In *Democracy and its Discontents in Latin America*, edited by Joe Fowraker and Delores Treviso, 149–169. Boulder, CO: Lynne Rienner.

Pitanguy, Jacqueline. 1996. "Movimento de mujeres y políticas públicas en Brasil." In *Triángulo de poder*, edited by Geertje Nijeholt, Virginia Vargas, and Saskia Wieringa. Bogotá: Tercer Mundo Editores.

Pitkin, Hanna. 1967. *The Concept of Representation*. Berkeley: University of California Press.

PNUD. 2010. *Desarrollo Humano en Chile. Género: los desafíos de la igualdad*. Santiago, Chile: Programa de las Naciones Unidas para el Desarrollo.

PNUD. 2014. *Ciudadanía Política: Voz y participación ciudadana en América Latina*. Buenos Aires: Siglo XXI Editores.

Power, Timothy J., and Matthew M. Taylor, eds. 2011. *Corruption and Democracy in Brazil: The Struggle for Accountability*. Notre Dame: University of Notre Dame Press.

Power, Timothy J., and Cesar Zucco. 2012. "Elite Preferences in a Consolidating Democracy: The Brazilian Legislative Surveys, 1990–2009." *Latin American Politics and Society* 54, no. 4: 1–27.

PRI. 2015. Dirigencias nacionales del PRI. http://pri.org.mx/TransformandoaMexico/NuestroPartido/Dirigentes.aspx, Accessed March 5, 2015.

Putnam, Robert. 1976. *The Comparative Study of Political Elites*. Englewood Cliffs, NJ: Prentice-Hall.

Quintero, Beatriz. 2005. "Las mujeres Colombianas y la Asamblea Nacional constituyente de 1991–participación e impactos." *Reformas Constitucionales y Equidad de Género* Santa Cruz de la Sierra: CEPAL.

Raczynski, Dagmar, and Claudia Serrano, eds. 1992. *Políticas sociales, mujeres y gobierno local*. Santiago, Chile: CIEPLAN.

Raile, Eric D., Carlos Pereira, and Timothy J. Power. 2011. "The Executive Toolbox: Building Legislative Support in a Multiparty Presidential Regime." *Political Research Quarterly* 64, no. 2: 323–334.

Ramos, Daniela, Eliana Graça, Gabriela Andrade, and Vera Soares, eds. 2014. "As mulheres nas eleições de 2014." *Eu Assumo Este Compromisso*. Brasília: Secretaria de Políticas para as Mulheres.

Reyes-Housholder, Catherine. 2013. "Presidential Gender and Women's Representation in Cabinets: Do Female Presidents Appoint More Women Than Male Presidents?" Paper presented at the Annual Meeting of the American Political Science Association. Chicago, IL. August 29, 2013.

Reyes-Housholder, Catherine. 2016a. "Presidential Power, Partisan Continuity and Pro-Women Change in Chile: 2000–10." In *The Gendered Executive*, edited by Janet M. Martin and MaryAnne Borrelli, 229–249. Philadelphia: Temple University Press.

Reyes-Housholder, Catherine. 2016b. Presidentas Rise: Consequences for Women in Cabinets? *Latin American Politics and Society* 58, no. 3: 3–25.

Reyes-Housholder, Catherine, and Leslie A. Schwindt-Bayer. 2016. "The Impact of Presidentas on Women's Political Activity." In *The Gendered Executive*, edited by Janet M. Martin and MaryAnne Borrelli, 103–122. Philadelphia: Temple University Press.

Reyes-Housholder, Catherine. 2017. "*Presidentas*, Power and Pro-Women Change." PhD diss. Cornell University, Ithaca, NY.

Reyes-Housholder, Catherine, and Leslie A. Schwindt-Bayer. 2017. "Citizen Responses to Female Executives: Is It Sex, Novelty or Both?" *Politics, Groups and Identities* 5, no. 3: 373–398.

Reynoso, Diego, and Natalia D'Angelo. 2006. "Las leyes de cuota y su impacto en la elección de mujeres en México." *Política y Gobierno* 12, no. 2: 279–313.

Ríos Tobar, Marcela. 2008. "Seizing a Window of Opportunity: The Election of President Bachelet in Chile." *Politics and Gender* 4, no. 3: 509–519.

Rivera-Cira, Tirza. 1993. *Las mujeres en los parlamentos Latinoamericanos*. Valparaíso, Chile: Centro de Estudios y Asistencia Legislativa—Universidad Católica de Valparaíso.

Roberts, Kenneth. 2003. "Social Correlates of Party System Demise and Populist Resurgence in Venezuela." *Latin American Politics and Society* 45, no. 3: 35–57.

Rodríguez, Victoria E. 2003. *Women in Contemporary Mexican Politics*. Austin: University of Texas Press.

Rodríguez Echeverría, Miguel Angel. 2006. "Getting Costa Rica Right." *Journal of Democracy* 17, no. 2: 161–164.

Rodríguez Gustá, Ana Laura, and Mariana Caminotti. 2010. "Políticas públicas de equidad de género: Las estrategias fragmentarias de la Argentina y Chile." *Revista SAAP* 4, no. 1: 85–110.

Rodríguez Valero, Luis Alfredo. 2013. "La representación substantiva de las mujeres en el Congreso Colombiano de 1998 al 2012: Una visión más allá del número total de legisladoras." *Documentos Del Departamento de Ciencia Política* 21: 1–37. https://c-politica.uniandes.edu.co/docs/descargar.php?f=./data/CP_Doc21_01_02_13.pdf

Romero, Karolyne, Marcus Figueiredo, and Clara Araújo. 2012. "Participação feminina e dinâmica de campanha no HGPE nas eleições 2010 para a Câmara dos Deputados." In *Mulheres nas eleições 2010*, edited by José Eustáquio Diniz Alves, Céli Regina Jardim Pinto, and Fátima Jordão. Rio de Janeiro: ABCP\SPM.

Rosas, Guillermo. 2005. "The Ideological Organization of Latin American Legislative Parties: An Empirical Analysis of Elite Policy Preferences." *Comparative Political Studies* 38, no. 7: 824–849.

Rosas, Guillermo, and Joy Langston. 2011. "Gubernatorial Effects on the Voting Behavior of National Legislators." *Journal of Politics* 73, no. 2: 477–493.

Roza, Vivian. 2010. "Gatekeepers to Power: Party-Level Influences on Women's Political Participation in Latin America." Ph.D. diss., Georgetown University, Washington, DC.

Rule, Wilma. 1987. "Electoral Systems, Contextual Factors and Women's Opportunity for Election to Parliament in Twenty-Three Democracies." *Western Political Quarterly* 40, no. 3: 477–498.

Ryan, Michelle K., and S. Alexander Haslam. 2005. "The Glass Cliff: Evidence That Women Are Over-Represented in Precarious Leadership Positions." *British Journal of Management* 16, no. 2: 81–90.

Sacchet, Teresa, 2009a. "Political Parties and Gender in Latin America." In *Governing Women*, edited by Anne Marie Goetz, 148–172. New York: Routledge.

Sacchet, Teresa. 2009b. "Capital social, gênero e representação política no Brasil." *Opinião Pública* 15, no. 2: 306–332.

Sagot, Montserrat. 2010. "Does the Political Participation of Women Matter? Democratic Representation, Affirmative Action, and Quotas in Costa Rica." *IDS Bulletin* 41, no. 5: 25–34.

Saiegh, Sebastian M. 2009. "Recovering a Basic Space from Elite Surveys: Evidence from Latin America." *Legislative Studies Quarterly* 34, no. 1: 117–145.

Saint-Germain, Michelle A. 1993. "Paths to Power of Women Legislators in Costa Rica and Nicaragua." *Women's Studies International Forum* 16, no. 2:119–38.

Saint-Germain, Michelle A., and Cynthia Chavez Metoyer. 2008. *Women Legislators in Central America: Politics, Democracy, and Policy*. Austin: University of Texas Press.

Saint-Germain, Michelle A., and Kathleen Morgan. 1991. "Equality: Costa Rican Women Demand 'the Real Thing.'" *Women and Politics* 11, no. 3: 23–75.

Samuels, David J. 1999. "Incentives to Cultivate a Party Vote in Candidate-centric Electoral Systems Evidence from Brazil." *Comparative Political Studies* 32, no. 4: 487–518.

Samuels, David J. 2002. "Pork Barreling is not Credit Claiming or Advertising: Campaign Finance and the Sources of the Personal Vote in Brazil." *The Journal of Politics* 64, no. 3: 845–863.

Samuels, David. 2003. *Ambition, Federalism, and Legislative Politics in Brazil*. Cambridge, UK: Cambridge University Press.

Samuels, David. 2008. "Political Ambition, Candidate Recruitment, and Legislative Politics in Brazil." In *Pathways to Power. Politcal Recruitment and Candidate Selection in Latin America*, edited by Peter Siavelis and Scott Morgenstern, 76–91. University Park: Pennsylvania State University Press.

Schenck, Marcela. 2015. "La candidata: Una mirada sobre la campaña de Constanza Moreira en las internas del Frente Amplio." In *Renovación, paridad: Horizontes aún lejanos para la Representación Política de las mujeres en las elecciones Uruguayas 2014*, edited by Niki Johnson. Montevideo, Uruguay: Cotidiano Mujer, ICP-FCS-Udelar.

Scherpereel, John A., Suraj Jacob, and Melinda Adams. 2014. "Ratchets and See-Saws: Exploring Temporal Patterns in Women's Political Representation." Paper presented at the ECPR Joint Sessions, Salamanca, Spain. April 10–15, 2014.

Schmidt, Gregory D. 2003a. "The Implementation of Gender Quotas in Peru: Legal Reform, Discourses and Impacts." The Implementation of Quotas: Latin American Experiences. Workshop Report. Lima, Peru. February 23–24 2003.

Schmidt, Gregory D. 2003b. "Unanticipated Successes: Lessons from Peru's Experiences with Gender Quotas in Majoritarian Closed List and Open List PR Systems." The Implementation of Quotas: Latin American Experiences. Workshop Report. Lima, Peru, February 23–24, 2003.

Schmidt, Gregory D. 2008a. "The Election of Women in List PR Systems: Testing the Conventional Wisdom." *Electoral Studies* 28, no. 2: 190–203.

Schmidt, Gregory D. 2008b. "Success under Open List PR: The Election of Women to Congress." In *Women and Legislative Representation: Electoral Systems, Political Parties, and Sex Quotas*, edited by Manon. Tremblay, 161–177. New York: Palgrave Macmillan.

Schmidt, Gregory D. 2011. "Gender Quotas in Peru: Origins, Interactions with Electoral Rules, and Re-Election." In *Diffusion of Gender Quotas in Latin America and Beyond*, edited by Adriana Piatti-Crocker, 98–113. New York: Peter Lang.

Schmidt, Gregory D., and Kyle L. Saunders. 2004. "Effective Quotas, Relative Party Magnitude, and the Success of Female Candidates: Peruvian Municipal Elections in Comparative Perspective." *Comparative Political Studies* 37, no. 6: 704–734.

Schmidt, Steffen W. 1975. "Women in Colombia: Attitudes and Future Perspectives in the Political System." *Journal of Interamerican Studies and World Affairs* 17, no. 4: 465–489.

Schwindt-Bayer, Leslie A. 2005. "The Incumbency Disadvantage and Women's Election to Legislative Office." *Electoral Studies* 24, no. 2: 227–244.

Schwindt-Bayer, Leslie A. 2006. "Still Supermadres? Gender and the Policy Priorities of Latin American Legislators." *American Journal of Political Science* 50, no. 3: 570–585.

Schwindt-Bayer, Leslie A. 2009. "Making Quotas Work: The Effect of Gender Quota Laws on the Election of Women." *Legislative Studies Quarterly* 34, no. 1: 5–28.

Schwindt-Bayer, Leslie A. 2010. *Political Power and Women's Representation in Latin America*. New York: Oxford University Press.

Schwindt-Bayer, Leslie A., and William Mishler. 2005. "An Integrated Model of Women's Representation." *Journal of Politics* 67, no. 2: 407–428.

Schwindt-Bayer, Leslie A. 2015. "Chile's Gender Quota: Will it Work?" *James A. Baker III Institute for Public Policy, Rice University.* https://www.bakerinstitute.org/media/files/files/947eca1e/LAI-pub-ChileGenderQuota-051915.pdf.

Schwindt-Bayer, Leslie A. and Catherine Reyes-Housholder. 2017. "Citizen Responses to Female Executives: Is it Sex, Novelty, or Both?" *Politics, Groups and Identities* 5, no. 3: 373–398.

Schwindt-Bayer, Leslie A. and Peverill Squire. 2014. "Legislative Power and Women's Representation." *Politics and Gender* 10, no. 4: 622–658.

Seligson, Mitchell. 2002. "Trouble in Paradise? The Erosion of System Support in Costa Rica, 1978–1999." *Latin American Research Review* 37, no. 1: 160–185.

Serna, Miguel, Eduardo Bottinelli, Cristian Maneiro, and Lucía Pérez. 2012. *Giro a la izquierda y nuevas elites en Uruguay: ¿Renovación o reconversión?* Montevideo, Uruguay: Udelar-CSIC.

Shair-Rosenfield, Sarah, and Magda Hinojosa. 2014. "Does Female Incumbency Reduce Gender Bias in Elections? Evidence from Chile." *Political Research Quarterly* 67, no. 4: 837–850.

Shugart, Matthew S. 2013. "Why Ballot Structure Matters." In *Political Science, Electoral Rules, and Democratic Governance*, edited by Mala Htun and G. Bingham Powell, 38–45. Washington, DC: American Political Science Association.

Shugart, Matthew Soberg, and John M. Carey. 1992. *Presidents and Assemblies: Constitutional Design and Electoral Dynamics*. Cambridge, UK: Cambridge University Press.

Shugart, Matthew Soberg, Erika Moreno, and Luis E. Fajardo. 2007. "Deepening Democracy through Renovating Political Practices: The Struggle for Electoral Reform in Colombia." In *Peace, Democracy, and Human Rights in Colombia*, edited by Christopher Welna and Gustavo Gallón, 202–266. Notre Dame, IN: University of Notre Dame Press.

Siavelis, Peter M. 2000. *The President and Congress in Postauthoritarian Chile: Institutional Constraints to Democratic Consolidation*. University Park: The Pennsylvania State University Press.

Siavelis, Peter M. 2006. "Accommodating Informal Institutions in Chilean Politics." In *Informal Institutions and Democracy in Latin America*, edited by Gretchen Helmke and Steven Levitsky, 33–55. Baltimore: Johns Hopkins University Press.

Siavelis, Peter M. 2009. "Elite-Mass Congruence, Partidocracia, and the Quality of Chilean Democracy." *Journal of Politics in Latin America* 1, no. 3: 3–31.

Siavelis, Peter M. 2014. "From a Necessary to a Permanent Coalition." In *Democratic Chile: The Politics and Policies of a Historic Coalition, 1990–2010*, edited by Kirsten Sehnbruch and Peter Siavelis, 15–41. Boulder, CO: Lynne Rienner.

Siavelis, Peter M., and Scott Morgenstern, eds. 2008. *Pathways to Power: Political Recruitment and Candidate Selection in Latin America*. University Park: The Pennsylvania State University Press.

Smulovitz, Catalina. 2015. "Legal Inequality and Federalism: Domestic Violence Laws in the Argentine Provinces." *Latin American Politics and Society* 57, no. 3: 1–26.

Soto Badahui, Lilian. 2014. "50 + 50 = paridad: Elementos para el debate por la igualdad sustantiva en la representación política en el Paraguay." Centro de Documentación y Estudios (CDE). *La Mitad Queremos Paridad*. http://www.cde.org.py/imd/nim/wp-content/uploads/2014/09/50-50-igual-paridad.pdf

Speck, Bruno Wilhelm, and Wagner Pralon Mancuso. 2014. "A Study on the Impact of Campaign Finance, Political Capital and Gender on Electoral Performance." *Brazilian Political Science Review* 8, no. 1: 34–57.

Staab, Silke. 2017. *Gender and the Politics of Gradual Change: Social Policy Reform and Innovation in Chile*. London: Palgrave Macmillan.

Staab, Silke, and Georgina Waylen. 2014. "Gender, Institutions, and Change in Bachelet's Chile." Paper presented at the ECPR Joint Sessions, Salamanca, Spain, April 10–15, 2014.

Staudt, Kathleen. 1998. "Women in Politics: Mexico in Global Perspective." In *Women's Participation in Mexican Political Life*, edited by Victoria E. Rodríguez, 23–40. Boulder, CO: Westview.

Stepan, Alfred, and Cindy Skach. 1994. "Presidentialism and Parliamentarism in Comparative Perspective." In *The Failure of Presidential Democracy*, edited by Juan J. Linz and Arturo Valenzuela, 119–136. Baltimore: Johns Hopkins University Press.

Stern, Steven J. 1997. *The Secret History of Gender: Women, Men and Power in Late Colonial Mexico*. Durham, NC: University of North Carolina Press.

Stevenson, Linda S. 1999. "Gender Politics in the Mexican Democratization Process: Electing Women and Legislating Sex Crimes and Affirmative Action, 1988–1997." In *Toward Mexico's Democratization: Parties, Campaigns, Elections, and Public Opinion*, edited by Jorge I. Domínguez and Alejandro Poiré, 57–88. New York: Routledge.

Stevenson, Linda S. 2012. "The Bachelet Effect on Gender-Equity Policies." *Latin American Perspectives* 39, no. 4: 129–144.

Stockemer, Daniel, and Manon Tremblay. 2015. "Federalism and Women's Representation: Do Federations have More Women Legislators than Centralized States?" *Publius: The Journal of Federalism* 45, no. 4: 605–625.

Taylor-Robinson, Michelle M. 2007. "Presidential and Congressional Elections in Honduras, November 2005." *Electoral Studies* 26, no. 2: 507–533.

Taylor-Robinson, Michelle M., and Roseanna M. Heath. 2003. "Do Women Legislators have Different Policy Priorities than their Male Colleagues? A Critical Case Test." *Women & Politics* 24, no. 4: 77–101.

Thames, Frank C., and Margaret S. Williams. 2010. "Incentives for Personal Votes and Women's Representation in Legislatures." *Comparative Political Studies* 43, no. 12: 1575–1600.

Thomas, Gwynn. 2011a. "Michelle Bachelet's *Liderazgo Femenino* (Feminine Leadership): Redefining Political Leadership in Chile's 2005 Presidential Campaign." *International Feminist Journal of Politics* 13, no. 1: 63–82.

Thomas, Gwynn. 2011b. *Contesting Legitimacy in Chile: Familial Ideals, Citizenship, and Political Struggle, 1970–1990.* University Park: The Pennsylvania State University Press.

Thomas, Gwynn. 2014. "Women Presidents and Troubled Coalitions: How Party Crisis Shapes Presidential Agendas and Government Capacity." Paper presented at the American Political Science Association Meeting, August, 28–31 2014, Washington, DC.

Thomas, Gwynn. 2016. "Promoting Gender Equality: Michelle Bachelet and Formal and Informal Institutional Change within the Chilean Presidency." In *Gender, Institutions and Change in Bachelet's Chile,* edited by Georgina Waylen, 95–120. New York: Palgrave.

Towns, Anne E. 2010. *Women and States: Norms and Hierarchies in International Society.* Cambridge, UK: Cambridge University Press.

Tremblay, Manon, and Gretchen Bauer. 2011. "Conclusion." In *Women in Executive Power: A Global Overview,* edited by Gretchen Bauer and Manon Tremblay, 171–191. New York: Routledge.

Tribunal Suprema Electoral (TSE). 2010. "Boletín Electoral Especial 3." San José, Costa Rica: Tribunal Supreme Electoral.

True, Jacqui, and Michael Mintrom. 2001. "Transnational Networks and Policy Diffusion: The Case of Gender Mainstreaming." *International Studies Quarterly* 45, no. 1: 27–57.

Udelar. 2014. *Estadísticas Básicas 2013 de la Universidad de la República.* Montevideo, Uruguay: Dirección General de Planeamiento-Universidad de la República.

UNDP. 2013. "How Much Progress We Made? An Analysis of Women's Political Participation in Subnational Governments in Latin America and the Caribbean." *United Nations Development Programme Report.* Regional Centre for Latin America and the Caribbean, Panamá.

United Nations. 1991. *Women in Decision-Making: Case-Study on Costa Rica.* Vienna: United Nations Office, Centre for Social Development and Humanitarian Affairs. New York: United Nations.

Valdés, Teresa E. 2012. "Introduccíon: 20 años de políticas públicas para de género." In *¿Construyendo igualdad? 20 años de políticas públicas de género,* edited by Teresa Valdés, 9–24. Santiago, Chile: CEDEM.

Vallance, Elizabeth. 1979. *Women in the House.* London: Athlone.

Van Cott, Donna Lee. 2005. *From Movements to Parties in Latin America: The Evolution of Ethnic Politics.* New York: Cambridge University Press.

Vázquez García, Verónica. 2010. "Mujeres y gobiernos municipales en México: Lo que sabemos y lo que falta por saber." *Gestión y Política Pública,* 19, no. 1: 111–154.

Vengroff, Richard, Zsolt Nyiri, and Melissa Fugiero. 2003. "Electoral System and Gender Representation in Sub-National Legislatures: Is there a National—Sub-National Gender Gap?" *Political Research Quarterly* 56, no. 2: 163–173.

Vidal Correa, Fernanda. 2014. "Federalism and Gender Quotas in Mexico: Analysing *Propietario* and *Suplente* Nominations." *Representation* 50, no. 3: 321–336.

Wängnerud, Lena. 2009. "Women in Parliaments: Descriptive and Substantive Representation." *Annual Review of Political Science* 12, no. 1: 51–69.

Walker, Lee Demetrius, and Genevieve Kehoe. 2013. "Regime Transition and Attitude toward Regime: The Latin American Gender Gap in Support for Democracy." *Comparative Politics* 45, no. 2: 187–205.

Watson, Robert P., Alicia Jencik, and Judith A. Selzer. 2005. "Women World Leaders: Comparative Analysis and Gender Experiences." *Journal of International Women's Studies* 7, no. 2: 53–76.

Waylen, Georgina. 2000. "Gender and Democratic Politics: A Comparative Analysis of Consolidation in Argentina and Chile." *Journal of Latin American Studies* 32, no. 3: 765–793.

Waylen, Georgina, ed. 2016. *Gender, Institutions, and Change in Bachelet's Chile.* New York: Palgrave Macmillan.

Weeks, Gregory, and Silvia Borzutzky. 2012. "Michelle Bachelet's Government: The Paradoxes of a Chilean President." *Journal of Politics in Latin America* 4, no. 3: 97–121.

Weyland, Kurt, Raúl Madrid, and Wendy Hunter, eds. 2010. *Leftist Governments in Latin America: Successes and Shortcomings.* New York: Cambridge University Press.

Wiesehomeier, Nina and Kenneth Benoit. 2009. "Presidents, Parties and Policy Competition." *Journal of Politics* 71, no. 4: 1435–1447.

Willis, Eliza, Christopher da C. B. Garman, and Stephan Haggard. 1999. "The Politics of Decentralization in Latin America." *Latin America Research Review* 34, no. 1: 7–56.

Wills, María Emma. 2005. "Cincuenta años de sufragio femenino en Colombia 1954: Por la conquista del voto. 2004: Por la ampliación de la ciudadanía de las mujeres." *Análisis Político* 53, no. 18: 39–57.

Wills, María Emma. 2007. *Inclusión sin representación: La irrupción política de las mujeres en Colombia (1970–2000).* Bogotá, Colombia: Norma.

Wills, María Emma. 2011. *La memoria histórica desde la perspectiva de género: Conceptos y herramientas.* Bogotá, Colombia: Comisión Nacional de Reparación y Reconciliación—Grupo de Memoria Histórica.

Wills, María Emma, and Angélica Bernal Olarte. 2002. "Mujeres y política en Colombia (1970–2000): Los caminos (insospechados) hacia una gradual apertura." In *Degradación o cambio: Evolución del sistema político Colombiano*, edited by Francisco Gutiérrez Sanín, 261–317. Bogotá, Colombia: Norma.

Wilson, Bruce M. 1998. "The Costa Rican General Elections of 1 February 1998." *Electoral Studies* 17, no. 4: 584–589.

Wilson, Bruce M. 2003. "The Elections in Costa Rica, February and April 2002." *Electoral Studies* 22, no. 3: 509–516.

Wilson, Bruce M. 2007. "Costa Rica's General Election, February 2006." *Electoral Studies* 26, no. 1: 712–716.

Wilson, Bruce M., and Juan Carlos Rodríguez-Cordero. 2011. "The General Election in Costa Rica, February 2010." *Electoral Studies* 30, no. 1: 231–234.

Wolbrecht, Christina, and David E. Campbell. 2007. "Leading by Example: Female Members of Parliament as Political Role Models." *American Journal of Political Science* 51, no. 4: 921–939.

World Bank. 2007. *World Development Indicators.* Washington, DC: World Bank.

Zamora Chavarría, Eugenia María. 2009. "Derechos políticos de la mujer en Costa Rica: 1986–2006." *Derecho Electoral* [*Revista de Tribunal Supremo de Elecciones*] 7: 1–44.

Zamora Chavarría, Eugenia María. 2012. El ejercicio político de las mujeres: Más allá de la paridad. Presented at the 35th Assembly of Delegates for the Inter-American Commission on Women of the Organization of American States. San José, Costa Rica. October 29.

Zamora Chavarría, Eugenia María. 2014. "El mecanismo de alternancia en el nuevo Código Electoral y su aplicación." *Derecho Electoral* [*Revista de Tribunal Supremo de Elecciones*] 17: 270–303.

Zaremberg, Gisela. 2009. "¿Cuánto y para qué? Los derechos políticos de las mujeres desde la óptica de la representación descriptiva y sustantiva." In *Género y derechos políticos: La jurisdiccional de los derechos político-electorales de las mujeres en México*, edited by Karina Ansolabahere Sesti and Daniela Cerva Cerna, 77–120. México, DF: Tribunal Electoral del Poder Judicial de la Federación.

Zetterberg, Pär. 2008. "The Downside of Gender Quotas? Institutional Constraints on Women in Mexican State Legislatures." *Parliamentary Affairs* 61, no. 3: 442–460.

Zetterberg, Pär. 2009. "Do Gender Quotas Foster Women's Political Engagement? Lessons from Latin America." *Political Research Quarterly* 62, no. 4: 715–730.

Zetterberg, Pär. 2011. "The Diffusion of Sub-National Gender Quotas in Mexico and Their Impacts." In *Diffusion of Gender Quotas in Latin America and Beyond,* edited by Adriana Piatti-Crocker, 53–69. New York: Peter Lang.

Zetterberg, Pär. 2012. "Political Engagement and Democratic Legitimacy in Mexico." In *The Impact of Gender Quotas: Women's Descriptive, Substantive, and Symbolic Representation*, edited by Susan Franceschet, Mona Lena Krook, and Jennifer M. Piscopo, 173–190. New York: Oxford University Press.

Zetterberg, Pär. 2013. "The Dynamic Relationship between Gender Quotas and Political Institutions." *Politics and Gender* 9, no. 3: 316–321.

Zimmer, Lynn. 1988. "Tokenism and Women in the workplace: The Limits of Gender-Neutral Theory." *Social Problems* 35, no. 1: 64–77.

Zovatto, Daniel. 2014. "Latin America: Re-election and Democracy." *Open Democracy: Free Thinking for the World.* https://www.opendemocracy.net/daniel-zovatto/latin-america-re-election-and-democracy. March 4, 2014. Accessed October 21, 2015.

Zúñiga Quirós, Isabel. 1999. "Las mujeres en el quehacer político del Partido Unidad Social Cristiana." *Revista Parlamentaria de la Asamblea Legislativa de Costa Rica* 7, no. 1: 287–316.

Note: Tables and figures are indicated by an italic *t* and *f*, following the page/paragraph number.